EVALUATING PUBLIC COMMUNICATION

Evaluating Public Communication addresses the widely reported lack of rigorous outcome and impact-oriented evaluation in advertising; public relations; corporate, government, political and organizational communication and specialist fields, such as health communication. This transdisciplinary analysis integrates research literature from each of these fields of practice, as well as interviews, content analysis and ethnography, to identify the latest models and approaches.

Chapters feature:

- a review of 30 frameworks and models that inform processes for evaluation in communication, including the latest recommendations of industry bodies, evaluation councils and research institutes in several countries;
- recommendations for standards based on contemporary social science research and industry initiatives, such as the IPR Task Force on Standards and the Coalition for Public Relations Research Standards;
- an assessment of metrics that can inform evaluation, including digital and social media metrics, 10 informal research methods and over 30 formal research methods for evaluating public communication;
- evaluation of public communication campaigns and projects in 12 contemporary case studies.

Evaluating Public Communication provides clear guidance on theory and practice for students, researchers and professionals in PR, advertising and all fields of communication.

Jim Macnamara is Professor of Public Communication at the University of Technology Sydney (UTS). Previously CEO of a leading research company specializing in evaluation of communication, he is the author of 16 books on media and communication, including, most recently, *Organizational Listening: The Missing Essential in Public Communication* (2016).

EVALUATING PUBLIC COMMUNICATION

Exploring New Models, Standards and Best Practice

Jim Macnamara

Routledge
Taylor & Francis Group

LONDON AND NEW YORK

First published 2018
by Routledge
2 Park Square, Milton Park, Abingdon, Oxon OX14 4RN

and by Routledge
711 Third Avenue, New York, NY 10017

Routledge is an imprint of the Taylor & Francis Group, an informa business

British Library Cataloguing-in-Publication Data
A catalogue record for this book is available from the British Library

Library of Congress Cataloging-in-Publication Data
Names: Macnamara, Jim author.
Title: Evaluating public communication : exploring new models, standards, and best practice / Jim Macnamara.
Description: London ; New York : Routledge, 2017.
Identifiers: LCCN 2017007988 |
ISBN 9781138228573 (hardback : alk. paper) |
ISBN 9781138228580 (pbk. : alk. paper) | ISBN 9781315391984
Subjects: LCSH: Communication--Social aspects.
Classification: LCC HM258 .M153 2017 | DDC 302.2--dc23
LC record available at https://lccn.loc.gov/2017007988

ISBN: 978–1–138–22857–3 (hbk)
ISBN: 978–1–138–22858–0 (pbk)
ISBN: 978–1–315–39198–4 (ebk)

Typeset in Bembo
by Sunrise Setting Ltd, Brixham, UK

CONTENTS

FIGURES

TABLES

ACKNOWLEDGEMENTS

The field of evaluation has evolved over more than half a century, with contributions made by many scholars, professional organizations and leading practitioners in a number of disciplines and fields. In researching and writing about this subject, it is inevitable and necessary that I have drawn on the work of many people. Throughout this text, I have endeavoured to recognize the contribution of others through citations and referencing, and to explain various perspectives in a manner that does them justice.

I particularly thank the organizations and agencies that agreed to have their evaluation activities reported as case studies in Chapter 10, and also the leaders in the field of public communication evaluation who agreed to be interviewed and comment, including: Walter Lindenmann; Michael Fairchild; Emeritus Professor Tom Watson; Fraser Likely; Professor Anne Gregory; Dr Glenn O'Neil; Barry Leggetter; Richard Bagnall; Paul Njoku, formerly of the UK Cabinet Office; and Neil Coffey, head of evaluation in the UK Department of Health.

I also acknowledge and thank the organizations and groups that assisted the research for this book, especially: the International Association for Measurement and Evaluation of Communication (AMEC) and the Institute of Practitioners in Advertising (IPA), headquartered in the UK; the Task Force on Standardization of Communication Planning and Evaluation Models in the US; the US Institute for Public Relations (IPR) and its Measurement Commission; the Evaluation Council of the UK Government Communication Service (GCS); the University of Technology Sydney (UTS); and The London School of Economics and Political Science where I worked as a visiting professor while researching this book.

In addition to all those cited and quoted, I thank Routledge — especially Niall Kennedy, editor, Media and Cultural Studies, and Kitty Imbert, editorial assistant, who supported this project from the outset and offered valuable advice throughout.

And, as always, I owe much to my colleague, intellectual partner and wife, Dr Gail Kenning.

Jim Macnamara PhD, FAMEC, FAMI, CPM, FPRIA

INTRODUCTION

On a number of occasions over the years, colleagues and delegates at industry and academic conferences have referred to my book on evaluation of communication, which has been intriguing. Until now, I have had to explain that I have not published a book on evaluation.

I have worked in the field of communication evaluation, conducted research into this field of practice and written so much about evaluation of public communication, such as media publicity, public relations (PR), advertising, social media, election campaigns, health communication programmes and other types of public communication, over the course of four decades that many assume I must have written a book on the topic.

Why write one now? Well, there are a number of reasons that explain this book, and which inform the approach and features of this study of evaluation of public communication.

First, as noted above, I have written many research reports and articles in professional and academic journals, and I have presented papers on evaluation at more conferences than I can recall. Therefore, I have accumulated a substantial body of literature and research findings.

Second, I have engaged in, thought a lot about and struggled with evaluation of public communication campaigns and projects as a public communication practitioner, as a professional researcher and as an academic. These three vantage points afford an empathy for the challenges and complexities faced, as well as the opportunities available. They combine the practical and the theoretical. Communication scholar Barbie Zelizer issued a timely caution in a recent special issue of *Communication Theory* that examined 25 years of theory-building, saying:

> Communication theory needs to reflect far more stridently on the relevance of practice. While the longstanding academic view has been that orienting

toward practitioners dumbs down intellectualism, the value of spanning practice and theory goes beyond the somewhat limited exemplar . . . offered most obviously by law and medicine.

(Zelizer, 2015, p. 414)

Third, despite more than 40 years of focus on evaluation in fields such as PR (Likely & Watson, 2013) and even longer in advertising, scholars and industry leaders around the world still bemoan the inadequacy of evaluation. Industry surveys show that 'to prove the impact of communication activities on organizational goals' is one of the 'major barriers' facing practitioners (Zerfass, Verčič, Verhoeven, Moreno & Tench, 2012, p. 36). This gap was confirmed in a recent study of evaluation practices in European intergovernmental organizations (IOs) and international non-governmental organizations (INGOs) by Glenn O'Neil, who reported that compliance with best-practice principles was lowest in relation to 'using a rigorous design' and 'linking to organizational goals' (2013, p. 572). Despite more than US$500 billion a year being spent on advertising (e-Marketer, 2016), independent marketing researcher and analyst Jerry Thomas says 'the advertising industry, as a whole, has the poorest quality-assurance systems and turns out the most inconsistent product . . . of any industry in the world' (2008, para. 1) – although this analysis identifies recent advances. Despite some noteworthy examples, a number of authors also note that programme evaluation has been poorly undertaken in the health communication and health promotion field (for example, Noblet & Lamontagne, 2009; Nutbeam, 1998). Researchers point out that many health communication campaigns fail to achieve their objectives (Gauntlett, 2005), resulting in the waste of large amounts of taxpayers' money. There is therefore still much to be learned and done in evaluation of public communication.

Fourth, even though there are a number of books that discuss evaluation of various kinds of public communication, most narrowly examine evaluation in particular fields of practice, failing to take advantage of models and methods developed and used in other fields. Evaluation has been extensively studied and used in education since the 1930s (Tyler, 1942). Programme evaluation is also highly developed in public administration. Even neighbouring public communication disciplines and fields fail to engage with each other. For instance, some discuss advertising research without considering the numerous models and extensive discussion of evaluating PR, and vice versa. Similarly, PR ignores much excellent work in evaluation of health communication, and so on. There is much to be learned from a transdisciplinary approach that synthesizes knowledge from various fields, as this analysis will show.

Case studies of evaluation of advertising, PR and specialist fields such as health communication practice are another feature of this book. In fact, this book grew out of a small booklet of case studies. That also was the result of comments that I received. At the 2015 Summit on Measurement, hosted by the International Association for Measurement and Evaluation of Communication (AMEC) in Stockholm, a delegate complimented me on a paper I presented, but asked 'Do you *do* any evaluation?' The question was not posed impertinently or in an accusatory way. It was a genuine and reasonable question that goes to the heart of the ongoing global debate about evaluation of advertising, PR and other public communication, such as health communication – the gap between theory and practice. What the delegate was asking me was whether evaluation theory can be applied in practice – or is communication evaluation theory normative and aspirational?

My answer to the question was: 'As a matter of fact, I do *do* evaluation as well as study others doing evaluation.' Even though I left practice some years ago – when I sold the media and communication research company[1] that I founded – to become an academic, government departments and agencies, and sometimes corporations, regularly ask me to provide, or advise on, evaluation as an independent researcher. Academics increasingly welcome such contract research projects as traditional grants for academic research dwindle in many countries. My independent position as a professor in a school of communication at a leading university is one of the reasons why I am commissioned to conduct evaluative research. But also, somewhat sadly, I have noticed a trend towards organizations calling in academic researchers because industry professionals often cannot do evaluation with the rigour and thoroughness that is increasingly required. Case studies reported in this book – including a few in which I was involved, as well as others – provide useful insights into evaluation of public communication in terms of both success stories, as well as shortcomings, and the challenges and barriers that lead to those shortcomings.

But this book is more than a review of established theories and 'war stories' from the past. Recently, there have been calls for standards for evaluation of communication (Michaelson & Stacks, 2011) and a number of initiatives to establish standards (for example, AMEC, 2012, 2016b). This analysis explores these initiatives, including the development of evaluation frameworks and standards by AMEC in the UK and by the Institute for Public Relations (IPR) and other groups in the US, and the implementation of accountability and governance in relation to public communication campaigns by a number of government organizations, including the Evaluation Council of the UK Government Communication Service (GCS, 2016a). Participation in, and review of, these projects have afforded me opportunities to closely study the latest developments in several countries in both the public and private sectors, and to work with leaders in professional practice, as well as the academy. So this book is informed by primary research, as well as an extensive literature review and synthesizing of knowledge about evaluation from a number of fields.

Furthermore, the communication and media landscape has transformed in the past decade. While traditional methods of communication remain important, new channels and practices of public communication have emerged through digitalization, the Internet and particularly social media. Evaluation needs to keep pace with these developments, which afford a range of real-time metrics and audience insights that present both opportunities and challenges ranging from technical skill requirements to ethical questions in relation to privacy. New digitalized and online forms and methods of evaluation that are not covered in most social science research books are closely examined, as well as emerging practices such as *behavioural insights*, which draw on behavioural economics and psychology, *econometrics* and *big data* analysis.

The result is that this analysis reviews 30 frameworks and models that identify or inform processes for evaluation in advertising, PR, health communication and promotion, and government communication and other specialist fields, and examines ten informal research methods and more than 30 formal research methods for implementing evaluation of public communication. Even then, it no doubt omits some, and I apologize in advance for any significant omissions. On the other hand, some may baulk at the breadth and detail of this analysis. Many yearn for a simple 'how to' book or guide – a 'Ten easy steps to success'. However, it is doubtful whether that is possible in a field as diverse and complex as human communication. Even if it is, that is not the purpose here. In a field characterized by, and rightfully criticized for, oversimplification and lack of rigour, this study has purposely set out to provide a comprehensive analysis of, and contribution to, this important field of practice.

Communication practitioners, researchers and service providers involved in evaluation will, in most cases, select and use only a few methods for most programmes. But, to make informed choices and apply methods appropriately, they need to be aware of what is available and understand the fundamental principles and procedures of programme evaluation and social research. The field needs to embrace complexity and depth if it is to have credibility. Standards need to be high – not simplistic short-cuts and made-up metrics with no scientific basis.

The methodology used in this analysis is outlined in Chapter 1. In summary, in addition to an extensive critical literature review spanning traditional and emerging digital approaches, the analysis and insights in this book are based on:

1. ethnography (first-hand observation and participation in major projects related to evaluation of public communication);
2. interviews with researchers and leaders in the field;
3. content analysis of documents such as frameworks, models, guides and manuals, and a wide range of evaluation reports, presentations and dashboards; and
4. analysis of case studies.

Through this empirical, as well as critical, transdisciplinary approach, this analysis offers new theoretical and practical insights for evaluation of public communication in the twenty-first century.

Note

1 The author founded CARMA International (Asia Pacific) as a franchise of the leading 'computer-aided research and media analysis' company and headed the successful company for 11 years, before selling it to Isentia (formerly Media Monitors) in 2006.

PART I

The foundations of evaluation

1

WHY WE NEED TO CRITICALLY EXAMINE COMMUNICATION

It is tempting to jump right in and start talking about evaluation methods and the tingling satisfaction of proving that a public communication campaign or project was effective in achieving its objectives and generating results. This discussion will get into the nitty-gritty very soon – but, first, it is essential to understand and remind ourselves of a few very important things about communication.

Communication is recognized as fundamental to all aspects of human society. John Dewey famously said that 'society exists . . . in communication' (1916, p. 5). Raymond Williams echoed Dewey in saying that 'society is a form of communication' (1976 [1962], p. 10). However, communication between humans is a far more complex, uncertain and variable process than most of us care to admit. We know that communication is something that all humans do to some extent from soon after birth. But to assume that attempts at communication are always, or even mostly, effective is to ignore the wars, divorces, breakdowns of friendships, family fallings-out, feuds, misunderstandings and other disruptions that occur every day in human society.

In an address to aspiring communication students some years ago, I reminded them that:

> Human history is one of lost letters, wrong numbers, downed wires, missed deliveries, misinterpreted messages, lost signals, no signal, failures to listen, incoherent speech and writing, mumbles, stammers and stutters, static, interference, not getting through, no one home, lost connections, errors, crashes, blackouts, breakdowns and dropouts, as much as it is of connection and communion.

> *(Macnamara, 2009)*

Communication: the 'registry of modern longings'

John Durham Peters poetically described communication as the 'registry of modern longings' (1999, p. 2). What he was referring to was the normative and aspirational expectations modern societies have of communication – what Pradip Thomas and Elske van de Fliert call the 'ceaseless quest for a communication utopia' (2014, p. 52). This involves an unfailing, but misguided, belief that communication will solve all of our problems and an unfounded confidence that communication will always work. Peters (1999) argues that we ask and expect too much of communication. We index almost everything against it to the extent that, when nations go to war or organization dissolves into chaos, we are surprised – as if human normalcy is a smooth flowing current of communication. Alas, that is not the case.

Peters says: 'That we can never communicate like the angels is a tragic fact, but also a blessed one' (1999, p. 2). He explains that giving up on the dream of instant unfailing communication is not at all to be driven into a nightmare of solitude or ignorance. He says that communication, in all of its fractures and mediations, is all we have. It is what makes us human. But the simple, inescapable and essential fact to recognize is: human communication often does not work.

It is surprising and somewhat frustrating that organizations, as well as individuals, continue to forget or ignore this. Our longing for, and faith in, the efficacy of human communication and a greatly inflated self-belief among many that they are 'good communicators' underlie the lack of evaluation in professional public communication practices that is the focus of this book.

Public communication

In contrast with interpersonal communication between two individuals (*dyads*) and within small groups, *public communication* refers to communication activities that take place in the *public sphere* (Habermas, 1989 [1962], 2006) rather than the private sphere (Chartier, 1989; Hansson, 2007) – albeit the separation of private and public is an increasingly blurred boundary in contemporary societies (Baxter, 2011). Also, public communication usually relates to matters of public interest rather than private affairs. Furthermore, those at whom it is aimed are commonly referred to as *publics*[1] (Eliasoph, 2004; Grunig & Hunt, 1984) and sometimes as *target publics* or *target audiences*. Individuals and groups with a vested interest in an organization, or which are directly affected by the activities of an organization, such as customers, shareholders, partners and affiliates, employees and sometimes local communities, are also referred to as *stakeholders*,[2] because they have a stake in the organization (Freeman, 1984). Sometimes, there are others who seek to have a stake or say in the activities of an organization and these are referred to in some literature as *stakeseekers*[3] (Heath, 2002; Spicer, 2007). In the interests of simplicity, this text will refer to all such groups as *audiences*.

Recognizing that communication is meant to be two-way, it should be noted that organizations that seek to engage in communication with various publics and stakeholders are also audiences – or at least they should be, as I argued in *Organizational Listening: The Missing Essential in Public Communication* (Macnamara, 2016a). Communication requires speakers and listeners – or authors and audiences – to interact reciprocally.

Communication between organizations and individuals, such as letters, emails and complaints processed through customer service call centres, may not always be public in terms of being open for all to hear or see, but they are public in the sense of being part of organization–public relationships, abbreviated in public relations (PR) practice to OPR (Broom, Casey & Ritchey, 1997; Heath, 2013). Similarly, internal communication inside organizations, commonly referred to as *organizational communication* – although it would be more accurately called 'intra-organizational communication' – is also public communication. While management and employees engage in private interpersonal discussions in relation to individuals' pay and performance, internal organizational communication addresses many or all members of an organization on matters of common concern. Internal organizational communication recognizes employees as key publics or stakeholders, and uses a range of public communication media and methods, such as the Internet, newsletters, videos, presentations, events and so on.

The website of the School of Communication at American University (2016) in Washington DC says of public communication: 'It's at the heart of our economy, society, and politics. Studios use it to promote their films. Politicians use it to get elected. Businesses use it to burnish their image. Advocates use it to promote social causes.'

Public communication *campaigns* are public communication activities that 'use the media, messaging, and an organized set of communication activities to generate specific outcomes in a large number of individuals and in a specified period of time' (Coffman, 2002, p. 2; Rogers & Storey, 1987, p. 821). Similarly, Charles Atkin and Ronald Rice say: 'Public communication campaigns can be defined as purposive attempts to inform or influence behaviours in large audiences within a specific time period using an organized set of communication activities and featuring an array of mediated messages in multiple channels' (2013, p. 3).

Despite their considerable cost in terms of both time and money, such campaigns are often not rigorously evaluated, partly because of the widespread assumption that communication efforts will have the desired effect This ignores the reality that others might have different views, beliefs, levels of literacy, and social and cultural influences. When hundreds of thousands, or even millions, of dollars, euros, pounds sterling or other currency units are spent on public communication, such as in major advertising, PR or public engagement campaigns, it is important to remember the famous statement by marketing pioneer John Wannamaker:[4] 'Half of my advertising is wasted; the only trouble is I don't know which half' (as cited by Albanese, 2007, p. 10, and in Stewart, Pavlou & Ward, 2002, p. 357).

Isabelle Albanese says that acceptance of Wannamaker's dilemma 'just doesn't cut it anymore' (2007, p. 10). A 50/50 chance of success is not acceptable in today's age of accountability, tight budgets and performance management. Even if one accepts Wannamaker's statement as a generalization, there is empirical evidence showing that public communication materials and campaigns, however creative and professionally packaged, regularly do not create the desired effects. A cover story in *Advertising Age* in 2006 reported market research that found 37.3 per cent of marketers' advertising budgets to be wasted because they are ineffective (Albanese, 2007, p. 10). The following section will present further evidence that much public communication fails to achieve the intended outcomes. That is not an indictment of the ability or work ethic of the instigators of that communication. Rather, it is a reflection of the complex range of variables that affect public communication, the susceptibility of audiences to other competing and contrary influences and messages, and sometimes the resistance of audiences (Knowles & Linn, 2004) – factors that necessitate evaluation.

Evaluation can apply to specific campaigns, or even to specific activities within campaigns, such as media advertising, publicity, events, websites and publications. However, a single communication initiative such as an event or website, and even a campaign, rarely has significant outcomes and impact. In discussing health communication, D. Lawrence Kincaid and colleagues point out that a single campaign is usually only one phase in a series of campaigns and other types of intervention designed to achieve desired results (Kincaid, Delate, Storey, & Figueroa, 2013, p. 305). Learning from evaluation of campaigns should be incorporated into planning of future campaigns to gain incremental improvement. Thus it is productive to think of evaluation beyond the scope and time scale of any one campaign.

Furthermore, the concept of campaigns narrows the focus to planned purposive communication designed to achieve specific results desired by an organization. As Brenda Dervin and Lois Foreman-Wernet say, 'no matter how carefully cloaked as attempts to "understand" and benevolently reach audiences, the intent of the campaign remains top-down social control – to entice audiences to comply with what experts deem appropriate' (2013, p. 148). Public communication needs to be understood and considered more broadly as the ongoing communicative interaction between organizations and their various audiences – and vice versa. Today, public communication occurs 24/7, not only within the semi-controlled confines of campaigns. Public communication occurs every time an official gives a speech, every time someone posts a tweet on Twitter and every time a photo is posted on Facebook, Instagram or Pinterest. Public communication other than that planned by a particular organization occurs regularly, such as independent media reporting, public complaints, protests, petitions, social media comments and various other day-to-day expressions of the 'will of the people'. Organizations need to monitor and evaluate what others say. Also, they often need to respond to communication initiated by others, such as letters, emails, website inquiries and social media discussion. Therefore, while this analysis of evaluation can be applied to campaigns, it discusses evaluation of *public communication*, not only of campaigns, recognizing that public communication is an ongoing, two-way process involving a range of channels and activities.

Throughout the twentieth century, it was common to refer to *mass communi-cation* in discussing public communication with large groups of people. However, this understanding of communication is mostly associated with *mass media*, such as newspapers, radio and television, which dominated the mediascape during the twentieth century, as well as the questionable concept of *mass society* (Hoggart, 2004; Williams, 1976 [1962]). *Public communication* is a more inclusive term than *mass communication* because it applies to all channels used for direct and mediated communication, and it recognizes a range of audiences with differing interests and views rather than one 'imagined' mass audience (Anderson, 1991 [1983]).

Communication effects: direct, limited and contingent

Unfailing faith in the power of human communication, and particularly in the growing array of technologies such as broadcast radio and television that made so-called *mass communication* technically possible in the twentieth century, led to what is referred to as *direct effects thinking* and a belief in the strong effects of media and public communication. Such views have been referred to colloquially as the *injection model*, the *hypodermic needle* concept of communication and *bullet theory* (Schramm, 1971a; Severin & Tankard, 2001), based on once-popular, but now largely discredited, one-way, linear models of communication such as those of Shannon and Weaver (1949), Schramm (1954) and Berlo (1960). These models are grounded in *basic systems theory* and early *cybernetics* (Wiener, 1948). Norbert Wiener (1950) and George Gerbner (1956) added 'feedback loops' to these early transmis-sional models, but much thinking about media and public communication in the first half of the twentieth century emphasized the primary power of the sender and assumed the efficacy of media channels. Media scholar James Lull summarizes: 'The first stage of media audience research reflects ... strong impressions of the ... media as powerful, persuasive forces in society' (2000, p. 98). A number of other scholars make similar observations and critique the one-way transmissional notion of communication, including the following.

The transmission view of communication is the commonest in our culture.
(Carey, 2009, p. 12)

Our basic orientation to communication remains grounded, at the deepest roots of our thinking, in the idea of transmission.
(Carey, 2009, p. 13)

Until late in the twentieth century, the transmission model served as the basis for conceptualizing communications activities by organizations.
(Hallahan, Holtzhausen, van Ruler, Verčič & Sriramesh, 2007, p. 20)

Contemporary theorists have criticized the current dominance of a transmission (sender-receiver) model of communication in everyday thinking.
(Craig & Muller, 2007, p. 1)

Challenges in communication

While the purpose here is to focus on evaluation, and particularly to explore new models and frameworks, emerging standards and new methods for the digital age, it is informative to reflect briefly on just some of the large number of studies that illustrate the highly contingent and often incongruous nature of public communication. For instance, for many decades, politicians, policymakers and some sociologists have argued that mass media content creates violence, sexual promiscuity and other social problems, and, conversely, that mediated communication campaigns can promote healthy behaviour, safe driving, patriotism, election victories and other desired results. The following are just some of the landmark studies that have examined the effects of media and public communication campaigns.

After major concerns emerged about the potential for films to influence children in negative ways, a number of research projects were conducted, including the extensive Payne Fund Studies, which involved a total of 13 studies published in ten volumes (Blumler, 1932; Sparks, 2006, p. 46). The research, conducted over five years from 1928 to 1932, examined the influence of films on children in relation to a number of topics, including violence, sex and knowledge of foreign cultures, and found that different children interpreted and reacted to the same films differently – that is, there were no consistent effects. Other factors believed to influence children more were age, gender, predispositions, social environment, past experiences and parental influences.

A major study of voting influences and behaviour in Erie County, Ohio, in 1940, commonly referred to as The People's Choice Study (Lazarsfeld, Berelson & Gaudet, 1944), found that personal contacts were more influential on voter behaviour than mass media and that reinforcement of existing views was more likely than conversion to alternative views (Sparks, 2006, p. 53). The study was conducted during the 1940 US presidential campaign, which saw President Franklin Roosevelt seek an unprecedented third term in office. Paul Lazarsfeld, Bernard Berelson and Hazel Gaudet of Columbia University supervised 15 interviewers, who interviewed 2,400 voters several times during the campaign to document their decision-making process. This study is most known for its identification of a *two-step flow* in public communication, which theorizes that while there are minimal direct effects of mediated communication, information and ideas flow from mass media to opinion leaders and from them to a wider audience (Severin & Tankard, 2001, p. 31; Sparks, 2006, p. 53).

Another early and widely discussed study that threw grave doubts on the effects of public communication such as films was the testing of the potential for war films to motivate US troops during World War II, conducted by Carl Hovland working for the US Army Information and Education Division. Hovland found that films depicting battles and war provided factual information, but did not increase troops' motivation to serve in the armed forces or change attitudes, such as heightening resentment towards the enemy. Hovland's work contributed to *learning theory*, but concluded that a single mass communication approach is unlikely to change strongly held attitudes or change behaviour (Hovland 1954; Hovland, Janis & Kelley, 1949; Hovland, Lumsdaine & Sheffield, 1953; Severin & Tankard, 2001, pp. 153–154).

The Stanford Three-Community Study of dietary behaviour designed to reduce disease and improve health was conducted between 1972 and 1975 in the communities of Tracy, Gilroy and Watsonville, California. A random sample of adults aged 35–59 was exposed to media messages on healthy nutrition and risk reduction, such as giving up smoking, as well as other interpersonal interventions, and examined annually to gain information on daily intake of nutrients, rate of smoking, knowledge of heart-disease risk factors, and laboratory and physical measurements of cholesterol, plasma renin, urinary sodium, blood pressure and weight. Mass media campaigns using television, radio and newspaper advertising were launched in Gilroy and Watsonville, while Tracy was used as a control group. This widely reported study claimed a statistically significant reduction in the composite risk score for cardiovascular disease as a result of significant declines in blood pressure, smoking and cholesterol levels (Farquhar, 1991; Stern, Farquhar, Maccoby & Russell, 1976), but there was considerable debate over the findings. Some of the researchers involved reported that a media-only campaign was able to bring about only small changes, while results for individuals for whom the media campaign had been supported with interpersonal contact were generally stronger (Flora, Maccoby & Farquhar, 1989, pp. 237–238).

The subsequent Stanford University Five Cities Project (officially named the Stanford Five City Multifactor Risk Reduction Project), aimed at reducing cardiovascular disease and conducted over 13 years from 1978 to 1991 in five northern California cities, reported even less impact. While smoking rates decreased by 14 per cent in the experiment group and the sample also experienced a 15 per cent decrease in risk score based on improvements in blood pressure, physical activity and cholesterol, David Gauntlett says that, overall, 'the effects of the enormous and very comprehensive campaign seem to have been marginal at best, and in several aspects were non-existent' (2005, p. 88). Evaluations of 'quit smoking' campaigns based on self-reporting are often unreliable and a significant number of quitters resume smoking after periods of abstinence.

One of the major areas of research to evaluate the effects of media communication has been in relation to the alleged effects of television violence. One of the most comprehensive studies of the effects of violence in television programming was conducted over a three-year period from 1970 to 1973 and involved 2,400 elementary school children (boys and girls) aged 7–12, plus a further 800 boys aged 12–16. The study took nine years to complete from survey to publication because the results were weak and inconsistent, with the data showing only very small effects. Researchers concluded that, on the basis of their extensive analysis, there was no evidence that television exposure had a consistent significant effect on subsequent aggressive behaviour (Milavsky, Kesslery, Stipp & Rubens, 1982, as cited in Gauntlett, 2005, pp. 38–39). Another three-year study by Wiegman, Kuttschreuter and Baarda, published in 1992, agreed with the 'no effect' result (as cited in Gauntlett, 2005, p. 140).

Susan Neumann conducted a review of studies of the alleged effects of television violence and found 'absolutely no evidence to support the claims of critics that television reduces children's attention spans, impairs their ability to think clearly, causes television "addiction", leads to illiteracy, or reduces cognitive abilities in any other way' (Neumann, 1991, as cited in Gauntlett, 2005, p. 51).

A meta-analysis, by Leslie Snyder and Jessica LaCroix (2013, pp. 123–124), of a large number of studies presents a number of other examples of public communication that have not been effective according to rigorous scientific testing, including the following:

- In campaigns to reduce alcohol use among youth, interpersonal interventions have been more effective than media campaigns, printed information materials and online information.
- In efforts to reduce smoking, media campaigns targeted at adults have a weak track record – although they have been shown to be effective in motivating people to participate in specialized quitting programmes and interpersonal interventions.
- In anti-smoking campaigns targeting youth, traditional media campaigns have also been shown to be less successful than interpersonal interventions. Research indicates that Internet- and phone-based communication offer greater promise with youth.
- The average effect for media campaigns promoting mammography (breast screening) has been found to be lower than for other types of intervention. The most effective approaches have been shown to be letters, phone calls, interpersonal communication and tailored programmes.

Snyder and LaCroix did find some successful uses of media, particularly in relation to campaigns to reduce obesity and promote healthy eating among adults, although impact on youth is significantly less (2013, pp. 124–125). Mediated campaigns also have shown significant effects in relation to prevention of HIV and sexually transmitted diseases (STDs) where interpersonal communication and other direct interventions can be confronting. But these examples show the variable effects of even major media campaigns.

Of course, public communication can include more than media campaigns, particularly traditional media. Online media including special websites (often referred to as information *hubs*), telephone hotlines offering support, such as smoking 'quit lines', and social media are increasingly part of public communication. Also, public communication professionals are recognizing the benefits of using direct audience engagement strategies, such as meetings, events and collaborative community-based projects. But there is a tendency among politicians, boards and senior management teams to commission mass communication campaigns using television, radio and print media advertising and publicity to address every marketing and social challenge that comes along.

There are a number of explanations for how audiences are able to avoid, block or disregard messages in media and other public communication, including the following:

- **Selectivity.** Audiences are selective at many levels, including: in what they read, listen to or watch (*selective exposure*); in how much attention they pay to content (*selective attention*); in how they interpret information and what they choose to believe (*selective perception*); and in what they retain (*selective retention*). It has been shown that various levels of selectivity operate as filters on information and images that audiences consume (Severin & Tankard, 2001, pp. 80–88, 143–145). For example, Joseph Klapper (1960) drew attention to the fact that people tend to favour information that reinforces their pre-existing views and to avoid contradictory information (that is, selective exposure). As well as working in negative ways, selectivity can operate in positive ways. For instance, a 2003 study conducted for the Broadcasting Standards Commission, the BBC and other bodies in the UK concluded unequivocally that even 'children are able to distinguish between fictional violence and violence that is "real"' (as cited in Gauntlett, 2005, p. 51) – which probably explains the lack of evidence that film and television depictions of violence actually cause violence.

- **Cognitive dissonance.** An important concept that remains as relevant today as ever is Leon Festinger's psychological theory of cognitive dissonance. Festinger (1957) based his theory on *balance theory* developed by Fritz Heider (1946), the notion of psychological *symmetry* proposed by Theodor Newcomb (1953), *congruity theory* developed by Charles Osgood (1954; see also Osgood, Suci & Tannenbaum, 1957) and what other psychologists call *consonance*, which identifies that humans seek a state in which their attitudes, knowledge and behaviour are aligned. When these are not aligned, humans encounter cognitive dissonance, according to Festinger (1957). Beyond merely identifying the mentally uncomfortable, and even stressful, state of cognitive dissonance, Festinger identified that humans employ strategies to deal with this mental state – and that those strategies may not always be logical or the best for them. For instance, a person who is overweight and is informed on the dangers of obesity will experience cognitive dissonance: their enjoyment or compulsion associated with eating will be in conflict with the rational information and argument to lose weight. One way of eliminating this dissonance is to comply with health communication messages and to control their diet. But humans, being the complex beings they are, are just as likely to rationalize their position with an inner argument that their weight problem is genetic or that they are 'big boned', so there is nothing they can do. Thus the strategies that humans deploy to deal with cognitive dissonance and regain consonance can be significant blockages to communication.

- **Reactance.** Another psychological factor that can block communication messages is reactance. This is a potentially strong form of resistance triggered when a person feels pressured to accept a certain view or to behave a certain way and that their freedom to choose is being restricted. Reactance can cause a person to strengthen a view or behaviour that is contrary to what is intended. This is commonly seen in people 'doing the opposite' of what is requested. What is colloquially called *reverse psychology* is a lay approach that recognizes this factor and employs strategies to combat reactance. Reactance is magnified by certain personality traits and predispositions, such as people with a resistance to authority. Parents of teenagers will be likely to identify with this psychological construct. Psychologists have developed measures of reactance (for example, Dillard & Shen, 2005) and public communication practitioners need to recognize the role of reactance in resisting persuasion (Quick, 2016).

- **Cultural factors.** In today's increasingly multicultural societies and in global communication, professional communicators also face the challenge of meaning-making across cultures with different values, attitudes, beliefs and practices. Understanding of multicultural and intercultural communication[5] is important for public communicators, because dominant Western approaches and Americentrism and Eurocentrism can not only lead to failures in communication, but also cause offence and disengagement (Crossman, Bordia & Mills, 2011; Kim & Ebesu Hubbard, 2007).

- **Information overload.** Also in today's connected online world, some audiences are simply overloaded with information and either heavily filter what they receive or ignore much of what is available.

As early as the mid–1950s, informed by some of the studies cited previously and their own research, Elihu Katz and Paul Lazarsfeld (1955) challenged direct effects thinking about mass media and mass communication with what became known as *limited effects theory*. In simple terms, they argued that, based on the evidence, mass media communication has limited effects. Their view was strongly supported shortly after by Joseph Klapper (1960), who reported in his landmark research that:

1. Mass communication ordinarily does not serve as a necessary and sufficient cause of audience effects, but rather functions among and through a nexus of mediating factors and influences;
2. These mediating factors are such that they typically render mass communication a contributory agent, but not the sole cause, in a process of reinforcing the existing conditions.

(Klapper, 1960, p. 8)

His conclusion was also referred to as 'the law of minimal consequences' – although this term is not in Klapper's book. It was reportedly coined by his wife, Hope Lunin Klapper, a faculty member at New York University at the time (Lang & Lang, 1968, p. 273).

The field of cultural studies that emerged in the 1970s and poststructuralist critical scholars threw more water on the flickering flame of direct effects arguments. The seminal essay titled 'Death of the author', written in 1967 in French as

La mort de l'auteur by French poststructuralist Roland Barthes and translated into English in the American literary journal *Aspen*, before appearing in books such as *Image, Music, Text* (Barthes, 1977), marked a turn towards the audience in terms of understanding communication. Of course, Barthes wished no harm to authors, but his essay was designed to shock literary and media studies researchers and educators out of the assumption that the author's intended meaning of texts is what audiences take from them. In his conclusion, he called for the 'birth of the reader' in understanding the meaning of texts and argued that achievement of this had to be at the cost of the 'death of the author' as the sole arbiter of meaning in literary works. This notion can be equally applied to all forms of texts, whether they are words or visuals, and communication ranging from documentary films to advertising.

Another landmark break from direct effects thinking was Stuart Hall's *encoding/decoding* research. Hall (1993 [1973]) pointed out that audiences can, and frequently do, interpret (*decode*) information and messages with different meanings from those intended (*encoded*) by the author. Hall posited three potential decoding positions that receivers of information can take:

1. dominant hegemonic (that is, the receiver accepts the connoted meaning);
2. negotiated (partly accepting of the encoded meaning, but also partly at variance); or
3. oppositional (rejecting messages and taking an opposing view).

(Hall, 1993 [1973], p. 94)

In cultural studies approaches to mass media, texts are viewed as *polysemic* – that is, they have multiple possible meanings 'even if a "preferred reading" is inscribed within the text by its producers' (Newbold, Boyd-Barrett & Van Den Bulck, 2002, p. 45). Noted media scholar James Curran agrees, saying 'the media have fractured meanings' (2002, p. 144), while James Lull uses the term 'multisemic' (2000, p. 162).

Audience reception analysis carried out by David Morley (1992) and others further advanced theories of audience power by shifting focus from messages to meaning and noted that meaning is created in the mind of an audience. This shift was part of a growing focus on human *agency*, leading to a growing body of *reception theory* (Hall, 1993 [1973]; Jauss, 1982) and the field of audience research that continues today.

John Fiske, one of the most strident cultural studies theorists, argues that it is the audience, not the media, which has the most power (1989, p. 127). However, many scholars say that Fiske 'hopelessly romanticizes the role of audience members' (for example, Lull, 2000, p. 168). Keith Tester says that 'Fiske's work confuses the possibility that the audience might carry out oppositional readings of media texts with the claim that they actually do carry out such readings' (1994, p. 70). Sonia Livingstone has noted a 'backlash' against some interpretations of Stuart Hall's theory on human agency that imply 'unfettered polysemy or excessive resistance' and present 'naïve celebrations of agency' (2015, p. 442).

Readers may have similar reservations about these apparent denunciations of the effectiveness, and therefore the value, of public communication. One might ask, for instance: what about *agenda-setting theory*? In their widely quoted study of undecided voters in Chapel Hill, North Carolina, during the 1968 presidential election contested by Richard Nixon and Hubert Humphrey, Max McCombs and Donald Shaw (1972) found a strong correlation between the volume of coverage of various issues reported and discussed in the media and 'the salience of those issues among voters' (McCombs & Reynolds, 2002, p. 2). Thus they concluded that mass media set the agenda of public issues.

However, their initial findings have been criticized and have evolved considerably. Since the Chapel Hill study, there have been more than 400 studies of the agenda-setting influence of news media (Griffin, 2009, p. 367). McCombs provides a useful review of 50 years of agenda-setting theory in his 2004 text *Setting the Agenda: The Mass Media and Public Opinion* in which he notes in the introduction that 'the theory of agenda-setting is a complex intellectual map still in the process of evolving' (McCombs, 2004, p. xiii). This evolution has included renewed attention to *framing theory* developed by Gregory Bateson (1955), sociologist Erving Goffman (1974) and Robert Entman (1993), as well as *priming* (Iyengar & Kinder, 1987; Iyengar, Peters & Kinder, 1982) and *agenda-building* developed by Gladys and Kurt Lang (1981, 1983). These and other theories have gained credibility as alternatives to, and even replacements for, the original notion of media agenda-setting, and offer more nuanced and contextual explanations of the effects of media and public communication. In a recent review, eminent media scholar Jay Blumler said that, in terms of ideas about message impacts on message receivers, 'these theories may be reaching their sell-by dates' (2015, p. 428).

Most modern researchers accept that a synthesis of influences comprising (a) the content mediated by the producers, (b) the semiotic complexity and efficacy of the medium, and (c) interpretations by the reader shape meaning from media texts. Newbold and colleagues summarize:

> The tradition of media effects has undergone a number of transformations . . . These . . . may be summarized as movements away from 'transmissional' models of effects towards a study of media within contexts of making of meaning, of culture, of texts and of literacy, in the interaction between media texts and media readers. Those who have asked how people make meaning from texts have had to look both at the ways in which texts are structured, and at the readers themselves.
>
> *(Newbold et al., 2002, p. 46)*

These authors conclude that 'media texts, including representations, do not affect audiences in a simple and direct way, but rather that this process is complex, ambiguous and at times even contradictory' (2002, p. 308).

Denis McQuail summarizes the evolution of mass media research as follows:

> In the early days of mass communication research, the audience concept stood for the body of actual or intended receivers of messages at the end of

a linear process of information transmission. This version has been gradually replaced by a view of the media receiver as more or less active, resistant to influence, and guided by his or her own concerns, depending on the particular social and cultural context.

(McQuail, 1997, p. 142)

While noting overly optimistic views on human agency to resist media messages and other public communication, Livingstone says: 'To assert that media influence is contingent is not to deny its existence' (2015, p. 442). David Morley similarly, and thoughtfully, advises: 'These models of audience activity were not ... designed ... to make us forget the question of media power, but rather to be able to conceptualize it in more complex and adequate ways' (2006, p. 106).

A large body of media and communication research, of which only a small part is summarized here, informs us that communication is contingent and contextual. The effectiveness of attempted communication depends on many external factors, including the credibility of sources (Hovland & Weiss, 1951), the similarity (*homophily*) of sources to the audience (McGuire, 2013 [1989]), preferences in relation to the channel and presentation of information, the presence of competing or contradictory information and cultural influences, as well as many internal psychological and phenomenological factors such as reactance, cognitive dissonance and the complex processes of *hermeneutics* (human interpretation).

Leading public communication researchers and editors of successive editions of *Public Communication Campaigns* Ronald Rice and Charles Atkin point out that 'research findings suggest that campaigns are capable of generating moderate to strong influences on cognition outcomes, less influence on attitudinal outcomes, and still less influence on behavioural outcomes' (2013, p. 13). They report that 'most experts conclude that contemporary public communication campaigns attain a modest rather than strong impact' particularly when it comes to behaviour change (Rice & Atkin, 2013, p. 15). Brenda Dervin and Lois Foreman-Wernet – who have developed some very interesting work on *sense-making methodology* that will be examined in Chapter 8 – say, in relation to compliance campaigns (for example, campaigns for driving safely): 'It is generally accepted that achieving behavioural change outcomes is difficult and costly and rarely results from communication efforts alone' (2013, p. 149).

Does this information present a negative and depressing view of public communication? To the contrary, research presents a realistic view of what public communication can achieve in contrast with the naive claims and hyperbole too often trotted out by communication agencies to win 'pitches'. Rice and Atkin go on to say that 'despite an array of barriers that diminish campaign effectiveness, the research literature shows many success stories' (2013, p. 15). Dervin and Foreman-Wernet's comment above gives one indicator of the path to success: public communication usually works best when it is integrated with other influences and 'levers', such as direct audience engagement and, sometimes, financial incentives (for example, making consumers pay for plastic bags in shopping centres to reduce non-biodegradable waste). Another necessary step towards success is evaluation conducted systematically and rigorously, as will be outlined in Chapter 2 to identify what communication is effective and when.

As Atkin and Freimuth say, drawing on the work of Eric Knowles and Jay Linn (2004) and W. J. McGuire (2013 [1989]): 'Perhaps the most elemental problem is reaching the audience and engaging attention to the messages. Other key barriers include underestimating susceptibility to threats, counter-arguing persuasive appeals, displaying reactance to compliance attempts, and exhibiting inertia' (2013, p. 54).

Sonia Livingstone warns us that audiences can be 'messy, unpredictable, hard to locate, and as liable to undermine the researcher [or public communicator] as they are to behave as desired' (2015, p. 441). A study by Lance Bennett and Shanto Iyengar (2008) has suggested that a new era of minimal effects might be emerging in today's world of media and audience fragmentation and 'communication abundance' (Blumler, 2015, p. 427).

One of the pioneers of communication audits, Professor Osmo Wiio is famous in Europe for his communication 'laws', which include several equivalents of 'Murphy's Law' for human communication. Translated from Finnish by Jukka Korpela (2010, n.p.), they include the following:

1. Communication usually fails, except by accident. Sub-laws of this are:

    1.1 If communication can fail, it will; and
    1.2 If communication cannot fail, it still most usually fails;
    1.3 If communication seems to succeed in the intended way, there's a misunderstanding;

2. If communication can be interpreted in several ways, it will be interpreted in a manner that maximizes the damage;
3. There is always someone who knows better than you what you meant by your message;
4. The more we communicate, the worse communication succeeds.

While written with some humorous intent, Wiio's 'laws of communication' are sobering reminders of the complexities of human communication, and the importance of formative research to understanding audiences and of summative evaluation to determining if and when communication has been achieved.

Increasing demand for governance, transparency and accountability

At the same time as our faith in the power of communication to facilitate human society and solve its problems took a hit, demands for accountability increased. Over the past few decades, pressure has mounted on all levels of management in the private and public sectors to be accountable and to report performance. Based on the influence of W. Edwards Deming (1986), who is credited with founding the quality movement, and Howard Dresner (2008), who introduced the term *business intelligence* in 1989 and pioneered *business performance management* (BPM), and others, modern management today widely utilizes measurement systems and methods such as *key performance indicators* (KPIs) and *key results areas* (KRAs), *balanced scorecards* as developed by Robert Kaplan and David Norton in the 1990s (Fleisher & Mahaffy, 1997), dashboards, *return on investment* (ROI), *cost–benefit analysis* (CBA) and *cost-effectiveness analysis* (CEA).

In public companies, shareholders demand strong performance and results. Likewise, a wave of performance management and accountability has swept through government in most developed and fast-developing countries, particularly in those with large expenditures of public funds. For example, in the UK, the Government Communication Service (GCS) is subject to the government's professional assurance processes. These include a requirement to submit plans for all major public communication expenditures to the government's Efficiency and Reform Group (ERG) and a GCS Evaluation Framework has been mandated, requiring detailed evaluation of all public communication campaigns on a regular basis. The GCS Evaluation Framework will be examined in detail in Chapter 3 as an example of contemporary evaluation practice.

Many government organizations have faced accusations of wasting of taxpayers' money on advertising, PR and other public communication, and many non-governmental organizations (NGOs) and non-profit organizations face increasing demands for accountability and proven efficiency if they are to maintain public support. So pressure is increasing for evaluation in both the public and private sectors – a challenge that the field of public communication practice has not adequately met to date. Conversely, opportunities exist to engage more effectively with audiences, to operate efficiently, and to demonstrate outcomes and impact that are important for organizations, their stakeholders and society.

The essentiality of evaluation

Informed by extensive research that illustrates the contextual and contingent nature of communication effectiveness and increasing expectations and demands for accountability, it is clear that evaluation is not an optional stage or activity in public communication. Evaluation is essential.

Evaluation is not only necessary to find out *if* the intended outcomes and impact are achieved. Even when desired results are achieved, public communication practitioners need to be able to show that their communication activities were responsible. There is an aphorism that 'success has many fathers and mothers, but failure is an orphan'. This is true in evaluation. When desired outcomes are achieved, many are likely to claim credit. For example, an increase in sales is likely to be hailed as a result of the efforts of the advertising agency, the marketing director who commissioned the advertising, the chief executive officer (CEO) and possibly others, such as PR and publicity staff or consultancies, as well as the sales staff who actually took the orders. *Causality* is a particular challenge in evaluation that will be investigated later in this analysis. For now, it is important to shed any doubt that evaluation of public communication is a 'must do'. No excuses will suffice – although there are many of those, as will be shown shortly.

Defining measurement and evaluation

The terms *measurement* and *evaluation* are often used interchangeably, and not infrequently measurement is used as an umbrella term for the range of activities involved in these practices. For example, the International Association for Measurement and Evaluation of Communication (AMEC), after using both terms in its name, brands its peak annual event the AMEC 'Summit on Measurement'. One of the long-established industry publications in this space is *The Measurement Standard*. In management, there is considerable focus on *performance measurement*, although ultimately this is seen as part of the wider field of BPM. To examine theories and practices in this field, credible and workable definitions must first be established, based on the research literature.

While measurement is a key part of what this discussion is about, *measurement* literally means 'taking measures'. Measurement is the collection and analysis of data in relation to a particular object, process or condition. We measure the height and weight of our children as they grow and develop. We measure our own weight for both health and aesthetic reasons. Our doctor measures our blood pressure and other variables, such as cholesterol levels. When we are driving, we refer to instruments that measure our speed and how much fuel we have. But none of these measures (call them *metrics* if you like) provides us with any more than statistics and descriptions. We might weigh 90 kilograms (200 pounds). We could be driving at 100 kilometres per hour (60 miles per hour). But what does that mean? What is the effect or likely impact?

Evaluation is defined in both Oxford Dictionary (2016) and Merriam-Webster (2016) as 'to judge' or 'making a judgement' about the value or significance of something. Evaluation involves interpretation of information, which calls into play various analytical techniques and human subjectivity. In addition, and very importantly, interpretation is informed by *context*. In the preceding examples, a body weight of 90 kilograms (200 pounds) could be judged to be healthy for a male football player, but not so if the person weighed is a young woman or a teenager. Driving at 100 kilometres an hour (60 miles per hour) would be considered acceptable and quite normal if driving on a highway or freeway, but the same speed in a narrow urban street near a school would be considered irresponsible and dangerous.

In the Research Methods Knowledge Base, William Trochim says 'evaluation is the systematic acquisition and assessment of information to provide useful feedback about some object' (2006, para. 3). In educational literature on evaluation, Ron Owston defines evaluation as 'the process of gathering information about the merit or worth of a program for the purpose of making decisions about its effectiveness or for program improvement' (2007, p. 606). These definitions are useful for drawing attention to the *assessment* that is part of evaluation and to the *learning* for programme improvement that evaluation provides in addition to identifying *effectiveness*. An even more specific definition of evaluation describes the process as 'the systematic application of research procedures to understand the conceptualization, design, implementation, and utility of interventions (Valente, 2001, p. 106). Noteworthy in this definition is that, in addition to emphasizing a systematic approach, it stipulates that research procedures should be used for evaluation – not casual observation, anecdotal information or 'black box' automated systems based on secret algorithms. Valente goes on to spell out that a comprehensive evaluation framework should include:

- assessing needs;
- conducting formative research to design messages;
- designing activities (referred to as *treatments* or *interventions* in health communication), instruments and monitoring methods;
- process research;
- summative research; and
- sharing results with stakeholders and other researchers.

(Valente, 2001, as cited in Rice & Atkin, 2002, p. 428)

A review of evaluation literature in the health communication field by Jane Sixsmith, Kathy-Ann Fox, Priscilla Doyle and Margaret Barry on behalf of the European Centre for Disease Prevention and Control (ECDC) describes this definition as 'comprehensive' and 'especially relevant as it encompasses the importance of integrating evaluation research throughout the project' (2014, p. 5). While identifying the importance of management steps such as initial assessment of needs, designing evaluation and sharing results, like Valente (2001, 2002), Sixsmith and colleagues (2014) identify three main stages of research for evaluation: *formative, process* and *summative*.

Michael Scriven (1967) reportedly first used the term *formative* in relation to educational assessment, although it and summative evaluation came into popular use in education through the *Handbook on the Formative and Summative Evaluation of Student Learning* (Bloom, Hastings & Madaus, 1971). Formative evaluation involves the use of *ex ante* research before planning and designing a campaign or project to identify factors such as pre-existing levels of awareness, pre-existing perceptions and attitudes, audience interests and concerns, and communication channel preferences. Such data provides a baseline for *ex post* comparison, and informs selection of channels, creation of content, and even tone and style of communication. Formative research also includes pre-testing of concepts, messages and pre-production mock-ups of designs and storyboards of proposed videos, which is a very important step of evaluation. Research shows that pre-testing is quite reliable in identifying the likely acceptance and effectiveness of communication (Dillard, Weber & Renata, 2007).

'Process evaluation identifies whether target groups were exposed to, and participated in, the intervention and whether stakeholders and partners engaged with it,' according to evaluation specialists in the health field, Adrian Bauman and Don Nutbeam (2014, p. 51). In simple terms, *process* evaluation involves progressive monitoring and tracking to identify whether or not milestones are being met. For example, audience *reach* of advertising and the placement of media publicity, which are commonly reported by advertising agencies and PR practitioners as 'results', are part of process evaluation. They show that information has been distributed and that it potentially could influence the intended audience. But such measures provide no empirical evidence that communication has been achieved – or even that the audience consumed and considered the information. Bauman and Nutbeam add that process evaluation also 'encompasses assessment of the short-term impact of an intervention' (2014, p. 51), but the emphasis here is on 'short-term' and one must be cautious in using the term *impact* in this context. It is used to denote longer-term, downstream effects, as we will see in examining evaluation models in Chapter 3.

Bauman and Nutbeam broadly support a three-phase approach to evaluation in their work in relation to health promotion. In their slim, but very useful, guide to evaluation, they list *formative* and *process* evaluation, but also emphasize the need for '*impact* (or outcome) evaluation' (Bauman & Nutbeam, 2014, p. 35).

Julia Coffman of the Harvard Family Research Project says that 'there are four basic types of evaluation: *formative, process, outcome,* and *impact*' (2002, p. 2), further emphasizing the need to look beyond processes to outcomes and impact – two key stages that are identified in programme logic models, which will be examined in Chapter 3. As Coffman acknowledges, outcome and impact evaluation are both summative, or what she calls 'back-end' evaluation, so this approach is similar to the three-phase formative–process–summative approach discussed by other researchers.

The US General Accounting Office (GAO, 2011) also proposes four types of evaluation, which it describes as *process, outcome, impact* and *cost–benefit analysis/cost-effectiveness analysis.* This nominates a very specific method for evaluating outcomes and impact, and illustrates a focus on financial results, which is not uncommon and which can be problematic for public communication professionals working to achieve social benefits or other so-called intangibles, such as quality of life, satisfaction, public trust or reputation.

A University of Wisconsin-Extension (UWEX) program teaching and training guide on evaluation models similarly identified four types of evaluation, but described these slightly differently as 'needs/asset assessment', 'process evaluation', 'outcome evaluation' and 'impact evaluation' (Taylor-Power & Henert, 2008, Handout 54).

In an extensive review of evaluation approaches, Daniel Stufflebeam (2001) identified 22 types of evaluation, which he arranged into four categories:

1. *pseudo-evaluations* – a type noted and lamented by public relations scholar David Dozier (1985);
2. *questions and/or methods-oriented;*
3. *improvement/accountability;* and
4. *social agenda/advocacy.*

These 22 approaches to evaluation are shown in Table 1.1 in the order in which Stufflebeam listed them.

TABLE 1.1 Twenty-two approaches to evaluation

No.	Approach	Description
1	Public relations (PR) studies	Criticized because they usually begin with an intention to show that a programme was sound and effective
2	Politically controlled studies	Often illicit because the evaluator withholds the full set of findings and may selectively use information
3	Objectives-based studies	Widely used approach that addresses specific needs of management
4	Accountability (particularly payment by results)	Narrows inquiry to particular outcomes and incentivizes the finding of results
5	Objective testing	Typically used in schools to test students against norms
6	Outcome evaluation as value-added assessment	Involves recurrent testing (e.g. annually) to identify trends over time
7	Performance testing	Tests authentic responses to questions, typically life-skills-oriented questions; used extensively in schools
8	Experimental studies	Sophisticated scientific methods such as randomized controlled trials (RCTs)
9	Management information systems	Provide data, mainly quantitative; data sets selected can be arbitrary
10	Cost–benefit analysis (*also* benefit–cost analysis)	Quantitative method that compares costs of a programme with benefits gained, usually measured in financial terms
11	Clarification hearing	Judicial approach to evaluation that effectively puts a programme 'on trial', with 'defence' and 'prosecution' arguments
12	Case studies	Critical analysis method that examines selected individual cases or can compare cases
13	Criticism and connoisseurship	Based on art and literary criticism; relies on the evaluator having special knowledge and expertise
14	Programme theory-based	Applies established theories of how programmes work
15	Mixed-method studies	Combines quantitative and qualitative evaluation
16	Decision/ accountability-oriented	Similar to accountability (see above), but emphasizes learning to improve decision-making
17	Consumer-oriented studies	Focuses on consumers and consumer benefits
18	Accreditation/certification	Evaluation associated with gaining formal recognition, e.g. membership of a professional body
19	Client-centred studies	As the name suggests, highly response to client needs

(Continued)

TABLE 1.1 (Continued)

No.	Approach	Description
20	Constructivist	Highly philosophical approach that rejects arbitrary targets and assessments to seek benefit for all involved
21	Deliberative democratic	Democratic approach that involves collaborative deliberation to reach decisions
22	Utilization-focused	Focuses on gaining specific evaluation data to apply to future planning; the servant of utility

Source: Based on Stufflebeam (2001)

Stufflebeam (2001) assessed 20 of the evaluation approaches that he identified (that is, minus two pseudo-evaluation approaches) against the criteria of the Joint Committee on Standards for Educational Evaluation (1994). He reported that the 'nine approaches that appeared most worthy' were then further analysed to identify what he considered to be the best and worst. He rated the nine best approaches as being what he termed *decision/accountability, utilization-based, client-centred, consumer-oriented, case studies, deliberative democratic, constructivist, accreditation* and *outcome/value-added assessment*. Perhaps not surprisingly, Stufflebeam rated *politically controlled* evaluation studies among the worst. More controversially in the context of this analysis, he also rated *PR* approaches among the four worst, along with *accountability based on payment by results*, and he was not very impressed with *programme theory-based* approaches either.

Some qualifications need to be made in relation to Stufflebeam's categorization and ratings. First, his list is heavily oriented towards education applications, such as school assessment and student testing. Second, his categories are complex and hardly parsimonious. Third, some of the so-called approaches are, in fact, research methods that can be applied in any approach – for example, experiments, case studies and cost–benefit analysis. Similarly, *mixed methods* is a research approach that simply refers to using both quantitative and qualitative methods – something that can be applied in many of the approaches listed. There is also considerable overlap between the approaches. For example, a *client-centred* or *consumer-oriented* approach could also be *outcome evaluation* or *utilization-focused*. Stufflebeam's list of approaches to evaluation mixes broad fields such as politics, management, PR and the arts, with specific specialized evaluation methods used in schools. As such, this typology is not altogether helpful for evaluating public communication. However, Stufflebeam's categorization and his *context–input–process–product* (CIPP) model (Stufflebeam, 1973) draw attention to some key issues in evaluation, including a focus on outcomes (not only processes), the importance of evaluation as a source of learning to inform programme improvement (not simply retrospective reporting) and the fact that there is no one single approach or method.

A later review by Ron Owston (2007), who examined evaluation from the perspective of technology programmes, identified four main approaches as:

1. *programme evaluation* based on programme theory (referred to by Stufflebeam as *programme theory-based evaluation*);
2. *decision-making evaluation*, in which he included the CIPP model developed by Stufflebeam (1973) and *utilization-focused* evaluation advocated by Patton (1978);
3. *naturalistic evaluation*, which emphasizes qualitative methods; and
4. the *four-level model* developed by Donald Kirkpatrick (2001), which focuses on reaction, learning, behaviour and results (Owston, 2007, p. 608).

This plethora of terms and descriptions of evaluation used across education, health, communication, business and other fields can be confusing and shows the difficulty of establishing standards. In literature related to public communication, a more manageable three-phase approach is most commonly recommended, as identified by Rice and Atkin:

1. *formative* evaluation;
2. *process* evaluation; and
3. *summative* evaluation, which they note is also referred to as *outcome* evaluation.

(2013, p. 13)

In his more recent writing, Thomas Valente also identifies three main phases of evaluation as formative, process and summative (Valente & Kwan, 2013, p. 83).

Some research texts (for example, Scriven, 1972; Trochim, 2006) collapse the types or phases of evaluation into two broad purposes of research: *formative* research, undertaken before activities to inform strategic planning (*ex ante*); and *summative* research, undertaken after activities to identify outcomes and impact (*ex post*). In Trochim's view, needs assessment and process evaluation are part of formative evaluation, while outcome and impact evaluation, including specialized methods such as cost–benefit analysis, are part of summative evaluation.

What emerges from analysis of evaluation literature across a number of disciplines is a number of fundamental points that inform understanding of evaluation, as follows.

- Evaluation is not done only at the end of a campaign, project or period – although this is how evaluation is often conceptualized in industry literature (for example, WPP, 2015) and in some academic discussions. For example, PR planning and implementation models such as the *research–action–communication–evaluation* (RACE) model proposed by John Marston (1981), the *research–objectives–programme/plan–evaluation* (ROPE) model championed by Jerry Hendrix and Darryl Hayes (2010), the *research–adaptation–implementation–strategy–evaluation* (RAISE) model proposed by Robert Kendall (1997) and Sheila Crifasi's (2000) *research–objectives–strategies–implementation–evaluation* (ROSIE) model all list evaluation at the end of the process. But evaluation must be done, at a minimum, *before* and *after* public communication (formative and summative evaluation). It is also advisable to conduct some evaluation *during* public communication activities, particularly those running over a long period, to identify whether activities are on track to achieve objectives and to incorporate progressive learning into fine-tuning or adjusting activities if required.

- Measurement is part of the process of evaluation, but, on its own, measurement provides only raw statistics (metrics) and descriptions. Measures can be meaningless without interpretation and context. Evaluation involves making judgements about the value and significance of findings and results within a context and within the terms of objectives set, and it applies these judgements to both reporting and planning of future strategies, as will be discussed in the following section. It is therefore more appropriate to refer to the field of practice as *evaluation* (albeit informed by evidence gained through various types of measurement) rather than simply as *measurement*.

- Measurement and evaluation should be undertaken using systematic, reliable and robust social science and humanities research methods and data analysis. Unreliable or highly subjective methods run the risk of misleading an organization and audiences, and can lose credibility and respect for those who use them.

- Evaluation at all stages requires focus on *audiences*. In public communication, it is audiences who determine whether or not communication is effective, particularly at the ultimate stages of attitude or behaviour change. Robert Stake, a well-known author on case study research, is quoted as saying, 'When the cook tastes the soup, that's formative. When the guests taste the soup, that's summative' (as cited in Scriven, 1991, p. 169; Shute & Becker, 2010, p. 7).

- Understanding audiences in most instances requires *qualitative*, as well as *quantitative*, evaluation. Shaped by modernism and positivist/post-positivist thinking, which privileges 'the scientific method' and the STEM disciplines (science, technology, engineering and mathematics), management in contemporary developed societies frequently favours quantitative methods that produce statistical calculations and numbers, particularly in business. Drawing on Guba and Lincoln (1981), Valente and Kwan say that 'evaluators may want to employ both quantitative and qualitative methods as the findings from one will help to supplement the results of another', and add that '[t]he balance of emphasis between the two methods should be driven by their ability to answer the research questions being posed' (2013, p. 84). Ultimately, human feelings, perceptions and complex constructs such as trust and loyalty are based on emotional (*affective*) as well as rational (*cognitive*) processes, and are rarely fully revealed by numbers on arbitrary scales.

Despite a raft of evidence indicating that communication and media often do not have the desired effects on audiences, Gauntlett notes that 'money tends to be pumped entirely into campaigns, both general and targeted, without much going into evaluation' (2005, p. 101). Evaluation is not done well in most public communication campaigns and programmes, whether they be advertising, PR or specialist programmes such as health communication. For example, in an analysis of the effectiveness of advertising, long presumed to be a major influence in modern societies, Jerry Thomas says:

> The advertising industry, as a whole, has the poorest quality-assurance systems and turns out the most inconsistent product (their ads and commercials) of any industry in the world. This might seem like an overly harsh assessment, but it is based on testing thousands of ads over several decades . . . Unlike most of the business world, which is governed by numerous feedback loops, the advertising industry receives little objective, reliable feedback on its advertising. First, few ads and commercials are ever tested among consumers – less than one per cent, according to some estimates.
>
> *(Thomas, 2008, para. 1)*

Thomas' tough assessment is supported by a more recent assessment from Price-WaterhouseCoopers (PWC). In its *Global Entertainment and Media Outlook 2015– 2019*, the consultancy reported:

> Measurement is getting better, but understanding how media is consumed will remain a significant challenge . . . Metrics are now being adopted by publishers and advertisers that better reflect the quality of impressions rather than their quantity. Yet despite this progress, effective measurement . . . will remain a significant challenge.
>
> *(PWC, 2015, Key Insight 6)*

The advertising industry is criticized for its frequent reliance on mid-range measures such as reach and recall. *Reach* simply measures the potential audience reached through advertisements and commercials placed in print, broadcast and digital media, based on the circulation, audience ratings and online viewers of those channels. This metric provides no indication of whether the people in these audiences actually consumed or paid attention to particular content. *Recall* asks a sample of the potential audience if they can recall advertising content, such as a television commercial or a brand or product name. Several anomalies arise in recall testing, including:

1. many people cannot remember whether or not they saw or heard particular media content;
2. many falsely report recall – for example, 'I must have seen it on TV', even when there is no television advertising; and
3. even if people can recall advertising content, a brand or product, there is no evidence that they will ever buy the product or comply with other messages contained in the content.

The PR industry also uses reach and related metrics such as *impressions* (the total potential number of people reached over a period), also referred to as *opportunities to see* (OTS). Many PR practitioners go no further than reporting the volume of media articles that they generate, presented as *press clippings* in the case of print media or as PDFs and web links to digital and social media content. The 2015 *European Communication Monitor*, a survey of more than 2,000 communication professionals across 41 European countries, reported that more than 80 per cent relied on counting the volume of publicity as the main focus of their evaluation (Zerfass, Verčič, Verhoeven, Moreno & Tench, 2015, p. 72).

One of the most nefarious pseudo-evaluation practices in the PR industry is the calculation of so-called *advertising value equivalents* (AVEs). This practice was reported to be used by up to a third of PR practitioners in 2009 (Wright, Gaunt, Leggetter, Daniels & Zerfass, 2009) and is still perceived as a valid method by many (see USC (University of Southern California) Annenberg Center for Public Relations & The Holmes Report, 2016). This method involves the multiplication of the space and time gained as editorial content in press, radio, television and online media by the advertising rate of the medium or programme on the basis that the figure obtained represents what it would have cost if the organization purchased the time and space as advertising. Researchers point out a number of fundamental flaws in this practice. These are summarized in Chapter 4 in examining metrics used in evaluation.

In 2010, and again in 2015, AMEC condemned the use of AVEs, stating in its Barcelona Principles for measurement and evaluation that 'AVEs are not a measure of public relations' (AMEC, 2015). A practice of applying multipliers of between two and eight times to further inflate the alleged value of PR based on an assumption that editorial is more credible than advertising is particularly criticized as fallacious (Macnamara, 2000a; Weiner & Bartholomew, 2006).

As communication has moved to digital platforms including social media, a wider range of metrics has become available, often in real time. However, proponents of digital communication continue to use many traditional approaches, such as reach and impressions, along with a range of basic quantitative metrics peculiar to websites and social media, such as unique visitors, views, likes, follows, shares and retweets. These will be examined in detail in Chapter 4, which looks specifically at a range of metrics available to inform evaluation.

Despite some progress in evaluation in various fields of public communication and considerable advocacy by industry organizations, evaluation remains underused and is often poorly executed. Some public communication practitioners continue to not do any evaluation at all. Before moving on to examine ways of doing better evaluation, it is useful to review the reasons – along with a number of excuses – that are put forward to explain the deficiency in evaluation of public communication.

Overcoming barriers and obstacles to evaluation

A number of explanations have been put forward for why rigorous, reliable evaluation is often not conducted in the field of public communication. There has been no shortage of discussion about evaluation – indeed it is one of the most talked-about topics in the advertising and PR industries, and to some extent in relation to digital communication. However, as Jim Grunig, emeritus professor of public relations, lamented in his much-quoted *cri de coeur* about evaluation of PR:

> I have begun to feel more and more like a fundamentalist minister railing against sin; the difference being that I have railed for evaluation in public relations practice. Just as everyone is against sin, so most public relations people I talk to are for evaluation. People keep on sinning … and PR people continue not to do evaluation research.

> *(Grunig, 1983, p. 28)*

Cost

A time-honoured reason put forward for not doing evaluation has been its cost and lack of budget (AMEC, 2016a; Valente & Kwan, 2013, p. 84; Wright et al., 2009). However, Walter Lindenmann (2001) pointed out that 'research doesn't have to put you in the poorhouse'. In a paper with that title, he listed seven suggestions for doing research in highly cost-effective ways, including omnibus surveys, self-administered mini-surveys of small samples and online surveys. The *pyramid model of PR research* (Macnamara, 2002a, 2005a, 2012a) lists a wide range of informal, as well as formal, methods for evaluation, including a number of low-cost, and even no-cost, methods such as case studies, consultative groups, online feedback forums, response mechanisms and self-administered e-surveys (see Chapter 3).

Furthermore, with industry studies showing steady growth in PR budgets after a temporary decline during the global financial crisis – for example, an 8 per cent average growth worldwide and more than 20 per cent in fast-developing countries in 2012 (ICCO, 2013) – lack of budget is revealed as an excuse rather than a reason for lack of evaluation.

A yardstick for the cost of evaluation (formative, process and summative) is commonly cited as 10–15 per cent of total programme cost (Piotrow, Kincaid, Rimon & Rinehart, 1997; Valente & Kwan, 2013). However, this is somewhat arbitrary and impractical in many cases. A number of leading evaluation specialists argue that there is no standard budget percentage that should be set aside for evaluation, proposing instead that it depends on a number of factors, such as the amount of relevant existing research that is available, the level of risk (for example, how much money is being spent on a campaign or project) and the difficulty of the challenge faced, as well as the priorities and expectations of management. How to make evaluation practical is discussed in more detail in Chapter 9. But, as a general rule, the answer to the common objection 'I can't afford evaluation' is: if you can't afford evaluation, you can't afford to undertake the programme. Without evaluation (formative as well as summative), programme managers are 'flying blind'. Evaluation has to be seen as an integral part of communication activities.

Time

Similarly, lack of time and human resources is often advanced as a reason why evaluation is not done (AMEC, 2016a; Watson & Simmons, 2004). However, Walter Lindenmann (2001) and others, including this author (Macnamara, 2005a), have pointed out that there is a range of time-efficient, as well as low-cost and even no-cost, methods available to conduct some level of formative and summative research. Also, evaluation can be outsourced to market research or social research companies and/or one of the wide range of specialist suppliers in fields such as media content analysis and social media analysis (see examples in Chapter 4).

Lack of demand

A study of European providers and consumers of measurement and evaluation by Otis Baskin and colleagues found some evidence to support anecdotal claims by practitioners that employers do not want evaluation (Baskin, Hahn, Seaman & Reines, 2010). However, research presented in this analysis shows that employer ambivalence is more to do with the type of evaluation offered than it is a lack of interest in accountability and measurability. As noted previously, most evaluation reports activities and processes – what are termed *outputs* in the evaluation steps and models that will be discussed in Chapters 2 and 3. While some organizations may have unsophisticated needs and management approaches, the worldwide focus on accountability, transparency and efficiency discussed previously means that most organizations are under pressure to achieve results and to show that these have been achieved efficiently.

Ego

In an article titled 'Barriers to great advertising', Jerry Thomas charges that one of the major barriers to more effective advertising is 'the big creative ego' (2008, para. 6). He says that 'great advertising tends to evolve over time, with lots of hard work, fine-tuning, and tinkering' and is 'based on objective feedback from target consumers' (the advertising industry's term for audiences and people). He goes on to assert that '[b]ig creative egos tend to resist such evolutionary improvements. We have seen great campaigns abandoned because agencies would not accept minor tweaks to the advertising', and concludes that 'big egos lead to bad advertising'. Thomas further criticizes what he calls:

> a pervasive tendency of many (but not all) advertising agencies to delay, undermine, and thwart efforts to objectively test their creative 'babies'. Who wants a report card on the quality of their work? It's very threatening. The results can upset the creative folks.
>
> *(Thomas, 2008, para. 5)*

Self-delusion

In the same article, Thomas suggests that another barrier to evaluation is 'self-delusion', saying:

> Most of us believe, in our heart-of-hearts, that we know what good advertising is and that there is no need for any kind of independent, objective evaluation. Agencies and clients alike often think that they know how to create and judge good advertising. Besides, once agencies and clients start to fall in love with the new creative, they quickly lose interest in any objective evaluation. No need for advertising testing. Case closed.
>
> *(Thomas, 2008, para. 38)*

The same criticism can be made against PR practitioners and other public communication professionals, who often believe that they are intuitively 'good communicators', and that therefore their ideas and creations should be accepted without question or scrutiny.

The myth of the 'silver bullet'

Another barrier that has held back evaluation in some sectors such as the PR industry is a misplaced belief that a single model is available, or even a single evaluation method that will prove the effectiveness of communication. A number of researchers have identified signs of a search by practitioners for a 'silver bullet' (Gregory & White, 2008; Likely & Watson, 2013, p. 156). Even the likes of Microsoft attempted to develop a single score out of 100 to report PR effectiveness as recently as 2007 (Bartholomew, 2016, pp. 3, 183), as did the Canadian Public Relations Society, with its media ratings points (MPR) system launched in 2006 (Bartholomew, 2016, p. 41). As Bauman and Nutbeam say in their guide to evaluation of health promotion, 'there is no single correct evaluation design' (2014, p. 128), and researchers almost universally agree that there is no single metric that can express the value and impact of the diverse range of objectives and activities that comprise public communication.

Lack of standards

Wright et al. (2009) identified a lack of standards as a further obstacle to evaluation of public communication. More recently, Michaelson and Stacks (2011) reported that more than two-thirds of practitioners believe a common set of standards for measurement and evaluation is necessary, and a 2013 survey of practitioners similarly reported that 66 per cent of PR professionals cited 'lack of standards as the biggest problem with PR measurement' (Ragan/NASDAQ OMX, 2013). As Michaelson and Stacks noted, standards are important because they allow 'comparative evaluations' over time and they ensure that appropriate methods are used (2011, p. 4).

A series of international initiatives was launched in 2011 under the auspices of the Coalition for Public Relations Research Standards, established by AMEC, the Institute for Public Relations (IPR) and the Council of PR Firms (CPRF). The 'march to standards' (Marklein & Paine, 2012) expanded in 2012 to include the Social Media Measurement Standards Conclave, and involved 11 professional PR and communication organizations worldwide, as well as consultation with five media and advertising industry bodies and eight companies representing employer perspectives.[6] This initiative had some success in drawing together communication industry professional bodies and raising awareness, but it did not produce standards that were supported or adopted. One of the weaknesses identified in the so-called march to standards was that there was little involvement of academic researchers or social researchers. The initiative therefore lacked methodological knowledge and rigour. Recent and ongoing efforts to develop standards are reviewed later in this analysis.

Fear

A study by Lloyd Kirban in 1983 among Public Relations Society of America (PRSA) members in the Chicago chapter found that more than half the practitioners expressed a 'fear of being measured' (as cited in Pavlik, 1987, p. 65). While little research has addressed this issue since, it is likely that a number of the other reasons proffered for lack of evaluation are, in reality, attributable to a fear of being evaluated. Robust evaluation will show what is not working as well as what is effective. Interestingly, in most discussions of evaluation at industry conferences, the purpose of evaluation is frequently expressed as 'to demonstrate the success of campaigns' or to 'show the value of PR'. Practitioners look to evaluation as a means to gain endorsement, rather than as a productive opportunity for learning and refinement of their work. Many seem ill-prepared and disinclined to openly and honestly evaluate their work, and there are indications that this is because of nagging doubts and fear that their activities may not be effective.

Lack of knowledge and skills

A number of PR scholars have concluded that a primary obstacle to implementation of research-based evaluation is lack of knowledge (for example, Cutler, 2004; Walker, 1997; Watson & Noble, 2007; White & Blamphin, 1994), also expressed as a 'lack of expertise' (Baskin et al., 2010, p. 111). Cutler commented that 'understanding and application of appropriate methodology is a major issue for public relations researchers' (2004, p. 372). Tom Watson and Paul Noble noted that practitioners largely operate as technicians, rather than as managers or strategists, and need to 'break the technician mould' (2007, p. 46). In a 2014 interview as part of a 'Thought leaders in PR measurement' series (Gohr, 2013), Jim Grunig reaffirmed his view that lack of knowledge of research methods among practitioners is a major obstacle, saying that 'the one variable that consistently explains why public relations people do what they do is their level of knowledge' (Grunig, 2014, para. 4).

The advertising industry's long reliance on simple output measures such as reach and recall of ads, and more recently on automatically generated digital metrics such as clickthroughs, also indicates a lack of knowledge of research methods appropriate to evaluation of communication, as well as egocentricity, as charged by Jerry Thomas (2008), and perhaps a level of complacency and laziness. Progress in recent years is acknowledged, but as PWC (2015) notes, evaluation of the effectiveness of advertising remains a challenge.

In response to calls for increased knowledge of research, educators have focused on research methodologies and methods in undergraduate and graduate education. Studies informing this increased emphasis include the 2006 Commission on Public Relations Education report, which recommended that undergraduate education include 'research and results measurement' (VanSlyke Turk, 2006, p. 6), as well as research as a core component of graduate education (p. 7). Similarly, in addition to emphasizing research in academic graduate programmes focused on preparing students for a research career, the 2012 Commission on Public Relations Education report on standards for master's degrees recommended providing 'social science research and evaluation knowledge and skills', and incorporating 'research methods' as a core curriculum component in professional master's degrees (Commission on Public Relations Education, 2012, pp. 4, 12).

Professional institutes and associations in a number of countries have introduced professional development short courses in research, and numerous conferences, seminars and workshops open to practitioners, as well as academics, highlight measurement and evaluation – for example, the annual 'summits on measurement' instigated by Katie Paine in the US and later sponsored by the IPR, and the annual International Summit on Measurement hosted by AMEC.

The Institute of Practitioners in Advertising (IPA) established its annual effectiveness awards in 1980 and has published more than 1,300 award-winning case studies of evaluation of advertising on its website.[7]

The Digital Analytics Association (2013) publishes a number of guides, including definitions of key metrics such as reach and impressions – although some of these have not been updated in several years, and some are inconsistent with definitions in other sectors such as advertising and PR. The digital communication field also has to deal with issues such as in-stream videos that play automatically when a web page is opened, even if the web user does not want to view the video. Counts of audience reach and impressions can be inflated by in-stream videos. Ethical evaluators discount unintentional video plays of short duration and usually count only videos that are viewed by clicking a 'play' button or in-stream videos that play for at least 30 seconds, which indicates viewership.

Having challenged many of the claimed barriers and obstacles to evaluation, it is important to note that advocates of evaluation do not recommend spending so much time doing evaluation that it undermines other necessary public communication work such as strategic planning and production. At a health communication research conference, Robert Hornik told health communicators: 'Do what is possible and live with uncertainty' (2002, p. 91) This might sound contrary to much of the advice in this book. But it is important to be practical. Approaches to evaluation discussed in Chapter 2 include *realist* evaluation, also called *realistic* evaluation. While this involves more than a simple admonition to be realistic, it does emphasize an approach that is feasible within the resources available and the levels of risk involved.

There is an illustrative story told about Lee Iacocca when he was head of Chrysler. Iacocca reportedly asked a middle-ranking executive for a report on some aspects of the corporation's business. The executive duly wrote a report and brought it to Iacocca, who, upon glancing through it, asked: 'Is this the best you can do?' The executive was a little taken aback and apologized, explaining that, with more time, he could do more. So Iacocca sent him away. A few weeks later, the executive brought a revised report to Iacocca, who asked the same question again. Again, the executive hesitated and said there was more that could be done. This occurred three or four times. Finally, when Iacocca asked the question for the fourth or fifth time, the executive had had enough. He blurted out: 'Yes, given the resources, time and other responsibilities I have, that is the best I can do.' Iacocca reportedly smiled and said: 'Thank you. That is all I wanted.'

Lack of SMART objectives

There is one more barrier to effective evaluation that must be mentioned and highlighted. Surprisingly, industry research reports that many public communication activities and even whole campaigns are still implemented without *SMART objectives* – that is objectives that are specific, measureable, achievable, relevant and time-bound. *Specific* objectives contain details such as numbers, percentages and dates – for example, 'to increase membership by 10 per cent in the next 12 months'. An objective such as 'to increase membership' is not specific or *measurable* because even if membership is increased by 5 per cent, management may have expected 15 per cent. *Time-bound* means that objectives should be achieved within a specified time frame. *Relevant* requires that objectives of public communication are aligned to overarching objectives and to an organization's strategic plan. It should be obvious that objectives need to be *achievable* and methods to ensure this are part of what is termed *formative* evaluation, which will be discussed in the next chapter. Understanding communication theory, programme theory and approaches such as realist evaluation, as well as close liaison with senior management, will help to ensure that objectives are SMART.

Research questions of this study

Based on the key issues summarized in this introductory chapter – namely, that the outcomes of communication are contingent and variable, and therefore that evaluation is essential; that most fields of management and administration today demand accountability; that new digital forms of communication offer new opportunities;

but that evaluation of public communication is often not done well and sometimes not done at all – five key questions are addressed in this analysis, as follows:

1. What are the fundamental concepts, principles and theories of evaluation of public communication identified in scholarly and professional literature?
2. What are the most widely used and endorsed approaches, models and methods of evaluating public communication?
3. How can new technologies enable new, improved and/or more efficient methods of evaluating public communication?
4. What other initiatives are necessary to improve evaluation of public communication to show the effectiveness and cost-effectiveness of public communication?
5. Are standards for evaluation of public communication possible and, if so, what do or should these involve?

Research methodology of this analysis

In addition to an extensive review of extant literature and synthesizing transdisciplinary knowledge, the findings and recommendations presented in this book are empirically informed by primary research undertaken over an 18-month period using three methodological approaches: *ethnography, participatory action research* (PAR) and *case study analysis*. Within these approaches, three qualitative research methods were used – namely, *observation/participation, interviews* and *content analysis* of documents – along with related techniques such as *journaling*, as explained in the following.

Ethnography

As Stanley Geertz (1973) notes, *ethnography* is a qualitative research method conducted to learn and understand cultural phenomena that reflect the knowledge and system of meanings guiding the life of a cultural group. In particular, Geertz described ethnography as *thick description*, meaning that such analysis is based on detailed observation and interpretation during an extended period of fieldwork – not simply casual observation over a short period. Barbara Tedlock notes that ethnographers ideally 'live in' the studied group or field for an extended period of time and gain first-hand observation, or even participation (2008, p. 151). Geertz (1973) similarly identified the primary research methods used in ethnography as participant observation and sometimes participation by the researcher. To bring rigour to the process, ethnographic information is collected in field notes, recordings, diaries and other data sources, such as minutes of meetings, letters, reports, papers and speeches. Also, ethnography typically includes interviews with those observed and fellow participants. All of these methods of data collection were used in this study, and content analysis was undertaken of notes and transcripts of interviews.

Interpretation of interviews and ethnographic reflections followed the principles of narrative inquiry – a process that recognizes the personal and social experiences of those studied as valid and important sources of knowledge (Clandinin & Connelly, 2000; Tedlock, 2008). That said, the author was reflexive in relation to his own subjectivity in interpretation, as well as potential influence on the participants and research findings, and addressed these risks by applying reflexivity and Maréchal's (2010) recommendation to connect observations to wider social, cultural and political meanings and understandings. For example, observations and comments gained in interviews and discussions were compared with published literature, documents such as official reports and archival records to verify claims wherever possible. Through these steps, this study produced findings that can claim *credibility, dependability, confirmability* and overall *trustworthiness*, as defined by Lincoln and Guba (1985), Silverman (2000), Shenton (2004) and other authors in describing the criteria for rigorous qualitative research.

First-hand observation and active participation was undertaken in a number of significant initiatives by organizations involved in attempting to develop standards and best-practice models for evaluation of public communication during the period of the study. The key organizations and initiatives studied included the following:

1. The International Association for Measurement and Evaluation of Communication (AMEC), based in London, during its 2015 revision of the Barcelona Principles (AMEC, 2015) and during the development of the AMEC Integrated Evaluation Framework (AMEC, 2016b) – as chair of the AMEC Academic Advisory Group, the author was directly involved in both of these projects during 2015 and 2016, respectively. Also, AMEC consulted with a number of other organizations, including the International Communication Consultants Organization (ICCO), affording wide exposure to industry and expert views.

2. The Evaluation Council of the UK Government Communication Service (GCS) in the UK Cabinet Office, Whitehall, which has established various frameworks, methods and tools for UK government communication to be applied by all departments and agencies – during 2015, the author participated as an external adviser in the development of the 2016 GCS Evaluation Framework (GCS, 2016a) and served as a member of the GCS Evaluation Council during the period June–December 2016, which provided access to review a wide range of UK government communication campaigns and activities.

3. The Task Force on Standardization of Communication Planning and Evaluation Models, an international collaboration of academics and public communication practitioners established in the US in 2015 to explore standards for evaluation of PR and communication – the author was a member of the task force throughout the period of research (2015–2017).

4. The Directorate-General for Communication (DG COM) of the European Commission, which provides a framework, guidelines and a code of conduct for

evaluation across European Union (EU) institutions and conducts evaluation of Commission communication activities – DG COM evaluation approaches and methods were examined, discussed and compared with international practices in a number of meetings with senior management and workshops with Commission communication practitioners in 2016.

5. The Department of Premier and Cabinet of the New South Wales state government in Australia – in 2015–2016, the author was involved in designing and implementing a framework and methodology for evaluating the state's AUS$100 million annual investment in advertising and other forms of public communication.

This stage of research also included interviews with the creators of a number of models and texts on evaluation of public communication cited in Chapter 3 to confirm historical facts, and to probe their thinking, influences and perspectives.

Also, the long-standing work of the Institute of Practitioners in Advertising (IPA) was closely examined, including its annual effectiveness awards. A number of winners of IPA Effectiveness Awards, along with winners of AMEC Global Effectiveness Awards, are included as case studies in Chapter 10. The IPA celebrated its centenary in 2017, having been founded in 1917 as the Association of British Advertising Agents (ABAA) before changing its name in 1927 to the Institute of Incorporated Practitioners in Advertising (IIPA), which was shortened to IPA in 1954. The IPA bills itself as 'the world's most influential professional body for practitioners in advertising and marketing communications',[8] with one of its five awards programmes focused on 'measuring marketing payback' (IPA, 2016a, para. 2).

Furthermore, this analysis drew on 36 case studies examined in The Organizational Listening Project, a two-year, three-country study that explored how and how well corporations, governments and NGOs listen to their stakeholders and publics, in which research was identified as one of the key methods of organizational listening (Macnamara, 2014a, 2015a, 2015b, 2016a, 2016b). These case studies afforded considerable insights into what research methods are used for formative, process and summative evaluation in practice.

Participatory action research

Action research, a qualitative method developed originally from the work of Kurt Lewin (1946) to explore specific issues and/or attempt to resolve specific problems *in situ* during the action or actions that are the subject of study (see also Greenwood & Levin, 2006), was adopted as a second method of primary research for two reasons. First, as noted previously, as well as being a close observer, the author was invited to be an active participant in recent evaluation initiatives by AMEC, the UK GCS and its Evaluation Council, the Task Force on Standardization of Communication Planning and Evaluation Models, and a number of others. In this sense, *participatory action research* (PAR) and ethnography overlap, blend and build on each other as methods of discovery.

Second, the UK GCS and several UK government departments and agencies agreed to implement and test a number of recommendations of The Organizational Listening Project, which proposed increased and improved formative and summative research, as well as other 'listening' methods, such as social media monitoring, to understand and engage audiences in effective communication (Macnamara, 2014a, 2015a, 2015b, 2016a, 2016b). This implementation and testing of various methods of research and analysis within several major government organizations afforded an ideal opportunity for action research.

In particular, this study used PAR (Kindon, Pain & Kesby, 2007), an application of action research that is based on collaborative inquiry by researchers and those responsible for what is studied. While action research and PAR are criticized by some scholars for their close association with applied research, PAR in particular offers significant benefits, including that:

- it takes advantage of the local knowledge of those involved in the problem being investigated;
- it gains deep understandings that are not available to 'outside' researchers 'looking in'; and
- it gains 'buy-in' and commitment from those involved to concretely address the research questions and find solutions to problems.

A rigorous social research approach is maintained by deploying systematic research methods to capture and analyse data, and by applying critical analysis, critical self-inquiry and reflection.

Specific methods used in PAR include journaling by participants, regular discussions such as meetings and forums, interviewing of key participants and stakeholders (often multiple times at various stages), and content analysis of research notes and interview transcripts to identify consensus or majority views. In this study, research notes from journaling and meetings, documents developed as part of the initiatives studied and email communication were analysed. Also, an interim report and a final report produced from PAR were circulated to all participants for their input, comments and verification.

By invitation, PAR was conducted in the Cabinet Office, Whitehall, and in the communication division of the UK Department of Health,[9] which included working closely with other divisions, such as policy, and with several of the department's arm's-length bodies that agreed to participate. These included NHS England, the national body in the UK's National Health Service (NHS) responsible for commissioning and administering healthcare service providers, such as medical practices and hospitals across the UK, and Public Health England (PHE), the agency responsible for conducting health-related public communication campaigns. The UK Department of Health and its agencies spend in excess of £75 million a year on public communication campaigns, excluding staff costs, addressing a wide range of audiences on important issues such as obesity and healthy ageing, as well as persuasive campaigns to solicit blood and organ donations and to change behaviours as part of preventative health care.

Evaluation case study analysis

The third research method deployed to inform this analysis involved examination of 12 contemporary case studies of evaluation of major campaigns or projects undertaken by corporations, as well as government, non–government and not-for-profit organizations, to explore contemporary evaluation practices. Because exemplar case studies were selected, as described in the following section, these provided insights into contemporary best practice, as well as further learning about the challenges, barriers, key enablers, opportunities and benefits of evaluation. Case studies were analysed qualitatively based on the techniques outlined by Robert Stake (2008) and Robert Yin (2009).

Sample

The organizations involved in ethnography and PAR comprised a purposive sample selected on the basis that they are sites of major contemporary initiatives in the development and/or implementation of best-practice evaluation of public communication. Also, participants in ethnographic and PAR were, of necessity, selected on the basis of their willingness to support and participate in the research. However, because no organizations refused to participate, the sample avoided bias associated with a convenience sample.

While some of the sites of PAR were public-sector organizations, there is no evidence to indicate that the findings cannot apply in private-sector organizations, such as corporations, and in non-profit organizations. Private-, public- and third-sector organizations all face increasing requirements for accountability today, and initiatives to promote professionalism among communication practitioners in advertising, PR and related fields include a focus on standards and effectiveness.

The case studies were also a purposive sample, selected on the basis of being exemplars in evaluation. This sampling method was appropriate given that the purpose of this study was to explore standards and best practice in evaluation Also, exemplars were considered to be best positioned to provide insights into response to the research questions (for example, organizations employing little evaluation would not be able to provide useful and relevant data). It should be noted that the exemplars in evaluation included some that found shortcomings and failures in the campaigns and projects evaluated – that is, the focus was on exemplary evaluation, not selection of only successful public communication programmes.

The case studies reviewed in Chapter 10 were identified during ethnographic research, and through access to the winners of AMEC's Global Effectiveness Awards[10] and the IPA Effectiveness Awards.[11] (The author was chair of the judges of the AMEC awards in 2016 and 2017, and also was an invited guest at the 2016

IPA awards, which afforded access and first-hand knowledge of cases.) As Wilbur Schramm stated, 'the essence of a case study . . . is that it tries to illuminate a decision or set of decisions: why they were taken, how they were implemented, and with what result' (Schramm, 1971b, as cited in Yin, 2009, p. 17). The case studies analysed are *descriptive* and *explanatory*, as defined by Yin, and also *revelatory*, in that they explain how evaluation was conducted and identify both things that worked well and those that did not (2009, p. 8).

Written consent was obtained from all organizations participating in interviews, ethnography and PAR, as well as for case studies reported.

The combination of (a) literature review, (b) ethnography, (c) participatory action research in major organizations involved in initiatives to develop and implement evaluation frameworks, models and standards, (d) interviews with the authors of widely used evaluation models and texts, and (e) case studies afforded academic, industry and client perspectives. Thus this analysis provides a 360-degree view of evaluation of public communication.

While it is presumptuous and ethnocentric for any researcher to claim global relevance for a study, primary research in this project included interviews, observation and participation in evaluation activities, and content analysis of documents in the US, UK, EU, Canada, Australia and New Zealand. In addition, case studies were obtained from these countries and regions, as well as countries in Asia and Africa, affording wide representation of practices.

Summary

- Evaluation of public communication is essential because human communication – particularly public communication with diverse audiences – is contingent on many factors that can result in failure to achieve intended outcomes and impact. Many of these are beyond the control of public communicators.
- Evaluation is poorly conducted in most fields of public communication, including advertising, PR, health communication (despite considerable research in this field) and even in digital communication. Emphasis is mostly placed on measuring *outputs*, such as placement of advertisements and media publicity, and proxy indicators of effectiveness, such as reach, share of voice, likes, follows, shares and retweets. It is apt to remember that, during planning and production of outputs, public communication functions are cost centres; it is only when outcomes and impact are demonstrated that they become value-adding centres.
- Measurement is part of evaluation, involving the collection and analysis of data. However, evaluation includes making judgements about the *value* and *significance* of measurement findings in the context of the organization's objectives and the prevailing circumstances and environment, as well as the interests of stakeholders and society (see further discussion of intended and unintended impacts in Chapter 3).

- Evaluation requires *SMART objectives* for public communication – that is, objectives that are specific, measurable, achievable, relevant and time-bound. *Relevant* means that objectives for public communication must support organizational objectives. Long-time PR evaluation evangelist, blogger and self-professed *Metrics Man*, the late Don Bartholomew, wrote in his blog in December 2010 that the number one thing for the communication evaluation field to learn in 2011 was 'measurable objectives' (Bartholomew, 2010). That practitioners were still to learn how to set *measurable* objectives in 2011 is concerning, and attests to the lack of knowledge and skills identified as a barrier to evaluation earlier in this chapter.
- Evaluation is not something that is done at the end of activities. Evaluation should be conducted progressively in three stages: *formative* evaluation (before communication activities begin to identify baselines and gain insights to inform planning); *process* evaluation (during activities to identify if things are on track and adjust activities if necessary); and *summative* evaluation (after activities to identify changes compared with formative data).
- A number of professional bodies are working with academics and social researchers to develop evaluation frameworks, models and standards, and these are investigated in the following chapters.

Notes

1 Public relations scholars Jim Grunig and Todd Hunt (1984) advocate the term 'publics' (plural) to refer to groups of people with whom interaction is desirable or necessary. The concept is also advocated by sociologists and political scientists such as Nina Eliasoph (2004), who has called for broad-based replacement of the singular term 'public' with the plural 'publics' to recognize social plurality and diversity. Kate Lacey says 'the idea of a singular, overarching public is a rhetorical fiction' (2013, p. 15).
2 'Stakeholders' is a term proposed by R. Edward Freeman (1984), in his book *Strategic Management: A Stakeholder Approach*, to draw attention to those affected by or affecting organizations beyond stockholders. Stakeholders can include employees, suppliers, distributors, retailers and local communities.
3 'Stakeseekers' is a term that broadens the concept of stakeholders to include individuals and groups without a direct relationship with an organization, but who seek to have a say or influence (Heath, 2002; Spicer, 2007).
4 John Wannamaker (1838–1922) was a prominent American retailer and political figure, regarded as a pioneer in modern marketing. He also served as US Postmaster General for a time.
5 Studies of *cross-cultural* communication, which were popular in the 1970s and 1980s, focused on differences and similarities between cultures, and suggested a binary or opposition between cultures. *Multicultural* and *intercultural* are more inclusive recommended terms, according to researchers (e.g. Crossman et al., 2011; Kim & Ebesu Hubbard, 2007).
6 Membership of the Social Media Measurement Standards Conclave included the three founding Coalition members – the Association for Measurement and Evaluation of Communication (AMEC), the Council of Public Relations Firms (CPRF) and the Institute for Public Relations (IPR) – as well as the Global Alliance for Public Relations and Communications Management, the International Association of Business Communicators (IABC), the Public Relations Society of America (PRSA), the UK Chartered

Institute of Public Relations (CIPR), the Society for New Communications Research (SNCR), the Federation Internationale des Bureaux d'Extraits de Presse (FIBEP), the Word of Mouth Marketing Association (WOMMA) and the Digital Analytics Association (DAA). In addition to the extensive collaboration by PR organizations worldwide, the Coalition and the Conclave have worked in consultation with the Media Ratings Council (MRC), the Interactive Advertising Bureau (IAB), the American Association of Advertising Agencies (AAAA), the Association of National Advertisers (ANA) and the Web Analytics Association (WAA).

7 See www.ipa.co.uk/effectiveness.

8 The plural term 'communications' is often used interchangeably with 'communication'. However, *communications* is widely used to denote technologies and systems used for transmission and broadcasting, such as computers, the Internet, telephone networks and satellites. *Communication* refers to the processes of meaning-making between humans or other species (some animals have capabilities for communication) and is the term used in this text.

9 The participatory action research stage of this study involved a six-month attachment of the author to work within the UK Government Communication Service (GCS) and the UK Department of Health (1 July–23 December 2016), as well as serve as a member of the Evaluation Council of the UK GCS and work with the other organizations participating in the research.

10 AMEC conducts annual Global Communication Effectiveness Awards that are based on independent expert judges' review of evaluation. The awards are made to research companies, communication agencies and in-house professionals in more than 15 categories, including 'Best measurement of a public-sector campaign', 'Best measurement of a consumer campaign', 'Best measurement of a business-to-business campaign', 'Best use of measurement for a single event', 'Best use of social media measurement' and 'Best use of a measurement framework'.

11 The IPA Effectiveness Awards are described as 'the most rigorous effectiveness awards scheme in the world' for advertising (IPA, 2016c, para. 2).

2

EVALUATION OF COMMUNICATION

Key concepts, principles and theories

While the purpose of this analysis is to examine methods for evaluating public communication, it is important to recognize that evaluation did not begin in the field of communication. Any approach to evaluating public communication that is grounded in theory and best practice must begin with understanding the major approaches and bodies of knowledge about evaluation that exist in the disciplines that have focused on this practice for some time, such as public administration, education, organizational psychology, and international and organizational development, as well as performance management in business.

This chapter critically examines major theories, approaches, and key concepts and principles advanced in relation to evaluation. This is a chapter not only for scholars to position the following analysis within a sound theoretical framework, but also for progressive and thought-leading practitioners. To underline this point, a quick word about *theory*.

As I noted some years ago in a textbook written for undergraduate and graduate students, mention of the word 'theory' makes many students' eyes glaze over (Macnamara, 2012a). Media scholar Dan Laughey says that 'theory, like a virus, spreads fear and trepidation among the student population' (2007, p. 3). Theory is often seen even more prejudicially by practitioners, who consider it abstract and unrelated to the 'real world'. However, this reaction is a result of a misunderstanding of theory – or perhaps of academics doing a poor job in explaining theories.

Many years of working as a practitioner and then as an academic have revealed to me that people commonly confuse 'theoretical' with 'hypothetical'. The two could not be more different. As most know, *hypothetical* refers to one or more hypotheses, which are conjectures or ideas put forward for proving or disproving. Hypotheses become theories only when they have been proved with a high degree of probability, usually through multiple experiments or testing using social science research methods and sometimes practical testing such as clinical trials.

There are many definitions of *theory*. Researcher David Silverman describes theory as 'a set of concepts used to define and/or explain some phenomenon' (2000, p. 78). In the widely used textbook *Theories of Human Communication*, Stephen Littlejohn and Karen Foss similarly define theory as 'an organized set of concepts, explanations and principles of some aspect of human experience' (2008, p. 14). Well-known media scholar Denis McQuail says that theory is 'any systematic set of ideas that can help make sense of a phenomenon, guide action or predict a consequence' (2005, p. 14). Public relations (PR) scholars Alan Center, Patrick Jackson, Stacey Smith and Frank Stansberry say that 'theory is the application of knowledge that has been verified and confirmed to consistently "work" in consistent situations' (2008, p. 13). In simple terms, theories explain how various things work. They explain and guide action, and can even help us to predict likely outcomes. That should immediately show their relevance to evaluation of public communication.

While the above definitions state that theories are systematic and organized, what is not emphasized sufficiently is that theories are *proven* explanations – or at least proved to the best of our knowledge and available data at a point in time. Theories do frequently need revision (for example, it was once a theory that the world was flat), and that is the work that academics do on a regular basis and the purpose of analyses such as this. However, as a starting point it is important to recognize that, in simple terms, theory is accumulated well-established knowledge. To go further, here is an even more simplified definition of theory that I give to my students.

> Theory is what others before us in other places have discovered, proved as far as humanly possible with a body of evidence, and documented.

In this context, it is foolhardy and foolish to ignore theory. Practitioners sometimes erroneously see theory as oppositional to, or competitive with, practical knowledge. All academics worth their salt acknowledge that there are several types of knowledge, including *traditional* knowledge handed down to us from previous generations and *practical* knowledge gained from personal experience, and some also recognize *intuition* – what is commonly called instinct or 'gut feel' (Frey, Botan & Kreps, 2000, pp. 8–11; Kerlinger & Lee, 2000). However, not all of the knowledge that we need in our modern world can be derived from tradition and none of us can have first-hand practical experience of every situation we may face. An example is handling crisis communication for an airline after a crash. Very few of us have had the experiences of being on an aircraft that crashed or of having to face families and media following a crash – and hopefully we never will. So how do most practitioners know how to handle such a crisis? The answer is: by drawing on theory. They apply learning from documented cases and research produced by others to plan for such eventualities – and so should we in examining evaluation.

There are three very practical benefits that come from identifying and applying relevant theories, and the principles and concepts embodied in those theories, as follows:

1. Theories help us to avoid mistakes that others have made in the past.
2. Theories help us to save time, because we can leverage the learning of others and implement proven methods, rather than waste time on unproven or speculative approaches.
3. Theories help us to identify best practice in a field.

As sociologist Kurt Lewin said, 'There is nothing so practical as a good theory' (1951, p. 69) – a truism repeated by Carol Weiss (1995) in the title of a book chapter on evaluation.

Logical framework approach (*log frames*)

One of the earliest frameworks for evaluation of programmes including communication was the *logical framework approach* (LFA), developed and used in the evaluation of aid programmes and development communication from the early 1970s by organizations such as the US Agency for International Development (USAID) (Practical Concepts Inc., 1971). Often abbreviated to *log frames* or *logframes*, LFA has been described as 'a historical precedent' to the contemporary logic models that will be discussed in following sections of this chapter (Henert & Taylor-Power, 2008, p. 2).

The LFA, or log frame, approach identified a number of stages of programmes, and applied a series of 'if' and 'then' statements, as illustrated in Figure 2.1, to denote the interim steps and dependencies involved in achieving goals. The names of the first two stages (*inputs* and *outputs*) are carried through in programme logic models and will be familiar to most, while the third stage of the four-stage log frame was called *purpose* and the fourth stage was termed *goal*. The term 'purpose' is somewhat ambiguous and is perhaps one of the reasons why the log frame was replaced by other frameworks and models. 'Purpose' in log frames is the answer to the question 'what is to be changed?', and therefore is equivalent to *outcome* in other frameworks and models. The logic of this framework is:

> If inputs are managed properly,
> Then outputs will be produced.
> If the outputs are produced,
> Then the purpose will be achieved.
> If the purpose is achieved,
> Then this will contribute to achievement of the goal.
>
> *(Practical Concepts Inc., 1979, Section 2, p. 5)*

It is important to understand that the *logic* of this or any framework or model is not based on an assumption that stages or steps automatically lead from one to the

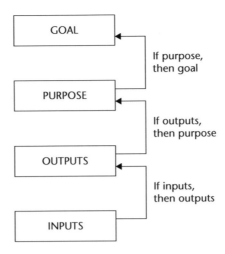

FIGURE 2.1   The logical framework approach

Source: Practical Concepts Inc. (1979, Section 2, p. 6)

next. 'Logic', from the Greek term *logike*, involves the study of the validity of arguments. The stages of logical frameworks and logic models are presented as a series of arguments (hypotheses) about alleged connections that have yet to be proved or disproved through evaluation research.

Programme theory

Building on the early logical framework approach, a body of programme theory was developed that underpins much thinking about evaluation today. The field of programme theory was pioneered by Joseph Wholey (1979, 1983, 1987), a professor of public administration at the University of Southern California for more than 30 years, followed by Peter Rossi and Huey Chen, who have championed the notion of theory-driven evaluation (Chen, 1990; Chen & Rossi, 1983; Rossi, Lipsey & Freeman, 2004). Other influential figures in developing programme theory for evaluation include Carol Weiss (1972, 1995, 1998), Sue Funnell (Funnell & Rogers, 2011) and Patricia Rogers (2008).

Wholey summarizes programme theory as that which 'identifies program resources, program activities, and intended outcomes, and specifies a chain of causal assumptions linking program resources, activities, intermediate outcomes, and ultimate program goals' (1987, p. 78).

More specifically, programme theory comprises two parts: (a) an *impact theory*, which is the explanation of what a programme is meant to achieve; and (b) a *process theory*, which is an explanation of how that impact will be achieved. It is significant that these components are listed in this order. Too many would-be evaluators start by planning their activities and only then try to work out what those activities will achieve. Programme theory starts with identifying the intended impact and then works backwards to identify the processes that need to be implemented to achieve that impact based on available evidence such as formative research, case studies of similar programmes and theory. The intended impact should include both *proximal* (short-term and intermediate) outcomes and *distal* (longer-term) outcomes.

Another important early step in programme theory proposed by Wholey (1987) is *evaluability assessment*. This involves three key questions, as follows:

1. Is the planned programme likely to achieve the intended outcomes and impact (proximal and distal)?
2. Is the programme measurable?
3. Are the proposed outcomes and impact aligned to the expectations and needs of management?

If the answer to any of these questions is 'no' or the response is doubtful, the programme should not proceed.

This is the stage at which objectives are set, expectations are identified, and the information needs of programme managers and senior management are confirmed. Evaluation theory suggests that evaluators should work with those managers who are likely to use evaluation results to determine their information needs and expectations, as well as others, such as researchers and data analysts, who can help in evaluability assessment (Wholey, 1987).

Even though some think theory is mostly normative, Wholey's concept of evaluability assessment is quite practical and pragmatic, because it suggests that evaluation should be undertaken only when the objectives are clear and realistic and have been agreed with management. Too many practitioners attempting evaluation simply accept the objectives given to them by management, with the result that they are often not SMART objectives, as discussed in Chapter 1.

In the tradition of log frames, programme theories are often developed as a series of 'if' and 'then' statements – for example, *if* women aged 50–70 are given information about (a) the risks of breast cancer and (b) the capacity for early detection by breast screening (that is, mammograms) to reduce those risks, *then* there will be an increase in breast-screening rates and improved health outcomes. Importantly, the 'then' statements (objectives and goals) should not be overly ambitious or fanciful. Programme theory advises that there needs to be some solid evidence or some well-established connection between the 'if' and the 'then'.

A good programme theory also should reflect the reality that change happens in stages – and sometimes much more slowly than we might think or hope. There are usually a number of things that have to happen before any significant behaviour change will occur (that is, proximal or short-term and intermediate changes). For example, people usually change their behaviour only after first learning some new information, developing a new skill or changing their attitude about something. Even then, W. J. McGuire warns us that 'correlations between how a given communication affects *knowledge* about a topic, *feeling* regarding it, and *behaviour* toward it tend to be modest' (2013 [1989], p. 139, emphasis added).

Programme theory evaluation

Programme theory evaluation (PTE) takes the baton from programme theory and moves on to look specifically at how evaluation will be done based on programme theory – although that is a rather simplified summary. In a historical review of the development of PTE, Patricia Rogers, Anthony Petrosino, Tracy Huebner and Timothy Hacsi (2000) note that a number of different names are used for the theory-based approach discussed here. These include *programme theory* (Bickman, 1987, 1990), *theory-based evaluation* (Weiss, 1995, 1998), *theory of action* (Argyris & Schön, 1978) and *programme logic* (Funnell, 1997). As Rogers and colleagues summarize, 'PTE consists of an explicit theory or model of how the program causes the intended or observed outcomes and an evaluation that is at least partly guided by this model' (2000, p. 5).

Programme theory evaluation does not get down to the detail of activities or evaluation tasks such as a 'to do' list; rather, it is a model showing a series of intermediate outcomes through which a programme is expected to lead to achievement of its objectives. The idea of basing programme evaluation on a causal model is far from new: it dates back to Edward Suchman's notion of a 'chain of objectives' (1967, p. 55). In this sense, it is easy to see why terms such as 'programme logic' are used to describe the process of planning in programme theory and PTE. After identifying the short-term and intermediate outcomes that are required to achieve the desired impact in programme theory (the programme logic), PTE adds in the 'evaluation bits' to answer questions such as 'how will we know when we have achieved various outcomes?'

This theoretical approach to evaluation and its practical use is highlighted by Don Nutbeam, Elizabeth Harris and Marilyn Wise (2010) in their *Theory in a Nutshell: A Practical Guide to Health Promotion Theories*, in which they present a planning and evaluation cycle for health promotion and communication (see Figure 2.2). While this uses an anti-clockwise directional flow instead of the more traditional clockwise progression of models, it identifies seven stages beginning with problem definition and progressing through creation of a strategy (possible solution), implementation of activities and evaluation of immediate outcomes to ultimate outcome assessment, showing the contribution of theory at several stages. However, it should be noted that this model uses the term 'impact' in a different way from most programme logic models that will be examined in following sections of this chapter and in Chapter 3.

Programme evaluation

Once a programme theory has been developed, including an impact theory and a process theory, evaluability assessment has been conducted to identify whether the programme can be evaluated and whether it is likely to achieve its objectives based on available evidence, and PTE has been planned, it is time to start doing evaluation.

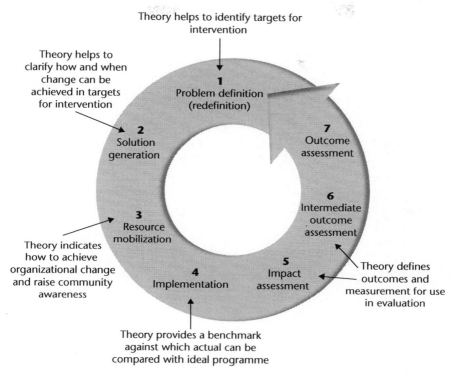

Theory helps to identify targets for
intervention

Theory helps to
clarify how and when
change can be
achieved in targets
for intervention

1
Problem definition
(redefinition)

2
Solution
generation

7
Outcome
assessment

6
Intermediate
outcome
assessment

3
Resource
mobilization

Theory indicates
how to achieve
organizational change
and raise community
awareness

4
Implementation

5
Impact
assessment

Theory defines
outcomes and
measurement for use
in evaluation

Theory provides a benchmark
against which actual can be
compared with ideal programme

FIGURE 2.2   The planning and evaluation cycle

Source: Nutbeam et al. (2010)

Supporting previous definitions of evaluation (formative, process and summative) and the fundamental role of research in evaluation, Peter Rossi and colleagues say that programme evaluation is synonymous with 'evaluation research'
and describe it as 'a social science activity directed at collecting, analyzing, interpreting, and communicating information about the workings and effectiveness of
social programs' (Rossi et al., 2004, p. 2). While they refer to *social* programmes,
this definition is applicable to other types of programme, such as marketing programmes. It usefully adds to the key principles of evaluation cited in Chapter 1
by highlighting the importance of analysis, interpretation and communicating the
findings – for example, to management, as well as to the programme team for
learning – and incorporating what is learned into future programmes as part of
programme improvement. As they go on to say:

Evaluations are conducted for a variety of practical reasons: to aid in
decisions concerning whether programs should be continued, improved,
expanded, or curtailed; to assess the utility of new programs and initiatives;
to increase the effectiveness of program management and administration;

and to satisfy the accountability requirements of program sponsors. Evaluations also may contribute to substantive and methodological social science knowledge.

(Rossi et al., 2004, p. 2)

Turning to another field, the US General Accounting Office (GAO) defines programme evaluation as:

> systematic studies conducted periodically or on an ad hoc basis to assess how well a program is working. They are often conducted by experts external to the program, either inside or outside the agency, as well as by program managers. A program evaluation typically examines achievement of program objectives in the context of other aspects of program performance or in the context in which it occurs. Four main types can be identified [as cited in Chapter 1], all of which use measures of program performance, along with other information, to learn the benefits.

(GAO, 2011, p.1)

Programme logic models

Models are a visual illustration of a process to explain complex steps simply (recognizing that a picture is worth a thousand words) and are applied to a wide range of processes including programme evaluation in the form of *programme logic models*. Logic models represent the logical (that is, rational and reasoned) connection or relationship between elements, and are used to conceptualize the flow and linkages in the process of change. The development and use of programme logic models goes back to Edward Suchman (1967) and Carol Weiss (1972), two pioneers in programme evaluation already cited, and they are informed by, and designed to operationalize, Joseph Wholey's (1979, 1983, 1987) evaluability assessment and programme theory. USAID used an early form of programme logic models in the early 1970s in what it called its 'log frame'.

Figure 2.3 is a basic programme logic model illustrating five key stages of a programme, described as *inputs*, *activities* (also called 'actions' by some), *outputs*, *outcomes* and *impact*. These terms for the main stages of a programme have become widely

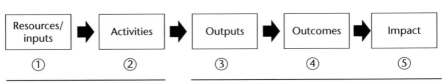

FIGURE 2.3   A basic programme model

Source: Kellogg Foundation (2004 [1998], p. 1)

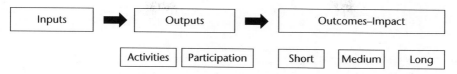

FIGURE 2.4 A programme logic model developed by UWEX

Source: Taylor-Power & Henert (2008, p. 5)[1]

used, because this model developed by the Kellogg Foundation has been applied in a large number of organizations worldwide.

In some programme logic models, *outcomes* are divided into short-term, medium-term (or intermediate) and long-term, in which *long-term* outcomes equate to *impact*, as in the case of the programme logic model developed by the University of Wisconsin-Extension (UWEX) program shown in Figure 2.4. This model also breaks *outputs* into *activities* and *participation*. Thus this model can be read as identifying four main stages – that is, *inputs–outputs–outcomes–impact* – or as representing six stages in total – that is, *inputs–activities–participation* (with *activities* and *participation* collectively described as *outputs*)–*short-term outcomes–medium-term outcomes–long-term outcomes* (also referred to as *impact*).

There are a number of variations in programme logic models, as the seven-stage model proposed by Knowlton and Phillips (2013) in their *Logic Models Guidebook* illustrates (see Figure 2.5). This lists resources as the first stage, while others prefer the broader term 'inputs', and it lists impact as separate from long-term outcomes. In practice, it may be hard to tell the difference between long-term outcomes and impact – a 'substitution' problem (Broom, 2009, p. 358) encountered by many practitioners in using programme logic models that will be discussed in later chapters focused on implementing these models for evaluation.

Some of the most extensive uses of programme logic models can be seen in the work by United Way, the largest volunteer non-profit organization in the United States, following publication in 1996 of *Measuring Program Outcomes: A Practical Approach* (Hatry, Houten, Plantz & Greenway, 1996). There are many variations of United Way programme logic models, but most closely follow the basic stages and principles of the Kellogg Foundation and UWEX models – particularly the latter.

One of the perceived limitations or weaknesses of logic models is that they imply a linear process and can be misinterpreted as suggesting a 'domino effect' – that is, that achievement of one stage leads automatically to the next. Writing in the UWEX guide, Taylor-Power and Henert note that many are uncomfortable

FIGURE 2.5 A basic logic model

Source: Knowlton & Phillips (2013, p. 37)

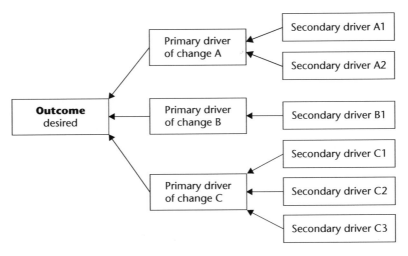

FIGURE 2.6 A 'driver model' of change

Source: Svoronos & Mate (2011)

with this apparent or suggested linearity (2008, p. 6). This has prompted some users to add feedback loops to each stage of programme logic models to emphasize that findings from evaluation at each stage should be used to review and adjust the programme as necessary. In their *Logic Models Guidebook*, Lisa Knowlton and Cynthia Phillips (2013) offer a circular programme logic model to illustrate the cyclical nature of the process of planning and evaluation. This avoids the seemingly simple linear approach of traditional programme logic models, but it is not a model that lends itself easily to the insertion of details about what happens at each stage – a next step in the process of implementing theory-based systematic evaluation. Whether or not programme logic models include arrows denoting that the findings of, and learning from, progressive evaluation at each stage are applied to fine-tune or revise strategy and activities, this should be read as implicit in all models.

The same basic principles of a series of causally connected activities leading to change are represented in the 'driver model' developed by Theodore (Teddy) Svoronos and Kedar Mate (2011), as shown in Figure 2.6. This employs the common business terminology of 'drivers' of success, but it is not used as extensively as programme logic models.

It can be seen from these models and the preceding discussion that programme logic models describe programmes from beginning to end – in fact, they start even before programmes begin. It is important to recognize that evaluation needs to be planned and designed before programmes get under way, and also that some evaluation needs to be conducted *ex ante* (formative evaluation) as well as *ex post* (summative evaluation). This is one of the most misunderstood aspects of evaluation: practitioners too often think about evaluation towards the end of a programme, by which time it is too late to gain benchmark data or to pre-test activities and materials, and too late to fine-tune or adjust tactics if there are indications that the programme is not achieving the intended outcomes and impact. One of the major contributions of theory to evaluation is to slow down the rush to production and delivery, which is particularly characteristic of creative fields such as advertising and PR, and instead to draw on existing knowledge (theory and research) to inform the design of the proposed programme. Programme logic models also can serve as a general strategic planning tool to map the process of activities and outputs through to outcomes and impact, with the advantage that evaluation is integrated into overall communication planning and design.

Theory of change

Theory of change emerged from the field of programme theory and programme evaluation in the mid-1990s as a way of analysing initiatives that seek to create change and explain how change is achieved, whether that is social, political, economic or commercial change. Theory of change draws from organizational and environmental psychology, and also, to some extent, from sociology and political science. Applications related to communication also draw on human communication theories, as might be expected.

Theory of change has been developed and applied to evaluation most notably by the Aspen Institute Roundtable on Community Change (Anderson, 2005) as a means of modelling and evaluating community initiatives, with leading programme evaluation researchers including Huey Chen, Peter Rossi, Carol Weiss, Michael Patton and Hélène Clark contributing to its development. In a chapter in an influential book, *New Approaches to Evaluating Comprehensive Community Initiatives*, Carol Weiss (1995) argued that a major obstacle to evaluation of many programmes is that managers and stakeholders are unclear how change will occur, and pay little attention to the short-term and mid-term changes needed to achieve longer-term outcome and impact. Weiss is recognized as popularizing the term 'theory of change' to describe two key steps in all programmes: (a) identifying the 'mini-steps' that lead to longer-term goals; and (b) identifying the connections between activities and outcomes and impact – that is, what drives what.

The Center for Theory of Change, a non-profit centre established by Act-Knowledge in New York City, says on its website that theory of change 'is focused in particular on mapping out or "filling in" what has been described as the "missing middle" between what a program or change initiative does (its activities or interventions) and how these lead to desired goals being achieved' (2016a, para. 1).

Beyond its basic admonitions to think hard about what interim steps, stages and milestones are required, and to draw on research to provide empirical evidence to support assessments and decisions in the process of developing and delivering programmes (Clark, 2004), theory of change adds one more important principle to the *modus operandi* for planning evaluation. This process of designing activities and outputs to produce outcomes and impact is done backwards. In what it calls 'backwards mapping', the Center for Theory of Change says that the theory is applied:

> by first identifying the desired long-term goals and then works back from these to identify all the conditions (outcomes) that must be in place (and how these related to one another causally) for the goals to occur. These are all mapped out in an outcomes framework.
>
> *(Center for Theory of Change, 2016a, para. 1)*

It adds that:

> After the first step of laying out the long-term goals and a simple change framework, comes a more detailed stage of the mapping process. Building upon the initial framework, we continue to map backwards until we have a framework that tells the story we think is appropriate for the purposes of planning. Sometimes, this will require much more detail because stake-holders want to identify the 'root' causes of the problem they hope to resolve. In other cases, the map will illustrate three or four levels of change, which display a reasonable set of early and intermediate steps toward the long term goal.
>
> *(Center for Theory of Change, 2016b, para. 1)*

The difference between programme theory and theory of change can be summed up as follows.

- *Programme theory* and its constituent elements, including PTE and programme evaluation, tell us if a particular programme is likely to work beforehand and whether it did work afterwards. Programme logic models graphically show programme components such as inputs, outputs and outcomes. Programme theory and programme logic models usually relate to particular programmes or activities at a particular point in time.
- *Theory of change* starts with a goal, and is a more comprehensive explanation of the determining factors for desired outcomes and impact. Theory of change tells us *why* and *how* programmes work, by identifying the preconditions to change at each stage, and provides insights into how to replicate that change in future. Thus theory of change informs us more generally about ways of creat-ing change than does a particular programme theory.

For example, a programme logic model and programme evaluation may show that a 'Get fit, be healthy' programme succeeded in achieving a specific objective to increase enrolments in exercise classes by 10 per cent. But a research-based theory of change may show that people enrolled in fitness programmes need to attend classes for at least six months to maintain the health outcomes desired, and then go on to identify the steps necessary to maintain enrolments and attendance. Theory of change may also identify that emotional factors (for example, desire to look good) have greater effect than rational appeals (reducing heart disease), which can be applied to other health campaigns.

To some extent, what Weiss (1995) says about theory of change – and even programme theory – may seem like common sense. Perhaps it is. But, in the hectic hurly-burly of day-to-day work, the managers of many programmes rush to meet deadlines and are under pressure to produce 'deliverables', which are mostly associated with visible outputs. In the case of public communication, success is often prematurely associated with producing an advertising campaign, developing a website or getting headlines and publicity in news media. Programme theory, PTE, programmes and programme evaluation, illustrated through programme logic models and theory of change, provide a structure and systematic process for undertaking evaluation.

Realist evaluation

Another approach to evaluation that has gained attention and support is *realist evaluation*, also less commonly referred to as *realistic evaluation*.[2] To the novice, this name might seem to be stating the obvious: surely *all* evaluation should be realistic? However, *realist* evaluation refers to several particular characteristics of evaluation.

Perhaps the most important principle in realist evaluation is an ontological one: it sees the 'actors' (audience and programme managers) involved in programmes and the activities undertaken (referred to as *interventions* in health communication) as embedded in a social reality and inextricably linked to, and affected by, that social reality. In simple terms, realist evaluation places great emphasis on *context* and uses *context–mechanism–outcome* (CMO) as the main structure for undertaking evaluation (Better Evaluation, 2016; Salter & Kothari, 2014). This involves first closely examining context, then implementing various mechanisms designed to effect change and finally evaluating outcomes. Ray Pawson and Nick Tilley (1997), who first developed realist evaluation, say that the key question in evaluation is 'what works in which circumstances and for whom?', rather than merely 'does it work?' Recent literature goes further and says the 'complete realist question' in evaluation is: 'What works, for whom, in what respects, to what extent, in what contexts, and how?' (Better Evaluation, 2016, para. 3). Thus 'realist', in this context, refers to evaluation anchored in social, cultural, political and economic reality.

Pawson argues that 'programs are not stable, single entities emitting some steady force for change' (2013, p. 48). Rather, he and Tilley (1997) say that whether information and ideas presented will 'cement' in the minds of audiences depends on what they call the 'four Is':

1. the *individual* capacities of audience members and the programme team members;
2. the *interpersonal* relationships created as part of, or concurrent with, the programme;
3. *institutional* factors; and
4. the wider *infrastructural* resources that either support or undermine the objectives of the programme.

Realist evaluation sees the processes of awareness, attitudinal and particularly behavioural change as more complex than some simple evaluation models suggest. Also, Pawson and Tilley (1997) say that 'evaluation research is cursed with *short-termism*', and advocate a number of principles for implementing realist evaluation, including:

- Always speak of evaluations in the plural. Rather than a one-off approach, evaluation should include an iterative series of inquiries.
- Use multiple methods and multiple data sources. Realist evaluation is method neutral, with most proponents advising that both quantitative and qualitative research are usually desirable.
- Never expect to know what works, just keep trying to find out.

(Pawson & Tilley, 2001, pp. 322–323)

Realist evaluation is also concerned with *knowledge translation*, which, according to the Canadian Institutes of Health Research, is 'the exchange, synthesis and ethically-sound application of knowledge within a complex system of interactions among researchers and users' (Salter & Kothari, 2014, p. 2). In short, knowledge translation is the process of translating theory and research findings into practice. The realist approach notes that traditional programme evaluation efforts – particularly evaluability assessment in programme theory and PTE – attempt to provide an *a priori* estimate of programme effectiveness based on existing knowledge (for example, case studies) and through the assessment of one or more outcomes in the case of summative evaluation (Salter & Kothari, 2014). In contrast, realist evaluation emphasizes ongoing theory-building. Realist evaluation starts and ends with theory, often creating new theory as it develops findings, but always grounded in the social reality of particular programmes and audiences.

Performance measurement and management

In the business world and some areas of administration, programme evaluation is closely associated, and sometimes seen as synonymous, with *performance measurement*, which is part of performance management. The US GAO, for example, describes performance measurement as follows:

Performance measurement is the ongoing monitoring and reporting of program accomplishments, particularly progress toward pre-established goals. It is typically conducted by program or agency management. Performance measures may address the type or level of program activities conducted (process), the direct products and services delivered by a program (outputs), or the results of those products and services (outcomes). A 'program' may be any activity, project, function, or policy that has an identifiable purpose or set of objectives.

(US GAO, 2011, p. 2)

This description of performance measurement is useful in explaining the nature of a *programme* as the term is used in measurement and evaluation literature – that is, 'any activity, project, function, or policy' – to which we could add 'campaign'. It also closely resembles the GAO's definition of programme evaluation. Some evaluation specialists see the practices as similar and advocate that the evaluation fraternity should embrace performance measurement (McDavid, Huse & Hawthorn, 2013). In business, in particular, performance measurement has gained widespread adoption, so linking programme evaluation to this practice could help to make evaluation mainstream in the business and corporate sector. However, others are sceptical, saying that performance management is a tool managers use to serve the needs of organizational management and that it is mostly focused on internal functions (for example, Feller, 2002, and Perrin, 1998, as cited in McDavid et al., 2013, p. 4). The strong association of performance management with maximizing human resource (HR) productivity and economic efficiency is also seen as much narrower than the role of programme evaluation.

Other approaches to evaluation

There are a number of other approaches to evaluation. In a claimed 'typology' of evaluation 'models', Hanne Hansen lists five other approaches in addition to programme theory:

- *Results* models focussed on specific goal attainment and effects;
- *Explanatory process* models designed to identify how a program has worked such as identifying any implementation problems and whether levels of activity are sufficient;
- *System* models used to examine how systems and procedures have performed;
- *Economic* models, which (as the name suggests) evaluate productivity and economic efficiency using methods such as cost–benefit analysis and cost-effectiveness analysis;
- *Actor* models, which focus specifically on the reaction of specific clients or stakeholders.

(Hansen, 2005, p. 449)

This typology – which identifies other broad approaches, rather than specific models – provides further insights into the focus and purposes of evaluation, and particularly highlights benefits such as learning for programme and system improvement during evaluation in explanatory and system approaches. However, some of the approaches can be seen to be narrow – for example, results and actor approaches typically focus on results related to organization objectives (that is, they are organization-centric) or the interests of specific groups, and economic models explore only financial benefits, while ignoring other potential outcomes and impact. The issue of organization-centricity in evaluation and the pluses and minuses of particular methods will be discussed further in Chapters 3 and 8.

Information processing and communication

To evaluate public communication, we need to have a clear understanding of how communication works, as well as of evaluation theories and approaches. This might seem obvious – and indeed the term 'communication' is used very liberally as if it is a simple thing to accomplish. The history of human relationships tells us that this is not the case, as noted in Chapter 1. Effective communication involves a number of steps and stages, and to evaluate public communication, the evaluation framework adopted needs to be mapped on to the steps involved in communication – whether the evaluation framework is a programme logic model (for example, Kellogg Foundation, 2004 [1998]; Wholey, 1979), a driver model (Svoronos & Mate, 2011) or a CMO structure (Salter & Kothari, 2014).

The purpose here is not to discuss human communication theories in detail – there are many other texts that do that (for example, Craig & Muller, 2007; Griffin, Ledbetter & Sparks, 2015; Littlejohn & Foss, 2008) – but simply to draw out of the large body of knowledge about how human communication works some key principles and concepts that provide the basis of what we should evaluate. We cannot evaluate if we do not know what it is we should be evaluating.

Evaluation of communication is informed to some extent by all of the 'seven traditions' of communication study and research identified by Robert Craig (1999), as well as by more recently identified traditions of communication studies, such as *pragmatism* (Craig, 2015, p. 361; Russill, 2008) and the *ethical* tradition (Griffin, 2000).[3] But evaluation is particularly informed by four bodies of communication theory – namely:

- *systems* theory (also known as the *cybernetic tradition*), which focuses on processes, channels and technologies – particularly information-processing models;
- *socio-psychological* theories, which focus on how humans think, interact and behave in a social context;
- *phenomenological* theories, which focus on human interpretation (hermeneutics); and
- *sociocultural* theories, which focus on social interaction and the influences of culture and the environment that humans inhabit.

(Craig & Muller, 2007; Littlejohn & Foss, 2008)

Of the other traditions of communication studies identified by Craig and others, *rhetorical* and *semiotic* theories provide some insights into audience interpretation, but mainly inform the design of communication programmes and materials. The *critical* tradition focuses on reviewing and critiquing public communication from a political economy, poststructuralist/postmodern, cultural studies or feminist perspective, rather than in terms of effectiveness. All perspectives are important, but systems, socio-psychological, phenomenological and sociocultural human communication theories provide some very specific insights into how people process, interpret and respond to information and influences.

Beyond Lasswell and Shannon & Weaver

A key to evaluation in public communication is moving on from simplistic trans-missional notions of communication that were widely accepted in *mass communication* and *mass media* theories for most of the twentieth century, based on Shannon and Weaver's (1949) *mathematical model of communication*, and similar thinking by David Berlo (1960) and others. Even though Harold Lasswell described communication as 'who says what, in which channel, to whom, with what effect' (1948, p. 12), his faith and that of many mass media and mass communication theorists resided uncritically in the power of senders to influence audiences. A large investment in propaganda studies between and after the two world wars was based on this premise.

As noted in Chapter 1 and in the major traditions of communication studies research referred to above, human communication is now recognized as a two-way transactional process that is affected by numerous internal and external factors. As W. J. McGuire (1969, 1985, 2001) says in *The Handbook of Social Psychology* and other writing, *meaning-making* – the locus of communication – is a complicated process involving a number of steps, of which presenting information is only the first. It is important to briefly reflect on some of the key steps in human communication to identify the milestones and metrics that can populate an evaluation framework for public communication.

The 6–13 steps of communication

In his early challenges to simple transmissional thinking about human communication, McGuire (1968, 1969) identified six important steps, as shown in Figure 2.7. He pointed out that, beyond (1) *presenting* or distributing information or messages, communication requires that (2) the *attention* of those with whom one wishes to communicate must be gained, (3) audiences must *understand* the messages, (4) they must *accept* them rather than reject or disregard them, (5) they need to *retain* them to have any lasting effect and (6) a *change* of attitude or behaviour may occur.

McGuire (1976) went on to expand this to 8 steps – and then to 12 steps (McGuire, 1989) – and, most recently, to 13 stages of communication (McGuire, 1999, 2001), as follows:

1. Exposure.
2. Attention.
3. Liking and interest.
4. Comprehension.

FIGURE 2.7 Six steps of communication

Sources: McGuire (1968, 1969)

5. Cognition – particularly cognitive elaboration (thinking about the message).
6. Acquiring the skills or knowledge required to deal with the issue.
7. Attitude change – particularly to agreement (what McGuire calls 'yielding').
8. Storing information in memory (retention).
9. Retrieving information (that is, recall).
10. Deciding to act in accordance with information (intention).
11. Action/behaviour.
12. Cognitive integration of behaviour (for example, reinforcement).
13. Encouraging others to behave similarly – what McGuire called 'proselytizing' and what is commonly regarded in modern marketing as *advocacy*.

This model of communication illustrates the fallacy of believing that communication is about producing content containing *messages* and distributing (that is, *transmitting*) information. The common industry catchphrase 'content is king' is reductionist and misleading (as well as being a gendered statement), and even the recent refocusing on story-telling (Mead, 2014) is only part of the process of communication. McGuire's 13 steps and the traditions of communication studies identified by Craig (1999, 2015) and others demonstrate the importance for public communication practitioners to have a sound understanding of human *communication* – not only of channels and technologies of *communications* and the creative and technical skills required to produce information materials, which are often the focus of industry training and practice.

Communication–persuasion matrix

From the steps of communication that he identified, McGuire (1989) developed his widely applied *communication–persuasion matrix*, which further informs approaches to evaluation. McGuire arranged his steps of communication on a matrix, on the vertical axis of which he listed output variables. He then drew on the models of Shannon and Weaver (1949) and Berlo (1960) to arrange 'source', 'message', 'channel', 'receiver' and 'response' (also called 'destination' and 'target') across the horizontal axis as input variables. Thus the communication–persuasion matrix is a basic *input–output model*.

While this matrix drew attention to the interacting factors that contribute to communication, and began a process of separating inputs and outputs in communication models, there are a number of flaws in the communication-persuasion matrix and in terms of how it is applied.

- The steps of communication identified by McGuire – particularly in his advanced 13-step model (McGuire, 1999, 2001) – go well beyond outputs. Action/behaviour, cognitive integration of behaviour (for example, reinforcement) and encouraging others to behave similarly (advocacy) are what most researchers and commercial and social marketers would consider to be *outcomes*. Also, storing information (retention) and attitude change can be outcomes if the objectives of a programme are awareness creation or changing attitudes.

- The matrix gives no consideration to *context*, such as the social, cultural, political and economic environment in which communication attempts to inform or persuade. As discussed in this chapter and in Chapter 1, a range of factors beyond the source, message and channel affect communication.

- The main criticism of the matrix is that it is one of a number of *hierarchy of effects* models. Such models and the thinking they represent rely on a highly contested notion that there is a logical progression from *cognitive* to *affective* to *conative* effects and that audiences need to move, or be moved, through those three stages to achieve behavioural outcomes. Such a view is now disputed in advertising and marketing literature (for example, Barry & Howard, 1990; Scholten, 1996) and by a number of communication theories, some of which will be briefly mentioned in the next section.

Notwithstanding, the communication–persuasion matrix has been widely applied and is the basis of a number of planning tools and models used in advertising, such as the attention–interest–desire–action (AIDA) model of advertising, as will be discussed further in Chapter 3, and contains many elements relevant to evaluation of public communication.

Other key communication theories that inform evaluation

While this is not a text on communication theories, as noted already, it is useful to briefly draw attention to some other important explanations of how humans communicate or fail to communicate – particularly those that inform an approach to public communication evaluation.

Elaboration likelihood theory

Developed by Richard Petty and John Cacioppo (1986), *elaboration likelihood theory* (ELT), also referred to as the *elaboration likelihood model* (ELM), goes some way towards showing why the notion of hierarchy of effects is problematic. This theory identifies two main routes in the way in which humans process information, which Petty and Cacioppo parsimoniously call the *central route* and a *peripheral route* (1986, p. 7). *Elaboration* refers to 'the extent to which a person carefully thinks about issue-relevant information'. Central-route information processing is also referred to as *active information processing* and *active cognition*, because, in this approach to information processing, people rationally analyse and reflect, often considering empirical information (that is, facts), and 'mull over' (that is, elaborate on) an issue. Engagement of the central route is triggered by a number of factors – particularly level of *involvement*, which is largely influenced by the personal relevance of an issue or problem, personal predisposition towards critical thinking and the influence of others such as peers (Littlejohn & Foss, 2008, p. 74).

In contrast, peripheral-route information processing relies on instinctive reactions: heuristics, which are also referred to as *mental shortcuts* (Griffin, 2009, p. 194), schemata and sometimes emotion. The same understanding is referred to as *systematic* versus *heuristic* information processing by others (Chaiken, Liberman & Eagly, 1989).

Heuristics are experience-based 'rules of thumb' that humans use to make sense and meaning, and to expedite decisions. Commonly applied heuristics include credibility (including source credibility), liking someone or something (we tend to agree with people whom we like) and consensus (that is, trust in the majority, such as a perception that 'everyone' is doing or thinking something) (O'Keefe, 1990, pp. 186–187). Heuristics applied to processing information and making decisions also include habit (such as voting a party ticket in elections) or buying a brand that we have always bought. Heuristics and other mental shortcuts bypass active cognition. A similar approach is explained in the *heuristic–systematic model* (HSM) of information processing (Chaiken et al., 1989).

Schemata (plural of schema) are mental categories that humans create based on their past experiences and which they use for categorizing new information that is received (Wrench, McCroskey & Richmond, 2008, pp. 130–133). W. James Potter points out that a number of synonyms and similar terms are used for the same concept, including *frames*, *cognitive maps*, *social scripts*, *cognitive structures* and *memory organization packets* (2009, p. 121). Doris Graber (1988) and others note that schemata are also similar to the psychological concept of *constructs* discussed in *constructivism*. Schemata or constructs function as mental templates into which new information and experiences are inserted. For instance, if we meet someone wearing a large hat, a check pattern shirt, pants with a large buckle and boots, we may quickly decide that the person is a cowboy because of a mental construct or schema. The person could, in fact, be a professional rodeo rider, a person going to a party in fancy dress or a member of a country-and-western band. The important ramification of schemata or constructs is that they inform us that humans do not analytically and rationally process all of the information that they receive. Often, they simply group new information into existing categories of information and assign the meanings already existing for that category. This is necessary, according to psychologists, because people cannot carefully and analytically process all information that they encounter – particularly in today's information-saturated world. People need to achieve some level of what psychologists call 'cognitive economy' by being 'cognitive misers' (Fiske & Kinder, 1981), or what McGuire (1969) calls 'lazy organisms'.

Elaboration likelihood refers to the probability or otherwise that people will either process information elaborately (that is, think deeply about it) or rely on heuristics or make an emotional response.

Diffusion of innovations and two-step flow

Another theory of communication worth highlighting for the way in which it informs evaluation is Everett Rogers' explanation of the *diffusion of innovations*. Rogers defines the diffusion of innovations as 'a social process in which subjectively perceived information about a new idea is communicated. The meaning of an innovation is thus gradually worked out through a process of social construction' (1995 [1962], p. vii). More specifically, information about new things is passed down from opinion leaders and influencers to others, thus linking this theory to the *two-step flow* understanding of communication – albeit, in diffusion theory there may be two, three, four or many more cascades of information.

A further important point to make about diffusion of innovations is that Rogers and Shoemaker found that 'early knowers' of information more often rely on media sources and 'late knowers' more often rely on interpersonal sources (1971, pp. 259, 348), suggesting a key role of media in reaching opinion leaders. However, this theory equally highlights the importance of peer influence in gaining wide acceptance of information and ideas. The widely used innovation adoption model identifying innovators, early adopters, early majority, late majority and laggards is based on Rogers' work.

Cognitive dissonance, reactance and other socio-psychological theories

There are many other socio-psychological theories of communication that are applied in advertising and other fields of public communication practice, such as health communication, but this is not the place to examine them in any detail. However, it is important for public communication practitioners to have at least a basic knowledge of key communication theories. Without this, they are likely to develop communication programmes that are bound to fail. Some other communication theories worth reading up on include the following:

- **Cognitive dissonance.** As already discussed in general terms in Chapter 1, Elizabeth Crawford and Charles Okigbo say that 'many communication campaigns fail on account of audience members resisting the messages because they contradict adopted habits and ingrained behaviours' (2014, p. 11).
- **Reactance.** As already discussed in Chapter 1.
- **Self-efficacy.** Researchers in many fields, including health communication, identify the importance of self-efficacy in determining communication effectiveness. Self-efficacy is an individual's perceived capability to successfully perform specific behaviours in a specific situation (Bandura, 1997; Egbert & Reed, 2016, p. 203). It is a psychological construct because self-efficacy refers to an individual's *perceived* capability, not *actual* capabilities such as physical or intellectual ability. For instance, a person may be physically capable of losing weight, but may perceive themselves as unable to do so.
- **Social learning theory.** This theory posits that learning is a cognitive process that takes place in a social context, not only in formal educational settings, and that it can occur through observation as well as direct instruction. Furthermore, learning occurs through the observation of rewards and punishments (Bandura, 1977). Social learning affects many public communication programmes. Another key consideration in public communication is whether

or not learning is required to achieve objectives. In some cases, audiences may need to learn if they are to behave in the way intended. For example, the introduction of calcium supplements to help women to avoid osteoporosis first required an education campaign to make women (who are particularly prone to this condition) aware of the risks and causes. In contrast, learning is not necessary and may even be a distraction in marketing fashion products, which are mostly purchased based on emotion or heuristics such as a desire to fit in with the crowd or be seen to be 'on trend'.

- **Social cognitive theory (SCT).** This theory builds on self-efficacy and social learning theory, and holds that a person first has to believe that they can perform a behaviour requested of them (self-efficacy), then must have the abilities and skills required, and finally requires motivation, such as incentives or reward (Bandura, 1977, 1986). Social cognitive theory also incorporates social learning theory in the sense that observation of others being rewarded or punished for certain behaviours can lead to the observer replicating a rewarded behaviour and avoiding a punished behaviour.

- **Theory of reasoned action.** This theory is one of three classic persuasion models derived from psychology, and gives insights into how well audiences are likely to engage in a requested behaviour and how long they are likely to maintain that behaviour. Research shows that the strength of behaviour is primarily determined by intention to perform that behaviour – that is, how committed those involved are to the action. Further, it shows that two key factors influence intentions: (a) a person's own attitude towards the behaviour; and (b) a person's subjectively perceived norms in relation to the behaviour – that is, how they think others perceive it (Ajzen & Fishbein, 1980). For example, if a person is inclined towards a certain behaviour and believes that others think the person should perform the behaviour, there is a high likelihood that they will adopt the behaviour. The theory of reasoned action draws on peer influence, but also highlights the reasoning process that audiences may go through in reaching decisions related to behaviour. However, some feel that we make too much of reasoned action, noting humans are emotional, as well as rational, beings.

- **Integrative theory of behaviour change.** As the name suggests, integrated theory of behaviour change brings together knowledge from a number of theories – particularly social cognitive theory, theory of reasoned action and the health belief model, in the case of health campaigns. It shows that a behaviour is most likely to occur when (a) a person has a strong intention to perform the behaviour, (b) the person has the necessary skills and abilities required to perform the behaviour and (c) there are no environmental constraints preventing that behaviour (Cappella, Fishbein, Hornik, Ahern & Sayeed, 2001). This theory, which has been applied in major campaigns such as the National Youth Anti-Drug Media campaign in the US, highlights the importance of identifying constraints and barriers, as well as focusing on messages and the distribution of information.

Social and cultural context and social interaction

Having highlighted a number of important theories grounded in psychology and socio-psychology that inform public communication, it is equally important to recognize that public communication is also significantly influenced by social and cultural factors. The sociocultural tradition of understanding human communication identified as one of seven traditions of communication scholarship by Robert Craig (1999) combines insights from sociology and cultural studies. Beyond simple notions such as the influence of peers and peer pressure, sociocultural theories of communication draw our attention to how human understanding of the world is based on *social constructionism*, which was first highlighted in texts such as *The Social Construction of Reality* by Peter Berger and Thomas Luckmann (1966). Concepts such as family, work, the role of women, gender identity, a home, appropriate dress and behaviour, and many other central aspects of people's lives, while being partly constituted and shaped by laws and conventions and having some physical attributes, are essentially what societies have decided them to be through discourse – that is, they are socially constructed. In addition to having a physical identity, British philosopher Anthony Giddens (1991) says that people create *narratives of the self* to describe who they are to themselves as well as others. One's identity is a social construction as much as or more than it is our physical body and name.

Giddens (1984) created the term *structuration* to denote a combination of structuralism (structure) and interaction to convey his view that human society is shaped by both social structures (laws, the state, the church, institutions, etc.), as well as individuals influencing each other through social interaction. American communication scholars Marshall Scott Poole, David Seibold and Robert McPhee (1985) applied Giddens' structuration theory to communication in their *adaptive structuration theory* to show that organizations are largely social constructions. They pointed out that while organizations have their structuralist elements (that is, organizational hierarchy, policies, rules, procedures, buildings, financial capital, etc.), they are also largely composed of conversations among people such as what staff and customers say and how people interact. Organizational reputation, for example, is very much a social construction made up of what people hear, see and read, and the perceptions that they have formed through interaction.

In recent times, many surveys have found peers to be the highest rated source of influence for many people (Edelman, 2015; Nielsen, 2015, p. 4). The phenomenal growth of social media is testament to the thirst that people have for social interaction and also the influence of social interaction. Therefore, all evaluation has to be mindful of how social and cultural factors and social interaction influences public communication. Other significant sociocultural theories that inform communication include the following:

- **Habitus.** In noting that they live in social space, as well as physical space, Pierre Bourdieu posited that people individually and collectively 'internalize their position in social space' (1990, p. 110) – that is, they unconsciously take on the rules, values and dispositions of the social space around them and accept them as their 'lot' in life. He asserted that people inhabit *cultural fields* in which there are rules, rituals, conventions, categories of description, designations, titles and so on, and that, in these fields, they accumulate more or less *cultural capital* depending on their circumstances. As well as requiring *social capital* (for example, networks of relationships and status, such as a senior position), Bourdieu said that people's capacity to think and act is shaped by their cultural capital (for example, education and general knowledge, communication skills and identity, dress or collective groups). In some public communication programmes, it is necessary to develop the cultural and social capital of audiences to enable them to comply with messages such as 'get fit', 'stop smoking', 'vote', 'send your children to university' or 'invest in pensions'.

- **Symbolic convergence theory.** Also known as *fantasy themes*, this theory refers to a human tendency to converge around certain narratives. For example, themes such as 'David and Goliath' (the small guy beats the big guy), the successful quest, the pot of gold at the end of the rainbow or journey's end, and so on, are near-universal stories that captivate audiences. Many such themes are used in public communication because of their symbolic efficacy.
- **Dialogical, or dialectical, theory of relationships.** Developed by Leslie Baxter (2011), this theory draws on Hegel's dialectic and phenomenological theories of communication, such as Mikhail Bakhtin's (1981, 1984 [1963]) *dialogism* and Martin Buber's (1958 [1923], 2002 [1947]) discussion of *dialogue*, to highlight the importance of the to-and-fro of debate and argument in communication, rather than monologue and 'monologue disguised as dialogue' (Buber, 2002 [1947], p. 22).

It bears repeating that it is important for public communication practitioners to have a good understanding of a range of human communication theories that inform how communication works, as well as the various blockages and forms of resistance that exist. There are many excellent reference texts that summarize these, such as Craig and Muller's (2007) *Theorizing Communication: Readings across Traditions* and Littlejohn and Foss (2008) *Theories of Human Communication*. These summarize the 'seven traditions' of human communication research based on systems theory, rhetoric, semiotics, psychology and sociology, phenomenology, cultural studies and critical thinking.

Stages of communication: inputs and outputs to outcomes and impact

Once we have recognized that human communication, including public communication, progresses through a number of stages and steps, with various obstacles and barriers along the way, as well as incentives and supporting factors, we can start to combine this information and knowledge to examine how public communication might be arranged and structured to enable timely and rigorous evaluation.

In terms of mapping the process, the tool that is most widely used in programme evaluation is the programme logic model, because of its capacity for visualization, which introduces a degree of simplification to otherwise complex processes. However, principles from other approaches, such as realist evaluation, also should be applied in developing an evaluation framework and working model.

Figure 2.8 provides an example of a five-stage programme logic model, adapted from the Kellogg Foundation's (2004 [1998]) model to show communication objectives and how these are linked to support overall organization objectives. The model also illustrates feedback loops from each stage, and makes it explicitly clear that outcomes and impact are the end point, not simply producing and distributing outputs.

Figure 2.9 populates the model shown in Figure 2.8 with examples of some typical *inputs, activities, outputs, outcomes* and possible *impacts* from public communication. Public communication outputs include paid media advertising, editorial media publicity, social media communication, websites, publications such as newsletters, events, sponsorships and community projects. Inputs and activities include the preparatory steps to plan, design and produce these.

The outcomes and impacts listed in Figure 2.9 are examples of what can result from effective communication. Not all public communication will include such a wide array of activities, outputs, outcomes and impacts, although integrated programmes involving multiple strategies and interventions are increasingly common. Figure 2.9 is a hypothetical programme logic model for public communication. It does not show how evaluation should be conducted, which will be the subject of the next chapter in which a number of models from various sectors of public communication, including advertising, PR and health communication, will be critically examined.

Cost centre vs value-adding centre

Breaking down public communication into these stages allows for the graphic illustration of another important reason for doing evaluation at outcomes and impact stages in addition to those outlined in Chapter 1. In the first three stages of the programme logic models for communication shown previously and in Figure 2.10, public communication is a *cost centre*, in management terms. It involves assembling resources, including people and money, and the production of often expensive activities and outputs, such as media advertising, events, sponsorships, publications, websites, and so on. It is only when outcomes are generated – and particularly when impact is achieved in line with organization objectives – that public communication becomes a *value-adding centre* or function in an organization (see Figure 2.10). Thus the public communicator who measures and reports only outputs such as advertising reach and the volume of publicity generated is likely to be perceived as a cost centre with no evidence of how these outputs add value to the organization. In all programme logic models, whether they identify three, four, five or six stages, roughly half of the process involves costs and investment; only the

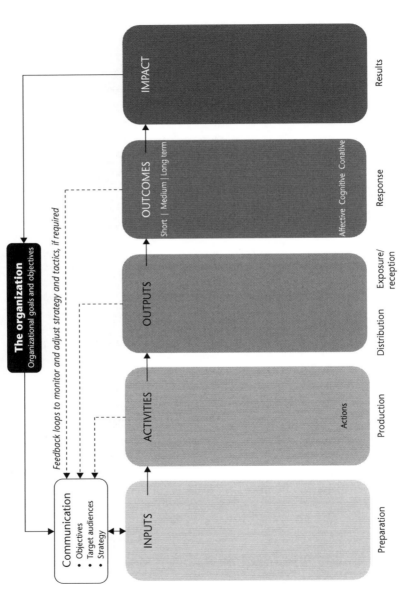

FIGURE 2.8 The basic stages of a programme logic model for public communication

Source: Adapted from Kellogg Foundation (2004 [1998])

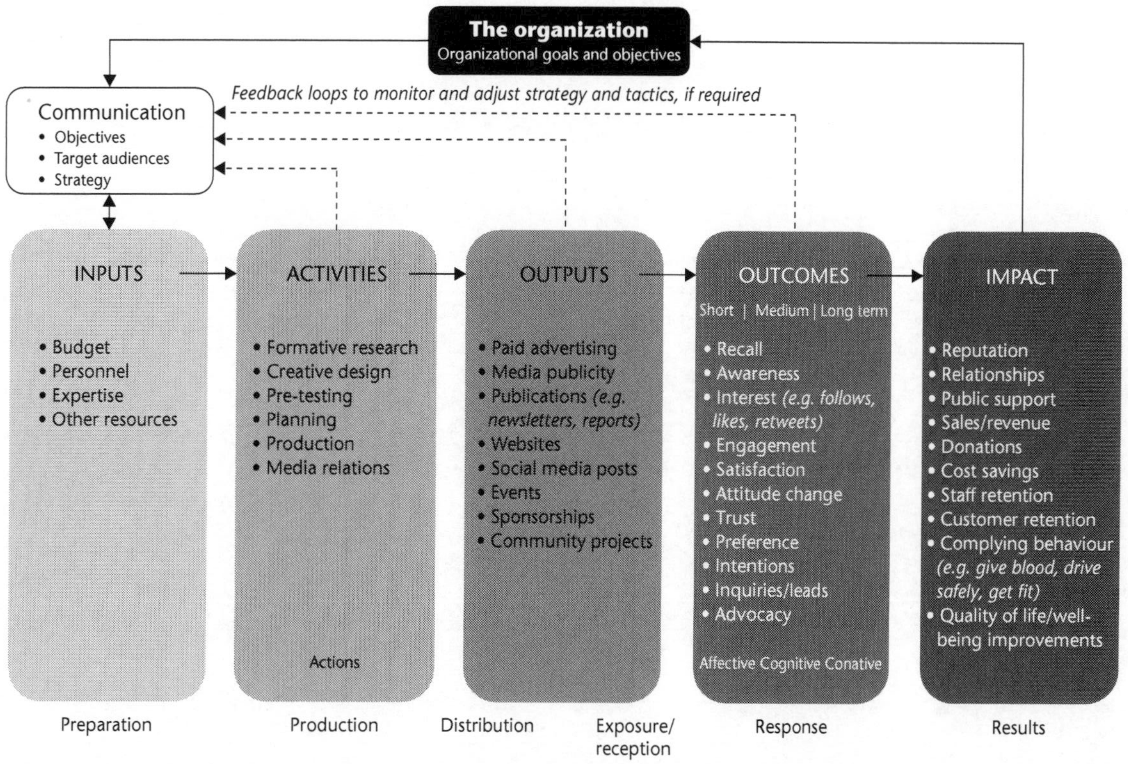
The organization
Organizational goals and objectives
Communication
• Objectives
• Target audiences
• Strategy
Feedback loops to monitor and adjust strategy and tactics, if required
INPUTS
• Budget
• Personnel
• Expertise
• Other resources
ACTIVITIES
• Formative research
• Creative design
• Pre-testing
• Planning
• Production
• Media relations
Actions
OUTPUTS
• Paid advertising
• Media publicity
• Publications (e.g. newsletters, reports)
• Websites
• Social media posts
• Events
• Sponsorships
• Community projects
OUTCOMES
Short | Medium | Long term
• Recall
• Awareness
• Interest (e.g. follows, likes, retweets)
• Engagement
• Satisfaction
• Attitude change
• Trust
• Preference
• Intentions
• Inquiries/leads
• Advocacy
Affective Cognitive Conative
IMPACT
• Reputation
• Relationships
• Public support
• Sales/revenue
• Donations
• Cost savings
• Staff retention
• Customer retention
• Complying behaviour (e.g. give blood, drive safely, get fit)
• Quality of life/well-being improvements
Preparation
Production
Distribution
Exposure/ reception
Response
Results

FIGURE 2.9 A programme logic model for public communication, with typical inputs, activities, outputs, outcomes and impacts

Source: Adapted from Kellogg Foundation (2004 [1998])

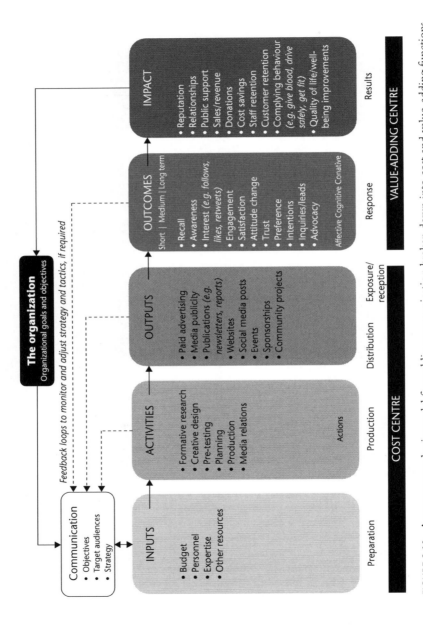

FIGURE 2.10 A programme logic model for public communication broken down into cost and value-adding functions

Source: Adapted from Kellogg Foundation (2004 [1998])

latter stages produce value. Being a cost centre is a precarious position to occupy in most organizations, because rationalizations, changes of senior management and efficiency drives see budgets cut and, sometimes, staff made redundant. Conversely, value-adding centres are maintained, often attract increased budgets and facilitate successful careers.

Causality: linking activities to outcomes and impact

One more key concept that is often poorly understood must be addressed before we conclude this chapter and look in detail at models and methods of evaluating public communication: the issue of *causality* – also referred to as *causation*.[4] In addition to showing that outcomes and impact have been created, there has to be evidence that the activities evaluated caused, or at least contributed to, the outcomes and impact identified. Many evaluations identify *correlations* and often confuse correlation with causation, or simply make assumptions about cause and effect. For example, media content analysis conducted by a PR firm or department may claim that an increase in the share price of a public company is the result of positive media coverage when the two occur in the same period. In so doing, they fail to consider other possible causes of the stock price gains, such as favourable analyst reports, the appointment of a new chief executive officer (CEO) or a rumoured acquisition. It may even have been that the stock price was increasing before the media coverage appeared and that the favourable reporting was the result of the company's performance – not vice versa. Advertising agencies often claim credit for sales increases without considering other possible influences, such as price reductions, retailer promotions, PR or competitor price increases – although, fortunately, these practices are becoming less common and best practice pays close attention to causality, as illustrated in some of the case studies reported in Chapter 10.

The presence of correlations between public communication and desired outcomes and impact does not establish causality. The three key rules of causality or causation that must be applied are as follows:

1. Temporal precedence. The alleged cause must precede the alleged effect or impact.
2. Covariation of cause and effect. There must be a clear relationship between the alleged cause and effect (for example, there must be evidence that the audience accessed and used information provided).
3. There must be *no plausible alternative explanation* – that is, other possible causes of the effect must be ruled out as far as possible.

Causality can be difficult to establish, particularly when multiple influences contribute to outcomes and impact, as is often the case. A lack of connection between communication activities and outputs and outcomes and impacts that achieve organizational objectives has been a failing particularly in PR evaluation, as noted by Ansgar Zerfass, Dejan Verčič, Piet Verhoeven, Angeles Moreno and Ralph Tench

(2012). However, there are techniques for establishing causality. Simple informal techniques include using different web links, email addresses or contact phone numbers in advertising, PR, events, and so on, which allows identification of the sources of inquiries and requests. In digital communication, tagging of content with embedded metadata allows precise tracking of what information leads to inquiries, registrations, sales or other actions. These methods are discussed in Chapters 4 and 5, and formal research methods to identify the impact of different channels, such as market mix modelling, are discussed in Chapter 8.

Summary

- Evaluation should be based on *theory* – that is, bodies of knowledge collected in various disciplines and fields of practice that explain processes and inform a systematic approach to evaluation, rather than ad hoc and subjectively based approaches. This tenet is based on understanding theory not as hypotheses or abstract notions unconnected to the 'real world', but as accumulated, well-established knowledge about what works and what does not work (what industry might call *best practice*). Theory-based evaluation is therefore not abstract or normative; it is grounded in social science and humanities research.
- *Programme theory* is one of the major underlying bodies of theory (knowledge) that informs evaluation. Its constituent concepts, including *programme theory evaluation* (PTE), ensure that planned programmes are tested against theory, formative research and case studies of similar programmes conducted previously, and that any pre-testing data is available long before the programme begins. Also, as Joseph Wholey (1987) advises, evaluators should work with management to identify their information needs and expectations. Then, evaluation can be designed at *formative*, *process* and *summative* stages for specific programmes.
- *Realist evaluation* also contributes important ideas for evaluation – and, as its name suggests, emphasizes the grounded nature of evaluation theory and its application to practice. Realist evaluation particularly draws attention to the *context* of public communication and the need for an ongoing iterative series of evaluations that cumulatively builds programme improvement and results. Like theory of change in many ways, the central question asked in realist evaluation planning is: 'What works, for whom, in what respects, to what extent, in what contexts, and how?' (Better Evaluation, 2016, para. 3).
- As detailed knowledge about what works, when and for whom accumulates, a *theory of change* can be developed. This is a theory because the body of knowledge developed can be applied to other programmes with similar objectives and similar target audiences – that is, it provides insights beyond a particular programme.
- Understanding of human *information processing* includes identifying the stages and steps between distribution of messages and outcomes and impact, such as attitudinal change or behaviour change or action. This is important to identify the interim 'mini-steps' that lead to, and cause, outcomes and impact, which

allows systematic evaluation to be carried out progressively (at formative, process and summative stages), affording opportunities for adjustments to strategy and tactics, if necessary. Information processing also brings into focus a number of important socio-psychological theories that explain how human meaning is produced. Public communication practitioners need to be familiar with key theories (that is, knowledge about how people make up and change their minds, and how and why they act as they do).

- Along with important psychological and socio-psychological theories and concepts, public communication is influenced by social and cultural factors including social interaction among audiences and between audiences and organizations. Sociocultural theories explain how these factors influence meaning-making and the effectiveness of public communication.

- Programme evaluation proceeds progressively from the early stages of planning to ensure that the appropriate *inputs* are gained, that *activities* are planned based on sound formative research, and that *outputs* produced and distributed are aligned to audience interests, needs and tastes, as well as the organization's objectives. Very importantly, programme evaluation must proceed to identify what *outcomes* and *impact* have been achieved and how these contribute to the organization. Some programmes are designed to contribute to stakeholders and society, and this broader aspect of outcomes and impact will also be examined, as well as unintended outcomes and impact.

Notes

1 *Developing a Logic Model: Teaching and Training Guide* by Henert & Taylor-Power (2008) was removed from the University of Wisconsin-Extension website in 2016 and replaced by an earlier guide (Henert, Jones & Taylor-Power, 2003). This guide was also then removed. However, the 2008 guide is available on other websites such as www.alnap. org/pool/files/logic-model-guide.pdf.

2 The book that first outlined this approach was titled *Realistic Evaluation* (Pawson & Tilley, 1997), but subsequently the authors settled on the term *realist* evaluation 'because it has become the preferred nomenclature of other authors' (Pawson & Tilley, 2004, p. 3).

3 Communication scholar Robert Craig used the term *traditions* to refer to the main approaches to studying human communication based on different underlying worldviews and perspectives, such as those focused on channels and media (*systems*), the structure of texts including visuals (*semiotics*), persuasive techniques in speech and writing (*rhetoric*), human cognition and emotions (*psychology*), interpretation (*phenomenology*), social and cultural influences (*sociocultural*), and critical perspectives.

4 Causality and causation are often used interchangeably. However, purists point out that *causality* is the relation between cause and effect, while *causation* refers to the act of causing an effect.

3

MODELS INFORMING EVALUATION OF COMMUNICATION

This chapter critically reviews a number of evaluation frameworks and models that are published and used in public communication practice. This analysis does not attempt to examine every model in existence – that would be impossible in one book and daunting to a reader – but it discusses more than 20 models that identify recommended processes for evaluation in advertising, public relations (PR), health communication and promotion, and specialist fields such as development communication, as well as a number of other models of communication and behavioural change that inform evaluation. Critical analysis of models is important because, as George Box said, 'all models are wrong' (1976, p. 792). There is no perfect model, no single solution. However, analysis can reveal useful features and insights that certain models provide, as well as weaknesses and flaws to note. This analysis also attempts to go further than existing models to provide recommendations that draw on the latest research and thinking from several disciplines and fields of practice.

Advertising evaluation models

The advertising industry has many models for explaining what it does and how it does it, some of which are highly complicated. For example, Jack Healey (1974) developed a model of communication impact and consumer response when he was a doctoral candidate in the Graduate School of Management at the University of California, Los Angeles. This identified three exogenous variables (Y1, Y2, Y3) and four endogenous variables (X1, X2, X3, X4), and then produced formulae for advertising awareness effect as:

$$Y_1 = Y_{10} + B_{13}Y_3 + Y_{11}X_1 + Y_{13}X_3 + Y_{14}X_4 + U_1$$

and for purchase and usage as:

$$Y_3 = Y_{30} + B_{32}Y_2 + Y_{31}X_1 + Y_{34}X_4 + U_3$$

where U is the error term for the equation.

It is perhaps not surprising that few have taken up and used Healey's formulae. Some of the more widely used – and much simpler – models for planning and explaining how advertising works are as follows.

AIDA model

An acronym for *attention–interest–desire–action*, the *AIDA model* is probably the best-known model used to plan and evaluate advertising (see Figure 3.1). The acronym is attributed to American advertising and sales pioneer Elias St Elmo Lewis in the late 1800s – although, in their comparison of 24 advertising models, Thomas Barry and Daniel Howard (1990) said that Lewis promoted only AID (that is, awareness–interest–desire) as a sales approach, without the second 'A'. The AIDA model, as it came to be widely used, was published by Edward Strong (1925). The model draws on W. J. McGuire's (1989, 2001, 2013 [1989]) information-processing model, but is very simplistic, incorporating only four of McGuire's original six (later, 13) steps of communication. Nevertheless, it is the basis of the *sales funnel* that is widely applied in marketing to denote that a large number of potential customers need to be made aware of a product or service, with a progressively smaller number developing interest and desire, and an even smaller number taking action (for example, purchase).

The oversimplification inherent in the AIDA model has led to a number of variants. Some have added a 'C' to the model for *conviction*, although others claim that this should be *confidence*, leading to AIDCA or AICDA. Others argue that

FIGURE 3.1   The AIDA model of advertising

Source: Strong (1925)

satisfaction is important to achieve sales, particularly repeat sales, leading to AIDAS (Sheldon, 1911), while still others argue for *attention–interest–confidence–conviction–action* (AICCA) (Hall, 1915, as cited in Barry & Howard, 1990, p. 100). In a recent critique of hierarchy of effects models, including the AIDA model, Bambang Sukma Wijaya (2012) has proposed AISDALSLove, which stands for *attention–interest–search–desire–action–like/dislike–share–love/hate*. There is no doubt that, in so doing, Wijaya is attempting to bring the model up to date by adding terms such as 'search' and 'like' – but it is puzzling why 'action' is in the middle of the model, when this is usually the outcome sought, whether it is buying a product as a result of commercial marketing or committing to a behaviour sought in social marketing. While Wijaya's critique of hierarchy of effects models (more about those later) is justified, his particular attempt to breathe new life into the AIDA model results in a clumsy acronym and a dubious model.

The sales funnel

It could be argued that the *sales funnel* is a separate, more sophisticated, model than the AIDA model, because there are myriad variations involving many more than four stages. Sales funnels are a way of attempting to identify the progression of informative and persuasive communication from reception of information to behaviour such as purchase and repurchase (that is, repeat sales). Some argue that the sales funnel is 'dead' as a useful concept or model in the age of digital disruption and social media, in which traditional channels and pathways to persuasion are increasingly being bypassed or ignored, but it remains a popular approach to planning and evaluation in marketing communication (Ritson, 2016). Some versions of the sales funnel simply replicate the four stages of the AIDA model or variations of them, such as *awareness–consideration–decision–action* (Zhel, 2016), while others propose more sophisticated expanded versions, such as what Philip Kotler, Neil Rakman and Suj Krishnaswamy (2006) refer to as the 'buying funnel', because it is developed from the customer's perspective. This involves 'customer awareness, brand awareness, brand consideration, brand preference, purchase intention, purchase, customer loyalty, customer advocacy' (Kotler et al., 2006, p. 11).

DAGMAR model

Another variant on the original AIDA model is the so-called *DAGMAR model* proposed by Russell Colley (1961). The name is an acronym for 'defining advertising goals for measured advertising results'. Despite the promising title, this simplistically maintains that, in buying a product or service, a person passes through four stages: awareness; comprehension; conviction; and action (see Figure 3.2).

In the first edition of *Advertising Management*, David Aaker and John Myers (1975) attempted to expand the DAGMAR model to incorporate other individual and contextual factors. However, a contemporary website discussing the DAGMAR model argues that 'if buyers have a sufficient level of awareness, they

FIGURE 3.2 The DAGMAR model of advertising

Source: Colley (1961)

will be quickly prompted into purchase with little assistance of the other elements of the mix' (Drypen, 2008, para. 10). This makes a rather large assumption and reveals a key problem that besets evaluation in public communication. This can be broadly summarized as the assumption of 'domino' effects from information reception to awareness to attitude change to behaviour. Research shows that awareness does not automatically, or easily, lead to action. Furthermore, awareness can be negative awareness – that is, a person being aware of a product or service and having a very low opinion of it. The website is also self-contradictory, saying later that 'awareness on its own may not be sufficient to stimulate a purchase' (Drypen, 2008, para. 14), and it recommends that potential buyers need *knowledge* about a product as well as conviction. The last point is also contestable, because knowledge is sometimes required to gain action, but on other occasions people rely on heuristics or mental shortcuts to make decisions, as discussed in Chapter 2. For example, consider buying toilet paper: do most people really want to know much about toilet paper? More often, they choose a brand because it feels soft or because of the cute puppy in the ad and on the pack. We all need to be 'cognitive misers' and 'lazy organisms' occasionally in today's information saturated world.

Hierarchy of effects model

The *hierarchy of effects model* created by Robert Lavidge and Gary Steiner (1961) proposed six steps of communication along the route to behaviour: *awareness–knowledge–liking–preference–conviction–purchase*. This model is referred to as a 'hierarchy of effects' model because it assumes an ordered progression from cognitive processing (learning and thinking to become aware) to affective connection to a conative result (action). This approach also assumes that awareness and knowledge combined with emotion are necessary precursors to action and generally must precede action – and hence a belief in a hierarchal relationship between the elements.

However, in effect, all of the advertising models discussed here are hierarchy of effects models, because all assume that cognitive processing precedes and leads to affective connection, which in turn leads to behaviour. Many of the models make reference to, and draw on, the steps of communication outlined by W. J. McGuire, particularly his early work (for example, McGuire, 1969, 1976, 1985), and his *communication–persuasion matrix*, as well as diffusion of innovations theory advocated by Everett Rogers (1995 [1962]). However, because these advertising models were based on McGuire's early work in which he initially identified only six steps of communication, the models mostly lack sophistication. Also, many in the advertising industry grossly oversimplified the work of McGuire, as well as that of other psychologists and sociologists.

In an extensive critical review of 24 advertising models, most of which presume a hierarchy of effects, Barry and Howard note that, in fact, there are six potential combinations of cognition, affect (emotion) and behaviour, as follows:

1. Cognition–affect–conation;
2. Cognition–conation–affect;
3. Affect–conation–cognition;
4. Conation–affect–cognition;
5. Conation–cognition–affect;
6. Affect–cognition–conation.

(Barry & Howard, 1990, pp. 103–104)

For example, it has been shown that emotional connection can lead directly to action, such as impulse buying, buying on the basis of habit or simply doing something because one 'feels like it'. Spur-of-the-moment decisions to buy something, to go to a favourite restaurant, and so on are usually affect-based, with little cognition involved. Most advertisers now know this well and use emotional appeals frequently in advertising.

Elaboration likelihood theory and heuristics, as discussed in Chapter 2, give insights into the various routes to behaviour change. It is also not uncommon for behaviour to occur first, with positive cognition and affective responses occurring afterwards. For instance, enforcement campaigns that use heavy fines as levers to create change often face cognitive and affective resistance initially, but this subsides as people are forced to adopt the behaviour and come to accept it. An example is the introduction of compulsory wearing of seat belts in motor vehicles. Initially, motorists in many countries were opposed to wearing seat belts based on years of driving habits. There were arguments that drivers could be trapped in their cars in an accident and burn to death in the case of fire. But as the wearing of seat belts become entrenched under the influence of policing and heavy fines, attitudes changed. Today, most people would 'feel' unsafe if they were to drive without wearing a seat belt and would fear for the safety of their children and other passengers if they were not to wear them. As a result, most now 'think' that wearing seat belts is sensible (that is, a conative, affective, cognitive process). Also, a person may think rationally about something (cognition) and decide to do it (conation) – such as eat broccoli and kale, because they are healthy foods – even if the person is not particularly fond of these foods (disaffect).

A further factor casting doubt on the widely assumed hierarchy of effects model is that the cognitive and affective systems in humans are closely entwined. They can even operate simultaneously. For example, every time a working parent walks out the door to work, are they not feeling negative emotions at leaving their loved ones, but also rationally deducing that they must work hard to pay the rent or mortgage and put food on the table? Either influence may take precedence at various stages of life. Barry and Howard concluded that 'our empirical review led us to conclude that something was amiss in the hierarchy debate' (1990, p. 105).

Innovation–adoption model

A further variant of hierarchy of effects models was the *innovation–adoption model* based on Everett Rogers' (1995 [1962]) *diffusion of innovations*, which proposed five steps towards behaviour: *awareness–interest–evaluation–trial–adoption*. ('Evaluation' in this context refers to potential consumers of products and services evaluating them with a view to purchase, not the subject of this book.)

Communications model

A somewhat grandly named *communications model* was also popular in the halcyon days of mass advertising, as noted by Philip Kotler (1991, p. 573). This listed the stages of persuasive communication as being *exposure–reception–cognitive response–attitude–intention–behaviour* (see Table 3.1).

More recently, McKinsey consultants have expanded the traditional sales funnel – or what they call the *customer decision journey* – to involve awareness, familiarity, consideration, purchase and loyalty, noting that the funnel narrows, with a reducing number of potential consumers at each stage (Court, Elzinga, Mulder & Vetvik,

TABLE 3.1 Five advertising models widely used for planning and evaluation

Stages	AIDA model	DAGMAR model	Hierarchy of effects model	Innovation–adoption model	Communications model
Cognitive	Attention	Awareness Comprehension	Awareness Knowledge	Awareness	Exposure Reception Cognitive response
Affective	Interest Desire	Conviction	Liking Preference Conviction	Interest Evaluation	Attitude Intention
Conative (behaviour)	Action	Action	Purchase	Trial Adoption	Behaviour

2009). But this still includes a relatively small number of stages and implies a smooth progression towards outcomes and impact. Customer decision journeys and what is also referred to as *customer journey mapping* are discussed further in Chapter 8.

Advertising has been heavily influenced by psychology, such as the work of W. J. McGuire, as well as sociologists and communication scholars, such as Everett Rogers. Interestingly, while advertising has taken up new technologies for delivery of messages such as the Internet, social media and mobile devices, most of the models listed and still cited in advertising and marketing literature date back to the 1920s. Some authors and practitioners advocate applying the AIDA model to digital marketing (for example, Elliot, 2014).

As noted previously, the most widely used methods of evaluating advertising continue to be *reach* and *recall* of ads and commercials, or of products or brand names, promoted in advertising. As will be discussed in more detail in Chapter 4, these are metrics related to distribution of, and exposure to, messages, but do not measure outcomes or impact. Digital advertising is changing approaches to evaluating advertising, with more data available on engagement and response by recipients (for example, liking, sharing, viewing videos or demos, making inquiries, and so on). However, despite the massive expenditure on advertising – more than US$500 billion a year worldwide in 2015 and forecast to exceed $600 billion a year by 2018 (E-marketer, 2016) – John Wannamaker's lament that half of his advertising was wasted is now almost certainly an understatement. Some studies estimate that, in the twenty-first century, a maximum of 5 per cent of advertising messages reach their target audiences – and only 1 per cent of targeted consumers actively process advertising messages (Kroeber-Riel & Esch, 2000, p. 15). For this reason, there is an ever-greater need for evaluation.

Behavioural advertising

One approach that is changing advertising planning and evaluation in the fast-growing world of online advertising is audience buying based on people's online behaviour. Traditionally, advertising has been targeted and evaluated based on *audience context*, using proxy data such as time of day, geography or content genre to identify likely audiences. For example, television advertising aimed at children has typically been scheduled in late afternoon and early evenings, when children are assumed to be watching. Advertising aimed at elderly people is frequently placed in daytime reruns of classic films or series. When advertisers want to reach farmers, they use early-morning programmes on regional and rural broadcast media, or specialist publications produced for farmers. These decisions are made based on the context in which audiences are considered to exist, not on actual audience signals. This method of evaluating audiences is 'modestly accurate', in the frank words of a senior executive of one of the world's largest advertising and media industry groups (Norman, 2014, p. 3), who adds: 'Advertising in the broadcast age was about shouting as loudly as possible in the general direction you hoped your audience was' (p. 3).

In contrast, online digital advertising uses *audience behaviour* for targeting and evaluation. As web users click into a page, they send a signal that identifies them as a potential 'impression' for content related to that on the page. Advertisers can buy space adjacent to content on a web page (for example, banners or side bars) on a regular ongoing basis, or increasingly they can bid in auctions to place their advertising on web pages based on information about particular users (for example, information collected through 'cookies').[1] Google AdWords works on an audience-buying basis, with advertisers bidding to buy key words used in online searches. In other systems, the web server asks advertisers if they would like to pay to place their content in front of particular users. For instance, if a user has recently searched for information on hiring a dinner suit in London, chances are that ads for formal-wear hire companies in London will start appearing on web pages that user accesses (as they did *ad nauseam* after this author attended a black-tie dinner for the Institute of Practitioners in Advertising awards). This is *behavioural advertising* at work – also referred to as *behavioural targeting*. In short, it is advertising placement based on the actual behaviour of people within the advertiser's target audience – not on broad contextual factors. These ad-serving processes are triggered by algorithms that process vast amounts of data in milliseconds. The systematic collection and use of such data for planning advertising placement is referred to as *programmatic advertising*.

Evaluation of digital advertising is similarly based on behavioural data such as identification of the types of information that a user accessed previously, rather than broad descriptions of assumed or 'imagined audiences' (Anderson, 1991 [1983]). Furthermore, much advertising is now conducted on a *pay per click* (PPC) basis – that is, the advertiser pays only when a web user clicks on its ad, sponsored search term or promotional video. Clicking on an ad or video still does not mean that a potential consumer will buy a product or change their opinion or behaviour, however. Also, behavioural targeting is under scrutiny in some countries because of privacy concerns, and regulations may restrict what information can be collected and used, as well as give citizens rights to remove data about themselves. Nonetheless, behavioural advertising is an emerging method of both planning and evaluating advertising in the digital age using empirical data.

Political communication evaluation

In a recent book edited by Leah Lievrouw (2014), *Challenging Communication Research*, David Karpf, Daniel Kreiss, and Rasmus Kleis Nielsen say that 'over the past decade cracks have appeared in the edifice of political communication research', going on to point out that 'most political communication research is quantitative" (2014, p. 44). Furthermore, two leading political communication scholars, W. Lance Bennett and Shanto Iyenger (2008), have argued that practices in the field have not kept pace with technological change – a view echoed more recently by Patricia Moy, Bruce Bimber, Andrew Rojecki, Michael Xenos and Shanto Iyenger (2012). In the same vein, Kevin Barnhurst (2011) says that the field faces a crisis because it continues to rely on theories and research methods developed for the mass media environment of the mid-twentieth century.

The problematic popularity of opinion polls

Political communication, as distinct from government communication,[2] is dominated by election campaigns, which some argue have distended into the *permanent campaign* (Canel & Sanders, 2012, p. 87) focused on winning and holding power rather than governing and serving the public interest in the three, four or five years between elections. Evaluation during electioneering, and even in much policy-making, is primarily based on polling. Polls are surveys (that is, a social research method), but polls are usually based on relatively small samples – sometimes only a few hundred and rarely more than a few thousand. For instance, in the 2015 UK national election, the average sample size of four major opinion polls in England published in UK newspapers during the election campaign was 1,168; in Scotland, it was 1,047; in Wales, just over 1,200 (Britain Elects, 2015). The US National Council of Public Polls (2015) reports a similar average sample size of around 1,000 adults. Samples of this size can yield quite accurate results if they are statistically representative of the population. However, many polls use *quota* samples, which are neither statistically reliable nor necessarily representative (discussed further in Chapter 6). Therefore, despite claims of accuracy, opinion polls regularly get it wrong. Following the highly significant June 2016 UK referendum vote to leave the European Union (EU), for example, the National Centre for Social Research (NatCen, 2016a) tabulated all of the major opinion poll predictions (that is, Kantar TNS, ComRes, Opinium, YouGov, Ipsos MORI and Populus), arriving at an average of 52 per cent to remain and 48 per cent to leave. The actual result of the referendum in the UK was, of course, exactly the opposite.

Another reason for the inaccuracy of simple polls is what they ask – and what they do not ask. Usually, polls are highly structured and restricted to a few questions – sometimes even a single question. Participants do not get to say what they want to say; they can respond only to fixed questions – and sometimes only to one such as 'who would you vote for if the election was next week?' Karpf and colleagues recommend that, to really understand voters' concerns, interests, needs and views, in-depth qualitative methods of research are required, such as 'first-hand observation [ethnography], participation, and interviewing in the actual contexts where political communication occurs' (2014, p. 44). A two–year, three–country study of organizational listening found that political parties and governments listen 'sporadically at best, poorly, and sometimes not at all' to their stakeholders and publics (Macnamara, 2016a, p. 236). How organizations can listen better – which is a fundamental requirement of formative, process and summative evaluation – will be discussed further in the following chapters.

Yet another reason for the inaccuracy of polls in predicting results is that, in effect, every poll preceding a public vote is a 'push poll'. *Push polling* refers to campaigning and marketing techniques that attempt to change or reinforce people's views under the guise of conducting a survey (Feld, 2003). For example, in a political context, a push poll question might ask: 'Will the fact that Candidate X was charged with fraud ten years ago affect your voting decision?'The question is designed to inform potential voters of the candidate's flawed past and thus to damage the candidate's election chances rather than to elicit information about voting patterns. Apart from such nefarious practices, all pre-election polls have a push effect when the results are published, which is common because many political polls are funded by major media groups.This is illustrated in the case of 'Richard's mother' (a real case de-identified). Following the highly controversial referendum in which the UK voted to leave the EU, Richard (a staunch EU supporter) found out that his mother had voted to 'leave', but had then been shocked at the result and had said that she really wanted the UK to remain in the EU. Perplexed, Richard asked his mother why she had voted 'leave' when she supported 'remain'. She replied: 'Because the polls said most people would vote to remain, so I thought I would vote the other way to avoid the government having a landslide win.' Richard's mother changed her vote because of poll predictions – and so did many other UK citizens, it seems, given widespread shock at the result.

Political communication sometimes uses in-depth interviews and focus groups to gain deeper insights into citizens' attitudes and interests, but polling remains a problematic default method for evaluating public attitudes and needs in Western democratic politics.

Health communication planning and evaluation models

In the mid-1970s, health communication practitioners began to take ideas from the commercial marketing sector, in which consumer research and analysis had proved to be a critical aspect of successfully promoting products to target audiences.This led to the development of *social marketing*, which applied commercial marketing approaches to objectives such as improving public health and other social goals. Over the past 30 years or so, health communication and the related field of health promotion have substantially used research (Kim & Dearning, 2016), including a major focus on evaluation (Shiavo, 2007;Valente, 2002).

Health belief model

The *health belief model* (HBM) dates back to the 1950s, when it was applied to try to explain the lack of uptake of a free tuberculosis (TB) X-ray screening programme offered by the US Public Health Service.The HBM is based in part on *expectancy–value* theory, which claims that attitude and behaviour change can be gained, and even predicted, based on (a) belief in the likelihood that an action or behaviour will lead to certain consequences, and (b) the perceived value of that behaviour to the individual concerned. Like most theories, the expectancy–value equation, which was developed by psychologist Martin Fishbein (1963), has evolved. In the 1970s and 1980s, Fishbein and Icek Ajzen expanded expectancy–value theory into the *theory of reasoned action* (Fishbein & Ajzen, 1975; Ajzen & Fishbein, 1980), and later Ajzen (1988) presented the *theory of planned behaviour*, a central tenet of which is that a major determinant of social behaviour is what *influential others* (sometimes called *orientational others*) expect a person to do in a particular situation, referred to as *subjective norms* (Ajzen, 1985).

The HBM originally involved five key elements made up of four risk perception concepts (that is, perceived susceptibility, perceived severity, perceived benefits and perceived barriers) combined with the concept of 'cues to action'. Cues, or triggers, to action can include interpersonal communication with family, friends and peers, interaction with health professionals such as doctors, or media messages about a particular health condition. More recently, the important concept of self-efficacy has been added to the list of preconditions to the model. However, despite this development, the HBM has had mixed results (Park, 2016, p. 26), probably because it has not expanded to include social influences that are recognized in theory of planned behaviour and other models, such as the social and behaviour change model discussed in the next section. The HBM also does not readily translate into a graphical representation and, as such, is more a theory than a model.

In *The Handbook of Global Health Communication*, Elizabeth Fox (2012) notes that terminology and the names of approaches and models have changed, and continue to change, in the health communication field. What was originally known as the *behaviour change model*, based on the work of W. J. McGuire, evolved to become the behaviour change communication model, and then further into a more sophisticated model that recognizes the importance of social factors and environments in the shape of the social and behaviour change communication model.

Behaviour change communication (BCC)

Behaviour change communication (BCC) refers to an approach to communication that is theory- and evidence-based, and which, as the name suggests, focused on changing behaviour drawing on *behavioural science* and recent specialist fields of research and practice such as *behavioural economics* (Samson, 2016) and *behavioural insights* (Thaler & Sunstein, 2008). Behavioural economics and behavioural insights are discussed as methods that can be used for evaluation in Chapter 8.

Behaviour change communication has been widely applied in attempts to achieve health outcomes over many decades and continues to be used. For example, Public Health England (2016) uses a four-stage bespoke behaviour change model in its public health campaigns focused on changing knowledge to 'alert' audiences to risks, on changing beliefs to 'motivate' audiences to change, on providing 'support' to help audiences to change, and on providing ongoing information and support to 'sustain' changed behaviour. This is based on an extensive body of research in relation to behaviour change (for example, Gibbons & Gerrard, 1997; Gibbons, Gerrard & Lane, 2003). The explicit emphasis on behaviour change as an outcome highlights the need for a thorough understanding of the range of influences, internal and external, that determine why people do what they do and how to stimulate changes in behaviour (Glanz, Rimer & Viswanath, 2008).

As well as relying on empirical evidence gained through primary research, BCC applies a number of theories of communication, including health belief theory, the theory of reasoned action, the theory of planned behaviour, social learning theory and diffusion of innovations. Behaviour change communication initially relied largely on psychological theories relating to individual cognition, emotional responses and behaviour influences (Story & Figueroa, 2012), but health behaviour change researchers and professionals have increasingly recognized the importance of community engagement and community mobilization, as well as social context.

Social and behaviour change communication (SBCC)

A growing understanding that behaviours are grounded in a social context has led to a shift from BCC to *social and behaviour change communication* (SBCC). The latter model is guided by a comprehensive ecological theory that incorporates both change at the individual level and change at broader environmental and structural levels. Social and behaviour change communication is driven by epidemiological evidence and 'client'[3] perspectives and needs.

Behaviour change and social change have often been seen as distinct approaches, requiring different strategies and skill sets. However, leaders in this field, such as the United Nations Children's Emergency Fund (UNICEF), see them as complementary approaches to address individual and social influences. In this focus on social context as well as internal factors, SBCC is similar to the *communication for social change* (CFSC) model, which describes an iterative process whereby 'community dialogue' and 'collective action' work together to produce social change in a community that improves the health and welfare of all of its members (Figueroa, Kincaid, Rani & Lewis, 2002, p. iii). By engaging collaboratively with audiences and paying close attention to their social and cultural context, the CFSC and SBCC models incorporate what others refer as the *social ecology* model.

Social ecology model

Contrasting previously used top-down modernist approaches to health communication that have been widely criticized by health communication researchers such as Mohan Dutta and Rebecca de Souza (2008), researchers in health communication and promotion increasingly apply a social ecology model that 'focuses attention on the contexts of behaviour when designing, implementing or critically evaluating interventions' (Panter-Brick, Clarke, Lomas, Pinder & Lindsay, 2006, p. 2810). Specifically, Panter-Brick and colleagues say: 'We use the term social ecology to focus attention on the social and physical settings contextualizing behaviour as well as the interplay between human actors and external factors shaping their agency'

(2006, p. 2811). Informing this approach is that Panter-Brick and colleagues note that 'behaviour change is notoriously difficult to initiate and sustain' and observe that 'the reasons why efforts to promote healthy behaviours fail are coming under increasing scrutiny' (2006, p. 2810) – a further factor relevant to this study. In fact, citing a wide range of health communication literature, they say 'there are remarkably few examples of truly successful health interventions' (p. 2811). They make the following recommendation:

> To be successful, health interventions should build on existing practices, skills and priorities, recognize the constraints on human behaviour, and either feature community mobilization or target those most receptive to change. Furthermore, interventions should strive to be culturally compelling, not merely culturally appropriate: they must engage local communities and nestle within social and ecological landscapes.
>
> *(Panter-Brick et al., 2006, p. 2810)*

In what could be considered part of the social ecology model, Mohan Dutta, Agaptus Anaele and Christina Jones have recently advocated a *culture-centred approach* (CCA) to health communication that 'seeks to address health disparities by fostering opportunities for listening to the voices of those at the margins through a variety of participatory communication methods' (2013, p. 160). They describe these as including 'co-constructive data gathering and analysis', 'community dialogues', 'community-driven media advocacy' and 'town hall meetings', and say that *co-construction*, 'a process of collaboration and power sharing between academics and marginalized communities, lies at the heart of the CCA' (Dutta et al., 2013, p. 160). These theoretical frameworks, which draw on understandings of user-centred design, co-production and co-creation from other disciplines (for example, Tanaka, Gaye & Richardson, 2010), are relevant to all public communication, not only health communication. But, as noted earlier in this analysis, studies and practices of planning and evaluating public communication are largely siloed, and do not sufficiently borrow learning and ideas from other disciplines.

Social ecology models were first developed in the 1950s and 1960s by Chicago School sociologists, who drew attention to the importance of social influences on humans in contrast with earlier thinking, which focused on channels and the production and transmission of messages, and psychological research that focused on individual traits and cognition. One notable model that has influenced applications in many fields is Urie Bronfenbrenner's *ecological framework for human development*. While some aspects of this model have been criticized, including by Bronfenbrenner himself in revisions (Bronfenbrenner, 1999), it informs a number of social ecology models that are relevant to public communication. These models show the myriad influences on human attitudes and behaviour, and caution public communication researchers and professionals about making glib predictions of impact. A simplified social ecology model used by UNICEF, based on social ecology models developed by the Center for Disease Control and Prevention (CDC) in Washington, DC, is shown in Figure 3.3.

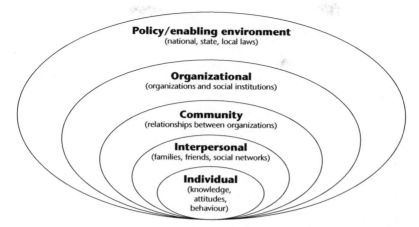

FIGURE 3.3 Social ecology model illustrating the range of influences on individuals who exist within social, cultural and political systems

Source: UNICEF and 3D Change (2009)

Development communication models

A number of models of public communication and evaluation of its effects have been produced in the field of development communication, including adaptations of social ecology models. In its simplest sense, *development communication* is the use of public communication to facilitate social development (Quebral, 1972–1973). More specifically, Nora Quebral – who coined the term and is sometimes described as the 'mother of development communication' – expanded this definition, to become:

> the art and science of human communication applied to the speedy transfor-
> mation of a country and the mass of its people from poverty to a dynamic
> state of economic growth that makes possible greater social equality and the
> larger fulfilment of the human potential.
>
> *(Quebral, 1972–1973, p. 25)*

Srinivas Melcote and Leslie Steeves (2001) refer to development communication as 'emancipation communication' aimed at combating injustice and oppression. However, this is substantially overstated and reflective of Western ethnocentrism – and, in fact, even Querbal's definition is optimistic, based on a faith in modernization through capitalism and technology.

Development communication evolved during a period of belief in direct and powerful media effects, when mass media communication was therefore the primary approach taken in projects and research, such as Daniel Lerner's 1958 study of communication and development in the Middle East. In the late 1980s and 1990s, this was replaced by a participatory approach, now often referred to as *participatory development communication* (Bessette, 2004).

Traditional approaches to development communication have faced considerable criticism on several grounds. In particular, traditional development communication has been attacked for its application of Western views and assumptions about modernization and growth, mostly defined in economic terms. In short, there has been an assumption that 'underdeveloped' countries should become like the dominant developed countries (Felstehausen, 1973). Today, the Center for Development Communication promotes *ethical* development communication, which it describes as 'audience-centred communication strategies taking individual, group and global needs into account' (CDC, 2016, para. 2).

June Lennie and Jo Taachi (2013a) have specifically addressed evaluation in a development communication context in their *Evaluating Communication for Development: A Framework for Social Change*, in which they criticize traditional measurement approaches that focus on upwards accountability reporting against organizational objectives and recommend instead continuous embedded evaluation using a participatory approach. They also call for 'an emergent adaptive evaluation approach' and 'holistic forms of evaluation' (Lennie & Taachi, 2013b, p. 2), which might sound vague and somewhat 'airy-fairy' to quantitative researchers, but what Lennie and Taachi are railing against is the dominant quantitative metrics approach in evaluation that reduces changes in human behaviour and the human condition to statistical calculations and algorithms. They advocate focus on context, networks and interrelationships, rather than looking for simple and simplistic cause-and-effect relationships, and they are cynical about logical frameworks, arguing that social change is complex, unpredictable, multi-causal and often illogical. Consequently, their recommended approach is qualitative, rather than quantitative, and participatory. As shown in the following example of a development communication evaluation model, evaluation is embedded in the communication programme and undertaken by the participants throughout the programme.

Integrated model of communication for social change

A model of evaluation that has received considerable attention in development communication, including publications by The Rockefeller Foundation, is the integrated model of *communication for social change (CFSC)*, as noted previously. Communication for social change describes an iterative, participatory process in which community dialogue and collective action are combined to produce social change in a community that improves the welfare of all of its members. The model emphasizes participation by those to whom Jay Rosen refers as 'the people formerly known as the audience' (2006, para. 1).

The integrated model of communication for social change is so-named because it integrates what the authors call 'catalysts' and others refer to as 'drivers' or 'levers', such as policy, technology and stimuli or 'change agents' (for example, regulation or financial incentives) with media communication. The catalyst in the model is the trigger that initiates community dialogue about an issue of concern or interest to that community. Proponents say that a catalyst is a missing piece in most of the literature on development communication, which often assumes that a community will spontaneously initiate dialogue and action once given information, or that media alone can trigger change (Figueroa et al., 2002).

One detailed report on CFSC and the integrated model of communication for social change outlines the 'social change process indicators [used] to measure the process of community dialogue and collection action' (Figueroa et al., 2002, p. 14). Because participation is seen as so central in this model, *participatory evaluation* is conducted involving *self-evaluation* by those involved. This is done through a number of forms that participants fill out as a project unfolds. As Figueroa and colleagues explain:

> It is important that most of the community participate in the evaluation process so that the lessons learned about what worked and why can be shared throughout the community. The result of the participatory evaluation should be a new reassessment of the current status of the community with respect to the problem . . . From here, the community is ready to renew the process, moving forward into further action for the same problem, perhaps, or on to a different problem.
>
> *(Figueroa et al., 2002, p. 10)*

One of the major lessons for evaluation of public communication in the integrated model of communication for social change is that improvement is shown as one of the primary outcomes of the process – an outcome supported by Lennie and Taachi (2013a). Another key learning for the effectiveness of communication generally is the focus on participation and collective action. Health campaigns have been leaders in showing that community-based activities are more effective than – or at least a necessary complement to – media campaigns in many circumstances.

It is not practical to show all, or even many, of the models used in health communication and development communication, because these are large and diverse fields. However, the models and approaches discussed offer insights for specialists in those fields and illustrate more generally that knowledge about evaluation resides in a number of them. Advertising, as well as PR (which will be discussed next), has adopted a siloed approach in evaluation, and failed to engage with the extensive body of communication theory and models for planning and evaluation that has emerged in other fields. Public relations has been perhaps the most siloed of all until recently.

Public relations evaluation models

Measurement and evaluation have been conducted by PR practitioners since the nineteenth century in basic forms such as media monitoring (Lamme & Russell, 2010). For instance, Tom Watson (2012) reported that the first press-clipping agencies were established in the US and UK in the late 1800s. Focus on a research-based approach to measurement and evaluation dates back to Edward Bernays, identified in US PR literature as the 'father of public relations' (Guth & Marsh, 2007, p. 70). Watson points out that whereas fellow US public relations pioneer Ivy Lee regarded his practice as an art, Bernays saw PR as an applied social science that should be planned using opinion research and 'precisely evaluated' (2012, p. 391). Fraser Likely and Watson also note the use of opinion research by Arthur Page in the early twentieth century (2013, p. 144).

Following the work of Bernays, Page and other pioneers, published literature on the importance of research for measurement and evaluation of PR began to proliferate in the late 1950s, when the second edition of *Effective Public Relations* was published. Having referred to the importance of public opinion research in the first edition (Cutlip & Center, 1952), in their second edition the authors added evaluation as the fourth step in the 'PR process' after 'fact-finding, planning and communicating' (Hallahan, 1993, p. 198).

Likely and Watson (2013), Watson (2012), and Watson and Noble (2014) identify a major focus on evaluation of PR from the 1970s. Likely and Watson (2013) say that a conference organized and chaired by Jim Grunig at the University of Maryland in 1977 was a 'prime catalyst' for scholarly attention to evaluation, as well as a special issue of *Public Relations Review* on 'Measuring the effectiveness of public relations' published in the same year. Other pioneering efforts in PR evaluation in the 1970s and the early 1980s were those of Walter Lindenmann (1979, 1980, 1993, 2003) of Ketchum, and Glen Broom and David Dozier from San Diego State University (Broom & Dozier, 1983; Dozier, 1984, 1985), as well as the eminent public relations scholar Jim Grunig (1979, 1983).

Before the end of the 1980s, John Pavlik (1987) published one of the first books on research for planning and evaluating PR, titled *Public Relations: What Research Tells Us*, in which he gave an early hint of the industry's struggle to evaluate its effectiveness when he said that 'measuring the effectiveness of PR has proved almost as elusive as finding the Holy Grail' (p. 65). Somewhat tragically, this view was echoed by Jacqui L'Etang near the end of the first decade of the twenty-first century, when she noted that 'evaluation has become and remains something of a "holy grail" for public relations' (2008, p. 26). Pavlik's small, but landmark, book was followed soon after by *Using Research in Public Relations: Applications to Programme Management*, a detailed text by Broom and Dozier (1990), and a review of PR evaluation studies by David Dozier (1990). Jim Grunig and Todd Hunt's (1984) seminal *Managing Public Relations* also contained considerable discussion of the importance of evaluation – particularly summative evaluation – as well as formative research for planning. Other pioneering research articles, book chapters and papers on evaluation of PR were published by William Ehling (1992), this author (Macnamara, 1992, 1999), Gael Walker (1994, 1997), and Paul Noble and Tom Watson (1999).

Industry bodies also began to produce position statements, manuals and guides on evaluation, such as the planning–research–evaluation (PRE) process developed by the UK Institute for Public Relations (now the Chartered Institute for Public Relations) in 2001 as part of its *Public Relations Research and Evaluation Toolkit* (Fairchild, 2001; Watson & Noble, 2014, p. 63). Updated since and renamed the *Research,*

Planning and Measurement Toolkit in 2010, this identifies five stages in the practice of PR as:

1. conduct research to audit 'where we are now';
2. set objectives;
3. develop a strategy and plan;
4. conduct ongoing measurement; and
5. evaluate results.

(CIPR, 2011)

Following in the footsteps of Edward Bernays, Arthur Page, Walter Lindenmann and other leading practitioners, Katie Paine, the founder and chief executive officer (CEO) of media analysis firm Delahaye, convened the first PR industry 'summit on measurement' at the University of New Hampshire, Durham, in 2003. This author was honoured to be a speaker at the second such summit in 2004, and again in 2006, 2007 and 2008, when the summit was moved to Portsmouth, New Hampshire. The formal summit proceedings were followed by stimulating debates that continued long into the night during a traditional clam bake at the woodlands home of Katie Paine on Shankhassick Farm near Durham, NH. The Public Relations Society of America (PRSA) has published a range of resources for evaluation over the past two decades, and Watson and Noble also note a number of other practitioner-developed models and tools, including dashboards and scorecards (2014, p. 72).

Nevertheless, despite considerable efforts and some progress, Gregory and Watson (2008) lamented a 'stasis' in PR evaluation, and a number of studies since have confirmed a lack of implementation of evaluation, particularly at the level of achieving organizational objectives (Cacciatore, Meng & Berger, 2016; Wright & Hinson, 2012; Wright, Gaunt, Leggetter, Daniels & Zerfass, 2009; Zerfass, Verčič, Verhoeven, Moreno & Tench, 2012). Scholars and practitioners alike have also lamented a lack of standards in PR evaluation (Michaelson & Stacks, 2011). As recently as 2015, a major survey of practitioners confirmed a continuing stasis in relation to evaluation (Macnamara, Lwin, Adi & Zerfass, 2016) and a 'deadlock' in advancing evaluation practice (Macnamara, 2014b, 2015c). Some of the reasons for this lack of progress have been discussed in Chapter 1, including cost (lack of budget), lack of time, alleged lack of demand and lack of standards. In addition, in a paper presented to the 2014 AMEC Summit on Measurement and in a subsequent journal article, Macnamara (2014b, 2015c) pointed to the conflation of measurement and evaluation, the primary focus being on measurement, as well as a 'backwards-looking' approach focused on justifying past programmes, rather than generating learning and insights to inform future strategy and programmes (see 'Measurement–analysis–insights–evaluation (MAIE) model of evaluation', later in this chapter).

The following sections summarize some of the most widely circulated models of PR evaluation – particularly the most recent versions that are attempting to break the deadlock and provide accountability for investments in PR.

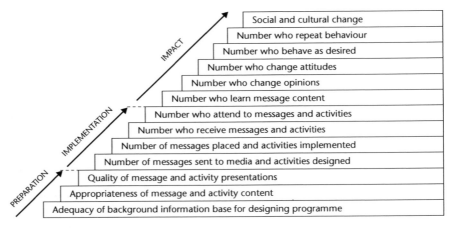

FIGURE 3.4 The planning–implementation–impact (PII) model

Source: Cutlip et al. (1985)

Planning–implementation–impact (PII) model

The earliest published and widely circulated model of PR evaluation is the *planning–implementation–impact* (PII) model developed by Scott Cutlip, Alan Center and Glen Broom (1985) in the sixth edition of *Effective Public Relations* (see Figure 3.4). This model is often nicknamed the 'step model' because it represents communication as a series of steps, from preparation to behaviour change and social and cultural change. It is interesting that its authors refer to 'social and cultural change', not only change designed to achieve the commercial objectives of corporations – a perspective that will be revisited later in this chapter.

While the PII model incorporated the inherent logic of programme theory and programme logic models, it did not follow the structure or terminology of programme evaluation other than in using the term 'impact'. It did, however, clearly identify that evaluation should occur in a number of progressive steps. As Charles Atkin and Vicki Freimuth say in their guidelines for evaluation research design for campaigns: 'As a means to attaining the bottom-line behavioural objectives, campaign messages must first have an impact on preliminary or intermediate variables along the response chain' (2013, p. 58).

Macro and pyramid models of PR research

The *macro model* of PR evaluation was published in 1992 in *International Public Relations Review*, and identified three stages of PR programmes and evaluation as inputs, outputs and results (Macnamara, 1992). This model followed basic programme logic model formats to some extent, but leaned towards the management language prevalent at the time in calling its final stage 'results'. However, it was the first model of evaluation for PR to be based, at least in part, on programme theory and programme logic models.

The macro model was later revised to fully incorporate a programme logic model approach in the *pyramid model* of PR research, which dropped 'results' and reverted to inputs, outputs and outcomes as the main stages (Macnamara, 2002a, 2005a, 2012a). In addition, in its revised form, this model deferred to the growing use of *outtakes* in the PR field, although it represented these as a subfield largely associated with short-term outcomes (see Figure 3.5).

An important contribution of the early macro model and the updated pyramid model of PR research is that they not only identified the main stages and key steps within each stage drawing on the PII model of Cutlip et al. (1985), but also added a list of formal and informal methods relevant for each stage. Despite frequent criticism of models for lack of application to practice, no previous models had – and few since have – attempted this translation into practice by adding details on applicable methods.

Lindenmann's PR effectiveness yardstick

A model that is widely claimed in US PR literature to be foundational in the development of PR evaluation is the *PR effectiveness yardstick* published by Walter Lindenmann (1993). This claim ignores earlier models such as the macro model of evaluation (Macnamara, 1992) and the early work of the International Public Relations Association (IPRA), which started in 1993 and was published in 1994.

Lindenmann's yardstick (see Figure 3.6) conceptualized PR evaluation as occurring at three levels, which he described as:

* Basic level for measuring *outputs*;
* Intermediate level for measuring what he called PR *outgrowths*; and
* Advanced for measuring PR *outcomes*.

(Lindenmann, 1993, p. 8, original emphasis)

Thus Lindenmann's yardstick introduced another term to the PR lexicon (*outgrowths*), which is not used in any other literature. He also took the common approach of using the term 'measurement' rather than *evaluation*. However, Lindenmann's yardstick was noteworthy for its emphasis on setting objectives as the first stage of all programmes and on conducting evaluation within the context of the objectives set.

Lindenmann's model became widely cited and adopted to some extent owing to Lindenmann's position as a practising researcher at Ketchum during most of this period, following more than a decade with Hill and Knowlton's research subsidiary, Group Attitudes Corporation, and his prolific writing on the subject of evaluation (for example, Lindenmann, 1979, 1980, 1990, 1997a, 1997b, 1998, 2003). Lindenmann himself acknowledges that he was influenced by the work of McGuire and other communication researchers, saying:

> The theory behind the model came primarily from well-known communication scholars, especially William J. McGuire, Wilbur Schramm, Everett Rogers, Charles R. Wright, Elihu Katz . . . and Jim Grunig. I was especially

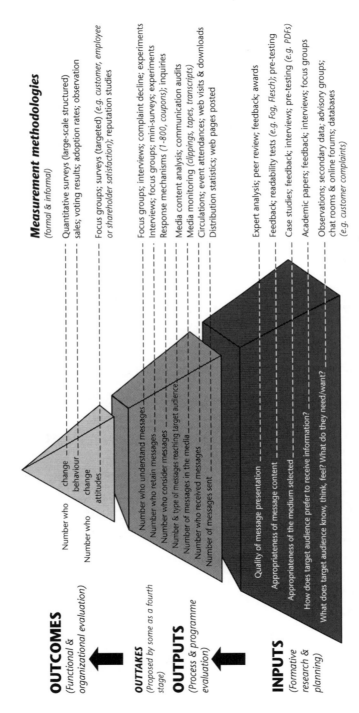

FIGURE 3.5 The pyramid model of PR research[a] derived from the macro model of evaluation[b]

Sources: [a] Macnamara (2002a, 2005a, 2012a); [b] Macnamara (1992, 1999)

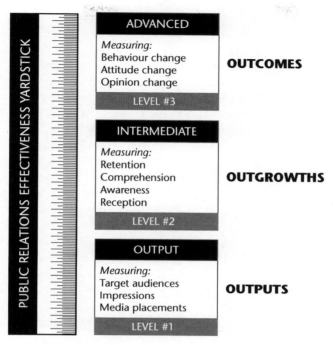

FIGURE 3.6 The PR effectiveness yardstick

Source: Lindenmann (1993)

taken with excellent essay of McGuire, 'Persuasion, resistance and attitude change' which appeared in the 1973 *Handbook of Communication*. McGuire had a matrix that he used in his essay, which I relied on heavily to explain the Yardstick model. The matrix and the arguments that McGuire presented led me to create the stages in the model the way I did.

(W. Lindenmann, personal communication, January 18, 2016)

International Public Relations Association (IPRA) model

In 1994, IPRA assembled an international committee under the leadership of then-president Jim Pritchitt to tackle the issue of evaluation. Pritchitt led an eight-member committee of practitioners and academics from Australia, the UK and South Africa in producing the IPRA Gold Paper on Evaluation (IPRA, 1994), comprising: Australian public relations practitioners Chris Hocking, Jane Jordan, Bill Sherman and this author (a practitioner at the time); Dr Gael Walker, an academic from the University of Technology Sydney (UTS); Sandra Macleod, the UK CEO of pioneering media analysis firm CARMA International; and Anna Mari Honnibal, a practitioner from South Africa (IPRA, 1994, Preface, n.p.).[4] The largely Australian composition of the committee was the result partly of Pritchitt being an Australian living and working in Australia. But several other factors indicate it was not simply a matter of geography. At the time, Australia had the third highest national IPRA membership in the world, after the US and the UK (Macnamara & Watson, 2014). Among those members, Walker was staunchly advocating evaluation in PR research and teaching at UTS (Walker, 1992) and, earlier that year, Walker (1994) had replicated in Australia a study undertaken by Lindenmann (1990) in the US. The IPRA model of evaluation cited and drew on this, as well as Cutlip and colleagues' PII model and the macro model. Another link between members of this group was that this author was in the process of founding CARMA International (Asia Pacific),[5] working closely with Sandra Macleod, and, furthermore, CARMA International sponsored the IPRA Gold Paper. There was thus significant academic and practitioner research expertise and a major commitment to evaluation among this group.

The IPRA model (see Figure 3.7) was the first to use the stages of *inputs*, *outputs* and *outcomes*, although most of these terms were used in the macro model of PR evaluation and they were also being talked about in the UK Institute of Public Relations (now CIPR). Yet neither the macro model nor the IPRA model is mentioned in the *Bibliography of Public Relations Measurement*, published by the Institute for Public Relations (IPR) in the US (Carroll & Stacks, 2004). The IPRA model also made it quite explicit that evaluation is an iterative process, with arrows indicating that the findings of each stage are used to inform following stages, including outcome evaluation providing insights for planning future programmes (see Figure 3.7).

Continuing model of evaluation

Tom Watson, another Australian, completed a PhD at Nottingham Trent University in the UK in 1995 with a thesis on PR evaluation and, shortly afterwards, published his short-term and continuing models of evaluation (Watson, 1996). While usefully emphasizing an iterative approach to evaluation, with feedback loops informing strategy and tactics, these models illustrate only broad stages, with few details. The *short-term model* was a simple diagram focused on media relations and media analysis (Noble & Watson, 1999; Watson, 1996). The *continuing model* of evaluation also was quite basic, showing stages of planning as comprising research, objective-setting, strategy development, tactical choices and effects identified through 'analysis', with no details (see Figure 3.8). Its purpose was to highlight the cyclical nature of evaluation, explicitly drawing attention to the importance of incorporating feedback gained during programmes into adjusting and fine-tuning strategy and activities. Watson criticized other models, including the macro and pyramid models (Macnamara, 1992, 1999), for their lack of feedback loops – although, as noted elsewhere, this is a misinterpretation of these models, because an iterative approach is emphasized in accompanying text.

In the same year, Anne Gregory (1996) published a chapter on evaluation in the first edition of her *Planning and Managing a Public Relations Campaign*, in which she attempted to integrate evaluation into PR planning and management, although she did not produce a model as such.

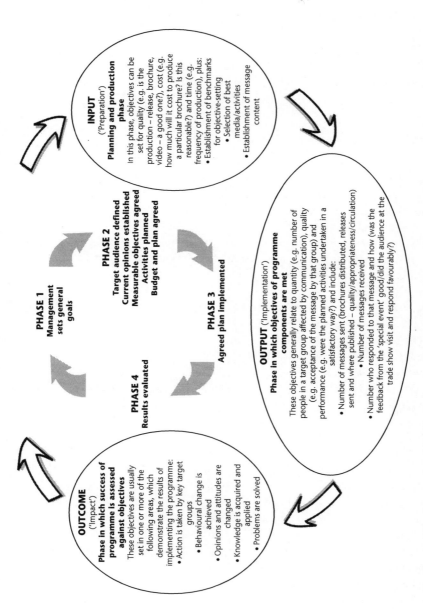

FIGURE 3.7 The International Public Relations Association model of evaluation published in *IPRA Gold Paper Number 11*

Source: IPRA (1994)

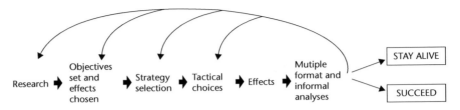

FIGURE 3.8 The continuing model of evaluation

Source: Watson (1996)

Fairchild's three measures – or four

The Institute of Public Relations (now CIPR) in the UK also began to develop a series of frameworks and models for evaluation in the mid-1990s. Michael Fairchild, a consultant working with the IPR and the International Committee of Public Relations Consultancies Associations (now ICCO), proposed three levels of evaluation, as follows:

- *Output* – which measures production of the PR effort as opposed to audience response (outtake or outcome). Output tells us whether the message was sent and aimed at the target audience;
- *Outtake* – the degree to which the audience is aware of the message, has retained and understood it;
- *Outcome* – clearly the greatest value is in knowing whether – and to what degree – public relations activity is actually changing people's opinions, attitudes and behaviour.

(Fairchild, 1997, p. 24)

Fairchild also hinted at a four-stage model including *input*. Thus Fairchild seems to be the first to use the term *outtakes* and the first to suggest four stages in PR programmes as *inputs, outputs, outtakes* and *outcomes*. Fairchild emphasizes that his focus was to integrate evaluation into 'the process of planning, research and evaluation', and 'to move beyond academic debate into pragmatic solutions' – although it must be noted that Lindenmann, Watson and this author all had practitioner backgrounds. In personal communication, Fairchild asserted that 'there was a need to show clients that we could evaluate the worth of what we did, but there was an equally pressing need to persuade PR practitioners that the whole approach to PR needed to be re-thought' (M. Fairchild, personal communication, May 24, 2016).

In the same year, in an early version of his *Guidelines and Standards* published by the IPR and in a number of industry journals, Lindenmann (1997b, 2003) dropped the term 'outgrowths' and renamed his three stages of PR programmes *outputs, outcomes* and *business/organizational outcomes*. He still did not include *inputs*. Six years later, in a revised *Guidelines for Measuring the Effectiveness of PR Programs and*

Activities,[6] Lindenmann (2003) adopted Fairchild's concept of *outtakes* in a four-stage model made up of PR outputs, PR outtakes, PR outcomes and business/organization outcomes. Fairchild says that several of the pioneers in PR evaluation communicated and shared ideas, including the rationale for outtakes as a stage. At the time of writing this, he reflected:

> Walt [Lindenmann] and I had a discussion about 'out-take' that seemed to fill an obvious gap: the need to know how you got from output to outcome; what did the audience understand from the output, indeed whether they got the message at all?
>
> *(M. Fairchild, personal communication, May 24, 2016)*

Unified evaluation model

In 1999, Paul Noble and Tom Watson presented a paper at the Transnational Communication in Europe: Practice and Research Congress in Berlin reviewing a number of models and introducing their *unified evaluation model* (see Figure 3.9). This identified the stages as *input, output, impact* and *effect* (Noble & Watson, 1999, p. 20), consolidating the concept of four stages, but introducing yet another term for results beyond impact – *effect*. Thus this model also fails to follow programme logic model terminology used widely in other fields. Nevertheless, Watson's unified model illustrated a broadening focus in PR evaluation, as he recalls:

> My research into measurement and evaluation started from a practitioner perspective. I wondered why some campaigns worked well and gained desired results and other, similarly-designed campaigns didn't. My reading of literature on evaluation methods identified work by Cutlip and Center, other PR texts, and Broom and Dozier's excellent book on research methods in PR. I was also aware of Jim Macnamara's early work. However, my testing of some models, particularly Cutlip and Center's PII model, in practice was not satisfactory. I felt they could not be implemented in practice. So, I developed four case studies as a central part of my PhD research to investigate the realities of measurement and evaluation. From these case studies, I identified two practice-related models – the short-term model for tactical activity and the continuing model that used iterative loops to undertake formative assessment during the length of a campaign.
>
> The unified model was an attempt by Paul Noble and me to create a more integrated model based on both our work in the mid-1990s and to position PR as a measurable strategic communication activity.
>
> *(T. Watson, personal communication, May 16, 2016)*

In the same year, Michael Fairchild and Nigel O'Connor (1999)[7] produced the first edition of the *IPR Toolkit for Measurement and Evaluation*, which continued to promote the stages of *outputs, outtakes* and *outcomes* within what they called the 'PRE process'

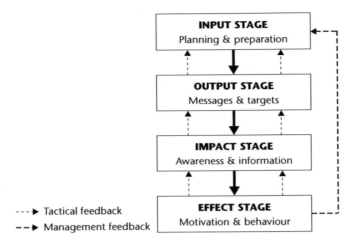

FIGURE 3.9 The unified evaluation model for public relations

Source: Noble and Watson (1999)

(*planning–research–evaluation*). Throughout this period, eminent US public relations academic Jim Grunig (1979, 1983) continued to advocate evaluation and, in 1999, he and Linda Childers published a paper on evaluating relationships in which they identified the key stages of evaluation as *outputs*, *outcomes* and *relationships* (Childers & Grunig, 1999), adding yet another term to the PR evaluation vocabulary.

Exposure–engagement–influence–action (EEIA) model

More recently, Don Bartholomew (2007) produced a model for PR evaluation, initially with three stages (exposure–influence–action) and then expanded to four stages, identified as *exposure–engagement–influence–action* (EEIA). Bartholomew's (2008) EEIA model is similar to the AIDA model used in advertising in that it is derived from the steps of communication identified by W. J. McGuire (2001). However, like the AIDA model, it selects only a few of McGuire's 13 steps of communication and seemingly assumes a logical progression from exposure to action. A further criticism of the model that applies to much of the PR literature is that it focuses almost exclusively on media content (traditional and social), identifying message inclusion, sentiment, share of online discussion, repeat visitors, duration of time spent, comments, links and other media-content-related factors as metrics to indicate effectiveness (see Figure 3.10).

Broad-based communication evaluation frameworks and models

There are also a number of models that have their roots partly in PR and partly in broader fields of practice, such as corporate communication and strategic communication management, which are used to plan and evaluate government

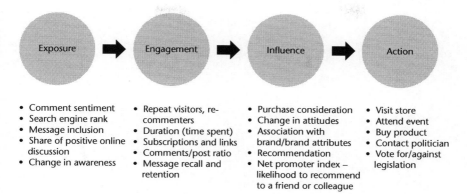

Exposure	Engagement	Influence	Action
• Comment sentiment • Search engine rank • Message inclusion • Share of positive online discussion • Change in awareness	• Repeat visitors, re-commenters • Duration (time spent) • Subscriptions and links • Comments/post ratio • Message recall and retention	• Purchase consideration • Change in attitudes • Association with brand/brand attributes • Recommendation • Net promoter index – likelihood to recommend to a friend or colleague	• Visit store • Attend event • Buy product • Contact politician • Vote for/against legislation

FIGURE 3.10 The exposure–engagement–influence–action (EEIA) model

Source: Bartholomew (2008)

communication, organizational communication and integrated communication programmes. The following are some examples, with particular emphasis on the most recent and advanced models.

Communication controlling model

As the twentieth century ended and the new millennium began, PR researchers working in the Deutsche Public Relations Gesellschaft (DPRG) and Gesellschaft Public Relations Agenturen (GPRA) in Germany produced the first of a series of 'communication-controlling' models, which identify four stages of PR programmes as input, output, outcome and *outflow*, thus introducing yet another term to PR evaluation terminology (DPRG & GPRA, 2000). Communication–controlling models have evolved over time, but continue to follow this basic four-stage structure (see Figure 3.11) (DPRG & ICV, 2009; Huhn, Sass & Storck, 2011; Zerfass, 2010).

Recent writing on this model emphasizes that communication controlling is more than a model for evaluation. For example, drawing on Zerfass (2007, 2010), who has championed this model, Huhn and colleagues point out that:

> Communication controlling is often mistakenly equated with 'monitoring' or 'evaluation'. But this is only one part of the functional tasks communication controlling needs to fulfil. From a management accountancy perspective, the term 'controlling' stands for the full management cycle comprising the planning, implementation, monitoring and evaluation of an organization's communication activities. It makes transparent how decisions are taken, how results relate to expenditure, whether resources are used efficiently and which results are achieved. As a support function, communication controlling provides methods and instruments for planning, steering and controlling corporate communication.
>
> *(Huhn et al., 2011, p. 11)*

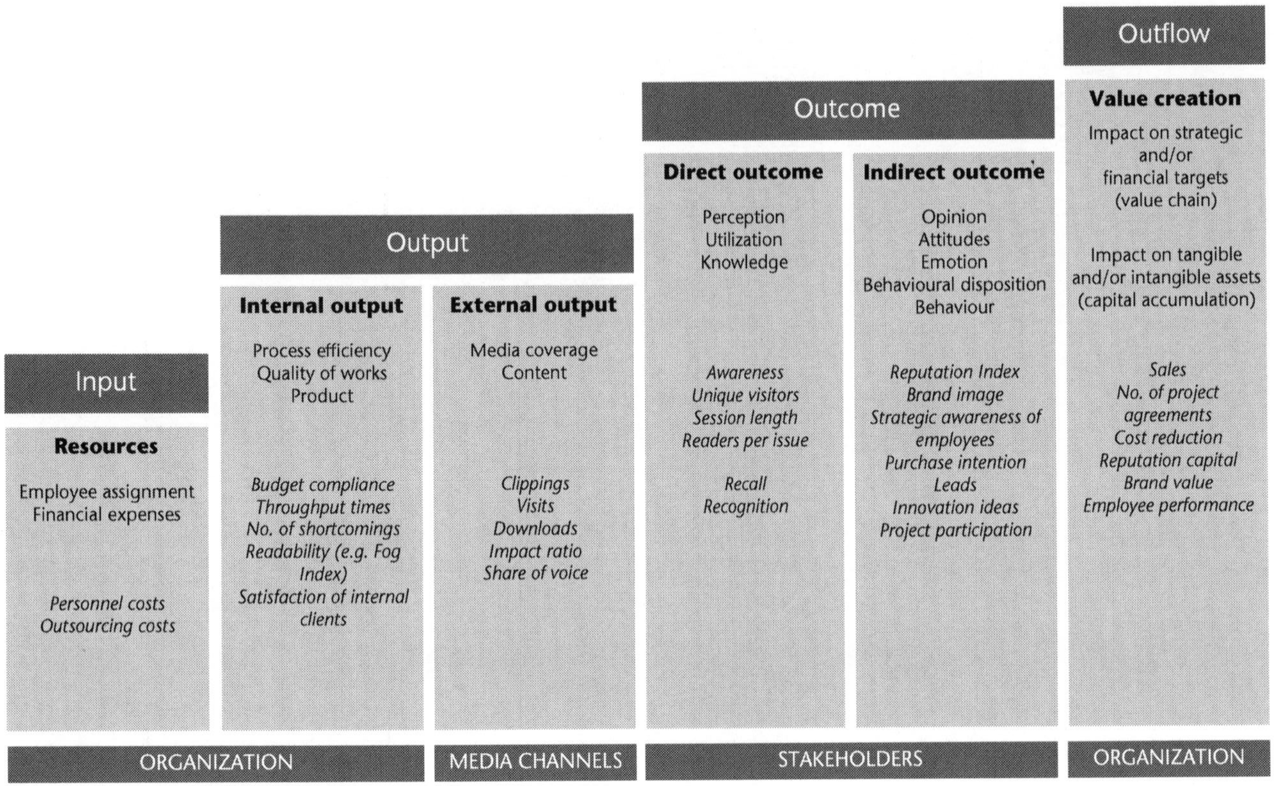

Input

Resources

Employee assignment
Financial expenses

Personnel costs
Outsourcing costs

ORGANIZATION

Output

Internal output

Process efficiency
Quality of works
Product

Budget compliance
Throughput times
No. of shortcomings
Readability (e.g. Fog Index)
Satisfaction of internal clients

ORGANIZATION

External output

Media coverage
Content

Clippings
Visits
Downloads
Impact ratio
Share of voice

MEDIA CHANNELS

Outcome

Direct outcome

Perception
Utilization
Knowledge

Awareness
Unique visitors
Session length
Readers per issue

Recall
Recognition

Indirect outcome

Opinion
Attitudes
Emotion
Behavioural disposition
Behaviour

Reputation Index
Brand image
Strategic awareness of employees
Purchase intention
Leads
Innovation ideas
Project participation

STAKEHOLDERS

Outflow

Value creation

Impact on strategic and/or financial targets (value chain)

Impact on tangible and/or intangible assets (capital accumulation)

Sales
No. of project agreements
Cost reduction
Reputation capital
Brand value
Employee performance

ORGANIZATION

FIGURE 3.11 The communication–controlling model

Sources: DPRG & ICV (2009); Huhn et al. (2011, p. 13)

Zerfass and Volk (forthcoming) say that communication controlling is a set of methods, structures, processes and metrics for planning, steering and evaluating communication that support communication management.

The creators and proponents of this model are aware of the negative connotations of the term 'control' in relation to communication and relationships with stakeholders and publics. However, in a position paper, they note and explain:

> Communication professionals and scholars might find it difficult to apply the term 'controlling' to a concept aimed at supporting management processes though providing transparency regarding decision making and performance ... However, linking communication to management requires communication practice to cross the borders of corporate functions and adopt management paradigms.
>
> *(Huhn et al., 2011, p. 4)*

They go on to argue that the concept of 'controlling' is well established in continental European management, as well as in global companies and consultancies based in Europe, and is recognized and understood by the Institute of Management Accountants (IMA) in the US, the International Federation of Accountants (IFAC) and the International Group of Controlling (IGC).

Huhn et al. (2011) also report that, with the support of academic researchers at the University of Leipzig and the University of Fribourg, 16 leading Austrian companies and institutions, including A1 Telekom Austria, Austrian Airlines, Bank Austria, OMV, ÖBB and Voestalpine, have collaborated to develop common processes, standardized metrics and benchmarks for their corporate communication, and have used a standardized set of indicators to monitor, direct and evaluate their communication activities since 2009. However, despite some take-up in business-oriented communication departments, this author considers the communication-controlling model unlikely to become a standard worldwide given the negative interpretations of the term 'controlling' in arts, social sciences and humanities, which are the disciplinary homes of most public communication practices.

Barcelona Principles

A number of significant developments have taken place in recent years in an attempt to address the limitations described. A starting point for reform in evaluation of PR was the declaration in 2010 of the Barcelona Principles, so-called because they were agreed by more than 200 delegates from 33 countries at an International Association for Measurement and Evaluation of Communication (AMEC) International Summit on Measurement in Barcelona (AMEC, 2010). In many ways, the Barcelona Principles are very basic, but they were a tipping point for a series of further developments, including a major revision of the Principles in 2015 (AMEC, 2015). Table 3.2 presents the Barcelona Principles as agreed in 2010 and the Barcelona Principles 2.0, both of which were jointly developed by

TABLE 3.2 The original Barcelona Principles of 2010 and the Barcelona Principles 2.0

	Barcelona Principles	*Barcelona Principles 2.0*
1.	Importance of goal-setting and measurement	Goal-setting and measurement are fundamental to communication and public relations
2.	Measuring the effect on outcomes is preferred to measuring outputs	Measuring communication outcomes is recommended vs only measuring outputs
3.	Effect on business results can, and should, be measured where possible	Effect on organizational performance can, and should, be measured where possible
4.	Media measurement requires quantity and quality	Measurement and evaluation require both qualitative and quantitative methods
5.	AVEs are not the value of public relations	AVEs are not the value of communication
6.	Social media can, and should, be measured	Social media can, and should, be measured consistently with other channels
7.	Transparency and replicability are paramount to sound measurement	Measurement and evaluation should be transparent, consistent and valid

Sources: AMEC (2010, 2015)

AMEC, the ICCO, the US IPR, the PR Consultants Association (PRCA) in the UK, the PRSA, and the Global Alliance for Public Relations and Communication Management.[8]

The Barcelona Principles 2.0 represent a necessary improvement on the original Principles in a number of respects, including the following:

- Principle 1 is broadened beyond PR to refer to 'communication'.
- Principle 3 is broadened from 'business results' to 'organizational performance', which is more inclusive of the work of public-sector and third-sector organizations.
- Principle 4 is broadened beyond 'media measurement'.
- Replicability is removed from Principle 7, because this is applicable only to quantitative research.

However, there is still room for improvement in the Barcelona Principles 2.0 and these should be read as a broad guide. For example, Principle 2 refers to 'measuring communication outcomes', but does not specify evaluation of *impact*, which is a stage beyond communication outcomes in most models, as discussed in Chapter 2, and while Principle 3 is broadened beyond a narrow focus on business, it remains restricted to evaluating the effect on organizational performance and does not give any attention to impact on stakeholders or social impact other than what the organization seeks to achieve. Further, the terms 'measurement' and 'measuring' are used extensively and often 'evaluation' is not mentioned.

Notwithstanding their weaknesses and generic nature, the Barcelona Principles have provided a framework for what several industry commentators call the 'march to standards' (Marklein & Paine, 2012). Two significant initiatives between 2010 and 2014, briefly noted in Chapter 1, were as follows:

- In 2011, the Coalition for Public Relations Research Standards was established by AMEC, the IPR and the Council of PR Firms (CPRF) to collaboratively develop standards for measurement and evaluation of PR within the framework of the Barcelona Principles. In 2012, the Coalition released its *Proposed Interim Standards for Metrics in Traditional Media Analysis* (Eisenmann, Geddes, Paine, Pestana, Walton & Weiner, 2012), which included definitions of key media content analysis terms such as 'items', 'impressions', 'mentions', 'tone' and 'sentiment', and described how these should be used.
- In 2012, the Conclave on Social Media Measurement Standards (known as the #SMMstandards Conclave, or simply 'the Conclave' for short) was established. The Conclave involved collaboration by 11 professional communication organizations worldwide, as well as consultation with five media and advertising industry bodies and eight companies representing employer perspectives. Membership of the Conclave included the three founding Coalition members (AMEC, CPRF and IPR), as well as the Global Alliance for Public Relations and Communication Management, the International Association of Business Communicators (IABC), the PRSA, the UK CIPR, the Society for New Communications Research (SNCR), the Fédération internationale des bureaux d'extraits de presse (FIBEP), the Word of Mouth Marketing Association (WOMMA) and the Digital Analytics Association (DAA). In addition, the Coalition and the Conclave consulted with the Media Ratings Council (MRC), the Interactive Advertising Bureau (IAB), the American Association of Advertising Agencies (AAAA), the Association of National Advertisers (ANA) and the Web Analytics Association (WAA). This was an important step in trying to achieve consistent terminology and compatibility of metrics across the public communication field. Corporations involved in the development of standards included Dell, Ford Motor Company, General Motors, McDonald's, Procter & Gamble, SAS, Southwest Airlines and Thomson Reuters.

At the fourth European Summit on Measurement in Dublin in 2012, the Coalition for Public Relations Research Standards released three documents as the first stage of social media measurement standards: *Valid Metrics for Social Media* (Daniels, 2012); *The Sources and Methods Transparency Table*; and *Social Media Standard Definitions for Reach and Impressions*, produced by the Conclave (2013 [2011]) in consultation with the DAA. Subsequently, between 2011 and 2013, the Conclave developed standards for 'content and sourcing', 'reach and impressions', 'engagement and conversation', 'influence', 'opinion and advocacy', and 'influence and impact' (Conclave, 2013 [2011]).

Despite enthusiasm and much hard work by those involved, the 'standards' developed by these groups mainly comprise a set of definitions. These are a useful contribution, but do not comprise a set of standards for evaluation of public communication. Also, some so-called standards are superficial and contrary to established research literature. For example, *engagement*, which is a multidimensional concept described in organizational psychology as involving cognitive, affective and conative dimensions (Macey & Schneider, 2008; Rhoades, Eisenberger & Armeli, 2001), and as 'two-way . . . give and take' between organizations and their stakeholders and publics (Taylor & Kent, 2014, p. 391), is described in terms of likes, comments, shares, retweets and video views in social media. Furthermore, the initiatives discussed above reveal a continuing focus on media, on 'business' outcomes and on retrospective reporting, as well as *Americentrism* with most members of these groups being Americans and all client organizations involved in these projects being US corporations.

Don Bartholomew repeatedly critiqued the preoccupation with media in PR, saying that 'public relations measurement has focussed on attempts to measure media relations value' (2016, p. 186), and that 'public relations research and measurement has historically been driven by content analysis' (2016, p. 15) in which 'the most common public relations metric . . . is impressions' (2016, p. 8). He referred to the 'measurement gap' (again illustrating the continuing focus on measurement), saying that 'the measurement industry today is focussed on media content analysis (outputs measurement) while organizations increasingly value public relations for our contributions in moving the needle on reputation, culture, or sales (outcomes)' (Bartholomew, 2016, p. 159).

Measurement–analysis–insights–evaluation (MAIE) model of evaluation: the shift to insights

A model designed to shift emphasis from 'rear-view mirror' reporting to forward-looking insights is the MAIE model of evaluation unveiled at the 2014 AMEC Summit on Measurement in Amsterdam (Macnamara, 2014b, 2015c). An acronym for *measurement–analysis–insights–evaluation*, MAIE is an illustration of a recommended evaluation process designed to make four important points, rather than a model of evaluation research. First, it separates the often conflated processes of measurement (M) and evaluation (E). When evaluation is undertaken as part of, or immediately after, measurement, it is limited and narrow in terms of the data analysed. Analysis is usually focused exclusively on *endogenous* data – that is, the data collected in the specific measurement process undertaken by the organization – and does not consider *exogenous* data, which may be available outside the measurement being undertaken or even outside the organization. Instead of fusing evaluation with measurement processes, the MAIE model proposes two additional stages be inserted between measurement and evaluation. The first of these is the second key feature of the model: it highlights and calls for analysis (A), and argues that this should be in-depth and undertaken for two purposes – first and foremost, to generate insights (I) to improve the communication programme and inform future organizational strategy; and, second, to provide data for reporting evaluation (E) of the effectiveness of the communication programme.

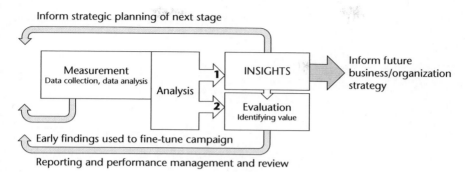

FIGURE 3.12 The MAIE model of the measurement and evaluation process
Source: Macnamara (2015c)

This forward-looking approach – designed to provide insights that contribute to future business or organization strategy, as well as inform future communication strategy and effectiveness – helps to bridge the gap between public communication, such as PR and corporate communication, and organizational outcomes. Rather than trying to link communication to business or organizational outcomes retrospectively, which can be seen as *post hoc* rationalization, this approach produces positive contributions to the future success of the organization. Insights that inform future strategy are generally perceived by management to be far more valuable than the reporting of past activities. Further detailed discussion of ways of generating insights is provided in Chapter 6.

A further initiative designed to move beyond definitions to more complete standards and to broaden focus internationally was the establishment in 2015 of the Task Force on Standardization of Communication Planning and Evaluation Models. Chaired by Canadian evaluation consultant Fraser Likely, the Task Force is made up of academics and professional researchers specializing in evaluation from Australia (including this author) and Europe, as well as the US, including some members of the US IPR Measurement Commission.[9] The Task Force is attempting to synthesize myriad models of evaluation, with a view to identifying approaches and methods that are theory-based and best practice, and are therefore capable of being a standard.

One of the first papers produced by members of the Task Force reviewed evaluation models published in PR and corporate communication literature from the early 1980s to the early 2000s and compared them with programme theory, programme theory evaluation (PTE) and theory of change models developed in the same period (Macnamara & Likely, 2017). The paper noted that some models of evaluation of PR and corporate, marketing, organizational and government communication broadly followed the stages and processes of *programme logic models*, but often modified or 'bastardized' these. For example, instead of the commonly used stages of *inputs*, *activities*, *outputs*, *outcomes* and *impact* advocated in widely used models such as those of the Kellogg Foundation (2004 [1998], 2010) and the University

TABLE 3.3 Basic and classic program logic models compared with PR and communication evaluation models from early 1980s to early 2000s (Macnamara & Likely, 2017).

Basic and classic logic models			PR and communication evaluation models			
Basic program logic model – UWEX (Taylor-Power & Henert, 2008)	*Expanded program logic model – UWEX (Taylor-Power & Henert, 2008)*	*Classic Program Logic Model (e.g. Kellogg Foundation, 1998/2004)*	*Cutlip, Center & Broom (1985) 'PII model'*	*Macnamara's 'Macro model' (1992)*	*Lindenmann's Effectiveness Yardstick (1993, 1997a)*	*IPRA Gold Paper on Evaluation (1994, pp. 10, 18–19)*
Input	Inputs	Inputs		Inputs		Inputs
		Activities	Planning			
Output	Outputs • Activities • Participation	Outputs	Implementation	Outputs	Outputs (*basic*)	Outputs
					Outgrowths (*intermediate*)	
Outcomes	Outcomes • Short-term • Intermediate • Long-term	Outcomes			Outcomes (*advanced*)	Outcomes
		Impact	Impact	Results		

(*Continued*)

TABLE 3.3 (Continued)

PR and communication evaluation models

Fairchild (1997, 2001); Fairchild & O'Connor, IPR Toolkit (1999)	Lindenmann Standards and Guidelines (1997b, 1997c)	Noble & Watson's 'Unified Model' (1999)	Grunig & Hon 'relationships' model	DPRG/ GPRA (2000), DPRG/ICV (2009) models	Likely Performance Measurement Framework (2000)	Macnamara's 'Pyramid' model (2000b, 2002a, 2002b)	Lindenmann's 'guidelines' (2002/2003)
Inputs (hinted)		Input		Input		Inputs	
Output	Outputs	Output	Outputs	Output	Outputs	Outputs	PR Outputs
Outtake					Outtakes	Outtakes	PR Outtakes
Outcome	Outcomes		Outcomes	Outcome	Outcomes	Outcomes	PR Outcomes
Business / organization outcomes		Impact	Relationships	Outflow	Outgrowths		Business / organization outcomes
		Effect					

of Wisconsin Cooperative Extension Program (UWEX) (Taylor-Power & Henert, 2008), PR practitioners and evaluation service providers have used terms such as *results*, *effects* and *business/organizational outcomes* and have created new terms, such as *outgrowths* and *outflows*, as shown earlier in this chapter.

The *Developing a Logic Model: Teaching and Training Guide* notes that 'many variations and types of logic models exist' (Taylor-Power & Henert, 2008, p. 2). The Kellogg Foundation similarly says that 'there is no one best logic model' (2004 [1998], p. 13). However, there are a number of common concepts and principles in programme logic models, as shown in Chapter 2. This author and Likely (Macnamara & Likely, 2017) produced a comparison of 12 of the PR evaluation models most widely used between the 1980s and the early 2000s, including many of those discussed in this section, and compared these with three classic programme logic models, as discussed in Chapter 2 (see Table 3.3).

As well as illustrating the fragmentation that has occurred in PR evaluation thinking, this comparison shows that, among 15 variants of models examined, the most commonly used stages are (in order of prevalence): *outputs* (14 times); *outcomes* (12 times); *inputs* (9 times); *impact* or closely related terms such as *results* (5 times); and *outtakes* (4 times). Arranged in 'logical' order, this suggests a model made up of at least four stages (*inputs*, *outputs*, *outcomes* and *impact*) and possibly five stages (*inputs*, *outputs*, *outtakes*, *outcomes* and *impact*). *Activities* is listed as a stage in classic programme logic models, but not in any PR evaluation models. *Outgrowths* is used twice (Likely, 2000; Lindenmann, 1993), but at two different levels, and *outflows* is used only once, suggesting that these terms are not widely supported (see Table 3.3).

The paper argued for a return to the 'disciplinary homes of evaluation' such as public administration, international development and education, and a refocusing on fundamental knowledge about evaluation, as summarized in Chapter 2 (Macnamara & Likely, 2017). In particular, it pointed towards the need to base evaluation of communication on programme theory (Weiss, 1972; Wholey, 1987), programme theory evaluation (Rogers, Petrosino, Huebner & Hacsi, 2000), theory of change (Anderson, 2005; Clark & Taplin, 2012), programme logic models (Funnell & Rogers, 2011; Julian, 1997; Knowlton & Phillips, 2013; McLaughlin & Jordan, 1999), and other systematic outcome and impact oriented approaches such as *realist evaluation* (Pawson & Tilley, 1997).

Since 2015, a number of new frameworks and models for evaluation of public communication have been developed based on transdisciplinary knowledge drawn from fields such as programme evaluation and other systematic approaches (Rossi, Lipsey & Freeman, 2004; Wholey, Hatry & Newcomer, 2010). These offer insights into best practice, as well as application of theory-based evaluation, and further point towards emerging standards, although inconsistency continues.

European Commission's Better Regulation Guidelines *and evaluation model*

The European Commission's (2015a) *Better Regulation Guidelines* uses the terms *inputs*, *outputs*, *results* and *impact* for the key stages of public communication, employing a further adaptation of programme logic model stages. However, the model of evaluation published in its *External Communication Network Code of Conduct on Measurement and Evaluation of Communication Activities* (European Commission, 2015b) notes that other contemporary PR and communication industry models use the terms *outtakes* and *outcomes* for the penultimate and ultimate stages, and presents an evaluation framework using these terms, indicating a shift towards standards (see Figure 3.13).

However, despite broadly following classic programme logic models, the Commission's evaluation framework omits *inputs*. Furthermore, it includes *relevance* as a stage after activities such as events have been undertaken. This confuses a characteristic of objectives with a stage of communication and is an ill-fitting element in this model. As discussed in Chapter 1, the 'R' in SMART objectives stands for *relevant* – that is, part of setting communication objectives is ensuring that they are relevant to the organization's overarching goals and objectives. So relevance of communication activities should be established at the time of setting objectives, long before activities are commenced. Another questionable aspect of the Commission's model is that it lists *engagement* as an outcome of communication, although it does go on to identify outcomes as 'indicators measuring the extent to which the communication activity led to either a discernible action being taken or a desired change in the target audience's perception' (European Commission, 2015b, p. 5). Others argue that engagement is an outtake or a short-term outcome at best, because engagement is rarely, if ever, the desired end point of communication. Usually, engagement is sought as a 'stepping stone' towards longer-term outcomes and impact, such as joining an organization, registering as a blood or organ donor, buying a product or service, and so on.

The 27-page Commission Code of Conduct on Evaluation goes on to provide details of a number of 'indicators and benchmarks', as well as metrics, methods and evaluation advice for a wide range of activities such as websites, videos, social media, print materials, events such as fairs, festivals, cultural events, conferences and workshops, stakeholder engagement, information centres, citizen dialogues and integrated campaigns.[10]

Glenn O'Neil, who has worked extensively in evaluating Commission communication programmes, rates the Commission as 'world-leading' in evaluation of communication, and says that this progress has been achieved because evaluation has been made mandatory for many types of project in Europe and increasingly has been applied to public communication. Referring to the *Better Regulations Guidelines*, Code of Conduct and evaluation model, O'Neil said:

> I have found that there is good awareness of these tools among the communication staff of the EC, as they are often referred to in the terms of reference that they outsource evaluation work. In this respect, communication evaluation is becoming more and more common, if not mandatory, in EC communication initiatives. The EC is also transparent in that it publishes many of its evaluation reports publicly.
>
> *(G. O'Neil, personal communication, November 11, 2016)*

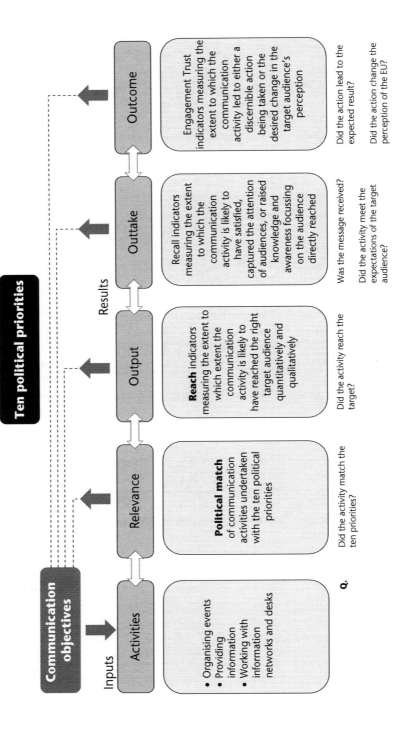

FIGURE 3.13 The European Commission evaluation model

Source: European Commission (2015b)

However, O'Neil has observed that evaluation of public communication campaigns and projects is widely outsourced to service providers in the Commission and other EU organizations, and as a result 'staff develop limited know-how and skills in this area'. Also, his observations echo studies of public communication evaluation practices elsewhere when he says that 'far too much evaluation occurs only as a post-measure . . . and objectives still remain vague and are often not SMART' (G. O'Neil, personal communication, November 11, 2016).

The Commission case study, 'Ex-smokers turn negative messaging to positive results in Europe', reported in Chapter 10, supports O'Neil's observation. Also, this author's ethnographic observations from a number of meetings and conducting workshops for the EC Directorate-General for Communication (DG COMM) and communication staff in Brussels confirm a lack of knowledge and skills in undertaking evaluation among many communication professionals. Even senior directors of communication acknowledged a need for further training, although it must be noted that many EU communication campaigns conducted by the European Commission itself and its numerous committees, agencies and representations are required to address multiple diverse audiences across the EU's 28 member states (at time of writing) and are therefore challenging.

The UK Government Communication Service evaluation framework

Following considerable focus on evaluation of communication within the European Commission (Henningsen, Traverse Healy, Gregory, Johannsen, Allison, Bozeat & Domaradzki, 2014), the UK Government Communication Service (GCS) has made a major commitment to evaluation of public communication among all UK government departments and agencies referred to in the UK as *arm's-length bodies* (ALBs). Under the leadership of Alex Aiken, the executive director of UK government communication, the UK GCS introduced an evaluation framework in 2015, which was updated in early 2016 (see Figure 3.14), as well as a range of other initiatives that have resulted in a substantial step forward in evaluation of UK government public communication and have gained international recognition.

The UK GCS evaluation framework (GCS, 2016a, p. 3) reflects the key concepts and principles of programme logic models, as well as communication and information-processing theory such as that of McGuire (2001), although, as shown in Figure 3.14, the framework retains the stage of *outtakes* introduced to PR evaluation models by Fairchild (1997) in the UK and then Lindenmann (2003) in the US. Furthermore, and importantly, it shows the process of planning and evaluating programmes starting with communication objectives and these being clearly linked to organizational objectives. The processes of evaluation of UK government communication are based on a five-stage programme logic model, with findings from formative, process and summative evaluation used as feedback to fine-tune and adjust programmes if necessary.

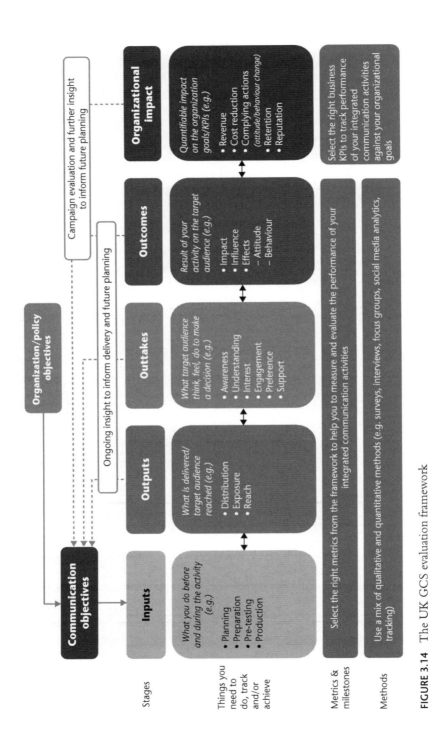

FIGURE 3.14 The UK GCS evaluation framework

Source: GCS (2016a, p. 3)

In reflecting on the UK GCS approach to evaluation, Paul Njoku, who was seconded by Aiken from Her Majesty's Revenue and Customs (HMRC) to lead insights and evaluation for the UK GCS between 2014 and 2016, identified four key factors that he feels contributed to a step change in evaluation within the UK government, as follows:

1. **Necessity.** Cutbacks in UK government expenditure put pressure on communication heads to justify their work.
2. **Strong leadership and governance.** Under the leadership of Alex Aiken, the UK GCS 'mandated' evaluation as a requirement across the 17 major departments and more than 300 ALBs that are responsible for spending around £300 million a year on public communication (GCS, 2015, p. 4), and set demanding standards for reporting. Anne Gregory, professor of corporate communications at the University of Huddersfield and a long-time advocate of evaluation, has said that this 'insistence that UK government communicators evaluate campaigns' has been 'one of the most important initiatives that have moved evaluation forward' in recent times (A. Gregory, personal communication, October 31, 2016).
3. **Evaluation culture.** A number of initiatives were taken to create a culture focused on evaluation, including the establishment of the GCS Evaluation Council, which reviews major government communication campaigns before implementation, and the creation of 'evaluation champions' in departments and ALBs to advocate and help to implement evaluation. While UK government policy requires that all proposals for public communication programmes costing more than £100,000 must be submitted to the Efficiency and Reform Group (ERG) for approval prior to implementation, the Evaluation Council examines a wide range of proposed public communication campaigns, and provides advice and suggestions, as well as mentoring, to departments and ALBs.
4. **Tools, training and support.** As well as producing an evaluation framework, as shown in Figure 3.14, the GCS has produced and distributed guidelines and instructions for each stage in a 12-page booklet available in both digital and printed form (GCS, 2016a), along with templates for reporting, and introduced an ongoing three-tiered professional development programme at 'foundation', 'practitioner' and 'advanced' levels. The content of the professional development programme is informed and guided by the GCS *Evaluation Capability Standards* (GCS, 2014), which are based on regular capability reviews of UK government communication staff to identify levels of knowledge and skills and areas for improvement.

In an interview in mid-2016, Njoku said:

> Professional development was very important to achieving implementation of best practice evaluation in UK government departments and ALBs. Many of the communication professionals working in the UK civil service were keen to evaluate, but lacked the knowledge and skills. We brought in experts

from many fields including academics and professional researchers to run regular master classes and do clinics with GCS staff and I think that was a big part of the success we achieved.

(P. Njoku, personal communication, August 19, 2016)

Anne Gregory agrees strongly. On a 0–10 scale on which 10 represents 'critically important' and 0 indicates 'not important at all', she rates 'professional development/ training of practitioners to include research skills' and 'evaluation being regarded as an essential phase in the strategic planning cycle' as 10, compared with obtaining bigger budgets for evaluation, which she rated 7, and outsourcing evaluation to specialist agencies/suppliers, which she rated 6 (A. Gregory, personal communication, October 31, 2016). To the interview question, 'If there was just one thing you could do to improve evaluation of communication, what would that be?', Gregory responded:

> Train all practitioners in how to do it properly and that includes training them in the full planning cycle from formative research to being able to set objectives appropriately and so on. Alternatively, make this a KPI [key perfor-mance indicator] for all practitioners.
>
> *(A. Gregory, personal communication, October 31, 2016)*

The templates produced for reporting the outputs, outtakes, outcomes and orga-nizational impact of UK government public communication include *dashboards*, which are used to present findings of media analysis, surveys, social media monitor-ing and internal analysis. These are highly graphic to allow information to be easily communicated to and digested by management. A lesson from the UK GCS is that simply introducing an evaluation framework or model does not result in rigorous evaluation; rather, the GCS approach has been a combination of policy, professional development and support, tools such as templates and a clear process identified in a framework.

Is the GCS framework, including its supporting materials, the optimum approach? Paul Njoku responded frankly, saying:

> Of course we can't say it's perfect. There's always room for improvement. Particularly in regard to the knowledge and skills of staff to implement evalu-ation – that's an ongoing process. But I believe we have got the fundamentals right. We have drawn on a wide range of published literature on evaluation and the advice of academics and social researchers and we apply social science research methodology. We also have combined that with a realistic appraisal of what evaluation can and should be done in the context of budget and other priorities.
>
> *(P. Njoku, personal communication, August 19, 2016)*

Ongoing research and critical analysis show that Njoku's modesty is justified. In late 2015, the GCS published its *modern communications operating model* (MCOM), which stated as a key principle that 'the modern communications team will be centred on a core powerhouse of functions', the first of which it listed as 'insight and evaluation' (Brown, 2015, p. 5). However, the MCOM Skills Survey 2016–2017, which gained responses from 2,034 of the 4,000+ GCS staff across the UK civil service, found that evaluation and audience insights were among the lowest rated skills within the GCS (GCS, 2016b). Subsequently, the Evaluation Council resolved to further focus on capability development in these areas.

The New South Wales government communication evaluation framework

In 2015, this author was engaged on a contract research project to review methods of evaluating advertising and other public communication undertaken by the state government of New South Wales (NSW), Australia's largest state, the capital of which is Sydney. The NSW government spends more than AU$100 million (almost US$80 million) annually on public communication, excluding staff salaries, so accountability for this expenditure and effectiveness is important. The result of the review was 20 recommendations for changes to the way in which government advertising and communication was commissioned, managed and evaluated, including the introduction of a new evaluation framework.

Figure 3.15 – which is described as a framework, rather than a model, because it is a broad outline of approach – closely follows classic programme logic models such as that of the Kellogg Foundation (2004 [1998], 2010), but customizes the inputs, activities, outputs, outcomes and impact stages to public communication. This framework is applied to advertising and also can be applied to evaluating media publicity, web communication, social media, events, community engagement projects and other public communication activities.

Within a month of being introduced, the NSW government evaluation framework for advertising and communication was applied to evaluating an anti-drugs campaign targeting youth. The resulting evaluation project won the Gold Award for 'Best use of a measurement framework' in the 2016 AMEC Global Communication Effectiveness Awards.

An important feature of this framework is that, in addition to achieving and reporting outcomes and impact that serve government or agency goals and objectives, it recognizes impact on, and response from, stakeholders and publics more broadly. While government communication should align with public interests, particularly in democratic states in which government ostensibly serves the people, corporate and marketing communication can potentially achieve an organization's goals and objectives while creating negative outcomes and impact for some stakeholders and publics. For example, the promotion of high-fat and high-sugar foods by companies may achieve their sales and profit objectives, but it contributes to obesity, increasing healthcare costs and potentially suffering and premature death among their consumers. All previously cited evaluation frameworks and models focus solely on achieving organizational objectives – an organization-centricity

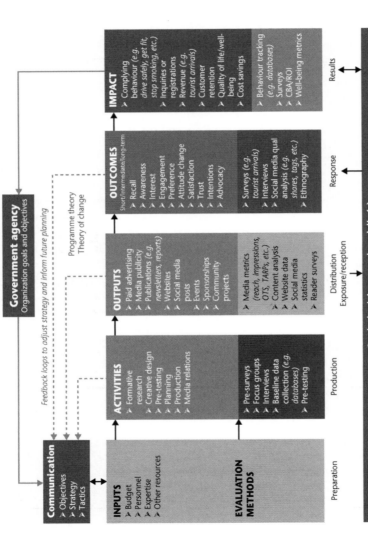

FIGURE 3.15 The NSW government evaluation framework

Source: DPC (2016)

that needs to be addressed in evaluation theory and practice. Recognition of the need to fully evaluate impact on stakeholders and publics, as well as the organization, aligns with programme evaluation theory and programme logic models (Kellogg Foundation, 2004 [1998]; Taylor-Power & Henert, 2008; Wholey et al., 2010) and with *excellence theory* of PR, which calls for evaluation to be conducted at (a) programme, (b) functional (for example, department or unit), (c) organizational and (d) societal levels (Grunig, Grunig & Dozier, 2002, pp. 91–92). (The need to broaden the focus of evaluation of outcomes and impact is further discussed in the last section of this chapter.)

The NSW government evaluation framework was not simply imposed on communication staff. Such an approach would be unlikely to succeed. The review undertaken included interviews with government communicators in a number of departments to understand their requirements, knowledge levels, concerns and contextual factors, as well as a global literature review of evaluation of government communication in other jurisdictions. A number of ideas were borrowed from the UK GCS and the European Commission. The framework was then presented for feedback to both senior government officials, including the Cabinet Committee on Communication and Government Advertising, and government communication staff. Fortunately, the feedback was positive. The framework was then implemented through a number of professional development workshops. Also, a number of new, simplified templates were developed for seeking approval to commission advertising and public communication programmes, and for reporting evaluation. Some of the recommendations of the review required legislative change, such as increasing the expenditure thresholds applying for Cabinet Committee approval, and these were a work in progress at the time of writing (for changing legislation can take a long time). What this and the GCS framework illustrate is that adopting valid, rigorous evaluation of public communication is not simply a matter of creating a pretty graphic model; it is actually the processes and resources behind the framework, which the graphic illustration represents in overview, that are the key.

The AMEC integrated evaluation framework

In mid-2016, AMEC launched a major revision of what began as the AMEC social media measurement framework and its valid metrics framework. After emphasizing setting clear objectives, the *AMEC integrated evaluation framework* (AMEC IEF) (AMEC, 2016b) also uses a programme logic model approach, albeit it applies a six-stage model involving inputs, activities, outputs, outtakes, outcomes and impact. In other words, it uses a classic five-stage programme logic model as used in other fields, but adds 'outtakes' as PR-oriented evaluators frequently do (see Figure 3.16). Only time will tell whether a six-stage framework will prove practical and popular. There is a chance that the potential overlap between outtakes and outcomes may only add to the confusion discussed in the next section. Nevertheless, the AMEC

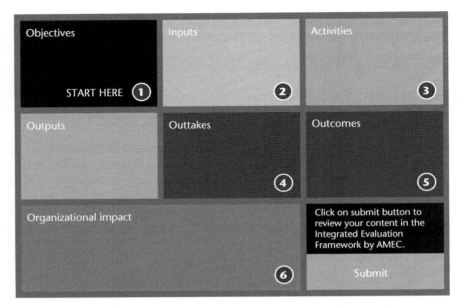

FIGURE 3.16 The interface of the AMEC integrated evaluation framework interactive online tool

Source: AMEC (2016b)

IEF was developed with considerable input from AMEC's academic advisory group,[11] of which this author was proud to serve as inaugural chair, working in collaboration with a committee of evaluation specialists led by Richard Bagnall, CEO of Prime Research in the UK. The framework takes its name from its integration of evaluation theory and academic research, existing industry matrices and models, and its capability to evaluate integrated communication involving *paid, earned, shared and owned* channels, referred to as the *PESO model* of media.

Some features particularly set the AMEC IEF apart and advance the field of practice considerably. The first is that the framework is an interactive online tool, not a static diagram.[12] This means that users can input data into the various steps and stages, including organization objectives and communication objectives, and then progressively add inputs, outputs and so on; hence it is a working tool.

A second key feature of the AMEC IEF that advances evaluation considerably for communication practitioners is that the framework is supported by a substantial range of online resources to guide practitioners through the process of evaluation. These include guidelines for setting SMART objectives, links to the *Dictionary of Public Relations Measurement and Research* (Stacks & Bowen, 2013) and a number of downloadable case studies that provide samples of the framework in use. In addition, one of the key resources in terms of using the framework is a *taxonomy of evaluation*, as discussed in the following section.

The AMEC IEF launched in 2016 was the result of many months of intensive work by a team most notably including Richard Bagnall, Paul Hender from Gorkana, Elayne Phillips from the UK GCS and Giles Peddy from Lewis (a London-based PR and marketing agency), strongly supported by AMEC CEO Barry Leggetter, the AMEC Academic Advisory Group (from which this author was able to observe, as well as participate in, the process) and a number of others who volunteered time to the project. Bagnall said of the process:

> It was a big undertaking. But we knew that we had to update our existing frameworks which many practitioners were finding informative but complicated to use. We also needed to support the newly revised Barcelona Principles 2.0 which provided a big picture view on what best practice looks like but not how to operationalize it. We realized that we needed to make the framework engaging and easy to use and felt that an interactive online tool would be critical to achieve this in the digital age. And we wanted to base the framework on sound academic theory. So we worked with academics as well as industry experts throughout the process.
>
> *(R. Bagnall, personal communication, October 15, 2016)*

The same question that was put to Paul Njoku was put to Bagnall: 'Is the AMEC framework the perfect solution for evaluation of public communication?' Bagnall responded:

> It would be a massive claim to say that AMEC's Integrated Evaluation Framework is perfect. No doubt it can be improved still further. It's unlikely that any model or framework could ever be perfect. But we believe this is a major step forward for the communication industry and accomplishes its remit to provide a step-by-step guide for aligning communication with organizational objectives, conducting formative research, planning and setting objectives, and measuring beyond outputs to also include evaluation of outcomes and organizational impact. Importantly, we also believe that it works for organizations of all sizes with differing objectives and budgets.
>
> *(R. Bagnall, personal communication, October 15, 2016)*

Barry Leggetter, CEO of AMEC, who has seen several AMEC evaluation models, matrices and frameworks developed during almost a decade with the organization, highlighted the importance of working collaboratively and internationally, saying:

> We fully engaged AMEC's Academic Advisory Group in developing the new integrated evaluation framework. Also we worked with professional researchers and communication practitioners. And, even after many months of development, a key step has been to put the framework out to a range of partner

organizations to test it and give us feedback for fine-tuning. So this truly is an industry initiative, and we believe it is a major step forward. But our work is not yet complete.

(B. Leggetter, personal communication, October 15, 2016)

Fraser Likely, a Canadian communication evaluation consultant, has posed a number of questions about the AMEC IEF, saying:

Is the IEF only for the evaluation of communication campaigns? Or, can its seven-stage process be used for a single message activity in any paid, earned, shared or owned (PESO) media channel? Does the seven-stage process apply equally to a comprehensive and dialogic stakeholder program?

(Likely, 2016, para. 5)

The answers to a number of Likely's questions are fairly clear in reading the menus and information pop-up boxes in the AMEC online framework. For example, the 'outputs' section lists advertising, publicity, websites, social media, events, sponsorships and even direct mail, email or e-marketing as possible outputs (AMEC, 2016). Also, the 'outcomes' and 'impact' sections in the AMEC IEF list 'trust', 'reputation' and 'relationships', which are applicable to evaluating relations with various stakeholders. The accompanying taxonomy of evaluation stages, steps, metrics and milestones, and methods elaborates on the range of activities that can be evaluated using the framework (see 'A taxonomy of evaluation').

Likely further states that 'the purpose of the IEF is to evaluate the "goods" that a communication department produces: *activities* (messages/channels); *campaigns*; and *programmes*' (Likely, 2016, para. 9, original emphasis). In this, he is mistaken: the framework – like most of the advanced frameworks and models outlined in this chapter – emphasizes a focus beyond activities and campaigns to include outcomes and impact, and explicitly lists these as the final stages of communication.

However, Likely makes a good point in noting that the AMEC IEF does not explicitly evaluate what he calls 'services – the immaterial exchange of value that a communication department provides' (2016, para. 10). In this, he is referring to the day-to-day services that communication professionals provide to management, such as speech writing, as well as the value of behind-the-scenes strategic advice that can help an organization to identify an opportunity or avoid a crisis. However, while the AMEC framework does not explicitly refer to this internal value, a number of the methods of evaluation recommended can easily be applied for this purpose. In this situation, senior management is the target audience or the 'client'. As Grunig et al. (2002) reported in the Excellence Study, interviews or surveys can assess senior management's satisfaction with, and appreciation of, communication activities. Grunig and colleagues found that senior managers evaluated public relations as returning up to 225 per cent of its cost (2002, p. 137).

Another way of assessing the value of services provided by communication staff in an organization and gaining a monetary value is to ask management, in interviews or surveys, 'how much would you be prepared to pay external suppliers for [name service or benefit] if it was not available from staff of the organization?' In the case of activities such as crisis communication, this can be quite substantial. This approach – that is, asking stakeholders how much they would be willing to pay for a benefit that does not have a direct financial value, a form of cost–benefit analysis referred to as the *compensating variation* – was first proposed more than 25 years ago by William Ehling (1992) and advocated by Jim Grunig and colleagues more than 15 years ago. It is an example of the existence of evaluation methods that have been overlooked or ignored by practitioners.

A taxonomy of evaluation

While these broad frameworks are useful, there is still the question of what goes where in terms of doing evaluation. In their leading PR textbook, Cutlip and colleagues noted repeatedly, in editions from 1985 to the late 2000s, that 'the common error in program evaluation is substituting measures from one level for those at another level' (Cutlip et al. 1985, p. 295; 1994, p. 414; Broom, 2009, p. 358). This warning has been echoed by Jim Grunig, emeritus professor of public relations, who said that many practitioners use 'a metric gathered at one level of analysis to show an outcome at a higher level of analysis' (2008, p. 89). The UWEX Guide to programme evaluation specifically states that 'people often struggle with the difference between outputs and outcomes' (Taylor-Power & Henert, 2008, p. 19).

In this author's work with the Task Force on Standardization of Communication Planning and Evaluation Models and the AMEC team in developing its IEF, a key step was synthesizing a wide range of literature that identifies the inputs, activities, outputs, outcomes and impact of public communication and the methods applicable to evaluating them. This enabled production of a taxonomy of evaluation for communication.

The term 'taxonomy' is used in preference to 'typology' because, even though the terms are often used interchangeably, a *taxonomy* categorizes empirical entities based on evidence, whereas a *typology* is typically a conceptual construct (Bailey, 1994, p. 6). The taxonomy of evaluation of communication identifies four levels in each of up to six stages of communication (inputs, activities, outputs, outtakes, outcomes and impact). Under each stage (the *macro* level), the taxonomy lists key steps required in that stage (*meso* level), then lists typical milestones and metrics for showing achievement of those steps (*micro* level), and finally lists typical evaluation methods to demonstrate milestones or generate metrics required for that stage.

By adding this detail, frameworks evolve towards a working model of evaluation for public communication. For example, if a practitioner has placed advertising or gained media publicity, the taxonomy identifies these as outputs at a macro level. In terms of key steps (meso level), these activities are part of 'distribution', 'exposure' and potentially 'reception' of messages. Looking down the outputs column of the taxonomy identifies that milestones and metrics relevant to evaluating these outputs include target audience ratings points (TARPs), audience reach data, publicity

TABLE 3.4 A taxonomy of communication evaluation showing stages, key steps, milestones and metrics, and evaluation methods for a six-stage programme logic model

Stages *Macro level*	Inputs	Activities	Outputs	Outtakes *Short-term outcomes*	Outcomes *Intermediate*	Impact *Long-term*
Short definition	What is needed to plan and prepare communication	What is done to produce and implement communication	What is put out that reaches and engages the target audiences	What audiences take out of and do with the communication	What effects the communication has on the audiences	What results are caused, in full or in part, by the communication[a]
Key steps *Meso level*	**Objectives** **Budget** **Resources** (e.g. staff, agencies, facilities, partnerships)	**Formative research** **Planning**[b] **Production** (e.g. design, writing, media buying, media relations, media partnerships, etc.)	**Distribution** **Exposure** **Reception**[c]	**Attention** **Awareness** **Understanding** **Interest/liking** **Engagement** **Participation** **Consideration**	**Learning/** **knowledge**[d] **Attitude change** **Satisfaction** **Trust** **Preference** **Intention** **Advocacy**	**Compliance/** **complying actions** **Reputation** **Relationships** **Organizational** **change** **Public/social** **change**
Example metrics and milestones *Micro level*	SMART objectives Targets/KPIs	Baselines/benchmarks (e.g. current awareness) Audience needs, preferences, etc. Strategic plan Evaluation plan Pre-test data (e.g. creative concepts) Content produced (e.g. media releases, websites) Media relations	Advertising TARPs Audience reach Impressions/OTS[e] CPM Publicity volume Share of voice Tone/sentiment/favourability Messages placed Posts, tweets, etc. E-marketing volume Event attendance	Unique visitors Views Response (e.g. follows, likes, shares, retweets) Clickthroughs Return visits/views Recall (unaided, aided) Positive comments Positive response in surveys, etc. Subscribers (e.g. RSS, newsletters) Inquiries	Message acceptance Trust levels Statements of support or intent Leads Registrations (e.g. organ donor list) Brand preference Trialling Joining Reaffirming (e.g. staff satisfaction)	Public/s support Meet targets (e.g. blood donations, cancer screening membership, etc.) Sales increase Donations increase Cost savings Staff retention Customer retention/loyalty Quality of life/well-being increase

(Continued)

TABLE 3.4 (Continued)

Stages Macro level	Inputs	Activities	Outputs	Outtakes Short-term outcomes	Outcomes Intermediate	Impact Long-term
Methods of evaluation	Internal analysis Environmental scanning Feasibility analysis Risk analysis	Metadata analysis (e.g. past research and metrics) Market/audience research (e.g. surveys, focus groups, interviews) Stakeholder consultation Case studies (e.g. best practice) SWOT analysis (or PEST, PESTLE, etc.) Pre-testing panels Peer review/expert review	Media metrics (e.g. audience statistics, impressions, CPM) Media monitoring Media content analysis (quant) Media content analysis (qual) Social media analysis (quant and qual) Activity reports (e.g. events, sponsorships)	Web statistics (e.g. views, downloads) Social media analysis (qual – e.g. comments) Feedback (e.g. comments, letters) Ethnography (observation) Netnography (online ethnography) Audience surveys (e.g. of awareness, interests, understanding, etc.) Focus group (as above) Interviews (as above)	Social media analysis (qual) Database statistics (e.g. identifying sources) Ethnography (observation) Netnography (online ethnography) Opinion polls Stakeholder surveys (e.g. re satisfaction, trust) Focus groups (as above) Interviews (as above) NPS[f]	Database records (e.g. blood donations, health outcomes, membership) Sales tracking Donation tracking CRM data Staff survey data Reputation studies Cost–benefit analysis ROI, ROMI, etc. (if there are financial objectives) Econometrics[g] Quality of life scales and well-being measures (e.g. QALYs, DALYs)[h]

(Continued)

Notes:

[a]As noted in Chapter 2, causation is very difficult to establish, particularly when multiple influences contribute to impact (results), as is often the case. The three key rules of causation must be applied: (a) *temporal precedence* – i.e. the alleged cause must precede the alleged effect/impact; (b) *covariation of cause and effect* – i.e. there must be a clear relationship between the alleged cause and effect (such as evidence that the audience accessed and used information provided); and (c) *no plausible alternative explanation* – i.e. other possible causes of the effect must be ruled out as far as possible.

[b]Some include planning in inputs. However, if this occurs, formative research (which should precede planning) also needs to be included in inputs. Most programme evaluation models identify formative research and planning as key activities to be undertaken as part of the communication programme. Inputs are generally pre-campaign/programme.

Notes: (Continued)

cReception refers to what information or messages are received by target audiences and is slightly different to exposure. For example, an audience might be exposed to a story in media that they access, but skip over the story and not receive the information. Similarly, they may attend an event such as a trade show and be exposed to content, but not receive information or messages (e.g. through inattention or selection of content to focus on).

dLearning (i.e. acquisition of knowledge) is not required in all cases. However, in some public communication campaigns and projects, it is. For example, health campaigns to promote calcium-rich food and supplements to reduce osteoporosis among women found that women first had to be 'educated' about osteoporosis (what it is, its causes, etc.). Similarly, combating obesity requires dietary education. While *understanding* refers to comprehension of messages communicated, *learning* refers to the acquisition of deeper or broader knowledge that is necessary to achieve the objectives.

eOTS = opportunities to see, usually calculated in the same way as impressions or gross audience reach.

fNPS = net promoter score, i.e. a score out of 10 based on a single question: 'How likely is it that you would recommend [insert name] to a friend or colleague?' Scores of 0–6 are considered 'detractors'/'dissatisfied; scores of 7–8 are satisfied, but unenthusiastic; scores of 9–10 are those considered loyal enthusiasts, supporters and advocates. (See www.netpromoter.com/know).

gEconometrics is the application of mathematics and statistical methods to test hypotheses and identify the economic relations between factors based on empirical data.

hQuality-adjusted life years (QALY) is an arithmetic calculation of life expectancy combined with a measure of the quality of life–years remaining, in which '1' equates to perfect health and '0' equates to death, with severe disability and pain assigned negative values. If an intervention were to provide perfect health for one additional year, it would produce one QALY. Similarly, an intervention providing an extra two years of life at a health status of 0.5 would equal one QALY. In evaluation, QALY calculations are related to cost of treatments and interventions – e.g. if an intervention costs US$5,000 per person and affords an additional 0.5 QALYs, then cost per QALY would be $10,000 (5,000 ÷ 0.5). Disability-adjusted life years (DALY) calculations sum years of life lost (YLL) as a result of premature mortality based on life expectancy data and years lived in disability/disease (YLD). Whereas QALYs can be used to estimate positive gains from various interventions and treatments, DALYs are a means of quantifying the burden of disease (see Chapter 4).

volume and tone, and possibly volume of posts and tweets in social media. Methods to acquire these data are then listed for this stage.

This taxonomy also clearly draws attention to the fact that outputs are barely halfway to achieving outcomes and impact. It points towards the need to go beyond distribution, exposure and even reception of information by audiences to gaining *attention*, creating *awareness* and *understanding*, generating *interest* or *liking*, creating *engagement* and *participation*, and, even further, *consideration*, which AMEC and some other models refer to as *outtakes* and some refer to as *short-term outcomes*. Furthermore, based on McGuire's (2001) steps of information processing, communication needs to go even further, sometimes to *learning* or creating new *knowledge* in audiences, *attitude change, satisfaction, trust, preference, intention* (for example, to buy or act) and *advocacy* (urging others to buy or act). Ultimately, impact is identified in terms of *complying action* or other results such as positive *reputation, relationships, organization change* or *public/social change*.

The taxonomy shown in Table 3.4 arranges key steps, milestones and metrics, and evaluation methods in six stages to match the AMEC IEF (Macnamara, 2016c). However, key steps in communication, milestones and metrics, and evaluation can be similarly arranged for five-stage (Table 3.5), four-stage (Table 3.6) and even three-stage (Table 3.7) logic models. In a five-stage framework, outtakes are reclassified as 'short-term outcomes' in line with classic logic models, with outcomes being 'intermediate' and 'long-term outcomes'. In a four-stage framework (inputs, outputs, outcomes and impact), outtakes are arranged as above (that is, as short-term outcomes) and activities are combined with inputs. In a three-stage framework (inputs, outputs and outcomes), impact is renamed 'long-term outcomes', as well as the other combined stages listed above.

These options recognize that there is unlikely to be a single standard evaluation framework or model. Nor is it possible to have a single evaluation method, given that different communication activities and campaigns have different objectives. Rather, most industries establish *standards* (plural) – a range of practices that conform to key principles that are agreed and formalized in manuals, guides and other publications.

The work of the IPR Measurement Commission, the Task Force on Standardization of Communication Planning and Evaluation Models, and evaluation frameworks developed by the UK GCS (2016a), the NSW Department of Premier and Cabinet for NSW government advertising and communication (DPC, 2016), and AMEC (2016b) are likely to be ongoing for some time. However, they represent significant advances in thinking about, and applying, evaluation.

Some argue that programme logic models are complex, and that practitioners cannot understand the difference between inputs, outputs, outtakes, outcomes and impact. This is somewhat hard to believe, given that most of these are quite simple terms – particularly outputs and outcomes – and there are definitions provided if needed. For instance, the *Dictionary of Public Relations Measurement and Research* defines outputs, outtakes and outcomes as follows.

TABLE 3.5 A taxonomy of communication evaluation showing key steps of communication, milestones and metrics, and evaluation methods for a five-stage programme logic model

Stages *Macro level*	Inputs	Activities		Outtakes *Short-term outcomes*	Outcomes *Intermediate*	Impact *Long-term*
Short definition	What is needed to plan and prepare communication	What is done to produce and implement communication	What is put out that reaches and engages the target audiences	What audiences take out of and do with the communication	What effects the communication has on the audiences	What results are caused, in full or in part, by the communication
Key steps *Meso level*	**Objectives** **Budget** **Resources** (e.g. staff, agencies, facilities, partnerships)	**Formative research** **Planning** **Production** (e.g. design, writing, media buying, media relations, media partnerships, etc.)	**Distribution** **Exposure** **Reception**	**Attention** **Awareness** **Understanding** **Interest/liking** **Engagement** **Participation** **Consideration**	**Learning/ knowledge** **Attitude change** **Satisfaction** **Trust** **Preference** **Intention** **Advocacy**	**Compliance/ complying actions** **Reputation** **Relationships** **Organizational change** **Public/social change**
Example metrics and milestones *Micro level*	SMART objectives Targets/KPIs	Baselines/benchmarks (e.g. current awareness) Audience needs, preferences, etc. Strategic plan Evaluation plan Pre-test data (e.g. creative concepts)	Advertising TARPs Audience reach Impressions/OTS CPM Publicity volume Share of voice Tone/sentiment/ favourability	Unique visitors Views Response (e.g. follows, likes, shares, retweets) Clickthroughs Return visits/views Recall (unaided, aided) Positive comments Positive response in surveys, etc.	Message acceptance Trust levels Statements of support or intent Leads Registrations (e.g. organ donor list) Brand preference Trialling Joining	Public's support Meet targets (e.g. blood donations, cancer screening membership, etc.) Sales increase Donations increase Cost savings Staff retention

(Continued)

TABLE 3.5 (Continued)

Stages Macro level	Inputs	Activities	Outputs	Outtakes Short-term outcomes	Outcomes Intermediate	Impact Long-term
		Content produced (e.g. media releases, websites) Media relations	Messages placed Posts, tweets, etc. E-marketing volume Event attendance	Subscribers (e.g. RSS, newsletters) Inquiries	Reaffirming (e.g. staff satisfaction)	Customer retention/loyalty Quality of life/well-being increase
Methods of evaluation	Internal analysis Environmental scanning Feasibility analysis Risk analysis	Metadata analysis (e.g. past research and metrics) Market/audience research (e.g. surveys, focus groups, interviews) Stakeholder consultation Case studies (e.g. best practice) SWOT analysis (or PEST, PESTLE, etc.) Pre-testing panels Peer review/expert review	Media metrics (e.g. audience statistics, impressions, CPM) Media monitoring Media content analysis (quant) Media content analysis (qual) Social media analysis (quant and qual) Activity reports (e.g. events, sponsorships)	Web statistics (e.g. views, downloads) Social media analysis (qual – e.g. comments) Feedback (e.g. comments, letters) Ethnography (observation) Netnography (online ethnography) Audience surveys (e.g. of awareness, interests, understanding, etc.) Focus group (as above) Interviews (as above)	Social media analysis (qual) Database statistics (e.g. identifying sources) Ethnography (observation) Netnography (online ethnography) Opinion polls Stakeholder surveys (e.g. re satisfaction, trust) Focus groups (as above) Interviews (as above) NPS	Database records (e.g. blood donations, health outcomes, membership) Sales tracking Donation tracking CRM data Staff survey data Reputation studies Cost–benefit analysis ROI, ROMI, etc. (if there are financial objectives) Econometrics Quality of life scales and well-being measures (e.g. QALYs, DALYs)

TABLE 3.6 A taxonomy of communication evaluation showing key steps of communication, milestones and metrics, and evaluation methods for a four-stage programme logic model

Stages Macro level	Inputs Resources/preparation	Activities	Outputs	Outtakes Short-term outcomes	Outcomes Intermediate outcomes	Long-term outcomes
Short definition	What is needed to plan and prepare communication	What is done to produce and implement communication	What is put out that reaches and engages the target audiences	What audiences take out of and do with the communication	What effects the communication has on the audiences	What results are caused, in full or in part, by the communication
Key steps *Meso level*	**Objectives** **Budget** **Resources** (e.g. staff, agencies, facilities, partnerships)	**Formative research** **Planning** **Production** (e.g. design, writing, media buying, media relations, media partnerships, etc.)	**Distribution** **Exposure** **Reception**	**Attention** **Awareness** **Understanding** **Interest/liking** **Engagement** **Participation** **Consideration**	**Learning/ knowledge** **Attitude change** **Satisfaction** **Trust** **Preference** **Intention** **Advocacy**	**Compliance/ complying actions** **Reputation** **Relationships** **Organizational change** **Public/social change**
Example metrics and milestones *Micro level*	**SMART** objectives **Targets/KPIs**	Baselines/benchmarks (e.g. current awareness) Audience needs, preferences, etc. Strategic plan Evaluation plan Pre-test data (e.g. creative concepts) Content produced	Advertising TARPs Audience reach Impressions/OTS CPM Publicity volume Share of voice Tone/sentiment/ favourability Messages placed	Unique visitors Views Response (e.g. follows, likes, shares, retweets) Clickthroughs Return visits/views Recall (unaided, aided) Positive comments Positive response in surveys, etc.	Message acceptance Trust levels Statements of support or intent Leads Registrations (e.g. organ donor list) Brand preference	Public/s support Meet targets (e.g. blood donations, cancer screening membership, etc.) Sales increase Donations increase Cost savings Staff retention

(Continued)

TABLE 3.6 (Continued)

| Stages | Inputs | Activities | Outputs | Outtakes | Outcomes | Long-term outcomes |
Macro level	Resources / preparation			Short-term outcomes	Intermediate outcomes	
		(e.g. media releases, websites) Media relations	Posts, tweets, etc. E-marketing volume Event attendance	Subscribers (e.g. RSS, newsletters) Inquiries	Trialling Joining Reaffirming (e.g. staff satisfaction)	Customer retention/loyalty Quality of life/well-being increase
Methods of evaluation	Internal analysis Environmental scanning Feasibility analysis Risk analysis	Metadata analysis (e.g. past research and metrics) Market/audience research (e.g. surveys, focus groups, interviews) Stakeholder consultation Case studies (e.g. best practice) SWOT analysis (or PEST, PESTLE, etc.) Pre-testing panels Peer review/expert review	Media metrics (e.g. audience statistics, impressions, CPM) Media monitoring Media content analysis (quant) Media content analysis (qual) Social media analysis (quant and qual) Activity reports (e.g. events, sponsorships)	Web statistics (e.g. views, downloads) Social media analysis (qual – e.g. comments) Feedback (e.g. comments, letters) Ethnography (observation) Netnography (online ethnography) Audience surveys (e.g. of awareness, interests, understanding, etc.) Focus group (as above) Interviews (as above)	Social media analysis (qual) Database statistics (e.g. identifying sources) Ethnography (observation) Netnography (online ethnography) Opinion polls Stakeholder surveys (e.g. re satisfaction, trust) Focus groups (as above) Interviews (as above) NPS	Database records (e.g. blood donations, health outcomes, membership) Sales tracking Donation tracking CRM data Staff survey data Reputation studies Cost–benefit analysis ROI, ROMI, etc. (if there are financial objectives) Econometrics Quality of life scales and well-being measures (e.g. QALYs, DALYs)

TABLE 3.7 A taxonomy of communication evaluation showing key steps of communication, milestones and metrics, and evaluation methods for a three-stage programme logic model

Stages *Macro level*	Inputs *Resources / preparation*	Activities	Outputs	Outcomes *Short-term outcomes*	Intermediate outcomes	Long-term outcomes
Short definition	What is needed to plan and prepare communication	What is done to produce and implement communication	What is put out that reaches and engages the target audiences	What audiences take out of and do with the communication	What effects the communication has on the audiences	What results are caused, in full or in part, by the communication
Key steps *Meso level*	**Objectives** **Budget** **Resources** (e.g. staff, agencies, facilities, partnerships)	**Formative research** **Planning** **Production** (e.g. design, writing, media buying, media relations, media partnerships, etc.)	**Distribution** **Exposure** **Reception**	**Attention** **Awareness** **Understanding** **Interest/liking** **Engagement** **Participation** **Consideration**	**Learning/ knowledge** **Attitude change** **Satisfaction** **Trust** **Preference** **Intention** **Advocacy**	**Compliance/ complying actions** **Reputation** **Relationships** **Organizational change** **Public/social change**
Example metrics and milestones *Micro level*	SMART objectives Targets/KPIs	Baselines/ benchmarks (e.g. current awareness) Audience needs, preferences, etc. Strategic plan Evaluation plan Pre-test data (e.g. creative concepts)	Advertising TARPs Audience reach Impressions/OTS CPM Publicity volume Share of voice Tone/sentiment/ favourability Messages placed Posts, tweets, etc.	Unique visitors Views Response (e.g. follows, likes, shares, retweets) Clickthroughs Return visits/views Recall (unaided, aided) Positive comments Positive response in surveys, etc.	Message acceptance Trust levels Statements of support or intent Leads Registrations (e.g. organ donor list) Brand preference Trialling Joining	Public/s support Meet targets (e.g. blood donations, cancer screening membership, etc.) Sales increase Donations increase Cost savings Staff retention

(Continued)

TABLE 3.7 (Continued)

Stages / Macro level	Inputs / Resources/preparation	Activities	Outputs	Outcomes / Short-term outcomes	Intermediate outcomes	Long-term outcomes
		Content produced (e.g. media releases, websites) Media relations	E-marketing volume Event attendance	Subscribers (e.g. RSS, newsletters) Inquiries	Reaffirming (e.g. staff satisfaction)	Customer retention/loyalty Quality of life/well-being increase
Methods of evaluation	Internal analysis Environmental scanning Feasibility analysis Risk analysis	Metadata analysis (e.g. past research and metrics) Market/audience research (e.g. surveys, focus groups, interviews) Stakeholder consultation Case studies (e.g. best practice) SWOT analysis (or PEST, PESTLE, etc.) Pre-testing panels Peer review/expert review	Media metrics (e.g. audience statistics, impressions, CPM) Media monitoring Media content analysis (quant) Media content analysis (qual) Social media analysis (quant and qual) Activity reports (e.g. events, sponsorships)	Web statistics (e.g. views, downloads) Social media analysis (qual – e.g. comments, letters) Feedback (e.g. comments, letters) Ethnography (observation) Netnography (online ethnography) Audience surveys (e.g. of awareness, interests, understanding, etc.) Focus group (as above) Interviews (as above)	Social media analysis (qual) Database statistics (e.g. identifying sources) Ethnography (observation) Netnography (online ethnography) Opinion polls Stakeholder surveys (e.g. re satisfaction, trust) Focus groups (as above) Interviews (as above) NPS	Database records (e.g. blood donations, health outcomes, membership) Sales tracking Donation tracking CRM data Staff survey data Reputation studies Cost-benefit analysis ROI, ROMI, etc. (if there are financial objectives) Econometrics Quality of life scales and well-being measures (e.g. QALYs, DALYs)

- Outputs – What is generated as a result of a PR program or campaign that may be received and processed by members of a target audience . . . the final stage of a communication product, production, or process resulting in the production and dissemination of a communication product (brochure, media release, website, speech, etc.).
- Outtakes – What audiences have understood and/or heeded and/or responded to . . . audience reaction to the receipt of a communication product, including . . . recall and retention of the message . . . and whether the audience heeded or responded to a call for information or action within the message.
- Outcomes – Quantifiable changes in awareness, knowledge, attitude, opinion, and behaviour levels that occur as a result of a . . . programme or campaign; an effect, consequence, or impact of a set or programme of communication activities or products [that] may be either short-term (immediate) or long term.

(Stacks & Bowen, 2013, p. 21)

In even simpler terms:

- *inputs* are what goes into creating public communication, such as formative research, information, materials and resources, such as money and time;
- *outputs* are what is *put out* (that is, distributed) to target audiences and reaches them;
- *outtakes* are what audiences *take out* of communication, such as awareness, interest, learning, and so on;
- *outcomes* are what *comes out* or eventuates as a result of communication – in particular, what audiences *do* as a result of the communication, such as buy a product or service, join an organization or movement, give up smoking, join a fitness class, etc.; and
- *impact* can overlap with, and be described as, intermediate and long-term outcomes, but usually refers to downstream, macro level results linked to objectives such as reaching sales, donation or membership targets, reducing obesity or the death toll on roads, or improving the well-being of a group or community.

Because the term 'impact' is used in daily speech for a wide range of even minor effects, some use terms such as *outflows* and *outgrowths* for the downstream results of communication, but *impact* or *long-term outcomes* are the terms that are more common in evaluation, as shown in the models reviewed.

International integrated reporting framework (IIRF)

Increasing recognition of the value of intangible assets including brands, reputation and relationships, which now account for more than 80 per cent of the market value of public companies such as the S&P 500 (Ocean Tomo, 2015), has led to

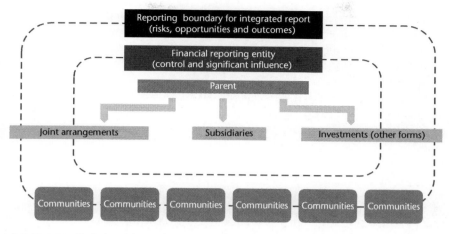

FIGURE 3.17 Relationships and interactions recognized as contributing value to an organization in integrated reporting

Source: IIRC (2013, p. 20)

a broadening of corporate reporting and increasing use of what is called *integrated reporting*. The International Integrated Reporting Council (IIRC) has developed an *international integrated reporting framework* (IIRF), which recognizes that value is created for organizations from relationships with communities, employees and stakeholders, such as investors, suppliers and business partners (IIRC, 2013, p. 10). Beyond paying mere lip service to this value, the IIRF broadens the notion of capital beyond financial assets, and treats these relationships and social interactions as forms of capital, saying: 'The capitals are stocks of value that are increased, decreased or transformed through the activities and outputs of the organization. They are categorized in this framework as financial, manufactured, intellectual, human, social and relationship, and natural capital' (IIRC, 2013, p. 4).

The IIRF has been endorsed by a substantial number of the world's leading corporations, including PepsiCo, Unilever, HSBC, Deutsche Bank, Hyundai Engineering and Construction, and National Australia Bank (NAB). While not specifically an evaluation model or framework for communication, the initiative to identify social and relationship capital requires evaluation of these elements, including methods to quantify their value. The IIRF also connects social interaction and relationships, which are formed and maintained through public communication, with organizational outcomes and value (see Figure 3.17) – a link that has long been missing in many areas of evaluation of public communication (Zerfass et al., 2012).

The Center for Corporate Reporting (CCR),[13] headquartered in Zurich, which supports integrated reporting by companies, as well as open transparent reporting generally, conducted a study in partnership with the University of Leipzig in

2015–2016 that identified major benefits of integrated reporting for organizations. These included 'enhanced resource efficiency as financial, sustainability and governance reports are merged', a 'strengthening of internal dialogue beyond departmental boundaries' and 'operational decision-making processes are expedited due to an improved consistency in individual reports' (CCR, 2016, para. 5) – although the study did report that a high level of internal coordination is required, which can result in a lengthy implementation period (para. 6).

No communication professionals interviewed were aware of these emerging models in the corporate and business sector, and very few communication industry organizations have engaged with organizations such as the IIRC or the Center for Corporate Reporting. This siloed approach has contributed to the fragmented nature of the communication evaluation industry (if it can be called that), a lack of standards and a continuing lack of empirical data to show the value of public communication – whether that is financial, in relationships, social benefits or other intangibles. Dr Kristin Köhler, CEO of the CCR, who has a communication background, including a doctorate in investor relations, said that her organization would welcome greater engagement with the public communication field (K. Köhler, personal communication, December 5, 2016).

Future directions in evaluation models

As well as new directions in corporate reporting noted in the previous sections, this author's programme logic model for communication presented as Figure 2.10 in Chapter 2 is updated and expanded in Figure 3.18 as a suggestion for further development and future directions. This author remains partial to five-stage programme logic models because these most closely follow classic programme logic models and those used in other fields – although others may prefer to use the term 'outtakes' as an additional stage or in place of short-term outcomes.

Highlighted in Figure 3.18, which is also a further evolution of the framework adopted by the NSW government for evaluation of advertising and communication, is that while distribution of information and communication messages is *to* stakeholders and publics, and response is *from* stakeholders and publics, impact is bidirectional. Stakeholders, publics and society, as well as the organization, are specifically represented in the model, and the bidirectional flow of impact is shown.

The two dimensions of impact need to be considered for two reasons.

1. As well as planned outcomes and impact on target audiences and the organization (such as gaining support for its policies, or achieving sales and revenue targets), two-way communication and engagement can potentially indicate that the organization needs to change. However, this potential impact is not widely accepted and seldom evaluated. The UK GCS evaluation framework narrowly defines *organizational impact* as 'contribution to the organization's goals/KPIs' (GCS, 2016a, p. 5). The AMEC IEF also lists the ultimate stage of strategic communication as 'organizational impact' and this section of its web-based

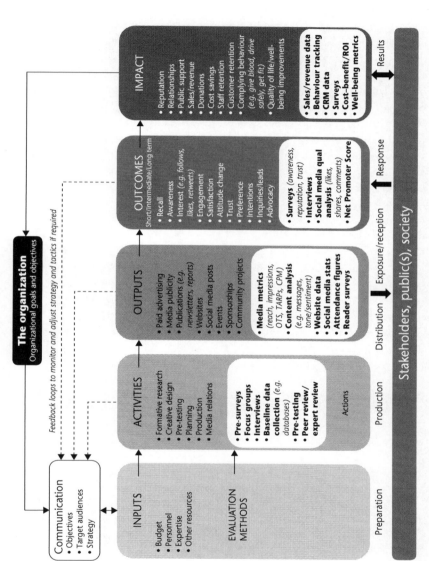

FIGURE 3.18 Integrated model of communication evaluation

interactive evaluation tool asks practitioners, 'How has the organization been impacted during the campaign?' (AMEC, 2016b, n.p.). While this might imply that the organization is open to change to align with the expectations and interests of stakeholders and publics, clicking through the interactive AMEC IEF reveals that impact is specifically defined as 'flow-on results related to *your* objectives which your communication achieved or contributed to' (n.p., emphasis added). There is no provision in most evaluation frameworks and models to identify and report how the views, needs and interests of stakeholders and publics might require the organization to change or do something other than what it has planned to do. Thus public communication and its evaluation remain one-way streets in most cases.

2. Beyond the desired outcomes and impact on target audiences in line with organizational objectives, public communication, such as corporate and marketing communication, can have broader impact on stakeholders and society, which should be considered. While some communication evaluation models, including the AMEC IEF launched in 2016, list 'social and cultural change' as factors to consider, the accompanying text again clearly indicates that this refers to change that the organization wants to create in line with its objectives. This narrow interpretation does not comply with major theories such as excellence theory of PR, as noted previously. Also, evaluation of impact only in terms of how an organization can achieve its objectives in influencing and persuading (sometimes manipulating) its stakeholders and publics to achieve its objectives does not align with contemporary understandings of ethical *strategic communication*, as it is described in contemporary literature such as Fransden and Johansen (2017) and the *International Encyclopedia of Strategic Communication* (Heath & Johansen, forthcoming).

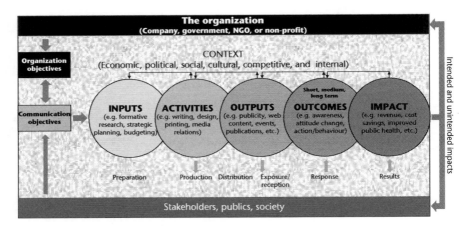

FIGURE 3.19 Proposed model of evaluation

Source: Developed collaboratively with the Public Relations Institute of Australia in 2017

A draft model being developed collaboratively with the Public Relations Institute of Australia (PRIA) at the time of writing explicitly addresses this concern, as well as criticisms in relation to the implied linearity of many evaluation models. Furthermore, it introduces another important dimension of evaluating public communication that is ignored in all other models.

The draft model shown in Figure 3.19 addresses the following three factors that are important in evaluation of public communication.

1. It overcomes the implied *linearity* of traditional programme logic models and various other models, such as the 'driver' model of change, by representing the stages as overlapping spheres instead of discrete separate 'boxes'. Like Figure 3.18, this model suggests five stages (inputs, activities, outputs, outcomes and impact), in line with the most common programme logic models, but outtakes could be included in the same way.

2. It illustrates that impact flows to the organization and to stakeholders, publics and society, and that this can include *unintended impacts* as well as intended impact. For example, a healthcare services company could decide to increase its profits by substantially increasing the price of its services based on a 'what the market will bear' philosophy and maintain sales through aggressive promotion. By taking advantage of the capacity of affluent consumers to pay more, the company could achieve its organizational objective of increasing profits – but the substantial price increase is likely to result in many poorer recipients of the services no longer being able to afford them, leading to hardship and social inequity and, most likely, criticism. The company may not intend to cause negative social impact through its marketing strategy – but it might and, regrettably, traditional approaches to evaluation would not consider this an outcome or impact. Thus evaluation is often not identifying the full impact of corporate, marketing and government communication. Michael Scriven (1972, 1991) is one of a few who have urged evaluators to examine and report unintended, as well as intended, outcomes and impact. In assessing impact, fundamental questions such as 'impact on whom?' and 'for whose benefit?' remain important matters for debate in the context of evaluating public communication.

3. It recognizes that *context* is a critical factor in evaluating public communication. All public communication occurs within a particular context. At a macro level, context includes the economic, social, cultural and political environment. Factors such as economic recession, a government policy change that affects business, global trade negotiations or a major event that overshadows a communication campaign (for example, an election) can fundamentally affect the outcomes and impact of public communication. At a micro level, contextual factors can determine whether or not communication progresses from one stage to the next. For example, at an inputs stage, contextual factors can include resource limitations. During implementation of activities, contextual factors that affect a programme include competitor activity and competitive messages. Thus the model shown in Figure 3.19 incorporates a *social ecology* approach to communication.

Practitioners seeking a single best method for evaluation fail to understand that every communication project and campaign operates within a unique context, with different objectives, different audiences, different resource allocations, different time scales, and different social, cultural, political and economic circumstances. This is recognized in *realist* evaluation and the *context–mechanism–outcome* (CMO) approach discussed in Chapter 2 (Better Evaluation, 2016; Salter & Kothari, 2014), but not in most other evaluation frameworks and models. The realist evaluation questions of 'what works?', 'to what extent?', 'in what context?' and 'for whom?' also speak to the previous point about the need for evaluation of outcomes and impact in relation to all affected parties, not only the organization (Better Evaluation, 2016; Pawson & Tilley, 1997).

The existence of a plethora of metrics, milestones and methods, as identified in the taxonomy shown in Tables 3.4–3.7, is thus not an unnecessary surfeit of information or theoretical indulgence. The breaking down of public communication into stages and the availability of many metrics, milestones and methods for evaluation are necessary and advantageous for making evaluation practical in a range of different circumstances.

The factors highlighted in Figures 3.18 and 3.19 – that is, avoiding simple linear thinking, recognizing organizational change as a possible outcome, considering broader social impacts, including unintended impacts, and evaluating context – indicate that there is still much more to be done in developing theory and practice in relation to evaluation of public communication.

Summary

- Advertising models have selectively appropriated concepts from psychology and social psychology, such as awareness, interest, desire and action (for example, in the AIDA model), but have ignored more than half of the 13 steps in communication identified by W. J. McGuire (2001). Careful attention needs to be paid to achieving the preliminary and intermediate variables along 'the response chain' (Atkin & Freimuth, 2013, p. 58).

- Some PR models of measurement and evaluation have incorporated elements of programme logic models, such as *inputs*, *outputs* and *outcomes*, but most have ignored *impact*, and many have made up additional stages such as *outtakes*, *outflows* and *outgrowths*. Don Bartholomew says that 'many public relations professionals get their outputs confused with their outtakes or outcomes', and claims that 'the terminology is confusing and is defined in different ways by different professionals' (2016, p. 10). It is doubtful that this confusion is attributable to the complexity or lack of clear definition of the concepts, because they are clearly defined and explained in the extensive body of programme theory and programme logic model literature. Rather, academics and practitioners need to address the lack of knowledge of evaluation theory and practice, which is the key barrier to evaluation, as noted in Chapter 1.

- A number of new frameworks and models for evaluation have been developed in recent years through collaboration between communication industry bodies and a return to fundamentals of programme evaluation. These adopt theory-based evaluation, as well as apply proven methods.
- Researchers agree that there is no single evaluation model, standard or method; rather, this chapter has presented a number of models that can apply to advertising, PR and corporate communication, government communication, specialist fields such as health communication, and integrated public communication programmes involving multiple channels, forms of content and activities.
- Irrespective of which model is used, evaluation should recognize that public communication is not a simple linear process with one stage leading automatically to the next.
- Evaluation also should recognize organizational change as a possible outcome of evaluation, broader social impacts including unintended impacts and context.
- Simply having a model or framework for evaluation does not ensure evaluation will, or can, be implemented. An evaluation framework or model is a graphic representation of a series of processes that usually requires supporting guidelines and resources such as samples and templates, professional development to increase knowledge and skills among users, and policy or directions to staff to embed evaluation in day-to-day work. Too often, evaluation is something that is not thought about until after a programme has finished. Mandating evaluation, and linking demonstrated performance through evaluation to staff performance assessment and reward, also substantially increases implementation of evaluation.

Notes

1 'Cookies', in Internet terms, are small data files containing information about an Internet user's online history, which are created by web servers when a user connects to them and then held in the user's computer. These records are sent to web servers by the user's web browser whenever the user connects to the Internet, thus providing information about the user's interests and online behaviour.

2 *Political communication* is defined as the 'process concerning the transmission of information among politicians, the news media and the public' (Norris, 2001, p. 11631), while *government communication* refers to the communication implemented by public officials in informing citizens about policies, services, and their rights and duties (Canel & Sanders, 2012; Holmes, 2011).

3 The health field is increasingly moving away from the term 'patients' towards referring to 'clients'. Providers of other services use other comparable terms such as 'customers', 'users' and 'participants'.

4 In his historical perspective on PR evaluation, Walter Lindenmann (2005) incorrectly attributes the IPRA Gold Paper as 'primarily the work of Jim Pritchitt' (p. 5, n. 3).

5 The author incorporated CARMA International (Asia Pacific) Pty Ltd in 1994 and the company began trading in 1995 as the exclusive franchise of CARMA International across Asia Pacific.

6 The Guidelines were produced in 2002, but dated the following year.

7 The first IPR Toolkit is often cited as 'Fairchild (1999)'. Michael Fairchild confirms that Nigel O'Connor, then head of policy with the UK Institute of Public Relations (IPR),

was the project manager for the work, and that he and O'Connor worked together on the 'Toolkit' (M. Fairchild, personal communication, May 24, 2016), thus confirming the citation by Carroll and Stacks (2004) as 'Fairchild and O'Connor (1999)' and of the second edition as 'Fairchild and O'Connor (2001)'.

8 The Global Alliance for Public Relations and Communication Management is a confederation of professional communication organizations representing some 160,000 practitioners and academics worldwide (www.globalalliancepr.org).

9 See www.instituteforpr.org/ipr-measurement-commission.

10 The European Commission has removed this publication and model from the Internet since this research was undertaken. However, it was an official guide until 2016.

11 At the time, the AMEC academic advisory group included (as well as the author): Dr Anne Gregory, professor of corporate communications, University of Huddersfield, UK; Dr Tina McCorkindale, CEO of the Institute of Public Relations, Gainesville, FL, US; Dr Brad Rawlins, professor of strategic communication, Arkansas State University, US; Dr Don Stacks, professor of public relations, University of Miami, FL, US; Tom Watson, emeritus professor, Bournemouth University, UK; and Dr Ansgar Zerfass, professor of communication management, University of Leipzig, Germany.

12 See http://amecorg.com/amecframework.

13 See www.corporate-reporting.com.

PART II

The practice of evaluation

4

METRICS, ANALYTICS AND BEYOND

The evolving evaluation landscape

Having looked at theories of evaluation, a range of frameworks and models to guide the process, and a taxonomy that overviews the stages, key steps, and milestones and metrics for evaluation of communication, this chapter is focused on collecting and generating the metrics and other evidence that demonstrate achievement of milestones at various stages. The term 'milestones', as well as 'metrics', is used both in the taxonomy presented at the end of Chapter 3 and here to refer to the 'preliminary or intermediate variables along the response chain' (Atkin & Freimuth, 2013, p. 58). The reason for this will become clear when examining the nature and role of *metrics* and the closely related term *analytics*.

Metrics and analytics

The evaluation landscape is awash with metrics and digital analytics. Reading industry and professional publications in the public communication and marketing fields, one might be led to believe that a golden age has dawned for evaluation, with digital platforms automatically generating data to show the results of programmes. There is a tendency, in marketing communication in particular, to fetishize metrics, believing that they signal success. The terms 'metrics' and 'analytics' have become buzzwords (Dykes, 2010), and are touted as *the* answer to all of an evaluator's questions. However, while metrics and analytics are important for evaluation, there are some things that need to be noted about their contribution and role.

First, as explained in Chapter 1, evaluation is something quite different from measurement. Metrics – which are generated from analytics, as well as various recording systems – are the basis of measurement. For example, the international standard for measuring weights, volume, distance and even currency in many countries, officially known as the International System of Units (*Système International*), is commonly referred to as the 'metric system'. But, as discussed in Chapter 1, evaluation involves assessing the value of the outcomes and impact of communication for an organization and its stakeholders and publics within the context of the objectives set and other factors (for example, the social, political and economic environment), as well as providing learning (insights) to inform future programmes and strategy. There is no metrics system or metrics-generating machine that can make such valuations or recommendations. Evaluation requires *interpretation* of data within particular, often complex, multidimensional contexts. Evaluation is also often qualitative, not only quantitative – which brings us to the second limitation of metrics and analytics.

Metrics

Metrics are numbers. In social science research, numbers usually stand as proxies for certain factors or conditions (that is, nominal, ordinal and even some interval variables). For example, reputation becomes a score on a scale. Satisfaction similarly becomes a rating, sometimes on an instrument as basic as a 0–5 Likert scale. A multidimensional concept such as public perceptions of an organization is frequently reduced to a single rating out of 10, such as a Net Promoter Score (NPS). Numbers are useful and necessary in public communication, because they allow large amounts of data to be condensed and processed quickly. But, as will be discussed a little later, not everything that counts can be counted.

Analytics

Analytics is the process of discovery and interpretation of meaningful patterns in data. It involves the application of statistics and computer programming to process large volumes of data to identify means (averages), significant trends, clusters and relationships.

The first level is *descriptive analytics*, which identifies patterns or trends in data, or finds explanations relating to past or existing circumstances. Where analytics becomes much more than data analysis is in the interpretation and application of findings to make predictions and recommendations for future decision-making and actions, referred to as *predictive analytics*. Descriptive analytics are of limited value, because they merely describe what happened in the past. As one senior manager of a large multinational organizational said, during an interview for this book, in relation to a descriptive media analysis report that he had received: 'That's all gone now. It's in the past. I can't change that. I need to know what I should do in the future' (Anon., personal communication, July 20, 2016). Many evaluation reports are descriptive rather than offering inferential or predictive analysis. This is particularly the case with some media analysis service providers, as Neil Coffey, head of evaluation for the UK Department of Health, noted with some concern in correspondence with this author (N. Coffey, personal communication, July 21, 2016).

Predictive analytics, often described as part of *advanced analytics*, requires advanced skills in computer science, statistics and mathematics, because it is usually produced from algorithms applied using specialist software and, increasingly, by utilizing emerging technologies such as *machine learning* and techniques such as *neural networks* to undertake predictive modelling. These skills are rarely possessed by public communication practitioners, so if predictive analytics is required, such projects almost certainly need to be outsourced to specialist service providers.

However, before public communicators rush to employ machine learning tools and hire predictive modelling experts, it is necessary to note that, despite a lot of hype, this field is far from precise. Remember that some of the world's largest research companies using these technologies still cannot predict the outcomes of elections or referenda in many cases. Why? Because humans are not machines. They do not behave predictably, and they do not always think and act systematically.

Interestingly, academic research itself is assessed and rated on the basis of metrics, as well as other methods, such as expert peer review. A range of metrics is collected by publishers, such as the number of times published work is read and how many times it is cited by other academics. An independent review of the role and use of metrics for evaluating academic research was conducted in 2014 and published in 2015, and noted that 'there are powerful currents whipping up the metric tide' (Wilsdon et al., 2015, p. viii). The study pointed towards growing pressures for audit and evaluation of public spending, demands by policy-makers for more strategic intelligence and the availability of real-time 'big data' (Wilsdon et al., 2015, p. viii). The review proposed what the research team called 'responsible metrics', which involve 'appropriate uses of quantitative indicators in the governance, management and assessment of research', and recommended that 'metrics should support, not supplant, qualitative expert judgement' (Wilsdon et al., 2015, p. x). The same principles should be applied in all cases of using metrics. In the case of academic publishing, a research paper might gain a high volume of citations (a metric), but many may be scholars criticizing the work and debunking its findings as flawed. Thus the metric is hardly a reliable indicator of a positive outcome and impact.

Beware meaningless metrics from 'measurement inversion'

Critique of metrics and analytics comes not only from qualitative researchers jealous of the attention and resources being assigned to their fashionable quantitative cousins, but also from experts in quantitative research and modelling. Douglas Hubbard, the developer of applied information economics and a widely published author on information technology (IT) and business evaluation (for example, Hubbard, 2010), says that many of the metrics used by performance measurement professionals have little value and can actually be misleading. For example, he says that the variables that are most valuable in return on investment (ROI) calculations are rarely represented in evaluation reports such as cost–benefit spreadsheets (Hubbard, 2007 [1999], para. 2). He refers to this as *measurement inversion*, whereby organizations get evaluation back to front – that is, easily available metrics, particularly those presented in impressive spreadsheets and colourful charts, are used whether or not they are the right ones, rather than the factors that are most important (Hubbard, 2007 [1999], 2010).

This is not an anti-metrics or anti-analytics tirade; on the contrary, data is fundamental for evaluation, and metrics and analytics are important components of most evaluation. The argument presented here is simply that metrics and analytics are not the total solution. Furthermore, organizations have much to learn about using data, metrics and analytics. Basing decisions on incomplete or selective data can be quite dangerous.

Online marketing specialist Jayson DeMers (2014) says that organizations need to 'democratize' their data and data analysis to gain reliable and useful findings and insights. He is referring to the tendency for organizations to have data locked away behind firewalls and security classifications, or siloed in departments and units, because of technical issues or internal politics. Despite the adoption of 'open government' policies and freedom-of-information laws, governments are particularly prone to these problems. Observation of data collection, data analysis and evaluation over several months in several of the largest government departments in the UK revealed that 'insights' units, social media 'listening' functions, public consultation teams and stakeholder engagement units in each collect large amounts of data. Each of the departments and their affiliated agencies was also revealed to regularly commission social research through companies such as Ipsos Mori, GfK and Kantar TNS. But most of this information remains inaccessible and even unknown to other departments, including those with related responsibilities and information requirements. Research found this to be because of a lack of a central insights database or 'knowledge warehouse', and also because of risk aversion in relation to privacy and data security. Interviews revealed a widely held view that it is a breach of an individual's privacy for government departments and agencies to share surveys, correspondence such as complaints or consultation data submitted by citizens. It is difficult to imagine that this is a correct legal interpretation, particularly if the data is anonymized.[1] Democratic governments are meant to be responsive to citizens. Furthermore, it is highly likely that, having gone to the trouble of writing letters, submissions or filling out surveys, citizens assume and expect that their voice will be heard by all departments and government agencies with responsibilities related to the issues raised. Recommendations to add an opt-out box to government surveys and public consultation templates to gain explicit permission to share data and to create a central knowledge base were solutions being considered at the time of writing.

DeMers says that data analysis requires data experts to set the vision and provide the capability for in-depth analysis and reporting, but that democratizing data also requires decision-makers and stakeholders throughout the organization to be 'empowered as much as possible to access data that they need and want' (2014, para. 9). Democratizing data requires breaking down siloes (technological and political) and making multiple data sets available through data 'warehousing', with searchable indexing and tagging. This enables *triangulation*[2] of multiple data sets relevant to an issue, *meta-analysis* of stored data and *longitudinal* analysis of studies that are repeated.

While more will be said on this issue under 'Big data' in Chapter 7, a key point to note now in relation to planning and evaluation is that metrics and analytics – particularly automatically generated, low-level metrics, such as clickthroughs and likes – do not constitute evaluation. They provide a useful contribution to the data required to inform evaluation. But usually other different types of data are also required, including unstructured qualitative data that is usually in text form such as transcripts of interviews or focus groups, comments and feedback, and audio or video recordings from interviews, focus groups and ethnography (observation). Also, interpretation of data sets is required to identify what they mean and what, if any, response is needed, by whom, when and how. This broader understanding of evaluation requires research, which will be explored in detail in Chapters 6, 7 and 8.

Beware vanity metrics

Another cautionary note is that there is a growing array of what are referred to as *vanity metrics* that masquerade as evaluation. These are usually imprecise and often exaggerated, designed to make people in an organization or investors feel good, and to justify jobs and budgets, rather than to critically inform strategy and tactics. Examples of vanity metrics are gross numbers of registered users, downloads and page views. High volumes of registered users can be gained by making an attractive offer such as a free copy of a report that requires a simple registration of a recipient's email address – but most who register do so only to receive the report and never return to the site. While some organizations use such techniques to claim X million registered users, responsible evaluation counts only *active* users, which is usually a small percentage of total registered users (often around 30 per cent). Likewise, some organizations and service providers report total page views – but many page views do not provide what visitors are seeking and they hit the 'back' button within seconds. More reliable metrics in terms of showing interest and engagement are page views with a reasonable 'duration' (for example, more than 30 seconds) and return visits. Other simple examples of vanity metrics are percentages cited without context, such as claims that something is 'up 400 per cent' – but 'up' compared with what? If the base number was very low, a 400 per cent increase would be insignificant and misleading.

Social media analysis is a field fraught with exaggerated claims based on vanity metrics, as noted by Don Bartholomew (2016, p. 97) and others. As online content marketer Sujan Patel wrote in *Forbes* magazine:

> The number of social media followers your social profiles have attracted is one of the most vain of all the vanity metrics you can attract, yet it often consumes far too much of the company's attention. Repeat after me – just because someone follows you does not mean they're engaged with your brand!

> *(Patel, 2015, para. 9)*

Instead, Patel and most researchers recommend metrics that indicate deeper engagement and communication, such as positive and supportive comments. Similarly, measurement of active users versus total registered users, return visitors and other more substantial metrics is recommended.

Beware invalid metrics

There are also some *invalid metrics* presented as purported evaluation that need to be avoided. The public relations (PR) industry is one of the worst offenders in this regard. Most notably, PR practitioners have long calculated alleged *advertising value equivalents* (AVEs), also referred to as *advertising value equivalency* and *equivalent advertising value* (EAV), as noted in Chapter 1. These are calculated by multiplying the space gained as editorial publicity in print media and the time gained in news, current affairs and talk shows in broadcast media by the advertising rate for the respective programmes and publications. Some even apply multipliers of the cost of an equivalent amount of advertising space or time, arguing that editorial publicity is more credible than advertising. Use of multipliers in the PR industry ranging from two to eight times have been reported by Walter Lindenmann (2003) and Mark Weiner and Don Bartholomew (2006).

Research studies over several decades have failed to substantiate so-called AVE of editorial publicity and studies have been particularly condemning of claimed multipliers (Cameron, 1994; Hallahan, 1999). In his guidelines for measuring and evaluating PR, Lindenmann reported that reputable researchers regard 'such arbitrary "weighting" schemes aimed at enhancing the alleged value of editorial coverage as unethical, dishonest, and not at all supported by the research literature' (Lindenmann, 2003, p. 10). Research by Samsup Jo (2004) found that when strong factual and logical arguments are available, editorial publicity outperforms advertising, but when weak arguments are available and persuasion based on emotion or other factors is required, advertising outperforms editorial.

Recently, PR researchers David Michaelson and Don Stacks have conducted several experiments to test the impact of similar advertising and editorial publicity. Following a pilot study (Michaelson & Stacks, 2006), they conducted an experiment in 2007 that involved production of quality print advertisements and mock-ups of editorial coverage for a fictitious product, Zip Chips, in a range of newspapers, including the *New York Times*. Professional designers and writers were used to simulate actual advertisements, and editorial coverage and layouts mirrored the style and format of food sections of the relevant media. Groups of potential consumers were then exposed to the advertising and editorial content promoting Zip Chips. This experiment found no significant differences in awareness, purchase intent or believability resulting from equivalent amounts of advertising and editorial publicity exposure (Michaelson & Stacks, 2007).

Responding to some incredulity and criticisms of their initial studies, Stacks and Michaelson repeated and extended the experiment in 2009, from which they concluded:

There are differences between advertising and editorial commentary but, as in the earlier study, these differences are not the difference expected. What we found was that both the editorial and the advertisement were equally effective in promoting the product, but no statistically significant differences existed between the editorial and the advertisement across measures of awareness, information, intent to purchase, and product credibility.

(Stacks & Michaelson, 2009, p. 12)

One difference found was that editorial publicity contributes to higher levels of product knowledge – which is not surprising, because editorial is usually a longer format than an 'ad' and thus contains more information. Nevertheless, Stacks and Michaelson concluded: 'We still failed to find a "multiplier effect"' (2009, p. 15). And even though these studies appear to show equivalency of advertising and editorial publicity, it must be borne in mind that they were testing carefully crafted editorial that was 100 per cent positive in relation to the product promoted. In reality, at least four factors make generalized AVE calculations invalid and spurious as a measure of the value of PR or publicity, as follows:

- The figure calculated is not the value of advertising; rather, it is the estimated *cost* if the same amount of space and/or time were bought as advertising.
- Most organizations would not purchase advertising in many of the media that publish or broadcast editorial content. Advertising is usually focused on priority media, while editorial content can be syndicated widely, including in less relevant media (Jeffries-Fox, 2003; Macnamara, 2000a).
- In most instances, editorial and advertising are not *equivalent*. Whereas advertising is controlled in terms of content and placement, editorial media coverage is highly variable in terms of placement and presentation. Editorial media content may not include key messages, and can even be critical and negative in relation to the organization or issue concerned. Editorial articles also often include information about competitors, sometimes even favourably comparing competitors or alternatives.
- The rates used in such calculations are often *casual* advertising rates, which inflate so-called values, because advertising campaigns usually access special rates – often at significant discounts in today's age of fragmenting audiences and cash-starved media organizations.

More recent experimental research by Julie O'Neil and Marianne Eisenmann (2016) has tested similar content in the full range of paid, earned, shared and owned media (the PESO model), including *native advertising*,[3] and again found that earned editorial publicity, while important, does not have greater impact on awareness, knowledge, interest, intent to purchase or advocacy. O'Neil and Eisenmann's experiment using various types of promotional content for a smartphone exposed to 1,500 participants found that the lines between various media content formats are blurring and that consumers access a range of sources of information. Overall, they found that media consumers today put less emphasis on content format and more on message quality wherever it appears, with reviews written by other consumers being the number one preferred source of information (O'Neil & Eisenmann, 2016).

As noted in Chapter 1, the Barcelona Principles, developed by the International Association for Measurement and Evaluation of Communication (AMEC, 2015) and endorsed by professional communication bodies worldwide, state emphatically that AVEs are not a valid measure of PR. Yet, at conferences and summits on evaluation, PR practitioners continue to argue that they have to provide AVEs because their clients or bosses ask for them. Other professionals, such as lawyers, auditors and accountants, are sometimes asked to do things that are improper and unethical, such as avoiding tax. Ethical professionals decline to provide such services and advise their clients of alternative approaches based on their expert knowledge. Public communication practitioners using AVEs need to consider whether they want to be recognized as professionals offering expert services or simply providers of low-end commodity products of dubious quality.

With these important qualifications about metrics in mind, the following sections summarize the key metrics that can be collected and used to inform evaluation.

Traditional media metrics

There are a number of metrics that are generated in traditional media placement and analysis. These can signal progress along the 'response chain' of preliminary and intermediate variables that must be achieved as stepping stones on the path to desired outcomes and impact (Atkin & Freimuth, 2013, p. 58). On their own, however, media metrics in particular mostly relate to counting outputs such as the following.

Media clip counts

One of the most basic metrics used in PR is *media clip counts* – that is, counting press coverage, traditionally referred to as 'clippings', because editorial stories were clipped from newspapers and magazines using scissors or a knife – along with transcripts, recordings or summaries of broadcast media coverage. For decades, PR practitioners have associated a high volume of media coverage with effectiveness and success. Of course, this is simplistic and may even be misleading as an evaluation metric, because media coverage can be negative. Also, editorial articles often only partially represent the organization's messages, and sometimes even discuss and favourably compare competitors. Furthermore, publication or broadcast does not mean that the target audience read, heard or saw the content. Media clips simply indicate that the information was put out into the public domain, so it is a basic output measure.

Reach

Another basic metric that has been widely used in advertising, PR and most forms of mediated public communication for many decades is *reach*. Reach relates to audience size and refers to the number of people within the intended audience who were potentially reached by the communication. Reach does not mean that the audience actually engaged with the content. As noted throughout this analysis and in the following sections in particular, reach is only an early step in communication. It is an *output* metric, because it provides data on the extent to which media content has been put out into the public domain. At the point of reach, communicators have not yet got to the 'response chain'. But, unless audiences are reached, there is no chance that information or persuasive messages can have any effect. So reach is an important basic output metric in evaluating public communication.

Reach is more specifically measured as *target audience reach* rather than total reach, because a gross figure can be misleading. For example, if a marketing campaign is designed to sell active wear to young women aged 18–24, advertising placed in a women's magazine with a total readership across all ages of 1 million is not reaching a target audience of 1 million. The proportion of young women aged 18–24 who read the magazine may be only 100,000. In advertising, *gross ratings points* (GRPs) refer to the percentage of the total audience reached, but the more common and useful reach metric is *target audience ratings points* (TARPs).

In television advertising, ratings are often referred to specifically as *TV ratings* (TVRs). If a television commercial is broadcast nationally across a UK network, for example, and claims to have delivered one adult network TVR, that means that 1 per cent of the UK's 50 million adults potentially saw the commercial – that is, 500,000. However, if the target audience is adults living in the London ITV region (population approximately 9.5 million), then one adult London TVR would be 95,000. If the target audience is ABC1[4] women aged 25–54 and there are approximately 27 million of them living in the UK, then the number of people in the target audience reached would be 270,000. It is important to remember that ratings points are percentages and that audience reach numbers vary, even for the same programmes on the same days, depending on the target audience.

Some other key points about reach to note are as follows:

- While reach is mostly calculated as a *percentage* of the total potential audience, such as in advertising rating points, reach is also sometimes calculated in terms of *volume* – that is, the number of people who potentially saw or heard the content.
- Reputable publishers and communication professionals use reach statistics based on independently *audited circulation* and *media ratings* data. For instance, reach through print media is typically based on audited circulation tracked by bodies such as the Audit Bureau of Circulation, which exist in many countries. Reach through television is estimated by organizations such as the Broadcasters' Audience Research Board (BARB) in the UK and Nielsen Media Research in the US, using meters installed in the homes of a survey panel. In online media (websites), reach is equivalent to *unique visitors*, which is the number of individuals – as identified by Internet Protocol (IP) addresses and 'cookies'[5] – requesting pages from the website during a given period, regardless of how often they visit.

- As indicated above, multiple viewings of content and multiple visits to websites by members of an audience do not increase reach. Some other statistics count multiple exposures, as discussed in the following sections.

In the era of social media, many advertisers and media agencies report paid reach and organic reach. *Paid reach* refers to the number of people or unique visitors who access paid content, while *organic reach* is achieved through shared content passed between web users (see also 'Shares' and 'Retweets, reblogs and regrams' later in this chapter).

Impressions and opportunities to see (OTS)

Impressions refer to the number of times that content is accessed, whether online, on air or in print – often crudely referred to as 'eyeballs' in marketing communication. For example, the *Dictionary of Public Relations Measurement and Evaluation* defines 'impressions' as:

> A metric that indicates the number of possible exposures of a media item to a defined set of stakeholders; the number of people who might have had the opportunity to be exposed to a story that has appeared in the media; also known as 'opportunity to see' (OTS); usually refers to the total audited circulation of a publication or the audience reach of a broadcast vehicle.
>
> *(Stacks & Bowen, 2013, p. 14)*

The Conclave on Social Media Measurement Standards, as discussed in Chapter 3, defines impressions as follows:

> Impressions represent the number of times an item has an opportunity to be seen and reach people, based on the simple addition of those audiences that have had the opportunity to see it . . . this term represents the gross number of opportunities for items to be seen, regardless of frequency of display, method of accessing the item, or audience duplication. It will typically count the same individuals multiple times.
>
> *(Conclave on Social Media Measurement Standards, 2013 [2011], para. 10)*

These definitions demonstrate the inconsistency in methods of evaluation and the lack of standards. The first states that *impressions* usually refers to the audited circulation of a publication or the audience of a broadcast programme. The second clearly defines *impressions* as 'the number of times' that content is accessed and adds explicitly that the metric typically counts the same individuals multiple times if they access content multiple times. In short, one refers to the *number of people* accessing content; the second refers to the *number of times* the content is accessed – quite different things.

In digital media, such as online advertising and social media, impressions are counted electronically as the number of times a web page is served to a user by a web server. Thus impressions can be a higher number than reach, because users may engage with content multiple times or multiple versions of content may be served to the same audience. For example, if three short videos are produced communicating the same messages in slightly different formats, some will view only one video, while others will view all three. If at least one of the videos is viewed by 200,000 people, the reach is 200,000. But if half of the audience viewed all three videos, while the other half viewed one, reach remains 200,000, but impressions total 400,000 (that is, a video has been served 400,000 times to a member of the audience). Most reputable media and agencies deduct short duration views to avoid inflated claims of reach and impressions (see 'Duration and bounce rate' later in this chapter).

Contemporary practice in digital communication and guidelines published by organizations such as the Digital Analytics Association (DAA)[6] indicate that the *Dictionary of Public Relations Measurement and Evaluation* is incorrect on this point. Impressions and *opportunities to see* (OTS) serve no purpose if they are the same thing as reach.

In any case, note the phrases 'opportunity to be seen', 'possible exposures' and 'might have had the opportunity to be exposed' in the above definitions of impressions. People leave television sets on when no one is watching and Internet users also leave web pages open for long periods without engaging with the content. Also, information consumers increasingly have and use a second, or even a third, screen, such as a television showing broadcast content, a tablet accessing web pages and a smartphone connected to Facebook, resulting in some accessed content not receiving significant attention.

Impressions data can also be overestimated when web pages present in-stream videos. *In-stream* is a format in which a video (for example, an ad) starts playing without a user clicking 'play'. In this case, impressions can be misleading, because many such impressions do not make much of an impression at all when visitors back out of pages or stop the video playing by clicking the pause or close button.

Like reach, impressions provide a useful basic metric at the *outputs* stage of public communication. But they tell us only what might have happened in relation to attempts at communication. More advanced metrics and research are required to confirm if audiences actually engaged with content and what effects it had, if any.

Share of voice

When the volume of media coverage of an organization and its key competitors and/or other organizations involved in similar issues is monitored, *share of voice* (SOV) can be calculated. Share of voice is not necessarily an indicator of influence, but it is a somewhat useful metric. If an organization has a dominant or sizeable SOV on issues in which it has an interest, it can be shown that it is 'getting its message across', at least at an output level. Conversely, if an organization has a small SOV, it is likely that it will struggle to have its views and messages known.

However, qualitative factors are also important, because large SOV could include negative and critical media coverage.

Cost per thousand (CPM)

Another basic metric used for paid media content is the *cost per thousand* impressions – the abbreviation CPM being derived from the Latin cost per *mille*. Media organizations often sell advertising on the basis of cost per thousand impressions, which is calculated by dividing the cost of an advertising placement by the number of impressions (expressed in thousands) that it generates. This metric is useful mainly for managerial purposes. For instance, it helps to identify whether public communication is cost-effective. If the cost per thousand to reach young women aged 25–34 is $10,000 in a prestige fashion magazine and only $1,000 in digital media, a much higher return will be expected from the magazine if it is to be cost-effective. The digital equivalents of CPM are *cost per view* (CPV) and *cost per click* (CPC), which are discussed in the following section.

Digital and social media metrics

Digital media have afforded a range of additional data for evaluating public communication, with most metrics available in real time, making digital metrics a favourite among marketing and media professionals. However, some digital metrics and so-called digital analytics fall into the category of vanity metrics, as discussed at the beginning of this chapter. Some of the most used and most important digital and social media metrics are briefly explained and critiqued in the following sections.

Unique visitors

Unique visitors refers to the number of people (more accurately, the number of Internet-connected devices) that visit a website and hence it is a web measure of reach. For some time and in some systems, uniqueness was determined by the IP address of the user's device. This meant that unique visitor data was reliable in the case of individuals with their own IP address. But most organization networks now channel all employee web access through a single IP address, so unique visitors based on IP addresses are only marginally reflective of who had accessed online information. However, since the advent of 'cookies', unique visitor data has been able to accurately reflect the number of individuals accessing a site.

Visits/sessions

It is important to understand the difference between unique visitors, visits and other metrics, such as page views. While unique visitors refers to the number of individual people accessing a website, *visits*, in web terms, denotes each continuous period that a user spends on a website before leaving. This metric is also referred to as *sessions*. For instance, if a person is on Twitter and clicks on a link to the *New York Times*, they start one visit to the *Times* website irrespective of how long they are there and irrespective of how many pages they access on that site.

Views/page views

Views, also called *page views*, are counted by tracking code embedded in websites that records each time a web page identified by a URL[7] is loaded by a web browser. A visitor may access multiple pages on a website during a visit or session. In the above example of a visit to the *New York Times* website, if the visitor looked at four stories, they will account for four page views.

Page view data is important for identifying which content is popular with visitors. Also, multiple page views per site are indications of interest and engagement. As well as providing information about web pages generally and access to documents such as media releases and reports, views are a key metric when evaluating the level of exposure of online videos and GIFs (short animations). Views can be obtained specifically for the URL of posted videos to show the number of times that videos are viewed, most commonly by clicking a 'play' button. Note that in-stream videos that play automatically on opening a web page are usually not counted in views data. The Interactive Advertising Bureau (IAB, 2014) recommends against views as a measure for in-stream videos and suggests other measures of engagement.[8]

Return visits and views

Return visits (that is, repeat visits) and *return views* are positive indicators of interest in content. While unique visitors is a useful metric to narrow down web traffic to the estimated number of people accessing a site (that is, reach), return visits and views count as impressions. Furthermore, beyond adding to impressions, return visits and views are a sign of deeper interest than a single visit suggests. Sometimes, Internet users return time and again to sites that they find informative, interesting or useful.

Duration and bounce rate

An important metric to use in combination with visitors, visits or sessions and views is *duration*. As any web user knows, many searches and links lead to pages that are not what the user is looking for, and the user clicks the 'back' button within a few seconds. Other web pages do not hold a visitor's interest and are closed after a short time. This is referred to as the *bounce rate*. Most honest and reputable measurement deletes page views and visits of less than 30 seconds from metrics collected and used. However, this is not always the case and misleading metrics can be generated. The bounce rate should be deleted from claimed web page visits.

Average duration is a useful basic metric when evaluating the appeal of web pages and videos, because this gives a better indication of how much attention was paid to the content than total visits.

Sometimes, a combination of duration and other metrics such as return visits is used to calculate engagement. However, as discussed later in this chapter, such calculations are quite superficial measures of engagement, which, as noted in Chapter 3, involves emotional and cognitive dimensions, as well as participatory actions, such as joining or supporting rather than simply clicking a mouse.

All of the preceding online metrics – unique visitors, visits or sessions, page views, return visits and views, and duration, as well as clickthroughs, which are discussed next – are *output* measures because they provide data on the extent to which information is distributed and accessed. While some practitioners consider the placement of ads and distribution of media releases to be outputs, these steps provide no information on whether the content actually reached the target audience. As many editors note, media releases frequently end up in the rubbish bin (physical or digital). Thus placement of ads, and writing and sending out media releases, are regarded as part of production and distribution at the *inputs* or *activities* stage of public communication. *Outputs* are considered to be informational or promotional content that can be shown to have reached the target audience.

Clickthroughs and clickthrough rate (CTR)

Digital advertising uses and tracks *clickthroughs* extensively. This is because advertising can present only short messages and visuals to gain attention, and more detailed information is usually required to motivate potential consumers towards buying products and services. This requires sending viewers of advertising to other pages where detailed descriptions of various models, types, prices, and so on can be provided. Also, clickthroughs send Internet users to order forms and organization contact details.

Clickthrough rates (CTRs) show which advertisements and web pages are working most effectively in directing visitors down a 'sales funnel' or towards more detailed information. Typically, pages and links with low CTRs are taken down and replaced, while those with high CTRs are promoted.

Conversions

A popular metric in marketing communication that collects data further down the 'response chain' is *conversions*. This refers to the percentage of visitors to a website who take an action that the content encourages them to, such as signing up to receive a newsletter, report or more information in some form, supporting a petition, joining an organization, and so on. The percentage of total visitors who take such actions is referred to as the *conversion rate*. For example, if a web page attracted 100,000 visitors and 5,000 responded with a desired action, this would equate to a conversion rate of 5 per cent. However, 'conversion' is a broad generic term for a wide range of actions. A more precise measurement and reporting approach is to identify specific responses, such as subscribing, inquiring, joining, trialling, and so on. The taxonomy of metrics presented in Tables 3.4–3.7 in Chapter 3 lists various types of conversion as outtakes and short-term outcomes.

Cost per click (CPC)

Like cost per thousand, *cost per click* (CPC) is mainly used as a managerial metric to ensure that online communication is cost-effective. Popular search engines such as Google, Yahoo!, Microsoft Bing, DuckDuckGo and Baidu in China, as well as major social media sites such as Facebook and Twitter, charge advertisers on a pay per click basis and some, such as Google's AdWords, auction key words to the highest bidder. Content sites usually charge a fixed price per click rather than a bidding system.

Cost per view (CPV)

Cost per view (CPV) is the average amount that advertisers pay when a viewer watches 30 seconds of their video (or the duration, if it is shorter than 30 seconds) or engages with a video in some way, such as liking it or commenting, whichever comes first. Clearly, advertisers and marketers want to pay the lowest possible CPV. This metric is used to evaluate the *cost-effectiveness* of campaigns rather than their effectiveness. Usually, online cost per view is less than 10 cents – often as low as 2–5 cents.

Likes

If you haven't already realized it, having online entities 'like' you or your organization on social media does not mean that they actually *like* you. There are a number of reasons why digital likes are only a basic, inconclusive metric for measurement and evaluation. First, there are limited options on most social media sites: Facebook, for example, has refused to accede to calls to add a 'dislike' button, even though one survey found that 38 per cent of users would like to be able to dislike (YouGov, 2015). Second, liking takes very little effort – a simple click of a button – so is not really an indicator of deep interest or engagement.

In early 2016, Facebook launched a range of *emoji*[9] to complement its famous 'like' button, including pictograms of round faces representing 'love', 'haha', 'wow', 'sad' and 'angry' as part of what it calls *Reactions* (Krug, 2016). It will be interesting to see whether evaluators count angry reactions on Facebook in the same way that many have claimed likes as measures of support and approval.

As shown in the taxonomy of evaluation presented in Tables 3.4–3.7 and the evaluation framework shown in Figure 3.18 in Chapter 3, likes are a basic indicator of *short-term outcomes*, or *outtakes* of public communication, if this stage is separately identified. They prove that those who like a website, page, video or story accessed it and took something from it – but they do not indicate engagement, as some claim. Return visits, positive comments and other higher-level responses, such as subscribing, are more indicative of engagement.

Follows

Similarly, studies have shown that having a million *follows* on Twitter has little to do with influence (Cha, Haddadi, Benevenuto & Gummadi, 2010). Lest some think that such statements are academic nit-picking, widely respected evaluation practitioner Don Bartholomew described quantitative claims of large numbers of followers, fans, friends, and so on as 'vanity metrics' (2016, p. 97). Follows on social media such as Twitter are even less of an indicator of engagement or support than likes, because many follow celebrities, politicians and even corporations simply to see what they are up to – sometimes so that they can criticize them. For example, in researching the use of social media in elections as part of *e-democracy*, a number of participants said that they follow politicians online to track their statements to identify contradictions and political 'spin'. Follows are another basic *short-term outcome* or *outtake* metric, and should be used cautiously in evaluation.

Shares

Shares of content online are a step up from likes and follows, for a number of reasons. While some share content that they dislike with others as a way of galvanizing opposition or outrage, most share content that they like and want to help to promote. People tend to share content that they find highly interesting, and which they believe their networks will find equally interesting and relevant. Because sharing is active and public – it sends links and messages to others – rather than passive and private, as in the case of following, people think twice before sharing. Therefore, it represents a higher form of *outtake* or *short-term outcome* than following or liking.

A further reason why shares are worth tracking is that this feature is widely available on websites, as well as being a feature of social media. It is common to find a row of buttons on most web pages to allow a user to instantly post a link to Facebook, Twitter, LinkedIn, Google+ and sometimes other sites. Share buttons are also a feature on these social media, as well as Pinterest, Instagram, YouTube and others.

Retweets, reblogs and regrams

Another even more active form of sharing is *retweeting* on Twitter, *reblogging* (for example, on Tumblr) or *regramming* on Instagram. This involves Internet users posting a tweet, blog post or photo from someone else's account to their own. Thus they are sharing it with their network. They are also effectively putting their name to it, indicating appreciation and support, although attribution to the original source is Internet etiquette. Retweets, reblogs and regrams are therefore further basic indicators of online liking and support.

Tweets and posts

A well as liking, sharing, retweeting and reblogging the online content of others, bloggers and social network users also initiate their own content, such as tweets on Twitter, wall posts on Facebook, photos on Pinterest and Instagram, short articles on blogs and videos on YouTube. While a large proportion of the zettabytes of web content produced weekly is not relevant to evaluation, tweets and posts about a specific organization or its products, services, policies, projects or campaigns are highly pertinent for the organization concerned. Social media have opened up a whole new world for evaluation, because they provide windows through which to view and listen in to conversations and discussions among networks, communities and individuals locally and globally. Furthermore, this content can be monitored and analysed in near real time, giving organizations quick insights and intelligence about relevant issues.

For example, if a company launches a new product, there is likely to be discussion in social media within hours, if not minutes, of the release. The company can monitor and analyse online tweets and posts to gain an early indication of reaction. Similarly, government departments, agencies and political offices can gauge the mood of citizens and the response of key stakeholders to a policy announcement, at least to some extent, through social media. Identification of response moves evaluation a little further along in the stages of communication identified in models discussed in Chapter 3. While analysis of tweets and posts requires research (*content analysis*), which will be discussed later in this chapter, simple metrics, such as the number of tweets and posts about a product, service, policy or issue, give an indication of response. Hence these are further basic-level *short-term outcome* or *outtake* measures.

However, it is an indictment of the public communication industries that most organizations have incorporated open interactive social media into their strategies and campaigns primarily for posting their own content and messages rather than monitoring and listening to others (Gibson, Williamson & Ward, 2010; Macnamara, 2014c; Macnamara & Zerfass, 2012; Vergeer, 2013; Wright & Hinson, 2012). An analysis summarizing the findings of a number of studies concluded that use of social media by organizations 'is largely a case of the new put into service of the old', referring to top-down, one-way mass media and mass communication practices of the past (Macnamara, 2012b, p. 84). Similarly, the Organizational Listening Project found overwhelming use of social media for 'speaking' rather than listening (Macnamara, 2016a). Thus social media represent a grossly underutilized source of insight and feedback.

A limitation of monitoring and analysing social media, it must be pointed out, is that tweets and posts including comments do not reflect a representative sample of views. Often, it is the most outspoken who pour forth their views in social media. Also, there is a widespread belief supported by research that social media are more often negative than positive towards business, politics and government. For example, in an analysis of the 2012 US presidential election campaign, the Pew Research Center (2012) reported that online discussion of both Barack Obama and Mitt

Romney was 'relentlessly negative' (para. 12). Social media discussion of business and products also tends to be more negative than positive according to studies (for example, Jalonen & Jussila, 2016). These factors need to be taken into account and illustrate why social media tracking alone does not provide reliable evaluation.

A number of metrics reporting online interactions such as views, likes, follows, tweets, retweets and shares can be obtained using web applications such as Brandwatch, Sysomos, BuzzSumo and SharedCount. Some can even be obtained for free using Google Analytics, Facebook Insights, Twitter Analytics and YouTube Insight. The features and vendors change rapidly in the online world, so it is necessary to do some homework or to talk to a specialist in digital analytics.

Tagging content

An important step for tracking online communication is *tagging content*. This refers to the embedding of metadata in content, which allows identification of what online content has been accessed and for how long, and also allows responses to content such as page views, video views, likes, shares, and so on to be linked back to specific forms of content and even specific messages. Through tagging, the effectiveness of various platforms, forms of content such as ads or videos and messages can be measured. For instance, if comments and inquiries are being generated from Facebook and not from Twitter, effort can be focused on Facebook. Tagging of specific pages allows site owners to identify which pages are generating responses. A key element and benefit of ongoing measurement and evaluation is that resources can be reallocated from ineffective and less effective activities to those that create the best outcomes and impact. New developments in *scroll tracking* (that is, how far visitors scroll down web pages) are also important for gaining information about content consumption.

Web programmers proficient in languages such as HTML, JavaScript and CSS can be engaged for this purpose. However, it is important that communication management sets out policies and guidelines on tagging, such as ensuring consistent tagging across various forms of web content. If a different system of tagging is used for online advertising, PR materials such as media releases and corporate reports, and other web pages, tracking and comparing the performance of content is impossible. Conversely, if a consistent tagging method is used, the effectiveness of each type of content can be identified and compared, and the source of responses such as inquiries, registering, joining or buying (causality) can be established. This is a good reason for integration of various forms of public communication, or at least close coordination.

Comments

Comments made on social media in response to content posted by organizations are a further indicator of audience reception and reaction. Comments can be made on an organization's own social sites, such as Facebook pages, blogs and on other websites that allow or even invite comment. The total volume of comments is an indicator of interest, although some basic categorization into positive and negative comments should be undertaken if this metric is to be meaningful. Political sites and Facebook pages and blogs of organizations involved in highly topical or controversial issues can attract hundreds and even thousands of comments – many of them critical. Ideally, the text of these should be systematically analysed, as will be discussed in Chapter 8. But the presence and volume of comments provide metrics indicating audience response, which constitutes a *short-term outcome* or *outtake*, as shown in Figure 3.18 and Tables 3.4–3.7 in Chapter 3.

While social media comments and other responses such as likes, follows, retweets, shares, and so on provide fast and low-cost indicators to inform evaluation, it must be remembered that these do not come from a representative sample. While increasingly popular, social media are not widely used by some demographic and socio economic groups such as the elderly and the poor. Also, those who are the most active commentators in social media are often atypical. As the self-professed 'measurement queen' Katie Paine colourfully told a 2016 measurement and evaluation summit in Oslo, the person commenting in social media 'could be a guy in a basement with a pet snake and a bunch of guns' (Paine, 2016b).

Sentiment, tone and favourability

Recognizing the potential for media content other than paid advertising to vary in messages, as well as quantitative factors such as size, reach and placement, content such as editorial publicity and online comment is commonly assessed in terms of *tone*, or what some call *sentiment* or *favourability*.

The terms 'tone' and 'sentiment' are used interchangeably in some literature, including proposed standards for evaluation (for example, Eisenmann, Geddes, Paine, Pestana, Walton & Weiner, 2012, p. 8), but there are important differences. *Tone* is related to voice and speaking – and media content is a form of speaking and voice. *Sentiment* is a human emotion, felt inside a person. Thus tone is the more appropriate term to apply to evaluation of content, such as media articles and online comment, while sentiment is more appropriately a measure of audience or public feelings towards a brand, product or organization. The difference is more than semantics. It can be concluded that tone is a measure of *output* (that is, how positive is content that is put out into the public sphere), while sentiment can be an *outtake* or *short-term outcome* (a human response). The development of standards for measurement and evaluation needs to recognize such differences.

Tone (or what some call sentiment) can be measured in a number of ways using various descriptive ratings or scales. The most common is a simple three-point rating of positive, negative or neutral. This form of rating suffers from a number of limitations.

1. It is often subjective, being applied by practitioners themselves, or by media monitoring or media analysis firms, without specific criteria to inform this categorization.

2. Tone is almost always applied from the perspective of the client organization. It is therefore not a generalizable rating of the content. What is negative for an industrial corporation may be positive for an environmental group.
3. A three-point scale lacks differentiation. Content that contains some minor criticism is bundled together with content that is savagely critical, while mildly affirming comments are not distinguished from highly positive advocacy. And how to rate items that contain both positive and negative content? Often, the crudeness of this method results in most content being rated neutral.

Nevertheless, positive–negative–neutral ratings are relatively quick and easy to apply, and give a broad (very broad) qualitative assessment of media content.

Members of the Coalition for Public Relations Research Standards have argued for 'balanced' as a fourth category for rating content that has an equal mix of positive and negative comments, noting that neutral content may have neither positive nor negative elements (Eisenmann et al., 2012, p. 9). But simple three-point scales are much more widely used for rating the tone of media content.

Some content analysis methods and systems calculate the favourability of content as an alternative to tone or sentiment. In a few cases, *favourability* is simply a synonym for positivity. But, in some systems such as CARMA® (an acronym formed from 'computer-aided research and media analysis'), favourability is a multivariate score that takes into account variables such as the size and length of the item, prominence, audience reach, topics or issues discussed, and messages contained in the item. Multivariate content analysis usually involves human coding requiring professional research skills and specialist software. Rigorous qualitative and mixed method content analysis is discussed in Chapter 8.

A word about automated systems and machine learning

A number of content analysis systems categorize, score and rate content based on *automated machine coding*. Automated machine coding of content, such as in terms of tone or sentiment, is based on algorithms (sets of instructions and rules) that match words in texts to 'libraries' of words and definitions held in computer systems. Computers can 'make sense' of words and phrases by directly matching them to definitions or instructions (for example, 'financial loss' = very negative) and by identifying defined words in close proximity (that is, context), such as the word 'medical' in close proximity to 'malpractice'. The appeal of fast, automated analysis of large quantities of text is strong and software promising to operate without human labour has proliferated.

However, while great claims are made for automated analysis systems by the technologists who produce them and great expectations are held by metrics-loving modernists, fully automatic coding is problematic for a number of reasons. Computers can match words and phrases in texts to digital libraries and stored instructions very quickly – but computers are quite poor at detecting nuance, sarcasm, colloquialisms, and local slang and dialect. Further, the libraries used need considerable customization to correctly interpret particular terms used in specialist fields such as health and medicine, engineering, education, and so on, as well as brand messages and tag lines. For example, Nike is likely to find hundreds of mentions of 'do it' online that are unrelated to its long-used slogan. Prominent author of research methods books W. Lawrence Neuman gives the example of the word 'red' and how it can be used with multiple nuances that are not visible to a computer:

> I read a book with a red cover that is a real red herring. Unfortunately, its publisher drowned in red ink because the editor couldn't deal with the red tape that occurs when a book is red hot. The book has a story about a red fire truck that stops at red lights only after the leaves turn red. There is also a group of Reds who carry red flags to the little red schoolhouse. They are opposed by red-blooded rednecks who eat red meat and honour the red, white and blue.
>
> *(Neuman, 1997, p. 275)*

Machine coding of the above text would be very unlikely to identify the range of meanings of the word 'red'. When content analysis is conducted across multiple languages and cultures, such as for global or non-Western media studies, the problems of machine coding become even more marked, because most automated coding systems work with English-language text only and computer translations are unreliable, except for the most rudimentary applications.

A second problem with fully automated analysis systems is that many use secret algorithms for coding and scoring – referred to as *black box* systems. This is contrary to the principles of research, which include transparency and replicability (that is, the facility for others to repeat the procedures with a likelihood of reaching the same findings). Secret algorithms are much vaunted in the commercial world, but are generally to be avoided in research. Professor Ken Benoit, head of the Department of Methodology at The London School of Economics and Political Science, says that 'black box' methods have no place in science (K. Benoit, personal communication, December 5, 2016).

A third, and perhaps the most important, reason to be extremely cautious in relation to fully automated analysis systems is that computers cannot consider the *context* of content. They only describe the *text* based on pre-set formulae. Gaining insights, learning and doing evaluation (as opposed to measurement) requires the interpretation of data. Contextualization is an important part of interpretation – and only humans can interpret data within the prevailing social, cultural, political and economic context.

An innovative alternative to fully automated rating of content is *active learning* systems that take advantage of the power of computers to process large volumes of text quickly, combined with the faculty of humans to instruct the system and correct 'codings', which the computer application in turn 'learns' and applies to subsequent processing. Such adaptive systems, which provide much more sophisticated analysis, and content analysis as a research method are discussed further in Chapter 8.

Audience research

It should be seen from the preceding sections that simple counts and machine-generated metrics provide early and basic indicators of audience reach and reaction, but, on their own, they do not provide deep insights or conclusive evidence of the outcomes and impact of communication. Beyond the collection of metrics, which is largely automated in the age of digitalization, quantitative, as well as qualitative, data can and should be collected and interpreted through *audience research*. The remainder of this chapter reviews and critiques some of the key metrics that can be generated from various social science research methods.

Recall

As noted in Chapter 1, *recall* has been one of the most commonly used metrics to measure (and allegedly to evaluate) advertising, along with reach. Several types of recall are measured. For a long time, the most frequently used approach was recall of ads. The IAB defines *ad recall* as:

> A measure of advertising effectiveness in which a sample of respondents is exposed to an ad and then at a later point in time is asked if they remember the ad. Ad recall can be on an aided or unaided basis. Aided ad recall is when the respondent is told the name of the brand or category being advertised.
> *(Interactive Advertising Bureau, 2012, n.p.)*

However, ad recall is somewhat short-sighted and self-serving. Many of us can recall television commercials for products that we would never consider buying. We also recall advertisements that are extremely annoying. While some argue that annoying ads gain 'cut through' and actually work, the popularity of ad blockers online is an indication that creating annoyance is not evidence of success. Also, even when audiences can recall ads, many do not know what they were for, which makes the communication pointless. For example, one of the most recalled television ads of the 1970s featured a gorilla in a cage beating up a suitcase, accompanied by voice-over pointing out that the product was so strong that even a 200-pound gorilla could not break it. However, later research found that most viewers assumed that the ad was for Samsonite, when it was actually for a new suitcase produced by American Tourister (Wasserman, 2013). A recent example reported in the *Advertising Benchmark Index* was Kmart's 'Ship my pants' ad, which became a viral hit, but which few people recalled as an ad for Kmart. This is referred to in the advertising trade as *brand linkage failure* (Wasserman, 2013).

Thankfully, ad recall is used less and less, in favour of measuring recall of brands and messages. *Brand recall* involves asking audiences what brands come to mind when they think of a particular product category (for example, airlines, washing liquid, banks, etc.).

Recall can be measured aided or unaided, referring to whether or not prompts are provided. *Unaided recall* testing is usually recommended for measuring brand recall, whereas *aided recall* can be useful or even necessary in some other situations. For instance, a further application of this metric is recall of *messages*. This involves asking people what they know about a particular organization, product or service, and identifying how well responses match the messages and information contained in the organization's public communication.

While recall has been mainly championed in the advertising industry, recall can be measured for other forms of communication, such as publicity, websites, social media and even word of mouth. In fact, it is more productive to conduct recall testing on an open-ended basis in terms of information sources and channels, because this allows comparative testing of recall via various forms of communication. People might recall seeing ads for a particular grocery store, but it might have been a neighbour's word of mouth that caused them to shop there. An example of an open-ended unaided (also referred to as *unprompted*) recall measure is asking people (for example, in surveys or focus groups) if they recall seeing, hearing or reading information about airlines recently, or asking them what airlines they can recall seeing, reading or hearing information about. Aided recall in this example is tested by asking people what they can recall seeing, reading or hearing about a particular airline.

Most recall studies test 24-hour recall (that is, recall 24 hours after exposure to information), but recall up to seven days is sometimes tested, and gives a more substantial indicator of recall and retention of information and emotional connection. Advertising research finds that recall is higher when content triggers an emotional response.

Recall rates of ads, brands and messages are *short-term outcome* or *outtake* metrics, because they indicate that the audience has taken something out of the content, but has not yet responded or acted in any desired way necessarily. Other metrics and research methods are required to move farther along the 'response chain' to advanced stages of communication.

Engagement

A metric that has become 'a prototypical buzzword' in marketing communication and other fields of public communication practice is *engagement* (Satell, 2013). A range of metrics, including some automatically generated in digital media, purport to show engagement. Some would have us believe that likes, follows, clickthroughs, and return visits to sites and content indicate engagement, but this denotes a low level of engagement that may be no more than curiosity or research (for example, comparing information on various makes of cars, most of which will be disregarded).

As briefly noted in Chapter 3, engagement is a complex, multidimensional, psycho-behavioural concept involving cognitive, affective and conative dimensions. More specifically, organizational psychologists and communication scholars point out that engagement involves:

- a psychological bond formed through a combination of cognitive processing of information and what scholars call *affective commitment* (that is, emotional attachment, such as a sense of belonging, feeling valued, etc.);

- *positive affectivity* – that is, a deep level of positive emotional engagement beyond liking or attraction, such as absorption, enthusiasm, excitement, pride and/or passion; and
- *empowerment* of those engaged, which is most effectively achieved through participation of some kind.

(Macey & Schneider, 2008; Meyer & Smith, 2000, p. 320;
Rhoades, Eisenberger & Armeli, 2001)

In short, true engagement involves cognition (thinking about), emotion and action of some kind. These multiple dimensions are not represented by any auto-generated metric. However, a combination of metrics can suggest engagement, such as an integration or triangulation of liking, sharing, retweeting and comments expressing positive sentiments, and some kind of participation, such as joining a group or subscribing. Hence engagement requires some data analysis before it can be evaluated and reported, as no single metric proves engagement.

Awareness

While recall of brands and messages gives some indication of *awareness*, recall testing does not probe deeply into what audiences know. Awareness can be measured in more detail using surveys, interviews or focus groups in which a number of questions can be asked. Surveys (a quantitative research method) are used if levels of awareness across a target population are required, while interviews or focus groups (qualitative research methods) allow awareness to be studied and understood in depth within smaller groups. These research methods are discussed in detail in Chapters 7 and 8.

Awareness is able to be expressed as a single metric such as on a scale from none to very high (for example, '0–5'), or as a percentage (for example, '65 per cent of women aged 35–50 are aware of the factors contributing to dementia and ways of offsetting or delaying the onset of dementia'). However, communication strategists and researchers usually want to go beyond simple ratings and percentages of aware-ness to understand what audiences think about the subject in question, what made them aware of it (that is, which channels, activities or experiences), and whether this awareness is likely to lead to attitude and/or behaviour change. Such questions require in-depth qualitative research. This expanding scope of insights and evalua-tion also leads on to the following even more in-depth metrics.

Attitudes and perceptions

Attitudes and perceptions are not easily described in numbers (metrics), because these are constructs with important qualitative dimensions. While it is possible to gen-erate metrics showing how many or what percentage of a target audience has certain perceptions or attitudes (for example, from *multiple-choice questions* or *scalo-grams*[10] in surveys), these are represented more comprehensively and with more fidelity in recorded responses or transcripts gained from interviews, focus groups or open-ended questions in surveys. The capacity of metrics to inform evaluation starts to break down when in-depth understandings are required. These concepts will be further discussed in Chapters 7 and 8 in reviewing the role of social science research methods, including surveys, depth interviews and focus groups.

Sometimes, identifying attitudes and perceptions at a single point in time is all that is required – for example, to understand an audience so as to plan communication and engagement. However, for evaluation of public communication activities or campaigns, attitudes and perceptions need to be measured before and after the programme, or even multiple times at intervals throughout the programme, to identify change.

Satisfaction

It seems that almost every merchant and retailer today (physical and online) sends customers a survey after they visit asking them about their experience. On one hand, this is good news – the importance of evaluation is increasingly understood. On the other hand, we might wonder about over-surveying and whether this is becoming self-defeating. I, for one, am getting tired of filling out customer satisfaction surveys – and their frequent landing in my inbox often decreases whatever satisfaction I might have had with the enterprise in question.

Satisfaction is a particular category of attitudes and perceptions. Therefore, as discussed in the previous section, metrics (numbers) offer only a limited capacity to evaluate satisfaction. Nevertheless, because satisfaction measurement is so commonly used, and because organizations want to incorporate a few key findings into their key performance indicators (KPIs) and evaluation 'dashboards', most satisfaction measurement involves structured surveys using scales. The most typical scales used are *Likert scales* (most often 0–5, with 0 representing 'very poor' or 'low' and 5 'excellent' or 'very high'). *Semantic differential* scales, which arrange opposite statements at each end of a 7, 9, or 11-point scale, may also be used (for example, 'Bright and modern' . . . 'Dull and old-fashioned'). A series of such questions can be tabulated to produce an overall satisfaction score or rating. (More detail on scales will be explored in Chapter 7.)

Satisfaction ratings can be gained to show *customer satisfaction* (commonly abbreviated to 'customer sat'), *employee satisfaction, member satisfaction, patient satisfaction* in health facilities such as hospitals, *student satisfaction* in schools and universities, and community or *ratepayer satisfaction* in local government areas, such as the California Report Card (Getuiza, 2014). (See also 'Net Promoter Score' later in the chapter.)

Intentions

Another specific type of attitude that is useful to identify is audience *intention*. This is usually assessed via surveys that ask participants questions about the likelihood of them taking certain actions in the future (for example, buying a product, giving up smoking, etc.). While intentions do not necessarily lead to outcomes, such as action or behavioural change, they do indicate another step along the 'response chain' and are particularly useful in evaluating long-term projects. For instance, a human organ donation campaign is unlikely to achieve its outcome (donation of kidneys, hearts, etc.) during the period of the campaign or immediately afterwards. In fact, one would hope that it would not. Barring unfortunate premature deaths, organ donation mostly occurs as people become older – often many years, or even decades, into the future. Interim steps that can be evaluated in organ donation campaigns include joining a register of organ donors (an intermediate action) and signalling intention to donate organs, such as recording wishes and permission on a driver's licence (intention).

Net Promoter Score (NPS)

A popular contemporary method of evaluating satisfaction and, to some extent, reputation is the *Net Promoter Score* (NPS). This is a score out of 10 given in response to a single question: 'How likely is it that you would recommend [name of brand, product, or organization] to a friend or colleague?' Scores of 9–10 are classified as *promoters* (that is, loyal enthusiasts who will keep buying from or supporting the organization); scores of 7–8 are referred to as *passives* (that is, those who are satisfied, but unenthusiastic and vulnerable to competitive offerings or views); and scores of 0–6 are *detractors* (that is, unhappy and liable to damage the organization through word of mouth, or 'word of mouse' online). Subtracting the percentage of detractors from the percentage of promoters yields the NPS, which can range from −100 (that is, minus 100) to a high of 100 if every person surveyed is a promoter (see Figure 4.1).

The benefit of the NPS is that it provides a simple single metric. Its weakness is that it provides no details about why people would recommend – that is, what are the characteristics that create the level of support and advocacy reported, or conversely the factors that create unlikeliness to recommend.

Reputation

Reputation is increasingly recognized as a valuable asset of organizations, as noted in Chapter 3. The 2012 World Economic Forum reported that reputation specifically accounts for 25 per cent of the market value of major public companies (Deloitte, 2014, p. 2).

While reputation is largely a qualitative construct, it is most commonly measured using surveys to produce metrics, such as scores and ratings. In some cases,

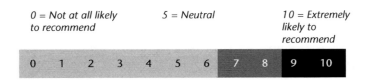

FIGURE 4.1 Net Promoter Score (NPS) calculation

reputation is reduced to a single metric, such as the NPS discussed above. Quantitative metrics applied in evaluating reputation are discussed here, but it should also be noted that surveys (discussed in Chapter 7) and qualitative research methods (discussed in Chapter 8) can be applied to evaluate reputation in customized and more in-depth ways.

At a personal level, *reputation* is defined as 'shared, or collective, perceptions about a person' (Nock, 1993, p. 2). This can be easily applied to organizations and is increasingly so, given that organizations, much like individuals, prosper or perish depending on their reputation. Nora Draper (2014) notes that people and organizations can influence their reputation to some extent through strategic self-presentation – a practice known as *reputation management* in the corporate communication field – but, ultimately, reputation is a construct formed in the minds of others based on their criteria and interpretations.

Well-known reputation studies include the Reputation Institute's RepTrak®[11] and the Harris Poll.[12] The Reputation Institute and the Harris Poll can provide bespoke research, but their most popular reputation studies are based on a standardized omnibus survey questionnaire that rates multiple companies and organizations. For example, for some time, the Reputation Institute promoted a *reputation quotient* (RQ) – that is, a six-dimension scale constructed from 20 attributes on which the company assessed all organizations. The RepTrak® System created in 2005–2006 expanded the initial set of attributes to include evaluation of emotional attachment, but still evaluates organizations based on an underlying set of dimensions and attributes (Reputation Institute, 2016). The Harris Poll, formerly conducted by Harris Interactive and now owned by Nielsen,[13] continues to offer an RQ. This is based on what the Harris Poll calls the 'six dimensions of reputation', which the company lists as: (a) products and services (for example, quality, innovativeness, value for money); (b) emotional appeal; (c) financial performance; (d) vision and leadership; (e) workplace environment; and (f) social responsibility (Harris Poll, 2016).

The Reputation Institute also produces a Public Sector RepTrak® study (for example, for the UK government). This makes only one major change to the corporate RepTrak® model, inserting 'development' in place of 'innovation'. Development in the UK public-sector study is defined as 'develops new ideas and initiatives (including digital communication) that improves the quality of users'/customers' lives' (Nielsen, Stokes & Laden-Anderson, 2015, p. 28).

Recently, Leonard Ponzi, former partner of Reputation Institute founder Charles Fombrun, joined ReputationInc[14] to create the CoreRep+ model for evaluation of corporate reputation, which he says is more flexible and which offers customization. This identifies five core 'drivers' of organization reputation as:

1. being 'open and honest';
2. 'personal connection' between stakeholders and the organization;
3. having 'appreciated products and services';
4. being 'dependable'; and
5. being 'ethical'.

(Ponzi, 2016)

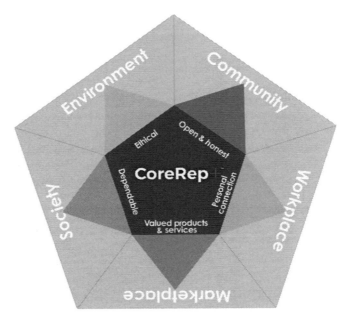

FIGURE 4.2 The CoreRep+ model for identifying and evaluating reputation

Source: Ponzi (2016)

The CoreRep+ model identifies that these five core attributes relate to five domains in which an organization operates – namely, the community, the workplace, the marketplace, society and the environment (see Figure 4.2). In addition, Ponzi (2016) says that other company-specific attributes can be added to the model, such as financial performance, culture, innovation, and so on, to design a customized reputation model to suit various organizations and their operating environment. Nevertheless, the CoreRep+ method remains relatively structured and formulaic.

While providing a broad picture of reputation and comparison of multiple organizations, studies based on predetermined and generic criteria to produce standardized metrics can result in misleading information. This occurs for two reasons, which will be discussed in Chapter 7 in relation to the use of customized surveys for a range of evaluation activities, including evaluation of reputation.

Trust

Draper (2014) argues that reputation is a proxy for *trust*. This is an interesting point because many evaluation programmes focus on reputation, while others specifically measure trust (for example, Edelman, 2015, 2016). Most researchers agree that trust is a key element of a good reputation. It is hard to imagine one without the other.

Trust is an undervalued and under-evaluated factor in corporations, government, non-government organizations (NGOs) and the non-profit sector. Charles Tilley's important study *Trust and Rule* identified trust as a fundamental condition for democracy and warned that 'a significant decline in trust threatens democracy' (2005, p. 133). More recently, Kate Lacey has argued that the loss of trust in politicians and government is a serious concern 'because of the role that trust plays in a representative political system' (2013, p. 187). Trust underpins legitimacy: if people do not trust a system, research indicates that they are likely to defect from it (Dobson, 2014, p. 125; Tilley, 2005). Low voter turnouts in elections signalling citizen disengagement and even the radicalization of youth in a number of democratic countries are, at least in part, an outcome of a breakdown in trust.

Trust between organizations and employees, customers, business partners and the communities in which they operate is also fundamental to business, but lacking, according to senior management consultants. Writing in the 2015 World Economic Forum blog under the title 'Why trust matters in business', Eduardo Leite, chairman of Baker & McKenzie US, said:

> Lack of public trust runs deep and it extends to both individual leaders and institutions . . . lack of trust is something we should all be worried about, because trust matters. For many companies, particularly professional services firms . . . trust is at the centre of the business model.
>
> *(Leite, 2015, paras 3, 5)*

He went on to say that, 'in business, trust is the glue that binds employees to employers, customers to companies – and companies to their suppliers, regulators, government, and partners' (para. 6), and that:

> Most companies appreciate that high trust levels lead to a stronger reputation, sustainable revenues, greater customer advocacy and increased employee retention. It is also likely that companies with higher levels of trust will bounce back from future crises far quicker than others.
>
> *(Leite, 2015, para. 7)*

As with reputation, there are generic studies that produce metrics in relation to trust in various institutions, such as the Edelman Trust Barometer (Edelman, 2016). Universities also conduct studies of trust, such as Harvard University (2015), which found in 2015 that only 14 per cent of young Americans aged 18–29 trust Congress, 20 per cent trust the federal government overall, 12 per cent trust Wall Street and only 11 per cent trust traditional media. Such studies are useful broad indicators of trust in business, government and media, and in other types of organization and institution. But understanding the causes of declining or growing trust in particular contexts requires bespoke research. This can be undertaken using surveys or qualitative methods, such as interviews or focus groups, with key stakeholders and publics, as discussed in Chapters 7 and 8.

Quality of life and well-being

The pursuit of metrics (quantitative data) has led many organizations, including governments, to overlook the fact that people and societies make decisions and measure their lives not only based on statistical and economic criteria. Governments concerned about public health, for example, often measure the outcomes and impact of programmes in terms of reducing health costs (that is, saving money). Similarly, the arts are often evaluated by governments and industry think-tanks in terms of their contribution to the economy. These are narrow and quite myopic perspectives that ignore many aspects of individual and social impact.

While there is a tendency to apply economic values to all aspects of life in neo-liberal capitalist societies, *quality of life* and human *well-being* are important factors. States and organizations whose objectives include a commitment to social equity, quality of life and the well-being of their citizens, employees, members, patients, students and other stakeholders (as all should be) need metrics that can inform evaluation of outcomes and impact related to these objectives. These factors are referred to as *intangibles*, although that term itself illustrates the secondary importance that is placed on important matters such as happiness and mental health in preference to financial earnings, ownership of assets and other so-called tangibles. Many public communication practitioners fail to recognize these factors and even those who do recognize their importance often do not know how to evaluate them.

The World Health Organization (WHO) defines health as 'a state of complete physical, mental, and social well-being and not merely the absence of disease or infirmity' (2014, para. 2). Despite some criticism that concepts such as well-being are 'fuzzy' – especially by those who favour quantitative data and 'scientific' rather than humanistic approaches – quality of life and human well-being are increasingly well defined in the literature (for example, Daniels, 2000; de Chavez, Backett-Milburn, Parry & Platt, 2005; Guttman & Levy, 1982) and recognized in public policy. For example, based on academic and social research, the European Union (EU) identifies what it calls '8 + 1' quality-of-life measures as:

- material living conditions (income, consumption and material conditions);
- productive or main activity (for example, work and creative activities);
- health;
- education;
- leisure and social interactions;
- economic and physical safety;
- governance and basic rights;
- natural and living environment; and
- overall experience of life – for example, including satisfaction and happiness.

(Eurostat, 2015)

To evaluate this broader concept of social impact and human well-being, a number of measurement instruments and tools have been developed, including:

- *quality of life* (QOL) measures (Barcaccia, Esposito, Matarese, Bertolaso, Elvira & De Marinis, 2013);
- *life satisfaction* (Neugarten, Havighurst & Tobin, 1961);
- *subjective well-being* (SWB) scales (Angner, 2011; Diener, 1984, 2006);
- *self-esteem* scales (Logsdon, Gibbons, McCurry & Teri, 2005; Ready & Ott, 2003); and
- the *human development index* (HDI) (Fukuda-Parr, 2003).[15]

One widely used metric for evaluating quality of life, particularly in the health field, is *quality-adjusted life years* (QALY). This involves an arithmetic calculation of life expectancy combined with a measure of the quality of life–years remaining, in which '1' equates to perfect health and '0' equates to death, with severe disability and pain assigned negative values. If an intervention such as a programme to quit smoking were to provide perfect health for one person for five additional years, it would be rated as producing five QALYs. Similarly, an intervention providing a person with an extra five years of life, but with a reduced health status of 0.5, would equal 2.5 QALYs.

The converse is *disability-adjusted life years* (DALY) calculations. This metric is gained by adding the years of life lost (YLL) as a result of premature mortality based on life expectancy data and years lived with disability or disease (YLD). Measuring DALYs is a means of quantifying the burden of illness and disease.

However, even in evaluating quality of life, there is often a focus on converting social outcomes into financial terms. For instance, QALY estimates are often related to cost of treatments and interventions – for example, if an intervention costs $5,000 per person and affords an additional 0.5 QALYs per person on average, then the cost per QALY is $10,000 (5,000/0.5).[16]

Summary

- A range of metrics (that is, numbers, ratings, scores, etc.), including automatically generated metrics, is available from websites and digital media, including social media. These provide raw quantitative data on potential audience reach, levels of exposure and some basic levels of interaction. As such, metrics mostly provide measures of *outputs*.
- Metrics such as audience reach, impressions, visits, page views and click-throughs, and even metrics such as duration of time spent with content, are not indicators of communication outcomes or impact. They tell communicators only that audiences accessed and interacted with the content in some way, and as such are measures of *outputs*. They are second base, in baseball terms, after inputs and activities to produce and distribute information.
- Metrics such as likes, follows, shares and comments go a little further in providing evidence that audiences are responding to content in some way. These

metrics are indicators of *immediate* or *short-term outcomes* – what some evaluation frameworks and models refer to as *outtakes*. These take evaluators to third base.

- Evaluating awareness, attitudes and perceptions are more advanced *short-term outcome* or *outtake* steps along the 'response chain'. However, evaluation of these usually requires social science research (see Chapters 6, 7 and 8).
- Reputation and levels of satisfaction and trust are important *intermediate outcome* metrics and, as with awareness, attitudes and perceptions, evaluation of these usually requires social science research (see Chapters 6, 7 and 8).
- Evaluation of the *outcomes* and *impact* of public communication, including establishment of *causality* (that is, evidence that particular communication activities caused the outcome and impact), almost always requires rigorous social science research, as discussed in the following chapters.

Notes

1 Anonymized data has all names and personal details removed and replaced with coded identifiers such as numbers. This is very important in fields such as health research, which may involve sensitive personal information, but also for research that has offered participants anonymity or de-identification.

2 While *triangulation* literally refers to the triangle and thus three, and applications in navigation involve three coordinates, in social science the term is used to refer to the use of two or methods.

3 *Native advertising* is 'the blending of advertisements with news, entertainment, and other editorial content in digital media' (US FTC, 2013, n.p.) or simply 'advertisements disguised as editorial content' (Hoofnagle & Meleshinsky, 2015, n.p.).

4 A widely used socio economic segmentation is the NRS social scale originally based on the National Readership Survey in the UK, which categorizes people as A, B, C1, C2, D and E, in which ABC1 generally equates to middle class, from senior managerial and professional to skilled workers, C2D equates to working class, from semi-skilled to unskilled, and E represents those dependent on welfare for income (Ipsos MORI, 2009).

5 *Cookies* are small packets of information about Internet users stored in their web browser, which are sent to web servers each time the user logs on, identifying the user and serving up details such as personal preferences, past browsing history, and so on.

6 See www.digitalanalyticsassociation.org.

7 URL stands for *unique resource locator*, which is code embedded into each page and each linked element on web pages.

8 The IAB website is a good source of information for digital advertising and marketing metrics information: see www.iab.com.

9 *Emoji* originated in Japan, the word meaning 'picture character'. An emoji is a small pictogram or ideogram available on websites and smartphones, whereas *emoticons* are typographic representations of facial expressions generated on computer keyboards, such as the well-known 'smiley'.

10 A scalogram, developed by Louis Guttman (1944), presents a series of statements in ascending or descending order of intensity from which participants select that which most closely matches their views or position.

11 See www.reputationinstitute.com.

12 See www.theharrispoll.com.

13 In November 2013, Nielsen Holdings agreed to purchase Harris Interactive for US$116.6 million. The sale was completed in 2014.

14 See www.Reputation-Inc.com.
15 Evaluators wanting to learn more about QOL measures and scales and indices for evaluating well-being can gain further information from specialist journals such as *Social Indicators Research* (www.springer.com/social+sciences/journal/11205), as well as the texts cited.
16 See the case study 'Ex-smokers turn negative messaging to positive results in Europe' in Chapter 10 for an example of QALY calculations.

5

INFORMAL METHODS TO EVALUATE PUBLIC COMMUNICATION

This chapter reviews a range of informal methods that can be used for evaluation of public communication. The line between formal and informal research and evaluation methods is a fine one, and it is often drawn on the basis of philosophical differences and intellectual 'paradigm wars'. Reflecting traditional scientific views, US public relations (PR) evaluation specialist Don Stacks (2011; Stacks & Bowen, 2013) regards case study analysis, content analysis and in-depth interviews as *informal research*, even though leading social science research texts identify these as systematic research methods (for example, Berger, 2000; Frey, Botan & Kreps, 2000; Neuman, 2006). In the *Dictionary of Public Relations Measurement and Research*, Stacks and Bowen say that any 'research methodology that does not allow the researcher to generalize to a larger audience' is 'informal' (2013, p. 15). Yet two of the above methods – case study analysis and content analysis – can be undertaken quantitatively, as well as qualitatively, and therefore are able to produce generalizable findings (Krippendorff & Bock, 2009; Neuendorf, 2002; Stake, 2008; Yin, 2009). This definition of informal research is therefore ambiguous and reflective of a bias towards scientific experiments and large-scale structured surveys, which will be further discussed in the next chapter.

While some define *formal research* as that using scientific methods, most researchers in the social sciences, humanities and arts, and in fields such as marketing, regard this as narrow and unhelpful. A more impartial and explanatory approach is to describe methods as *quantitative* or *qualitative* or *mixed*, and to identify whether methods involve *primary* or *secondary* data and whether or not they are based on *systematic* data collection and analysis procedures.

Here, the term 'informal' is used to denote methods of data collection and analysis that do not involve systematically conducted primary research. Notwithstanding, the methods discussed in this chapter can significantly inform evaluation and, importantly, can do so for very little cost – even, sometimes, no cost. Such methods therefore help to overcome one of the major barriers to evaluation discussed in Chapter 1 and a number of these informal methods are included in the pyramid model of PR research presented in Chapter 3.

The inclusion and discussion of informal methods ahead of social science research methods for evaluation is a matter not of priority, but rather of practicality. This approach recognizes that evaluation needs to be scalable, depending on the budget, time and resources available, the importance of the project, and management expectations and requirements for evaluation. This is not to suggest that evaluation should be scant or avoided if management does not insist on it or when a project is not top priority. However, practicality demands that fewer resources and less time are devoted to evaluating some small and low-priority projects compared with public communication programmes involving major investments and those with greater risk (for example, innovative and first-time programmes). Furthermore, this chapter recognizes that, in some situations, public communication professionals do not have budgets available to them for formal research. Hence this chapter addresses the 'lack of budget' obstacle (excuse) that is often cited, as discussed in Chapter 1. However, while noting the following informal methods and the contribution that they can make, it is important to read this chapter in conjunction with Chapter 6, which overviews social science research methods for evaluation, as well as Chapters 7 and 8, which examine specific research methods.

Secondary data

The starting point for any evaluation is to identify any relevant existing data. Secondary data is simply second-hand data – that is, data that someone else has acquired and used previously. While data can become out of date like any other commodity, many types of existing research are useful in evaluation, particularly in formative evaluation. For example, if several credible studies have found that teenagers reject anti-drug campaigns that feature authority figures, there is little or no need to do primary research or pre-testing of the influence of authority figures in such a role. Such secondary data can serve as formative evaluation and inform strategic planning. Unlike most second-hand products, secondary data are often freely available.

There are many, many sources of secondary data – far more than most communication professionals use or can even imagine. These include both internal and external sources, such as the following:

*   **Literature review.** One of the largest sources of secondary data is published research. Many thousands of research studies on an extensive range of topics are published in academic journals, as well as professional journals, and on the websites of universities, research institutes and centres, foundations, and government organizations ranging from departments, agencies and authorities in various countries to the European Commission and United Nations bodies such as the World Health Organization (WHO). All academic research

begins by conducting a thorough review of existing research literature. This is done for two main reasons: (a) to ensure that new research does not duplicate previous studies (unless this is done intentionally to re-evaluate findings); and (b) to frame future work and thinking within the context of existing knowledge. Existing research provides a 'jumping-off point' for future exploration and activity, and it can often answer many of the questions that communication professionals have at a planning stage. For example, in planning a campaign to increase awareness and understanding of breast screening (mammograms) for early detection of breast cancer and to increase screening rates among *culturally and linguistically diverse* (CALD) communities, also referred to as *black, Asian and minority ethnic* (BAME) groups, a global literature review revealed that mass media campaigns had been found to be mostly unsuccessful. Direct community engagement and collaborative community-based projects had proved more effective, according to a number of published research studies. This secondary data contributed significantly to formative evaluation and provided valuable insights to inform strategy (Macnamara & Camit, 2016). While academics extensively incorporate literature review as the first stage of research projects, it is curious and problematic that communication professionals rarely conduct a thorough literature review before setting out to design a communication programme. This is one key area in which professional communication practice can be improved.

In conducting literature reviews, researchers give preference to studies published in academic journals because these have been subjected to independent *expert peer review*, a process designed to ensure that only well-conducted research with reliable findings is published. While academics are often irked by critical reviews, they are an important part of research quality assurance. In addition, many research institutes and centres have earned a reputation for publishing quality research, which is often available free online. Examples include the Pew Research Center, a non-partisan, non-profit 'fact tank' headquartered in Washington, DC, and the Reuters Institute for the Study of Journalism, a research centre and 'think-tank' based at Oxford University in the UK. Also, major government and some non-government organizations (NGOs) such as WHO publish authoritative research-based reports that are rich sources of data that can inform public communication.

- **Other people's (OP) research.** Within organizations, there are frequently research studies conducted by marketing, human resources (HR), policy development and other departments and divisions that can be informative for public communication – what can be referred to colloquially as *other people's* (OP) research. Often, research is not shared across an organization and important information is ignored, or research is duplicated, as noted in the previous chapter. In conducting the Organizational Listening Project Stage II within UK government departments and agencies (Macnamara, 2017), this author found hundreds of research studies, records of public consultations and minutes of stakeholder meetings, and hundreds of thousands of items of correspondence, in various parts of government, but most were not accessed by anyone other than those who dealt with that particular function. There are both formal and informal ways of gaining access to information that is available within a large organization. Formal methods include establishing a *knowledge management* (KM) system in which pertinent information and research are recorded and indexed in a central place, so that they are available to others. Informal methods include networking and building relationships with other relevant departments, divisions and units, so that information can be shared. As one UK government communication strategist said in an interview: 'Sometimes you have just got to go and ask colleagues in other departments and divisions if they have anything relevant to what you're doing' (Anon., personal communication, August 2, 2016).

• **Data, data, everywhere.** As many reports and professional journal articles have noted, most large organizations in the private and public sectors are accumulating vast amounts of data, referred to as *big data*. This includes customer profiles and records, statistical data on sales by area and period, feedback through various mechanisms such as customer relations call centres, and so on. Today, most of this is in searchable digital form. But what do organizations do with it? A large amount of such data is poorly used or not used at all. Much of it sits on hard disks behind firewalls and is inaccessible. Alternatively, it exists in raw form that is unintelligible and meaningless without insightful analysis. To parody Samuel Taylor Coleridge's *Rime of the Ancient Mariner*, there is often 'data, data everywhere, but not a drop of information to use'. Big data will be discussed in more detail in Chapter 7, because detailed statistical or textual analysis is usually required to make sense of large data sets and to produce actionable insights.

Even before tackling complex sets of 'big data', communication practitioners should make literature review an essential first step in formative evaluation to gain access to useful external information and also to build networks to gain access to other data that is available inside their organization. In addition to human networking to share information, the growing mountain of data that is available indicates that data retrieval and analysis skills for both structured and unstructured data are fast becoming key competencies for public communication professionals. This will be further illustrated in the following sections.

Database records

While databases could be regarded as a site of secondary data and therefore as part of the previous section, they are singled out for special mention because they contain large sets of structured data that are available for analysis. Databases have inbuilt field creation, query and analysis tools for categorizing, coding, tagging and retrieving particular types of data, as well as export functions for producing customized reports drawn from the data. Databases containing useful statistical and textual information that can be used as part of evaluation exist publicly, as well as internally within organizations.

Examples of external databases include public records such as US Data and Statistics[1] and the Australian Bureau of Statistics,[2] which can provide extensive demographic information, as well as those of various government departments and agencies, the records of libraries and media databases. While many databases are proprietary, requiring special passwords and applications to access information, and much information is securely protected for privacy reasons, a vast amount of information is publicly available. Public communication professionals regularly draw on statistics such as media audience and circulation figures from media databases. But they can look further afield to find rich insights that inform evaluation. For example, to evaluate the outcome of the previously mentioned programme to increase the rates of mammograms among particular groups of women, evaluators accessed statistics from a Cancer Institute database, filtered by year, area and type of treatment, which enabled comparison of screening rates before and after the programme. This example is outlined in detail as an award-winning case study in Chapter 10.

Internal databases inside organizations typically include customer relations management (CRM) systems, membership records and complaints systems. These can be data-mined to identify increases or decreases in complaints, the primary reasons for complaints or increases in membership, the occupations and age of members, the sales levels of products and services, the profile of customers, and so on. Databases can also hold records of attendance at events, employee turnover rates and many other types of information that can provide baseline data as part of formative evaluation and the basis for comparison as part of summative evaluation.

By gaining familiarity with databases and the related processes of data collection, categorizing, data-mining and data analysis, public communication professionals can make suggestions to increase the capability of databases for evaluating effectiveness and performance. For example, simply adding a question to the script used by telephone sales staff that asks callers where they heard about a product or service can help to establish causality – one of the challenges in evaluation discussed in Chapter 2. The same information also can be captured in online inquiries. Also, additional data fields might be useful in databases to record information that can aid evaluation, such as capturing details on past behaviours and product preferences for future comparison.

Journalists are discovering that digitalization and the growth of databases offer new research and investigation opportunities referred to as *data journalism* or *computational journalism*. This involves the use of database search and data-mining techniques to access information, and sophisticated data analysis tools to identify patterns, trends and key issues (Flew, Spurgeon, Daniel & Swift, 2012). A 2012 report produced by the Tow Centre for Digital Journalism at Columbia University in New York argued that, in addition to having 'soft skills', such as the abilities to maintain networks and relationships with sources and to understand audiences, journalists in the twenty-first century need 'hard skills', including data literacy and even an ability to write computer code, as well as to tell stories using a range of technologies (Anderson, Bell & Shirky, 2012, pp. 36–39). In addition to gaining advanced computing skills, Philip Meyer (2002) and others explain that data or computational journalism utilizes social science research methods, including quantitative data collection, in the form of polling, surveying, archival records analysis, statistical analysis and text analysis, to collect and make sense of information.

Communication practitioners working in corporate, government, political and organizational communication, and specialist fields such as advertising, digital marketing, health promotion, and so on, equally need skills in database searching, retrieval and analysis. This growing imperative is something that educators need to note and address by incorporating such knowledge into the curricula of advertising, PR, and corporate, government, political and organizational communication courses. Also, professional industry bodies should further address such topics within their professional development programmes.

Readability tests

Some other informal evaluation methods are very simple and easy to implement. A basic, but useful, *ex ante* evaluation that can be applied to any form of writing is a *readability test*. A number of such tests are available and easily administered. For example, Robert Gunning, an American business teacher, distilled a word-length and sentence-length test into a formula for measuring readability, which became known as Gunning's *Fog Index*. The Fog Index calculated corresponds to the number of years of formal education required to understand the text. A Fog Index of 12 means that readers must have finished high school in most countries if they are to understand the text easily. A Fox Index of 15 indicates that only university graduates will be able to comprehend the writing easily and 20 or above means that there is unlikely to be an audience other than among doctorate-level graduates. The following demonstrates how Gunning's Fog Index is calculated (Ashe, 1972, p. 56).

Step One	Take a sample of around 100 words from the writing to be tested (complete sentences). Count the exact number of words.
Step Two	Divide the number of words by the number of sentences in the sample to identify the average sentence length.
Step Three	Count the number of words of three or more syllables (excepting compound words made up of two simple words such as 'book-keeper' and words that become three syllables or more after adding a suffix such as 'ed' or 'ing').
Step Four	Add the average sentence length and the number of long words together.
Step Five	Multiply the result by 0.4 to calculate the Fog Index.

Other commonly used methods for measuring readability include the *Flesch Reading Ease Test* developed by Rudolf Flesch and the *Dale–Chall Readability*

Formula developed by Edgar Dale and Jeanne Chall, which has been updated to the *New Dale–Chall Formula.* A number of these can be calculated online[3] or in writing textbooks. While basic, these are examples of simple tests that can be implemented to evaluate whether written communication is likely to be effective before money is spent on production and distribution.

Advisory and consultative groups

A very simple informal method of collecting qualitative feedback and insights from audiences is through *advisory boards* and *consultative groups.* These may be already existing, or they can be established specifically for the purpose of soliciting information and advice in relation to the views, needs, interests and concerns of particular groups. Too often, organizations establish such groups and then set about talking to them with corporate presentations and PowerPoint decks. Evaluation requires *listening*, as will be noted a number of times throughout this analysis. If trust is established, however, advisory boards and consultative groups can be very effective and cost-efficient ways of collecting information and insights, both pre- and post-programmes of various kinds.

Engagement with advisory and consultative groups can be made somewhat systematic by recording minutes of meetings, as well as documenting discussions in reports. This ensures that important feedback, requests, suggestions and proposals are not forgotten, and the records can then be analysed periodically using content or textual analysis techniques to ensure that key points and issues are captured and noted.

Feedback

Feedback also can be collected in a number of other ways. These include simple feedback forms, online feedback boxes, and simply asking key stakeholders and publics for feedback. Sometimes, research is just that: going out and asking people questions. In the case of informal evaluation, this will not involve statistically representative samples or require sophisticated data analysis, and hence cannot be treated as rigorous research or statistically reliable data. But feedback provides indications. If a lot of employees are saying that they do not understand the organization's vision and approach, this is a sign that there is a communication problem.

Many organizations ask for feedback, and it is important, in such cases, that the organization acts on the feedback and, ideally, reports back to those who went to the trouble of providing it. An example of gathering feedback that most readers will have encountered is airline passenger feedback forms. Most airlines distribute feedback forms randomly or systematically on flights and many passengers willingly provide information – but have you ever heard back from an airline, even when you have provided your name and email address? Furthermore, have you ever read or heard about what they learned and what changes were made as a result of feedback? This frequent flyer does not expect a personal response – but an article in the glossy inflight magazines that are distributed in seat pockets could easily thank passengers who provided feedback and report what has been done based on that feedback. Nonetheless, a search of more than a dozen airline inflight magazines over a 12-month period found that none reported passenger feedback or responses to passenger feedback.

The Organizational Listening Project[4] also found that a majority of organizations do not respond to feedback provided on their websites and that 25 per cent did not respond to direct messages requesting information (Macnamara, 2016a). Again, this makes the point that evaluation is more than collecting information. It also requires listening to what is received, which includes reporting back and addressing issues raised in some appropriate way.

Media monitoring

The most widely used method for data collection in the PR industry is *media monitoring*. Note that this is described as 'data collection' rather than evaluation. This is because monitoring what appears in media such as newspapers, magazines, radio, television or social media collects content that requires analysis of some kind before it affords any form of evaluation. At its most basic, media monitoring involves *counts* of articles and mentions (for example, of brands, products, services or issues). However, the volume of media coverage does not necessarily indicate communication success, because much of the coverage may be negative or it could fail to communicate key messages. An evaluation needs to be made of the effectiveness of the media coverage.

Many chief executive officers (CEOs) and other senior executives in business and government, as well as politicians, are obsessed with appearing in the media. Politicians, in particular, often associate media headlines and quotes with impact on audiences – a fundamental misunderstanding of communication as discussed in Chapters 1–3. This delusion derives from modernist beliefs in the power of mass communication to influence audiences conceived as passive receivers of information and persuasion. Along with growing awareness of the *agency* of audiences to interpret and even reject information, *audience fragmentation* in an era of declining traditional media consumption and growing use of myriad forms of social media challenges such notions (Anderson, 2006; Jenkins, 2006).

Nevertheless, media monitoring is a necessary activity for tracking public communication in many organizations. It is often through an article and comment in traditional or social media that an organization becomes aware of an issue or statements by others to which it needs to respond. Monitoring media content therefore provides early warning and intelligence. However, analysis of media content that takes into account audience reach and the positioning, size, messages and sentiment expressed is required to gain an understanding of what influence and impact the content might have and what response, if any, is required. Media content analysis is a formal research method discussed in Chapter 8.

Tracking online comments and reviews

A similar activity to media monitoring – and sometimes included in the expanding rubric of media monitoring – is *tracking online comments and reviews*. This is often included in social media monitoring, which is increasingly common internally in organizations or provided through service providers. Online comments can be posted on an organization's own blogs and social media sites (for example, Facebook pages). In addition, comments about an organization, its products or services, or issues relevant to an organization are frequently posted in social media users' own sites (for example, on Twitter, Facebook, YouTube, etc.).

All organizations today need to be aware of what is being said about them and their products, services, policies and relevant issues online. This may constitute positive feedback and advocacy or it may be criticism. If online comments related to an organization are ignored, this indicates to the source, and to that person's followers and friends, that the organization is not listening or does not care. When this occurs, online criticism can escalate. Thus social media monitoring is essential for organizations operating in the public sphere today.

Fortunately, a range of software applications are available that can monitor the Internet using key words. These include products such as Brandwatch, Tableau, Coosto, Social Mention and Traackr, among many others. Also, a number of service providers are available that provide services ranging from basic monitoring and alert systems to full quantitative and qualitative analysis. Examples include Radian6 (now owned by Salesforce), Gorkana[5] and Kantar Media (incorporating Precise) in the UK, Cision, Visible Technologies, Cymfony and Buzzlogic in the US, and companies that operate across multiple markets, such as CARMA and Meltwater. This list is far from complete and it is not an endorsement for any of the products or services mentioned as examples. Potential users should check out potential suppliers themselves, because this field is characterized by rapid change.

A particular form of online comment of concern to many organizations is reviews. Many industry sectors have trade media that publish reviews of products and services. The information technology (IT) and automotive industries are examples. Computers, smartphones, cars and sports utility vehicles (SUVs) are routinely reviewed. While such reviews relate predominantly to product performance rather than communication, the capacity of reviews to influence others is a concern for public communication professionals. Reviews therefore need to be monitored, and influential reviewers need to be provided with information and sometimes some professional PR support, which might include exclusive interviews, background briefings and extended product experiences. Pre- and post-programme analysis can then be used to evaluate the effectiveness of these activities.

Beyond professional reviews, the Internet and social media in particular have expanded reviews into the public domain. Today, everyone can be a reviewer. Reviews by non-professionals are not to be dismissed, because a number of studies show that peers are among the most trusted sources of information (for example, Edelman, 2015). What other users of products and services say about them can be very influential. TripAdviser is a well-known example of an online review site featuring customer reviews of travel destinations and service providers such as hotels, restaurants and transportation services. A bad review on TripAdviser can be very damaging to a business; gaining an increasing number of positive reviews can be beneficial. Reviews should consequently be reported in evaluation and even given special consideration.

How an organization responds to reviews is part of its public communication, and affects audience perceptions and behaviour. For example, a 'thank you' to negative, as well as positive, reviewers for their feedback and a promise to try to address the concerns of critical reviews can result in a favourable reaction and word of mouth (some say 'word of mouse' for online discussion). Evaluation can track reviews over time to identify trends such as the proportion of positive and negative reviews, the issues raised and the tone of reviews following response by the organization, which can inform strategy and provide data on communication effectiveness.

As well as discussing past experiences, many comments and reviews indicate future *intentions*, such as 'I will definitely go back' or, conversely, 'I will never go there again'. Furthermore, positive reviews can constitute or contain *advocacy* for a brand, product, service, event, policy or mode of behaviour. Thus even informal methods can evaluate *outtakes* and *short-term outcomes* in some cases.

Response mechanisms

Audience responses, such as inquiries and correspondence (for example, letters and emails), can be tracked and analysed to gain indications of stakeholders' and public reactions to events, campaigns, policy announcements and other activities, as well as their interests and concerns. These are often tracked and processed by specialist units or divisions within organizations, such as customer relations or correspondence units in government. Public communication professionals should establish working relationships with such functions to gain access to data that can contribute to evaluation.

In addition to spontaneous response, audience reactions can be stimulated through a number of *response mechanisms*, such as offering free hotline numbers, online inquiry and comment links, and email addresses for further information. Furthermore, response can be encouraged by offering incentives. Common examples include offering free copies of reports, booklets and even e-books that are appealing to a target audience in return for registering or participating in some activity. Other incentives to gain response include the opportunity to win prizes (for example, entering all inquiries into a draw).

Tracking and linking responses to particular activities to establish causality can be enhanced by using activity-exclusive numbers, links and email addresses rather than generic contact points. For instance, a free report can be made available via a web link that is not used elsewhere. Similarly, a series of different free hotlines can be used in advertising, publicity and online communication. These can all direct inquiries to the same information, but IT systems can identify and record the address to which inquiries are directed, thus enabling identification of the source of information that prompted the inquiry.

Response mechanisms are a simple, but useful, method for collecting information that demonstrates *reception* of information (an output metric), *awareness* (a basic outtake) and *interest* (an outtake further along the 'response chain' that is closely linked to *intention* and which is a precursor to action).

Diaries

Diaries are a much-overlooked method of gaining information ranging from media consumption patterns to in-depth qualitative information about participants' reactions to programmes and their perceptions of relationships. For example, communication researchers can ask a sample of their target audience to record the amount of time they devote to consuming media and the various types of media they encounter and use over a week or more (including press, radio, television and cinema advertising,[6] entertainment, and news content, outdoor advertising, websites and social media, and so on). Such metrics can be very useful formative evaluation on which to base public communication. Researchers tracking the reactions of participants in health programmes, ranging from diets to quit smoking, and attendance at detox facilities often ask those involved to maintain a diary recording their activities and feelings as they progress through the programme. This provides first-hand information on the reactions of participants and the effectiveness of such programmes, although more formal and systematic research is usually required to identify longer-term behavioural outcomes.

Diaries have the benefit of capturing experiences, perceptions and reactions over a period of time, and in a more deliberative and reflective way than those gained from surveys and interviews in which participants provide a top-of-mind response at a particular point in time. However, they do create more work for the participants and for the evaluator, given that the information is provided as text and so requires textual analysis.

Informal interviews and discussion groups

In addition to gathering feedback in day-to-day discussions with stakeholders and publics, as discussed previously in this chapter, there are often opportunities to conduct *informal interviews* or *discussion groups* that can serve as informal focus groups. For example, some questions can be included in meetings with key representatives of stakeholders or audiences to gain insights into their perceptions or their satisfaction with a relationship. These can be as simple as 'On a scale of 0 to 10, how would you rate the support you receive from our organization?'

Meetings with groups of people from a particular sector, location or audience category can sometimes be used to conduct informal formative and/or summative evaluation. Clearly, this must be done with the agreement of the organizer and chair, and with empathy for those attending. Hijacking a group meeting for one's own agenda is likely to be counterproductive and is not recommended, but a request to include a short discussion to gain the group's feedback on an issue is often looked upon favourably. Groups sometimes relish an opportunity to state their views on a matter, particularly if they feel it might influence management decisions. In other cases, groups are often happy to help if it might lead to improved communication. As an example, many years ago, when I found myself head of communication for a national farmers' organization with no budget for research, I learned that groups of farmers met every month all over the country to discuss issues and forward recommendations to the state and national bodies. To gain insights to inform a communication plan, I asked if I could attend a selection of these meetings in various locations and have 15 minutes of the agenda to discuss communication. I received a number of invitations and used these to canvass farmers' views on their preferred channels and the issues of most interest to them, and to test various ideas and proposals. The following year, I repeated the exercise, this time asking for feedback on the communication activities conducted, as well as their suggestions for improvements, thus gaining both formative and summative evaluation. The minute takers at the meetings helpfully recorded comments, which provided summaries of this informal research.

Informal interviews and discussion groups do not produce statistically representative, or even comprehensive, findings in a particular context, because they do not involve samples selected according to quantitative or qualitative research methodology. However, they can be done for little or no cost other than some investment of time – another example of how budget is not a barrier to evaluation – and they provide good indications to inform strategy and assess results.

Summary

- There are a number of informal methods of evaluation that are low-cost or even no cost – thus proving that lack of budget is not a barrier to some level of evaluation.
- These include secondary data (the reuse of existing data) gained from literature reviews and database records, feedback, advice from advisory and consultative groups, media monitoring, tracking online comments and reviews, response mechanisms, diaries, and informal interviews and discussion groups. Also, readability tests can be conducted on draft content to gain indications of likely understanding and resonance with audiences.
- While informal methods can provide some useful insights and data for evaluation, with the exception of database records, they are not statistically reliable or representative of the groups and contexts involved. Thus, in most cases, formal research methods are required for evaluation, as discussed in the following chapters.

Notes

1 See www.usa.gov/statistics.
2 See www.abs.gov.au.
3 At sites such as https://readability-score.com or www.readabilityformulas.com.
4 A two-year, three-country qualitative study of how, and how well, corporate, government, non-government and non-profit organizations listen to their stakeholders and publics (Macnamara, 2014a, 2015a, 2015b, 2016a, 2016b).
5 Gorkana in the UK became incorporated under the Cision brand in 2017.
6 Diaries were widely used for estimating television and radio audiences and ratings for many years, but have been replaced in most cases by meters.

6

RESEARCH APPROACHES AND KEY PROCEDURES

When it comes to doing research, there is no one proper approach or method; rather, there are two broad approaches, several methodologies and many methods. It is not simply a matter of identifying which one is 'best'. That is the equivalent of asking 'what is the best instrument for a surgeon or dentist to use?', or 'what is the best tool for a carpenter to apply in building a house?' Different instruments and tools do different jobs. Research methods textbooks describe these in detail, but a brief explanation of the main approaches (often referred to as research *paradigms*), *methodologies* and some of the key procedures that need to be followed are provided in this chapter as a framework for understanding and using research to evaluate public communication.

Scholars with a sound knowledge of quantitative and qualitative research methodology and practitioners trained in social science research will be familiar with the contents of this chapter. But numerous studies show that many public communication practitioners, and some academics working within particular disciplinary fields, lack knowledge and skills in the range of research methods available for evaluation of communication, as noted in Chapter 1. Also, even among practising researchers, there is often confusion and misunderstanding in relation to quantitative and qualitative research and the differing procedures that apply for each, as well as the differing uses and benefits of each. Therefore, this chapter examines the philosophical basis of the main research methods that are used to facilitate informed choices and identify the key procedures that ensure validity, reliability and trustworthiness in research.

The 'scientific method'

In contemporary developed societies, much research is conducted in accordance with the *scientific method*. This approach is the standard for research in the natural sciences, such as physics and chemistry, and related fields of practice, such as medicine, aviation and engineering, for good reasons. However, it is also applied to social research and it is important to understand its affordances, as well as its limitations, in this realm of knowledge construction. Some background helps in understanding the strengths and weaknesses of the scientific method.

After a long period of human history during which tradition, personal experience, religious beliefs, spiritualism, and even myths and superstition were primary sources of knowledge (Frey, Botan & Kreps, 2000), a number of major discoveries and breakthroughs in thinking were made over several centuries. This period of change is commonly described as beginning with the *Renaissance* (approximately 1300–1600 CE) and gathered momentum during the so-called *Enlightenment* (approximately 1600–1800 CE). While the Renaissance and the 'Age of Enlightenment' included an expansion of the arts and humanist thinking, such as the work of Leonardo da Vinci (1452–1519) and Michelangelo (1475–1564), and the philosophies of René Descartes (1596–1650), this period is particularly characterized by discoveries and inventions that formed the basis of modern science. These included, for example, those of da Vinci, Copernicus (1473–1543), Galileo Galilei (1564–1642), Francis Bacon (1561–1626), Christiaan Huygens (1629–1695), Isaac Newton (1643–1727), and polymath and founder of the 'American enlightenment' Benjamin Franklin (1706–1790).[1]

The terms 'renaissance' and 'enlightenment' are problematic, however, in the sense that the naming of epochs and eras oversimplifies and omits much of what happened in a period. Also, they are Eurocentric, ignoring Arab, Chinese and other knowledge that was developed at the same time or which even pre-dated Western 'discoveries'.[2] However, these overviews serve to draw attention to the emergence of knowledge based on *systematic* collection and analysis of *empirical* evidence and *rational* reasoning – the underlying principles of *science* (Kerlinger & Lee, 2000; Koyré & Cohen, 1972).

The ongoing expansion of science resulting from discoveries such as those of Charles Darwin (1809–1882) and Albert Einstein (1879–1955), together with inventions such as those of James Watt (1736–1819), Samuel Morse (1791–1872), Alexander Graham Bell (1847–1922), Thomas Edison (1847–1931), Guglielmo Marconi (1874–1937) and many others, paved the way for the Industrial Revolution and *modernism*.

Because it is believed to be *objective* and based on 'hard' evidence, the scientific method has become a dominant method of research and knowledge construction in developed modernist societies. As Jacquie L'Etang notes in her critical analysis of public relations (PR) and public communication, Western modernist societies are 'heavily influenced by rationalism and science' (L'Etang, 2008, p. 13). This is understandable and justified to a large extent, given the increased reliability of scientific research methods compared with some traditional methods of understanding and explaining the world.

Social science

As well as applying the scientific method to develop knowledge in the natural and physical sciences, such as biology, physics, chemistry and astronomy, in the nineteenth century scholars began to apply the scientific method to expanding knowledge of human society and the workings of the human mind, leading to the development of *social science*. Major social sciences include psychology, sociology, political science and early approaches to anthropology. Noteworthy examples of early social scientists include Émile Durkheim (1858–1917) and Sigmund Freud (1856–1939). Durkheim founded sociology as 'the science of institutions', which he defined as established belief systems and modes of behaviour in society, and he developed structuralist and functionalist theories of society based on what he described as 'social facts' (1982, pp. 34–47). Durkheim and other structuralist sociologists believed that human society can be understood in scientific terms. Freud, as is well known, is regarded as the father of psychoanalysis, a specialist application of psychology for therapeutic purposes. He (Freud, 1973) applied a clinical approach to interpreting human behaviour and psychoses, arguing that the unconscious could be understood and systematically interpreted through analysis of dreams and hypnotherapy, and that repressed emotions and experiences could be made conscious to cure various mental conditions. Freud's work led many to believe that human behaviour could be accurately predicted and controlled using scientific methods – a belief that lingers in behaviourist branches of psychology today.

It would be unfair to bracket all social science with early structuralist and rationalist approaches, such as those of Freud, because there have been many movements and 'turns' in sociology, psychology, political science and anthropology over the past century. Nor is this brief introduction to the philosophical paradigms that inform research methods intended to deny or diminish the substantial merit in the work of those authors. The purpose here is to provide a backdrop for understanding the various research methods in use today, why they take the approach they do and how they are used.

Positivist and post-positivist paradigms

Wide application of the scientific method led to a *positivist paradigm* of research and, to some extent, the *post-positivist paradigm*. While the term 'paradigm' is overused, it is useful to denote the broad body of underlying beliefs and assumptions that inform a field. Even before we do research, we arrive at the point of departure with beliefs and assumptions – what some refer to as our *worldview*. These are commonly grouped into *ontological* assumptions (beliefs about the nature of reality), *epistemological* assumptions (beliefs about how knowledge is best constructed, from the Greek term *episteme* meaning theoretical knowledge or science) and *axiological* assumptions (beliefs and understanding about values). These in turn lead to *methodological* assumptions and preferences. Many researchers remain unaware of, or skip over considering, these assumptions and jump straight into methodology, which contributes to the confusion that often surrounds various research methods.

The positivist paradigm of research based on the scientific method and the metanarratives of science – referred to as the *behaviourist* tradition in psychology, because it believes human behaviour can be scientifically understood, predicted and controlled – involves the following assumptions:

- **Ontology.** There is a singular reality (*realist*), one truth (*absolutist*) in each situation, and the discovered 'truth' and facts can be applied generally (*universalist*).
- **Epistemology.** Researchers are *independent* (that is, not influenced by the research participants or environment), *objective* and rational (*rationalist*).
- **Axiology.** Researchers are value-free and unbiased.

(Creswell, 2009; Frey et al., 2000)

These assumptions among some scientific researchers are contested by others, as will be shown. Such assumptions and beliefs lead to a confident, positive belief in the ability of researchers to discover reality and truth, based on rational thought and analysis of empirical data, collected through mainly *quantitative* methodology using research methods such as scientific experiments and statistical analysis. French philosopher Auguste Comte (1798–1857) was a leader in a movement to blend rationalism and empiricism in a new doctrine called *positivism* (Bhattacherjee, 2012, p. 8).

It must be acknowledged, however, that a number of scholars warn that few, if any, scientists in the natural or social sciences today ascribe to full-blown positivism in the sense of believing that the scientific method and empirical evidence are the only valid and reliable ways of understanding reality and human existence. Professor of psychology Philip Bell says that 'there are not many vulgar "science-as-facts" apologists still standing' (2010, p. 25). Bell argues that social scientists are 'not naive positivists' and have long recognized that 'mental phenomena could not be understood nor [*sic*] explained only as physico-chemical phenomena' (2010, p. 8).

The humanistic approach

In the twentieth century, some scholars – particularly those who ascribed to *postmodernism* – have critiqued the scientific method and early social sciences, arguing that their generalized laws, structuralist theories and empirical data do not fully explain the human condition and human society. For example, in the mid-twentieth century, British philosopher Karl Popper suggested that much human knowledge is not based on unchallengeable, rock-solid foundations, but rather on a set of tentative conjectures that can never be proved conclusively (Bhattacherjee, 2012, p. 8). Postmodernists argue that there are other useful and relevant ways of exploring and creating knowledge about human society that are *humanistic* and informed by *poststructuralism*.

In some contemporary discussions, all approaches that deviate from the positivist paradigm are described as *post-positivist*. However, this broad categorization does not lead to clarity, because many of the broad-minded scientists and social scientists to whom Bell (2010) refers describe their work as post-positivist (Denzin & Lincoln, 2013). Anol Bhattacherjee (2012) notes that post-positivism retains the positivist notion of objective truth and emphasis on the scientific method (p. 8). While some use the term *anti-positivists* for those who question and deviate from the tenets of positivism (particularly *critical* researchers), a more specific description of alternative non-scientific approaches is preferred by most researchers (for example, Creswell, 2009; Denzin & Lincoln, 2013; Frey et al., 2000; Guba & Lincoln, 2005; Neuman, 2006).

There is no single agreed name for approaches to research that take an alternative route to the scientific method, but they are commonly described as the *constructivist paradigm* (Denzin & Lincoln, 2013), the *interpretivist paradigm* (Neuman, 2006) or the *naturalistic paradigm* (Creswell, 2009; Frey et al., 2000). The *constructivist* description is designed to highlight the role and influence of social constructionism and constructivism[3] in creating human reality and meaning-making, while the *interpretivist* label emphasizes that all reality is, in fact, an interpretation. The so-called reality of research participants is their interpretation of their world and condition. Also, the findings of research involve interpretation, not simply 'crunching' numbers. The term *naturalistic* is often misunderstood as denoting a 'natural' unstructured way of doing research, which is misleading. In fact, this term emphasizes exploration of the views and perceptions of participants in their 'natural setting', based on the belief that artificial settings, such as laboratories or even focus group rooms with one-way mirrors, create unnatural responses.

The interpretivist, constructivist or naturalistic paradigm

In contrast with the positive paradigm, the variously named interpretivist, constructivist or naturalistic paradigm or approach is guided by the following assumptions:

*   **Ontology.** Much of what we call 'reality' is socially constructed. There are multiple realities and truths (that is, it takes a *relativist* position in which truth is relative to one's context, culture, etc.), and findings and beliefs cannot be generalized or univeralized to all humans, or even whole categories of people. Findings are context-specific.
*   **Epistemology.** Researchers are *subjective* and *interdependent*, working with research participants and possibly influencing them, just as they are influencing the researcher.
*   **Axiology.** Researchers are value-laden and biased, which they need to recognize and work carefully to minimize, or at least acknowledge, in conducting research.

These assumptions (or beliefs, if you prefer) lead to *qualitative* methodology and research methods such as in-depth interviews, focus groups, ethnography, case studies, action research, and so on, which will be discussed in Chapter 8. As the paradigmatic names suggest, the emphasis in this approach is on exploring the social constructions and contexts in which people live and work, and the *affective*, as well as rational, dimensions of their life worlds, plus interpreting what people say, rather than simply counting scores and ratings. As Arthur Asa Berger says: 'Facts don't speak for themselves; they have to be put into context and their significance explained' (2000, p. 9).

Quantitative vs qualitative

Young researchers and practitioners still ask, 'which is better, quantitative or qualitative research?' Like so many questions on complex issues, the answer is 'it depends'. The following discussion will put some meat on the bones of the high-level review of paradigms and approaches provided so far, and challenge some views commonly held about research.

Not everything that counts can be counted

The subtitle of a posthumously published book containing the blog posts of Don Bartholomew,[4] respected US advocate of evaluation for PR and corporate communication, states: 'It doesn't count unless you can count it' (Bartholomew, 2016). Whether Don actually wrote this line is debatable. Nevertheless, splashing it across the cover of a book that will no doubt be read by many communication evaluators means that it warrants challenge.

The statement is positioned as contradictory to that attributed to Albert Einstein, but more likely written by William Cameron (1963), that says: 'Not everything that counts can be counted and not everything that can be counted counts.' As noted in Chapter 4, metrics are important elements in evaluation, but they are incorrectly seen as the 'be-all and end-all' of evidence required for evaluation. The subtitle of Bartholomew's book is symptomatic of an obsession with numbers and quantitative methods that is particularly prominent in the US, and which leads to reductionism and a lack of deep understanding of many issues related to human communication.

At the risk of boring readers with a longish and somewhat whimsically written story, the following is the text of a paper I wrote for Master's degree students who were struggling to grasp the difference between quantitative and qualitative research methods, which I titled 'The tribal conflicts of science and humanities and the villages of Quant and Qual'. The paper, which spells out in simple terms the origins, focus, benefits and limitations of quantitative and qualitative research methods, goes like this:

> Once upon a time, all across the land people believed in spirits and superstition. This was much more pervasive than the occasional good luck charm or ghost story. Witchcraft was practised, invoking Black Magic to try to resolve problems. It was common to cut off the heads of goats and other animals in the belief that such sacrifices would bring favourable seasons and good crops, or good luck generally. Others believed fervently in religion, putting their faith in one or more Gods. Devotees of religion and spiritualism believed that whatever happened was the 'will of God' able to be influenced only by prayer and sacrifices.
>
> But those beliefs came under challenge from new ways of thinking that emerged among some tribes. Several centuries ago some areas experienced what was later referred to as the Enlightenment. This was a period in which many discoveries were made that changed how people understood their

world and thought about things. While religion remained important to many, and everyday ways of knowing such as tradition and custom continued to be respected and hold some sway, a new type of knowledge emerged.

One legendary example was a young radical called Copernicus who used an apparatus called a telescope to make observations of the sky (previously referred to as the heavens) that led him to conclude that the Earth was not the centre of the universe. Instead of this long-held geocentric (not to mention egocentric) view, he described a heliocentric solar system in which the Earth revolved around the sun, which was a star in space – not a powerful God as ancient Egyptians, Greeks and others believed. The traditionalists were not pleased by this challenge to their teachings and banished Copernicus, but followers such as Galileo Galilei used mathematical calculations to prove he was right.

Others who contributed to the Enlightenment included Ibn al-Haytham (also known as Alhazen) whose *Book of Optics* reported experiments combined with observations and rational argument to prove that light is emitted from objects rather than from humans' eyes, as was previously believed.

Over the decades and centuries, other progressives who called themselves scientists challenged other aspects of human knowledge. Isaac Newton, who is widely known for 'discovering' gravity, expounded on many aspects of the natural world in his landmark treatise *Philosophiæ Naturalis Principia Mathematica*. The title illustrates the central focus of this new band of thinkers. Rather than conceiving philosophy in spiritual and religious terms, attention turned to Nature and understanding Nature through mathematical principles and logical rational reasoning, referred to as the 'Scientific Method'.

Then there was Albert Einstein, perhaps the most famous scientist of all, whose mathematical equations changed human understanding of the material mass of objects and even time itself. Charles Darwin turned attention to humans themselves and theorized that, rather than being created by God, humans evolved like the animals and plant species on the planet and that there are natural laws governing human physical evolution and development.

Soon, inspired by Darwin and others (and perhaps jealous of their recognition and fame), those focussed on understanding human behaviour and how societies function turned their attention to the increasingly popular methods of science, calling themselves *social scientists*. Along with the empiricism and scientific scepticism of David Hume, the economic principles of Adam Smith, the scientific inventions of Benjamin Franklin, and the structuralist concepts and rules of human society advanced by Émile Durkheim, Sigmund Freud claimed that even the workings of the human mind could be understood scientifically.

With this new knowledge, the Science tribe expanded and became influential, with its members becoming known as 'experts'. The tribe's chieftains led many neighbouring tribes into the Industrial Revolution and a new era called Modernism. Soon the technologically-advanced Science tribe embarked on global colonization and eventually the 'Space Race' in which humans developed technologies to leave their planet and explore celestial bodies at which they once peered in awe.

Across the valley, the Humanities tribe lived on with very different views. It was not that they rejected the knowledge of the Science tribe. The members of the Humanities tribe welcomed medical science that helped eradicate many diseases, agricultural science that improved crop production far more effectively than killing goats, and their children were very excited about the development of computer science. But they did not accept that the laws of science that applied to rocks, chemicals, plants and other matter (i.e., the natural sciences) and rational reasoning could explain everything about humans. They believed that there are some innately human characteristics that give humans independence and *agency*, which rocks, gases, chemicals, and plants do not have – and which lead to diversity, variability, and even unpredictability. Also, they disagreed with some of the assumptions that scientists make in their methods for producing knowledge.

But back in the Science tribe, the leaders and their loyal followers saw the Humanities tribe as wedded to old-fashioned beliefs handed down from ancient Greeks such as Plato, Aristotle and Socrates and mysterious figures from the 'Far East' such as Confucius. Some were particularly critical of new-age mumbo-jumbo from postmodern poststructuralist thinkers and proponents of amorphous liberal arts and new-fangled disciplines such as cultural studies.

The worst in the Science tribe were the Positivists. These were the hard core who believed that absolutely everything could be explained and understood scientifically and that they could discover the truth about all manner of things with certainty through the 'scientific method' of research, which by the twentieth century of the Gregorian calendar had become *de rigueur* in most respectable academic and technical endeavours.

The result has been many skirmishes between the tribes over the years. Like many conflicts that unfold over centuries, the basis of dispute and tensions has become lost in time and is not understood by contemporary generations. But it is important for young knowledge seekers today to understand the historical, cultural, and ideological differences as they still influence what we know about the world, what we think we know, and how we know it.

Inspired by an 'innocent anthropologist'[5] and others who laboured for many years to refine how humans create knowledge, the following table (Table 6.1) summarizes some of the quite marked differences between the views of the Science tribe and the Humanities tribe in relation to what scholars call ontological, epistemological, axiological, and methodological issues. In simple terms, these shape how we understand the nature of reality and truth; the standpoint of the observer and how this affects what is seen (and not seen); the processes involved in producing knowledge and how they affect the outcomes; and the methodologies and methods employed, which also enhance or limit findings.

TABLE 6.1 Comparison of scientific and humanistic approaches to research and knowledge production

Key questions	Scientific view	Humanistic view
What is reality? (*Ontology*)	It is **Nature** and **matter** governed by natural laws.	It is: (a) **interpretations** of Nature by humans; and (b) **constructs** by humans, as well as elements of Nature (e.g. the family, national identity, masculinity and femininity, a 'year', etc., are social constructs collectively made by humans)
What it truth? (*Ontology*)	There is **one truth** (i.e. it is singular) and 'out there' (i.e. outside ourselves) in the universe, to be discovered.	Truth is **relative**, **multiple** and often an **internal** construct. Beyond some well-established truths in Nature (e.g. gravity), what is truth varies substantially between people (e.g. the truth about God, creation, life after death, the best job, the best place to live, etc.)
What is the standpoint or position of human researchers? (*Axiology*)	**Independent** **Objective** **Value-free** and therefore **Unbiased** **Rational and logical**	**Interdependent** (we learn and discover the world by interacting with, and being influenced by, others) **Subjective** (humans inevitably apply personal interpretation. At best, we can be *intersubjective* – i.e. arrive at shared subjective views) **Value laden** (all humans have values, and these vary and shape our views) **Biased** (all humans have biases, even when they try not to) **Emotional**, as well as rational
What are the best processes for producing knowledge? (*Epistemology*)	'**The scientific method**' (also called *positivist* or *empirical*), involving: Experiments in **controlled settings** (e.g. laboratories or in the field with predetermined parameters) Collection of **empirical data**, particularly numeric data such as counts (e.g. demographics), scores on scales, ratings, etc. **Rational logical reasoning** and cognition (thinking) **Mathematical/statistical analysis**	The **interpretative method** (also called *naturalistic* or *constructivist*), involving: Observation in the **natural setting** of what is studied (e.g. in the field, at home, at work, etc.) Collection of **participants' thoughts, perceptions and feelings**, as expressed in words, visuals such as drawings or through observation Recognition of **affective** (feelings), as well as cognitive, processing **Reflective/reflexive**[a] – **interpretative analysis**

(Continued)

TABLE 6.1 (Continued)

Key questions	Scientific view	Humanistic view
What are the best research methods to use? (*Methodology*)	Primarily *quantitative* e.g.: **Experiments** (laboratory or field) **Structured surveys** **Case studies** (in volume) **Content analysis** relying on counts of key words and phrases and units such as audience size **Meta-analysis** (i.e. re-analysis of existing data sets, including large data sets such as 'big data')	Primarily *qualitative* e.g.: **In-depth interviews** **Focus group discussions** **Case studies** (few studied in depth) **Ethnography** (direct observation) **Content, textual, thematic, semiotic, narrative, rhetorical, conversation and discourse analysis** using interpretative techniques (i.e. focus on meaning)

Note: ªMany confuse the terms 'reflective' and 'reflexive'. All research and writing should utilize *reflection* – that is, allow time to reflect on what you are thinking or writing (what writers often refer to as a 'gestation period'). *Reflexivity* refers to thinking about how your views, and even your presence, affects the research. Famous examples of distortion caused by the researcher include anthropological studies that reported certain ceremonies and rituals as daily behaviour in villages, but which were later found to have been especially staged to impress the visitor (Barley, 1983).

As occurs in many tribal conflicts, each side sees its value system and methods as superior to those of others. Nowhere has this been more marked than in the village of Quant occupied by researchers from the Science tribe and the village of Qual occupied by researchers from the Humanities tribe. The burghers of Quant have an air of confidence because, as they proclaim, their research is:

- *Scientific*, which is widely regarded as a highly desirable and superior method of conducting research and generating knowledge;
- *Objective* because of its 'scientific' methodology;
- *Statistically reliable*, which in common parlance is taken to mean accurate; and
- *Generalizable* – that is, findings of a study can be applied to the whole population category from which the sample is selected.

It sounds like a convincing case and it is perhaps not surprising that the marketers and Visitors Bureau in the village of Quant have been very successful in attracting support. At the same time, the burghers of Quant see the interpretative/naturalistic/humanistic research done in the village of Qual as:

- 'Unscientific', which is sometimes spoken with an air of paternalism bordering on pity;
- *Subjective*, with the implication that findings are little more than personal opinions;
- Not statistically reliable; and
- Not generalizable.

This has led to more than a few burghers of Quant and some confused visitors asking 'What good is qualitative research?' and some pronouncing

'Hail quantitative research; long live quantitative research.' It has to be acknowledged that in the case of the natural sciences the benefits and rigour of the scientific method are unquestionable.

However, the burghers of Qual have been fighting back in recent times in a movement that could be called the 'Social Research Spring'. They make a number of telling points about so-called 'scientific' research. For instance, consider these points in relation to surveys, which are the most popular quantitative research method used.

1. Surveys are generally self-administered. That is to say, participants fill out the questionnaires themselves with no validation that they are telling the truth and no supporting evidence. It is well established that people exaggerate when rating themselves on positive attributes, whether it is in relation to their skills, knowledge, proficiency, professionalism, creativity, innovation, or ethical standards. Thus surveys are prone to what is called 'response generation' which produces exaggerated and even false findings.
2. Unless they are conducted face-to-face or by telephone, there is no capacity for the researcher to query, challenge, ask for clarification, or seek more information to confirm responses, as there is in open-ended interviewing conducted as part of qualitative research.
3. Furthermore, structured surveys can tell us *what* people claim to do and think, but they usually tell us little about *why* (e.g., underlying reasons, motives, fears, feelings, influences, and so on). Often people will be reluctant to reveal these – and sometimes even intentionally hide them, thus not telling the whole story.
4. Many surveys are now conducted online. While convenient and quick, this makes controlling the sample difficult. The link for online surveys can be intentionally or accidentally leaked to people outside the desired sample. As the Science tribe knows well, having a carefully selected *random*, *representative*, or *purposive* sample is essential for *validity* and *reliability*. 'Convenience' or corrupted samples result in misleading data.
5. It is also well established that surveys are rarely completed by senior executives in organizations or heads of households. They are often passed on to someone else to fill out – sometimes a junior employee in organizations or a child in households.[6] This casts further doubts over the claimed rigour of the 'scientific method' in the case of surveys among such groups.
6. Even when filled out by the intended research participant, a survey questionnaire provides a fixed set of questions with a limited choice of responses. It is largely a 'tick the box' exercise. As such, surveys gain approximate answers (nearest match) and do not discover any of the richness, complexity, nuance, contradiction, or ambivalence that is common in human attitudes and thinking.
7. Yet another limitation of surveys and most quantitative research methods is that data analysis focuses on *means* (i.e., averages), and sometimes *medians* and *modes*. Average calculations produce findings about hypothetical cases

that often do not exist in reality – they are a statistical calculation that identifies a middle ground in a data set. Modes are better than means in this respect in that they at least identify the most commonly occurring response. But by virtue of focussing on averages, most statistical analyses exclude what are called 'outliers' in a data range – effectively they ignore all responses outside the normal 'bell curve' distribution, which can be a sizeable proportion of the population studied. While calculation of statistical significance (*p* values) and standard deviation (*SD*) can ensure statistical reliability of what is reported, it is what is *left out* of quantitative findings that is the most significant limitation. In focussing on averages and reporting arbitrary scores and ratings on limited numeric scales (often 0–10 or even 0–5), quantitative research is highly *reductionist*. It reduces the diversity and complexity of human views, perceptions, interpretations, and feelings to a few numbers, which despite the elegance of tables or charts in which they are presented, provide little by way of deep understanding and human insights.

Qualitative research also has its limitations. It is true that it is not statistically reliable and thus its findings are not generalizable to the whole population category studied. That is not its purpose. Whereas quantitative research produces aggregated and averaged data about broad groups and topics (which is often useful and even essential information), qualitative research seeks to provide deep insights into human thinking, perceptions, attitudes, and interpretations in particular contexts and situations. Also, whereas quantitative research reports *who*, *what*, and *where*, qualitative research is more interested in the *why* and *how*. Qualitative research also wants to understand the affective (i.e., emotions), not only the rational cognitive processes of those studied.

Interpretative analysis done in qualitative research does have to take into account the human subjectivity and values of the researcher, but at least qualitative research recognizes that humans are subjective, value-laden beings rather than claiming an unattainable objectivity.[7] Well-conducted qualitative research employs a number of techniques for minimizing the influence of the researcher's subjectivity and identifying the potential for their standpoint and values to influence the findings (see Table 6.1, note a).

It can be seen that the Science and Humanities tribes focus on different aspects of our life world, and the villages of Quant and Qual do different kinds of work. It is perhaps not surprising then that the tribes and villages have engaged in peace talks over recent years and negotiated a fair trade agreement that they call the *mixed method* approach. This recognizes the culture, politics, ideology, skills, and resources of both sides and advocates peaceful coexistence and cooperation between the Science tribe and the Humanities tribe and between the villages of Quant and Qual. The borders have opened up and researchers today increasingly travel through the tribal territories of each – albeit there is still occasional civil unrest and some border guards are known to maintain a stern decorum in dealing with methodological foreigners and visitors.

Mixed methods

As the concluding paragraph of the above paper circulated to my research students says, many, if not most, researchers now recognize the benefits and complementation of a *mixed-method* approach using both quantitative and qualitative research (Creswell & Plano Clark, 2007). It is important, however, to apply the correct procedures and rules to whichever methodology is being used — qualitative or quantitative. The oft-held view that qualitative research is easier than quantitative research, because it avoids complicated statistics, is misguided. Both qualitative and quantitative research require care in research design, sample selection, data collection and data analysis.

Key concepts and procedures in research

Because this is a study of evaluation theory and practice, not a text of research methods, only some of the most important concepts and procedures that need to be understood in doing research are summarized here. Public communication professionals who are unfamiliar with research procedures should seek deeper understanding from specialist texts, courses of study or professional development programmes. This section focuses on the research concepts and procedures most relevant to evaluation, particularly those that are frequently misunderstood or misapplied, to clarify these and also to define terms that will be used in the following chapters.

Units of analysis

All research examines one or more specific things. These are referred to as the *units of analysis*. These may be individual people, objects such as media articles, or groups or categories, in some cases. For example, in a survey, the units of analysis usually will be the individuals in the sample, while in a study of major stakeholders, the unit of analysis may be organizations. In a media content analysis, the unit of analysis may be articles or even specific messages.

Variables

Research examines a number of *variables* — in simple terms, things or conditions that can change, some of which communication professionals want to change. In quantitative research using the scientific method, there are three key types of variable:

- an *independent variable* that is introduced or manipulated to test its effects on other variables (for example, a stimulus, treatment or intervention);
- one or more *dependent variables*, which are the conditions against which the independent variable is tested to establish whether or not a causal relationship exists; and
- a *control variable*, which is used to help to prove *causality* by not being exposed to the independent variable.

The control variable should not change in the same way that dependent variables change. There will be further discussion of variables in relation to randomized controlled trials (RCTs) in Chapter 7.

Hypotheses

A *hypothesis* is a proposition that is tested in scientific quantitative research and either proved or disproved. One or more hypotheses (referred to as H^1, H^2, etc.) are written as declarative statements (for example, 'Increased exposure to positive publicity about a product increases propensity to buy the product'). If a hypothesis is not proved to an acceptable level of statistical reliability, a *null* finding is recorded and the hypothesis is rejected.

Research questions

Research questions (often listed as RQ^1, RQ^2, etc.) can be posed in quantitative research either in conjunction with or instead of hypotheses. Qualitative research always investigates research questions, because it does not produce statistically reliable generalizable findings to prove or disprove hypotheses. As noted previously, qualitative research investigates research questions in a more open-ended way than quantitative research. Thus qualitative research to investigate research questions is often referred to as *exploratory* or *discovery*.

For example, a research question for a qualitative study might be: 'What relationship is there between positive publicity about a product and propensity to buy among potential customers?' Whereas the hypothesis 'Increased exposure to positive publicity about a product increases propensity to buy the product' tests a binary proposition to gain a definitive finding (true or false), research questions explore a topic more broadly and may identify degrees of causality or context-specific findings. For example, positive publicity might influence some potential customers in some circumstances, but not influence others. Researchers might then want to further explore why this occurs.

Research questions should not be confused with the specific questions asked in surveys or interviews. Research questions state the overall purpose of the research. Usually, a study will comprise between two and five research questions, although there may be more. However, too many research questions means that a study will be very broad and will be unable to address the questions in sufficient detail to gain deep insights.

Sampling and samples

There is much confusion among practitioners who are not trained in research methods about sampling. Quantitative methods are sometimes applied to qualitative research or, alternatively, some believe that there are no rules or methods for qualitative research. As Arthur Asa Berger warns:

> Quantitative researchers are sometimes accused of being too narrow, basing their research on what they can count, measure, and observe and neglecting

other matters. Qualitative researchers, however, are often accused of 'reading into' texts things that are not there or of having opinions or making interpretations that seem odd, excessive, or even idiosyncratic.

(Berger, 2000, p. 13)

Quantitative research designed to produce statistically reliable and generalizable findings requires *probability sampling*. This is a statistical method designed to ensure that the sample selected is representative of the population under study – *population* being a term used to denote the total number of units within the category being studied, not necessarily the population of a city or country.

Probability sampling can be undertaken in a number of ways, including the following:

*   **Random methods.** These use a statistical method such as selecting every *n*th name from an alphabetical list (called the *skip interval*). In selecting a random sample, every person in the population has an equal chance of being selected for the study. Randomizer software is available to make random selection from lists easy.
*   **Segmented and stratified methods.** These include such methods as *systematic stratified random*, *segmented stratified* and *proportionate stratified*, which are designed to select samples within a number of specific groups based on statistical data.

Many falsely believe that the larger the sample, the more accurate the research. In fact, using the correct method for sampling is more important than total numbers. For a population of 10,000, a carefully selected probability sample of around 400 can produce reliable findings. However, most research texts recommend sampling ratios of 30 per cent for small populations of fewer than 1,000 (that is, a sample of 300), 10 per cent for large populations up to 10,000 (that is, 1,000) and 1 per cent for very large populations of more than 150,000 (that is, 1,500) (Neuman, 2006, p. 241). This still means that reliable results can be obtained from surveys with 300–1,000 responses, but it must be remembered that if breakdown by categories is undertaken (for example, by region, gender/sex, etc.), reliable conclusions can be drawn only if there are sufficient numbers in each category. Also, it should be noted that, for small populations, sampling may not be necessary, because it may be possible to survey everyone in the group (referred to as a *census*).

A common sampling method used in many polls and surveys is *quota sampling*. This segments a population into mutually exclusive groups, as in stratified sampling, and then selects participants from each segment based on a specified proportion. This second step is based on judgement, a client's requirements or arbitrary considerations. For example, a pollster may decide to interview 200 women aged 18–35 and 300 men aged 18–35 to identify attitudes towards driverless cars, on the basis that males in that age group buy more cars than females. Quotas usually have some rational basis, but this second step in selecting participants is not a probability sampling method. Therefore quota sampling is problematic when used for quantitative research such as surveys (as discussed in relation to polls in Chapter 7). Notwithstanding, many public opinion polls use quota sampling.

Sampling for qualitative research is often poorly described, and thus is confusing for many in terms of both the method of selecting samples and the size of samples required. Public communication professionals seeking to conduct their own qualitative research should refer to a research methods text specifically explaining qualitative methods, including some of the references cited here. This brief overview is designed to indicate the types and level of knowledge that are required to undertake rigorous evaluation research.

The first key principle of sampling for qualitative research that is a mystery to many is the method of selecting samples. In most cases, sampling for qualitative research is *purposive* – that is, it purposively selects participants on the basis of certain criteria rather than random, segmented or stratified methods. One of the most useful methods is the three-stage approach outlined by researchers Matthew Miles and Michael Huberman (1994), who recommend selecting equal numbers from three categories in the target population, as follows:

1. *typical* examples;
2. *exceptional, exemplar* or *discrepant* examples; and
3. *negative* or *disconfirming* examples (p. 34).

This method can be summarized as selecting some who are apparently at one extreme, some at the other extreme and some in the middle, based on available secondary data about the target population.

The follow-on question that arises is: how are typical, exceptional or exemplar, and negative or disconfirming, examples to be identified? Subjectively selecting samples for qualitative research based on one's own personal opinion can lead to invalid findings.

A case study can illustrate how an evidence-based approach can be taken in qualitative sampling. In conducting the Organizational Listening Project (Macnamara, 2016a), the findings of which will be referred to later for how they impact evaluation, Miles and Huberman's three-stage approach was used as follows. Exceptional and exemplary examples were identified from academic articles, media reports and announcements of specific initiatives in organizational listening that had attracted positive publicity and/or praise, such as the MasterCard's Conversation Suite (Weiner, 2012). Discrepant negative examples were identified from media and public criticisms of organizations for lack of listening and engagement with stakeholders and citizens, such as criticism of the UK government and its Department of Health in relation to complaints that led to the Mid-Staffordshire hospitals crisis (Francis, 2013) and official reports of customer complaints about energy, finance, telecommunications and other companies (for example, US FTC, 2015). Typical examples were chosen randomly from large well-known organizations. While selection of typical examples was somewhat subjective, this and the other stages of sample selection were guided by a *sampling frame* that prescribed (a) large organizations with significant investments in public communication as the subject of study, and (b) that a balance of corporate, government, non-profit and non-government organizations (NGOs) would be examined.

Other purposive qualitative sampling methods include *typical case sampling, extreme* or *deviant case sampling* when the purpose of the research is to study extreme or deviant cases specifically, *maximum variation sampling, revelatory case sampling* and *critical case sampling* (Patton, 2002; Teddlie & Yu, 2007). These sampling methods further illustrate the different purposes of qualitative and quantitative research. Whereas quantitative studies seek to find averages and typical findings, qualitative studies often are designed to gain insights into exemplar, extreme or deviant cases, or to intentionally seek insights from different ends of a spectrum to understand the range in a field of study.

The second key principle of sampling for qualitative methodology that confuses many is that there are no specific sample size requirements. From the outset, sampling for qualitative research should be informed by the conceptual question, not concern for 'representativeness' (Miles & Huberman, 1994, p. 29). Bryman similarly advises that qualitative research seeks 'generalizability of cases to theoretical propositions [or contexts] rather than populations or universes' (1988, p. 90), although his use of the term 'generalizability' can be confusing. Most researchers prefer to hold qualitative research to account for *credibility, dependability, confirmability* and *transferability,* which contribute to the overall *trustworthiness* of the research (Denzin & Lincoln, 2008, p. 32; Lincoln & Guba, 1985; Shenton, 2004). In qualitative research, trustworthiness relates to findings within a particular context. In simple terms, quantitative research learns a little about a lot of cases; qualitative research learns a lot about a specific group in a specific context.

While there are no numerical requirements on sample sizes for qualitative research, there are guidelines that determine whether or not the findings are credible and trustworthy. The size of the sample needed in qualitative research is most commonly determined by what is termed the *redundancy criterion* – also referred to as *information saturation, information redundancy, thematic redundancy* and *diversity exhaustion* (Morrison, Haley, Sheehan & Taylor, 2002). These terms refer to a point at which little or no new information is emerging in the research. Many think that the redundancy criterion will not be apparent until after hundreds of interviews or dozens of focus groups, whereas in practice, patterns emerge in data surprisingly quickly. Often, after three or four focus groups, a clear pattern in views is evident. Similarly, the redundancy criterion often occurs after as few as 20 interviews – sometimes even fewer in relatively homogeneous populations.

Data analysis

Because quantitative research primarily collects numbers, referred to as *structured data,* such as ratings, scores or selections on multiple-choice questions, each assigned a number, data analysis for quantitative research is usually done using specialist statistical software applications, the most popular of which is SPSS (Statistics Package for the Social Sciences), now owned by IBM. There are also many other statistics applications including SAS and MiniTab, as well as open-source software (OSS), which can automate many of the calculations required. In addition, statistical analysis can be undertaken with Microsoft Excel using formulae, macros and functions such as pivot tables to sort and filter data. However, users need to understand statistical concepts such as confidence intervals, p values (measures of statistical significance), t tests, standard variation (SD) and critical values, as well as have skills in writing and using formulae and macros. For this reason, most public communication practitioners are likely to use specialist service providers, such as research firms, or to hire data analysts to conduct statistical analysis.

Because quantitative research uses probability sampling to obtain representative samples, the findings of quantitative research are *generalizable* – that is, they can be read as indicative of the entire population studied within the proviso of the confidence interval and error rates reported. It is important to understand that this cannot be done with qualitative research findings, which have a different purpose. Also, because it follows scientific principles, quantitative research should be *replicable* – that is, the same researcher or someone else should be able to repeat the research and obtain the same, or closely similar, results. Replicability is an important feature of scientific research to confirm findings. For example, it is dangerous to put drugs on the market based on one study. Usually, pharmaceutical products are subjected to multiple studies, which have to replicate results before the product can be approved for use.

Specialized (albeit different) data analysis methods apply for qualitative research. Because qualitative methods involve open-ended discussion such as in-depth interviews and focus groups, analysis of documents such as transcripts or media articles and researcher notes, the data collected for analysis is often in the form of text, referred to as *unstructured data*. Hence qualitative analysis uses a range of *textual analysis, content analysis, narrative analysis, thematic analysis* and *discourse analysis* methods, all of which will be discussed in Chapter 8.

One aspect of data analysis that applies equally to quantitative and qualitative research is the importance of data display. Miles and Huberman say 'you know what you display' (1994, p. 11). Similarly Keith Punch says, 'good qualitative analysis involves repeated and iterative displays of data' (1998, p. 204). What they are referring to is how to make sense of, and gain insights from, large bodies of data, including unstructured data, such as text, which can be difficult to interpret. Data display involves data reduction, which is necessary to identify key themes, patterns and characteristics.

In quantitative data analysis, data reduction and display typically involve the creation of tables and charts that rank data by volume or frequency. Line, bar and pie charts are commonly used, as well as histograms, scatter charts and Venn diagrams. These can be produced in statistics programs or by exporting data into software such as Microsoft Excel for further manipulation. For example, A–Z sorting in an Excel spreadsheet allows data to be quickly ranked and re-ranked by various

FIGURE 6.1   Sample word cloud developed from analysis of transcripts of interviews

criteria arranged in multiple columns. In this way, data can be interrogated and reduced to key findings.

In qualitative data analysis, data display can include *word clouds* that proportionally display the most frequently occurring terms, concepts or themes in unstructured data (see Figure 6.1). Many word cloud applications are available, including free OSS such as Wordle,[8] WordItOut[9] and WordClouds,[10] to name but a few. For example, Figure 6.1 shows that 'government' and 'policy' were dominant themes in the text analysed, followed by discussion of 'issues', 'management', 'organizations' and 'the public'. Sometimes, qualitative analysis can also use bar, pie, line and scatter charts to show major topics, issues and themes, along with specialist applications such as social network mapping based on *social network analysis* (SNA), which is increasingly used in sociology, anthropology and communication studies. As well as assisting in data reduction to identify key findings, data display is also important in reporting evaluation to management, as discussed in Chapter 9.

Induction and deduction

Data analysis and interpretation use two broad approaches to logic and reasoning – deduction and induction. *Deductive reasoning* works from the general to the specific, which is the approach predominantly used in quantitative research – that is, it starts with a large representative data set and distils it down to specific generalizable findings. *Inductive reasoning* works from specifics to the general – that is, it looks into the data to find what emerges and then explores how widely those specifics apply. As a result, in colloquial terms, deductive reasoning is described as a 'top down' approach, systematically distilling the data using predetermined criteria, while inductive reasoning is a 'bottom up' approach, openly exploring what is in the data.

In practical terms, a deductive approach starts *outside* of the data by identifying hypotheses to prove or disprove and often identifying categories into which data will be categorized, while an inductive approach starts *within* the data, identifying key concepts, themes and patterns, and then grouping those into categories to form findings. For example, in conducting content or textual analysis, a deductive approach decides the categories into which data will be coded, while an inductive approach explores the data to identify the key concepts that emerge. While findings are deduced in deductive analysis, it could be said that findings from inductive analysis are emergent. One is not, however, better than the other; rather, they each serve different purposes and apply to different methodologies and methods. Both inductive and deductive analyses are important in conducting evaluation, and practitioners need to be familiar with both of these approaches.

As findings emerge from data analysis, whether this is quantitative or qualitative, deductive or inductive, researchers must remember and pay attention to the issue of *causality*, which was discussed as a key concept in research in Chapter 2. Data analysis will often reveal a number of *correlations*. For example, inquiries about a new service may increase following media publicity about the service. It may seem self-evident that the publicity caused the increase – yet correlation does not necessarily mean causation. Perhaps the service provider offered a 30-day free trial, prompting the increase. Often, there are multiple influences, or what some call *interventions*, that lead to changes in awareness, attitudes or behaviour. Hence the three key rules of causation must be applied in analysing data and identifying findings:

- *temporal precedence* – that is, the alleged cause must precede the alleged effect or impact;
- *covariation of cause and effect* – for example, there must be evidence that the audience accessed and used information you provided; and
- other possible causes of the effect must be ruled out as far as possible.

Descriptive, inferential and predictive analysis

As discussed in Chapter 3, evaluation should produce *insights* to inform future strategy, not simply report outcomes of past activities. Insights include learning that can be used to improve programmes, as well as potentially to identify opportunities for the organization that can add value (for example, identifying consumer needs or concerns that are not being met). Other examples of insights include identification of an opportunity to seize thought-leadership on an emerging issue, predicting a likely legislative initiative based on patterns of political comment, or spotting a mood swing among stakeholders that can be productively addressed at an early stage. The term 'insights' has become something of a buzzword at evaluation summits and conferences, often thrown around without any substance in terms of how insights can be generated. As identified in the measurement–analysis–insights–evaluation (MAIE) model discussed in Chapter 3, deep analysis is required to produce insights.

As early as 1952, in discussing content analysis, Bernard Berelson noted that analysis in research is conducted at several levels. He (Berelson, 1952) pointed out that analysis can be used to (a) describe message content, (b) make inferences in relation to the producers of content (for example, their interests and strategies) and (3) predict the effects of content on audiences. Kimberley Neuendorf (2002) describes four roles of content analysis as *descriptive, inferential, psychometric* and *predictive* (p. 53). While *psychometric analysis* refers to specialized medical and psycho-analytic uses of content analysis for interpreting the text of patient interviews or statements – one of the earliest uses of this method – the three other approaches are relevant and important in all analysis of research data.

Descriptive analysis that merely describes characteristics or conditions present at a point in time (for example, employees are dissatisfied or media coverage was negative) is of some, but limited, value. *Inferential analysis* takes findings a step further to infer certain causes of, reasons for and explanations of what has been studied, while *predictive analysis*, as the term suggests, informs predictions about future conditions, behaviours, trends, and so on. Researchers are cautious in relation to inferential and particularly predictive analysis, saying that research data is 'facilitating', rather than conclusive (Neuendorf, 2002, p 53). This is particularly the case with content analysis, as will be discussed in examining this method in Chapter 8. However, whenever possible, data analysis should extend beyond description to include inferential and predictive analysis.

When prediction is based on data-mining and statistical analysis, it is referred to as *predictive analytics*. Insights based in inferences and predictions can also be drawn from qualitative analysis – sometimes even more so than from numerical data.

In a paper presented to the 2014 AMEC Summit on Measurement in Amsterdam, it was pointed out that inferential and predictive analysis start by accessing all available data (Macnamara, 2014b). First, as noted in Chapter 5, beyond bespoke research conducted as part of evaluation, *literature review* can access relevant findings from research published in journals and on the websites of research institutes and other organizations. Often dozens, or even hundreds, of articles and reports are available reporting research that is relevant. Second, data can be obtained from research conducted by other parts of one's own organization (for example, marketing or human resources), by data-mining various databases, by accessing case studies or even from historical records. These *exogenous* sources of data are colloquially referred to as *other people's* (OP) research and are often free for the asking. This provides a deeper, richer data pool from which to produce findings.

Further, a range of analysis methods can be brought to bear on data collected. Beyond statistical analysis and specific methods such as content analysis, this can include *critical analysis*, as described in academic literature, as well as *market analysis*, *competitor analysis*, *business analysis* and *contextual analysis*.

The 'metrics to insights' model, illustrated in Figure 6.2, was developed collaboratively by this author and R. P. Kumar, executive vice president and global director of strategic planning, insights and research at Ketchum Global Research and Analytics, to summarize some of the techniques for undertaking deep inferential and

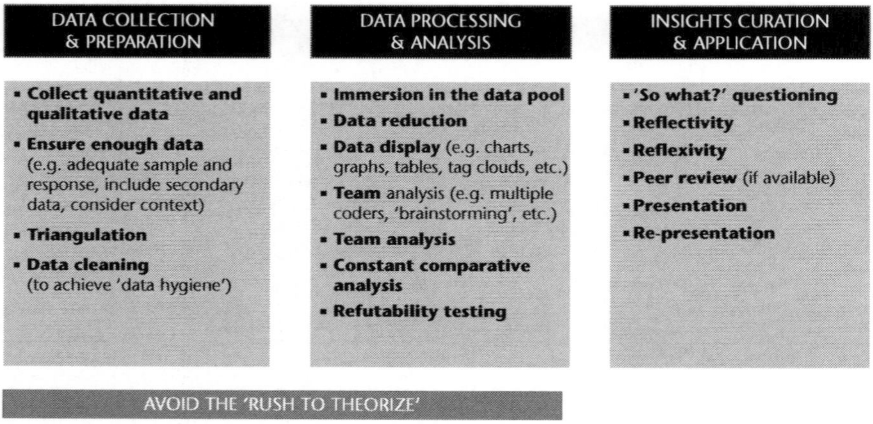

DATA COLLECTION & PREPARATION	DATA PROCESSING & ANALYSIS	INSIGHTS CURATION & APPLICATION
• **Collect quantitative and qualitative data** • **Ensure enough data** (e.g. adequate sample and response, include secondary data, consider context) • **Triangulation** • **Data cleaning** (to achieve 'data hygiene')	• **Immersion in the data pool** • **Data reduction** • **Data display** (e.g. charts, graphs, tables, tag clouds, etc.) • **Team** analysis (e.g. multiple coders, 'brainstorming', etc.) • **Team analysis** • **Constant comparative analysis** • **Refutability testing**	• **'So what?' questioning** • **Reflectivity** • **Reflexivity** • **Peer review** (if available) • **Presentation** • **Re-presentation**

AVOID THE 'RUSH TO THEORIZE'

FIGURE 6.2 Metrics to insights model
Source: Macnamara and Kumar (2014)

predictive analysis. As well as noting the importance of collecting both qualitative and quantitative data and having all of the relevant data available, this lists more than a dozen techniques for conducting deep analysis that can yield inferences and predictions, including:

- *triangulation* – that is, combining and comparing data gained from multiple methods or studies using the principle of navigation, whereby, when three or more measures point to the same position, there is a very high probability of that being accurate;
- *data cleaning* to remove irrelevant data;
- *immersion in the data pool* – that is, the researcher becoming intimately familiar with the data (Neuendorf, 2002);
- *data reduction and display*, as already discussed (Miles & Huberman, 1994), which distils data and makes trends, patterns, clusters and themes visible;
- *team analysis* – because bringing in 'another pair of eyes' often results in new discoveries or perspectives;
- using the *constant comparative method*, which involves iteratively drawing conclusions rather than waiting until the end of analysis and regular comparing them back to the data to see if they are supported;
- applying the *refutability* principle – that is, assigning team members to try to disprove preliminary findings, which often leads to some initial conclusions falling by the wayside and those that cannot be disproved being demonstrated to be those worth taking forward;
- regularly asking *so what?* (for example, 'If favourable media reporting has increased, so what?', 'What does this mean?', 'If employees are dissatisfied, so what?'), pushing analysis away from simple findings towards conclusions, inferences, predictions and recommendations;

- allowing time to reflect on data and findings – that is, *reflectivity* (commonly referred to as 'mulling over' or allowing a 'gestation period'), which often affords additional or revised perspectives (Ben-Ari & Enosh, 2011);
- applying *reflexivity*, an often misunderstood practice that involves considering one's own subjectivity, how this might affect the analysis and how the data would look from another perspective (that is, trying as far as possible to take oneself out of the research);
- *peer review* by one or more independent experts in the field, if possible, which is the technique from which academic research gains much of its rigour and credibility; and
- *presentation* and *re-presentation* of data – because it is often when one has to summarize and explain findings to others, and respond to questions, that key issues become clear.

The metrics to insights model recommends the use of several of these techniques in data analysis and avoidance of the 'rush to theorize' (Denzin & Lincoln, 2008, p. 20; Lofland & Lofland, 1984) – that is, avoiding jumping to conclusions until all relevant data has been accessed and in-depth analysis has been done.

Ethics

A final important note is that all research should be conducted in accordance with strict ethical standards. Research studies by universities and many research institutes require the approval of a human research ethics committee (HREC) before they are undertaken. The independent committee of experts will examine applications to ensure that a number of factors have been taken into account, including the following:

- *No harm* will be caused to participants (mental or physical).
- *Participants' privacy* will be protected unless explicit consent for identification is given. It is standard practice to obtain written consent from all participants in experiments, interviews, focus groups and observation studies. Surveys do not require consent, because respondents' completion of a survey constitutes consent. *Consent forms*, to be signed by each participant, should be accompanied by a *research information sheet* that outlines the research, its purpose, methodology and how data will be used, including whether data collected is *identified*, *de-identified* or *anonymized*.[11]
- *Security* of data files will be maintained, particularly when confidential information is involved, with details given of how data will be protected (for example, passwords, secure servers, etc.).
- *Publication* plans will be declared and acceptable (for example, whether the research is to be an internal confidential report or published in an academic or professional journal or book, and if so, whether the published work will involve identification or de-identification).

The same principles should be applied to all research, including applied commercial research. It ought also to go without saying that ethical research requires avoidance of any fabrication, distortion or even exaggeration in findings. It is not unknown for some client organizations to ask research or communication staff or agencies to delete, or 'dumb down', bad news or to highlight certain points that serve their own strategic or political purposes. Professionals must resist such pressures and point towards codes of ethics that apply to research, such as those of the Market Research Society (MRS)[12] or the Social Research Association (SRA)[13] in the UK, the Marketing Research Association (MRA)[14] in the US, and other similar bodies in other countries and specialist fields.

Based on this overview of some of the fundamentals of research methodology, the main methods for doing evaluation can now be examined. For rigorous evaluation, primary research using recognized social science research methods is often required. The following chapters examine the quantitative and qualitative methods commonly used for formative, process and summative evaluation of various types of public communication.

Summary

- While metrics, which are increasingly easy to obtain using digital technologies, and a number of informal methods can inform evaluation of public communication, rigorous evaluation will usually require social science research.
- When it comes to research, there is no one 'best' methodology or method. Rather, there are two quite different approaches to research – the 'scientific method', which is commonplace in the natural and physical sciences and is also applied in social science, and a humanistic approach, which is referred to variously as the interpretivist, constructivist or naturalistic paradigm.
- The 'scientific method' of research relies predominantly on quantitative methodology, and claims to be objective and reliable owing to its focus on empirical data. The humanistic approach, which pays attention to human interpretation, social construction, and seeks to study people and phenomena in their 'natural setting', uses qualitative research methodology.
- There is a bias towards quantitative methods of evaluation based on the dominance of the 'scientific method' of research and the belief systems of modernism. Metrics and analytics are about numbers and, while important, numbers tell only part of the story of human attitudes, perceptions, concerns, interests and preferences. Public communication practitioners need to be familiar and competent with qualitative research methods, as well as quantitative research.
- Also, to implement quantitative or qualitative research, public communication practitioners need to be familiar with methods of sampling and other procedures appropriate to each methodology. There is no getting away from it: no shortcuts; no magic wand. Communicators who want to do rigorous evaluation need to either be knowledgeable about research or hire someone who is. For too long, communication industries, such as PR, have applied gimmicky shortcuts.[15]

- Those undertaking evaluation of public communication need to know not only how to collect data, but also how to analyse various types of data, including unstructured data such as text gained from interviews, focus groups, public consultation submissions and correspondence. Textual data, such as public consultation submissions and correspondence, can provide rich insights into the perceptions, concerns and interests of their authors, but such data is often not analysed in detail and sometimes is not even recognized as data.
- All research needs to be conducted ethically in terms of how participants are treated, and in terms of how findings are gained and reported. This includes applying rigour and honesty in all aspects of research.

Notes

1 Benjamin Franklin is credited with a number of discoveries, including bifocals, the lightning rod and the Franklin stove, and he founded the first public lending library in the US.

2 In his *Book of Optics* published in 1021, Iraqi scientist Ibn al-Haytham (Alhazen) reported experiments combined with observations and rational argument to prove that light is emitted from objects rather than from eyes, as was previously believed (Gorini, 2003). Also, printing presses for block printing were first developed in China and Japan around the eighth century (Schirato, Buettner, Jutel & Stahl, 2010), and movable type printing was developed in China around 1040 – around 400 years before Gutenberg's printing press was invented in Europe (Needham, 1986).

3 Constructionism and constructivism are often used interchangeably. They are broadly synonymous, but have a different focus and emphasis. *Constructionism* is a term used in sociology to refer to the external (sociological) processes used by humans to construct reality, such as social interaction (Berger & Luckmann, 1966), while *constructivism* is a term used in psychology to refer to internal processes and constructs used by humans for meaning-making and learning.

4 Don Bartholomew died on June 1, 2015 from brain cancer.

5 Drawn from a book by Nigel Barley (1983).

6 Studies of market and customer surveys have found that 'busy executives will ignore them or delegate them to junior clerks', and concluded that most feedback comes from the least important and valuable sources (Reichheld, 2008, pp. 81–82).

7 In *The Social Construction of Reality*, Berger and Luckman (1966) argue that there is no such thing as true objectivity.

8 See www.wordle.net

9 See https://worditout.com

10 See www.wordclouds.com

11 *De-identification* involves removing names from data to be reported or published, but retaining records. *Anonymization* involves irreversibly severing a data set from the identity of the data contributor in a study.

12 See www.mrs.org.uk

13 See http://the-sra.org.uk

14 See www.marketingresearch.org

15 For instance, self-professed 'measurement queen' Katie Paine (see http://painepublishing.com/about/katie-paine) markets a 'Measurement 101 course for professors in a box' for US$247. It claims to provide a complete syllabus and lesson plan, videos, guides, and other resources to help lecturers to understand and teach evaluation research (Paine, 2016a) – which ignores the fact that professors spend between three and six years gaining their PhDs, and most are highly trained in a range of research methods.

7

QUANTITATIVE METHODS TO EVALUATE PUBLIC COMMUNICATION

Armed with an understanding of the key differences between various approaches and methodologies, specific research methods can now be examined, along with how they can be applied and for what benefit. This chapter reviews a range of the most frequently used quantitative research methods, not with detailed descriptions in the way that a research methods textbook would, but in terms of how they can be used for evaluation of public communication, with illustrative examples in many cases. Furthermore, various methods are analysed critically as part of exploring standards and best practice. As well as drawing on research literature, this review and the following chapter on qualitative research methods are based on interviews and case studies of evaluation in organizations. As noted in Chapter 1, some case studies and interviews are de-identified as both a requirement of ethics approval for this research and a courtesy to the individuals concerned. However, all reported interviews and case studies of public communication evaluation took place in 2015 or 2016 and are therefore reflective of contemporary evaluation practices.

Audited circulation statistics

Some of the most fundamental data required in public communication relates to the size and composition of the media audiences that consume various content such as advertising, news and current affairs, as well as entertainment. In the case of press (that is, newspapers and magazines), *audited circulation* statistics provide the most reliable data. Most countries have circulation audit boards or bureaux that independently collect and ensure the accuracy of press audience statistics. These include the Audit Bureau of Circulations (ABC), which operates in many countries worldwide, including the UK,[1] Canada,[2] and some European countries such as Romania and Serbia, as well as Australia, New Zealand and many Asian countries, including Singapore, Malaysia, Hong Kong, Korea and India.[3] In the US, the ABC changed its name in 2012 to the Alliance for Audited Media,[4] while the Canadian Circulation Audit Board (CCAB) is a subsidiary of BPA Worldwide, which also operates in the Middle East, as well as the US. A number of independent circulation auditing bodies operate in other European countries, such as the Centre d'information sur les media in Belgium, the Office de justification de la diffusion (OJD) in France, the Informationsgemeinschaft zur Feststellung der Verbreitung von Werbeträgern in Germany and the Instituut voor Media Auditing in the Netherlands. Similarly, institutes for the verification of circulations operate in South American countries such as Brazil and Argentina. Such services can be found through the International Federation of Audit Bureaux of Certification (IFABC), of which most national service providers are members.

It is important to access audited media circulation statistics in undertaking evaluation, because some publishers make exaggerated audience claims based on *readership* as a multiple of sales. While some research such as the National Readership Survey (NRS) in the UK suggests that there are between two and nine readers per copy of some publications (NRS, 2016), many readership claims are based on assumptions and arbitrarily applied ratios such as 2:1, 3:1 or more.

People meters

For many years, media audiences of television and radio — referred to as *ratings* — were measured using diaries completed by panels[5] comprising a sample of the audience, as well as various survey methods. These included:

* the *seven-day diary* method, in which media audience members recorded on paper or electronically what programmes they viewed or listened to;
* *telephone surveying* using recall questions, such as 'what did you listen to in the last 24 hours?', or co-incidental questioning, such as 'what are you listening to right now?'; and
* *personal interviewing* to measure recall from 24 hours up to seven days after exposure to media content.

Diaries are not particularly accurate, because participants frequently forget to record their viewing and listening practices, participants often recall only their favourite programmes and there is no verification of the accuracy of entries. As a result, diaries have been largely replaced by electronic meters for audience measurement. Arthur C. Nielsen, founder of the Nielsen research company, invested in the first television metering device in the US in 1936 (Nielsen, 2016a, para. 6). Another, more advanced, frequency-based meter was invented by the British company Audits of Great Britain (AGB), and successfully marketed in the UK and a number of European countries, before a failed attempt to enter the US market. Nielsen responded with its own people meter and a large national panel — albeit that the companies were later to join forces.[6]

The original people meter was an electronic set-top box about the size of a book, which was connected to a television set and operated via a remote control unit through which family members, each assigned a viewing button, recorded their viewing. However, even though the early people meters flashed lights to remind viewers to press buttons to record their viewing patterns, the system was prone to error. Children often operated the remote control units, and many users became fatigued and failed to record their viewing. Also, early meters identified content based on the transmission frequency of channels (VHF and UHF) and the time of day. These became obsolete with the introduction of direct-to-home (DTH) satellite dish transmission and digital broadcasting, which led to *time shifting*. Furthermore, early meters were hardwired, relying on a telephone line to send signals that recorded programmes and time slots viewed. Thus they could not record media consumption via the portable transistor radios that became popular in the second half of the twentieth century and the growing range of digital devices that proliferate today.

Increasingly, people meters have transitioned from manual systems that require audience members to press buttons to record data to automated systems that digitally record media viewing in real time. The *portable people meter* (PPM) was also developed in the US by Arbitron (now part of Nielsen), and is a wearable device similar to a pager that detects and logs inaudible signals embedded in a media network's broadcast or cable content.

Today, digital metering technology is the basis of the Nielsen television ratings process in the US and worldwide. The company claims that 'our tools capture not only what channel is being watched, but also who is watching and when, including "time-shifted" viewing' (Nielsen, 2016a, para. 3). Nielsen's television panels included almost 80,000 representative homes in 36 countries across five continents, as at the end of 2016 (Nielsen, 2016b, para. 6). Nielsen media audience measurement now covers not only conventional television sets, but also the growing viewership of content via computers and mobile devices.

Since 1981, the Broadcasters' Audience Research Board (BARB)[7] has delivered official viewing figures for UK television audiences. The Board commissions research companies such as Ipsos MORI, Kantar Media and RSMB (a research company jointly owned by Kantar and Havas) to collect data that represent the viewing behaviour of the UK's 26 million households with a television, based on a panel of more than 5,000 households. The Board accesses information codes from set-top boxes to measure Sky TV audiences and has developed technology to use metadata tags embedded by broadcasters to track online television viewing.

Nielsen Audience Measurement and Kantar TNS hold television audience measurement contracts across most European countries. A list is available from the International Television Expert Group (ITVE, 2010). In Australia, OzTAM[8] is the official source of television audience measurement covering the country's five main metropolitan markets and nationally for subscription television.

While television viewing is now mostly measured by people meters, radio audiences continue to be measured largely by diaries. The wearing of portable people meters is not popular and is unreliable because panel members forget to take the devices. Radio audiences consequently remain somewhat questionable, but comparative independent data is available in most countries.

Physiological testing: eye movement tracking to brain pattern analysis

A range of physiological testing methods have been developed by the advertising industry, working in conjunction with researchers and clinicians such as physicians and neurologists, in efforts to scientifically prove the effectiveness of advertising. These include:

- *pupillometric testing*, in which the dilation of a respondent's pupils is measured to indicate interest and reaction;
- *eye movement tracking*, in which a camera tracks the route that a respondent's eyes travel when looking at advertising, allowing advertising designers to identify entry and exit points and images or messages that hold attention (for example, information or images to which a participant returns);
- *galvanic skin (electrodermal) response*, in which a mild electrical current is used to measure a respondent's sweat gland activity, which is an indicator of tension and arousal that can be created by content such as images and videos;
- *blood pressure testing*, which tracks heartbeat as a way of measuring emotional response to content; and
- *brain pattern analysis*, in which a scanner monitors the reaction of the viewer's brain during exposure to various forms of content such as images and messages.

These methods are quite technical and are usually administered by specialists. For instance, special rooms are set up for eye movement tracking, pupillometric testing uses equipment and expertise borrowed from optometry, and brain pattern analysis requires qualified clinicians and laboratory equipment. Thus these forms of measurement are usually conducted only for major investments, such as seven-figure advertising campaigns.

Experiments including randomized controlled trials (RCTs)

Laboratory tests by clinicians in white coats come to mind for most people when 'experiments' are discussed. Certainly, this is often the case for medical and scientific research. However, experiments can be conducted in the field, as well as in laboratory settings, and can be used to measure human reactions to a wide range of stimuli, treatments[9] and interventions,[10] including response to public communication. An experiment is a scientific procedure, usually undertaken under controlled conditions, to make a discovery, test a hypothesis or demonstrate a known fact (Easton & McColl, 1997).

An experiment involves testing using at least two kinds of *variables*, a variable being any factor, trait or condition that can exist in differing amounts or types. These are the independent and dependent variables. The *independent variable* is that which is changed by the researcher. Only one variable is changed at a time in an experiment. If more than one is varied, it is not possible to establish the cause of any change that occurs in the dependent variables. The *dependent variables* are the things that the researcher measures to see how they respond to the change made to the independent variable. As noted in Chapter 6, there can be one or multiple dependent variables. In an experiment, the researcher is trying to find out whether the value of the dependent variables depends on the value of the independent variable. If there is a direct link between the two types of variable (independent and dependent), then a cause-and-effect relationship may be established.

Field experiments use similar procedures to laboratory experiments, but are undertaken in a natural setting (for example, in homes or workplaces) rather than in the controlled, but artificial and contrived, setting of a laboratory (Frey, Botan & Kreps, 2000, p. 195). Field experiments are the most common type in the social sciences, such as political science, sociology, and communication and media studies, although some sites of research such as media studios and focus group rooms could be considered 'laboratories' in social research terms.

In some (fairly rare) cases, an experiment may be what is termed 'natural' or 'found' (Gauntlett, 2005, p. 30). This is possible when the independent variable that is to be tested for causal effect does not exist within the group studied. For example, some years ago, social scientists researching the effects of television violence on audience attitudes and predisposition towards violence found a remote region in which no member of the community had been exposed to television. They were able to measure attitudes towards violence and the level of violence in the community, and then introduce exposure to violent television content to a sample over a period and measure any changes in attitudes or predisposition.

However, in most cases, careful attention must be paid to experimental design to avoid experimental bias caused by uncontrolled variables and other influences, such as the *placebo effect*.[11] In many instances, there can be contamination of groups participating in an experiment through accidental or unknown exposure to the independent variable or other variables that could cause observed effects. Experimental design therefore usually includes a third type of variable – the *control variable*. This is operationalized by establishing a *control group* – that is, a group that is identical as far as possible to the experimental group except for the fact that participants have not been exposed to the independent variable being tested. The variation in response between the experimental group and the control group is then able to be identified and attributed to the independent variable.

The 'gold standard' in experiments is *randomized controlled trials* (RCTs), also referred to as *random controlled trials*. These are quantitative, comparative, controlled experiments in which treatment effect sizes may be determined with less bias than in observational trials (see next section). An RCT is a scientific experiment with two or three distinctive features, as follows:

- It includes a *control group*, so that any changes in the experimental group after introduction of the independent variable (the stimulus, treatment or intervention being tested) can be compared with any changes in a group that has not been exposed to that variable.
- People participating in the experiment are randomly assigned to either the experimental group or the control group. *Randomization* minimizes selection bias. Selection of members of the experimental group and control group by

anything other than a random method can result in subjective factors influencing the research, either consciously or unconsciously. Even highly trained medical practitioners are not unknown to make remarks such as 'We should have Mrs Brown in the experimental group because she has a condition that will be very interesting to study.'
- In addition, 'gold standard' RCTs are usually *double-blinded*. This refers to concealing the identity of those receiving a stimulus, treatment or intervention from both the participants in the experiment (experimental and control group members) and the researchers, to avoid biases such as the *Hawthorne effect* – that is, a type of *reactivity* in which participants modify their behaviour as a result of their awareness of being observed.

(McCarney, Warner, Iliffe, van Haselen, Griffin & Fisher, 2007)

However, even RCTs are not foolproof. The extent to which the results of RCTs are applicable outside the RCTs (that is, in the 'real world') varies – in other words, the *external validity* of RCTs can be limited. Factors that can affect the external validity of RCTs include:

- where the RCT was performed (for example, what works in one country may not work in another);
- characteristics of the participants (for example, an RCT may include non-typical participants as a result of randomization or exclude some groups, such as those suffering ill health, the poor and disadvantaged, who may not be able to participate); and
- the study procedures (for example, in an RCT, participants may receive intensive treatments, attention and diagnostic procedures that would be difficult to achieve under normal circumstances).

Researchers also have noted that it is often difficult to 'blind' participants to their assigned group. For example, within education and training programmes, participants interact and share learning with each other, resulting in contamination of trial effects (Sullivan, 2011, pp. 285–286). Also, randomization may be achieved at the expense of relevance, according to some researchers (Cronbach, 1982) – that is, in some circumstances, researchers may want to purposively include the most relevant people in an experiment.

While RCTs are the gold standard in medical research and scientific fields such as physics and chemistry, even some quantitative researchers committed to scientific methods question their applicability in some situations. For example, medical researcher and educator Gail Sullivan says:

> Perhaps a more relevant clinical research model for educators is the 'pragmatic trial'. In a pragmatic trial, two or more medical interventions are compared in real-world practice. Patients are heterogeneous from a wide variety of practice settings, non-blinded, and may choose to switch treatments . . . However, a much greater number of subjects are usually needed to determine true differences (or equivalence) among interventions.

(Sullivan, 2011, p. 286)

Public communication practitioners do not work in medical or scientific laboratories, but instead operate in dynamic, 'real world' environments. Hence experiments and RCTs are not widely used. These methods – especially double-blinded RCTs, which may need to be conducted at multiple sites and with multiple groups to gain reliable results – are time-consuming and expensive in most cases.

However, experiments are not to be ignored and can form part of rigorous evaluation of public communication. For example, researchers at US universities have conducted experiments that show that *advertorials* – that is, advertising content camouflaged as editorial – are less likely to trigger the cognitive and persuasive schema normally associated with advertising such as scepticism. From two experiments, they concluded that:

> [R]eaders exhibited more positive attitudes toward advertorials than they did toward traditional advertisements due to decreased awareness of persuasive intent (Study 1) and advertorials' structure [presenting useful information before advertising a related product], which, in turn, increased willingness to purchase advertised products.
>
> *(Kim & Hancock, 2016, n.p.)*

Other uses of experiments in evaluation of public communication were cited in Chapter 4 in relation to testing claims of the equivalency between editorial publicity and advertising – that is, advertising value equivalents (AVEs) – and even more controversial claims for multipliers to calculate the value of public relations (PR).

Observational trials

Observational trials are similar to experiments involving expert observation to identify changes in groups when exposed to an independent variable. However, a key difference is that observational trials do not include a control group. Observational trials are also different from *ethnography*, a qualitative research method involving observation discussed in Chapter 8, in that quantitative observational studies typically use scientific instruments to record measures (for example, health checks and medical tests) and the researchers are located as observers outside the study.

Participants (the sample) in observational studies are typically cohorts or panels. *Cohorts* are groups of people with shared characteristics (for example, children born in 2001). *Panels* are made up of the same participants, who are studied throughout the course of the trial.

Surveys

The most commonly used quantitative research method is surveys. *Surveys* are a quantitative method because they involve mainly *closed questions* – that is, questions that require participants to select from a limited number of fixed responses, such as ratings, rankings or options, in multiple-choice questions – and they collect responses from probability samples, thus producing statistically reliable findings.

Most surveys also include some *open-ended questions*, but these are usually limited to 'other' options at the end of closed questions or a final 'any other comments' question to which participants can respond in their own words. Thus surveys can produce some qualitative information, but this is minimal and usually different research methods are applied to gain qualitative findings.

Scales for quantification

In addition to closed multiple-choice questions designed to measure nominal and ratio variables (that is, numbers that stand for categories such as gender/sex or occupation selected from a list, or real numbers such as age), easy comparison of responses in surveys and calculation of means, modes and medians is facilitated by the use of *scales*, a number of which measure ordinal and interval variables. Commonly used scales include the following:

- A *dichotomous scale* is a binary scale requiring 'yes' or 'no' responses. These are not used very often because they do not yield detailed information. However, a binary question can be very useful towards the end of a survey, in a question such as 'Overall, would you buy this brand again?' Sometimes, respondents give critical ratings in a survey, but then indicate that they would continue to support the brand or organization, which is a quite different (and better) finding than positive responses followed by an indication that they would not continue to support the brand or organization.
- The *Likert scale*, named after its inventor, psychologist Rensis Likert (1932), is a psychometric scale that contains equal numbers of positive and negative positions that are equidistant, and in which there is a neutral or balanced mid-point. The most popular form of Likert scale is a 5-point scale (see examples in Table 7.1). While simple 5-point Likert scales are widely used, they are subject to a number of biases and distortions, such as *central tendency bias* (many

TABLE 7.1 Examples of Likert scales

5-point Likert scale	5-point Likert scale	7-point Likert scale
Excellent	Strongly agree	Very positive
Good	Agree	Quite positive
Average	Neither agree or disagree	Slightly positive
Poor	Disagree	Neither positive or negative
Very poor	Strongly disagree	Slightly negative
		Quite negative
		Very negative

Innovator   ☐ ☐ ☐ ☐ ☐ ☐ ☐   Follower

Financially strong   ☐ ☐ ☐ ☐ ☐ ☐ ☐   Financially weak

High-quality products   ☐ ☐ ☐ ☐ ☐ ☐ ☐   Poor-quality products

Clear vision   ☐ ☐ ☐ ☐ ☐ ☐ ☐   No vision

Well managed   ☐ ☐ ☐ ☐ ☐ ☐ ☐   Poorly managed

Environmentally responsible   ☐ ☐ ☐ ☐ ☐ ☐ ☐   Environmentally irresponsible

Good corporate citizen   ☐ ☐ ☐ ☐ ☐ ☐ ☐   Poor corporate citizen

Good employer   ☐ ☐ ☐ ☐ ☐ ☐ ☐   Poor employer

FIGURE 7.1 A sample semantic differential scale used for measuring corporate reputation

respondents tend to cluster around the middle) and *acquiescence bias* (respondents lean towards agreement responses out of deference or fear of causing offence).

- A *semantic differential* is a rating scale designed to measure perceptions by using a set of adjectives or phrases arranged as opposites, with between five and seven gradient points between the poles. Seven-point semantic differential scales are the most popular. Figure 7.1 is an example of a simple semantic differential scale used for measuring corporate reputation, in which respondents tick or check one of the intervals from left to right. These ratings can be can be scored and averaged, thus producing statistical data.

- The *Thurlstone scale*, developed by Louis Thurstone in 1928, is used in psychology and sociology to measure attitudes. It is made up of a range of statements about a particular issue that are assigned a numerical value indicating how favourable or unfavourable each is judged to be. A Thurlstone scale is operationalized by, first, collecting statements on the topic to be studied from people holding a wide range of attitudes from extremely favourable to extremely unfavourable, and then sorting and summarizing the statements into 11 positions representing the range of attitudes from 1 (extremely favourable) to 11 (extremely unfavourable). Respondents are then asked to select the statements that they agree with and a mean score is computed, indicating their attitude.

- The *Guttman scalogram*, named after Louis Guttman, is a social distance scale that asks respondents to give a binary 'yes' or 'no' response to one option that most closely matches their view or position on an ordered scale in ascending order. For example, a Guttman scale could offer the following options:

A   I am aware of ABC organization;
B   I have a positive attitude towards ABC organization;
C   I would consider joining ABC organization;
D   I intend to join ABC organization;
E   I am applying to work with ABC organization.

A 'yes' response to one of these options can be taken to include all options lower on the scale. So a 'yes' response to C can be taken to mean that the respondent is also aware of, and positively disposed towards, the organization (that is, also agrees with A and B).

Guttman scales simplify responses and data analysis by allowing selection of one response on a progressive list of options in ascending order. A widely used example of a Guttman scale is the *Bogardus social distance scale*.

Another important type of question used in surveys is *rankings* whereby participants are asked to number a range of options in order of their perceived importance or priority (for example, from 1 to 10). Ranking questions can require all options to be numbered (that is, a *forced scale*), or ask participants to number only some options (for example, 1–5 or 1–10). To avoid misunderstanding and erroneous data, ranking questions should make the order of rankings very clear – for example, whether 1 or 10 is the highest ranking.

Types of survey

A number of different types of survey can be used, including the following:

- *Cross-sectional surveys* seek comparative information from a target population or a representative subset at a particular point in time. These are the most common type of survey. Cross-sectional studies are the opposite of *time-series studies*, which examine phenomena over a period of time.
- *Longitudinal surveys* are repeated at intervals over a period of time (that is, they are a time-series form of research). There are three types of longitudinal survey: (a) *trend studies*, which use different participants and can study different phenomena over time; (b) *cohort surveys*, which track certain phenomena in a sample of people with shared characteristics over a period of time (for example, working mothers); and (c) *panel surveys*, which study certain phenomena among the same participants over time.
- *Delphi method surveys* are used for measuring attitudes and views on particular issues using several rounds of questions. Delphi studies begin by canvassing a panel of experts or a sample to solicit a range of views and perspectives on a particular topic. Then, subsequent rounds of Delphi surveys ask a wider sample of respondents to rank or rate the views and perspectives collected. Sometimes, more than two rounds are conducted to 'boil down' the range of existing views and perspectives to those that are most highly rated by the target population. Delphi studies can be used to measure attitudes, issues of concern, priorities or forecasts about the future.

Surveys can be used for a wide range of purposes, including recall testing and measuring awareness, perceptions and attitudes, and for specialist purposes, such as evaluating reputation – although qualitative methods also need to be considered for evaluating reputation, as will be discussed in Chapter 8.

In the past, surveys were mainly administered by post. Today, online surveys are increasingly used based on publicly available web applications such as SurveyMonkey, SmartSurvey, Qualtrics, QuestionPro, Typeform and Google Forms, or using proprietary systems offered by a range of service providers. Online survey applications have the added benefit that most can automatically produce tables and charts for each question from responses collected. However, surveys can also be conducted by telephone using systems such as *computer-aided telephone interviewing* (CATI) or face-to-face interviewing (discussed in relation to structured interviews later in this chapter).

Surveys are undertaken by a large number of service providers, large and small. The four largest market research companies globally are Nielsen, the Kantar Group (part of WPP, which includes TNS), Millward Brown and IMRB International,[12] and a number of media analysis brands include Kantar Media and Precise, Ipsos MORI and GfK SE, the largest market research institute in Germany.[13]

As noted in Chapter 4, reputation is often evaluated using generic studies and reductionist metrics such as the Net Promoter Score (NPS). While these offer comparative and simple approaches, respectively, customized surveys can overcome some of the weakness of these methods noted in Chapter 4. In particular, a bespoke survey can be targeted and tailored to the most relevant audiences for a particular organization and ask questions relevant to that audience. As Charles Fombrun, Leonard Ponzi and William Newburry say, 'a company's overall reputation is rooted in the perceptions of its stakeholders . . . each of which responds to different signals or informational inputs' (2015, p. 4). This recognizes that reputation among *stakeholders* is most important – not necessarily the perceptions of everyone with a viewpoint. Furthermore, the second part of this description warrants unpacking because it is very important in terms of the methodology of reputation evaluation. In *The SAGE Encyclopedia of Corporate Reputation* (Carroll, 2016), Gillian Brooks elaborates on this point, saying:

> A firm's reputation is a function of the attitudes of the firm's constituents. Therefore, it is important that the . . . firm reach consensus regarding the pre-existing known categories and attributes that will be associated with it; these categories must align conceptually with those understood by the firm's constituents. One of the challenges faced by . . . firms in their attempt to form their own reputation is reaching consensus regarding these known categories and attributes.
>
> *(Brooks, 2016, p. 641)*

This author has long argued that reputation is *what the people who matter think about what they think matters* (Macnamara, 2005a, p. 210). Three key elements in this definition can be broken out to identify three key stages recommended for reputation research, as follows:

1. **The people who matter.** Not everyone has an interest or stake in a particular organization. Many people are outside the market, sector or field in which an organization operates, or may be marginally involved. The views

of these people are not materially important to the organization. The views of some other people, such as customers, employees and other key stakeholders, matter a lot. Reputation research should focus on those who matter most to an organization.

2. **Think.** Whereas brand is largely an emotional construct (Gobe, 2010), reputation is largely cognitive. It does include affective elements (emotion), but reputation is largely rationally and reflectively constructed. Reputation research should seek the considered, reflective views of participants based on all of their interactions with an organization, which can include customer service experiences, employment, observations of its corporate social responsibility (CSR), and so on.

3. **About what they think matters.** This is a key recommended stage that is missing from most reputation studies. Instead of asking the people who matter about what the organization thinks matters, reputation measurement should first ask participants what they think matters most in terms of the organization's operations and behaviour. It should then ask them to rate the organization in terms of these characteristics – not arbitrary criteria set by a research company. To illustrate, many reputation studies ask stakeholders to rate an organization in terms of factors such as innovation, leadership, world-class technology, and so on. But many stakeholders care little, or only marginally, about these characteristics; instead, they want good service, reliability and local contacts. A reputation study that rated an organization on the first set of criteria might come up with a high rating, but if these are not high priorities for stakeholders, that rating is misleading. Furthermore, if the stakeholders are less than satisfied with the organization in terms of the second list of characteristics (*what they think matters*), the organization has a false view and a hidden problem.

This suggests a fully customized approach to evaluating reputation. This can be accomplished in a two-part customized survey. In the first part, stakeholders can be asked to list or rate the attributes and criteria that are most important to them in relation to particular types of organization. In the second part, they can be asked to rate particular organizations in that sector in terms of those attributes and criteria that they believe are most important. This approach produces a much more grounded and reliable evaluation of reputation. It also allows for reputation to be identified in categories such as among customers, shareholders, employees and local communities, among each of which the reputation of the same organization can be quite different.

Polls

Polls are surveys that involve only a single question or a few questions on a single issue. Polls are commonly used in the run-up to elections, with questions such as 'who would you vote for if the election was tomorrow/this Thursday/next Saturday?' Polling is also used to gauge public opinion on issues. A benefit of polls is that results can be tabulated quite quickly. However, polls are not always accurate reflections of a population's views for a number of reasons. First, they ask a hypothetical question in many cases. If an election is several weeks away, preferences on a prior date are not necessarily an indication of voting behaviour. Many things can happen between pre-election polls and an election, including televised debates, gaffes by candidates, revelations in the media, and so on.

Second, people are forced to give responses to a very specific question, or narrow set of questions, in polls that do not necessarily capture their views. For instance, a British Social Attitudes survey published in June 2016, only a week before the UK's referendum on membership of the European Union (EU), reported that 60 per cent of UK citizens were in favour of retaining membership and only 30 per cent supported withdrawal (NatCen, 2016b). However, as was dramatically and historically shown on June 23, 2016, almost 52 per cent of those UK citizens who voted in the referendum, voted to leave the EU. What happened? There are many commentators with 20:20 hindsight, but it became clear that UK citizens voted in the referendum based on a range of concerns, including general dissatisfaction with the Conservative government led by David Cameron. Polls did not ask questions about public satisfaction with the government or key issues such as immigration, so they did not fully capture the mood of citizens or their range of related feelings and concerns. The vast majority of polls failed to predict the UK's momentous referendum decision to withdraw from the EU (colloquially known as 'Brexit') nor did they predict the election of Donald Trump as US president. In the aftermath of the Brexit decision, post-mortems in the UK Cabinet Office, and in discussions inside research companies such as Kantar TNS and Ipsos MORI, noted the bias of quota samples used by many polls, as well as the limitations of asking only one or a few questions.

Deliberative polls

To address the limitations of surveys, and particularly polls, a new approach designed to capture deeper and more accurate understanding of the attitudes, perceptions and views of groups is *deliberative polls*, also referred to as *deliberative surveys*. Deliberative polls use at least two waves of research. In the first, a random or representative sample is polled to gain insights into opinions, perceptions and initial reactions to questions. Then, rather than taking these responses as an accurate representation of views, deliberative polls allow the sample time (for example, one or two weeks) for reflection and deliberation. In this period, participants are encouraged to talk to friends, families and colleagues about the issues. Sometimes, factual information and/or a range of views and perspectives about the issues under discussion are circulated to participants. After allowing time for reflection, deliberative polls then invite participants to a second-round survey or a face-to-face meeting to discuss the issues raised. In some deliberative polling approaches, participants are engaged in dialogue with competing experts and in discussion groups. The idea behind deliberative polls is that whereas traditional polls and surveys capture 'off top of the head' responses, deliberative polls allow participants to reflect on the issues under discussion, to gain information about them and even to participate in debate (that is, to deliberate on the issues). Proponents of deliberative polls argue that they produce much more accurate and informed views compared with traditional surveys.

The downside of deliberative polls is that, because they involve two or more rounds of research and periods of information distribution and reflection in between, they are more time-consuming and therefore more expensive than traditional surveys. However, public communication evaluators should consider the benefits of deliberative polling, along with the weaknesses of 'in the moment' cross-sectional surveys, which have statistical validity and reliability, but may not tell much about the views, attitudes and perceptions of people as they think about and become informed about issues.

Structured interviews

Structured interviews are not to be confused with the qualitative research method of in-depth interviews. Structured interviews are a way of delivering quantitative surveys face-to-face or by telephone using CATI systems. Face-to-face methods include *intercept interviews*, also referred to as *button-hole interviews*, which involve intercepting people in a natural setting, such as on the street or at events (Atkin & Friemuth, 2013, p. 65). Intercept interviews usually do not provide a representative sample; rather, they provide a *convenience* sample, because they capture the views of those readily available to the interviewer and those willing to be interrupted as they go about their business. However, there are occasions on which intercept or button-hole interviews are a reasonable approach. For instance, one health project found it very difficult to access women of Indian and Sri Lankan backgrounds aged 50–65 to ask them about health issues – so the researchers used naturally occurring assemblies of these groups, such as Deepavali[14] celebrations, to conduct intercept interviews and captured far more responses than were gained online or by other methods (as shown in the case study 'Increasing breast screening among BAME/CALD communities 100 per cent above target' in Chapter 10).

Return on investment (ROI)

Return on investment (ROI) is a widely used method of measurement in business and management, but is controversial in public communication. The PR industry has tried to apply ROI and developed a range of quasi-ROI metrics that count intangibles in an attempt to demonstrate a 'bottom-line' result from communication. However, an international analysis by Tom Watson and Ansgar Zerfass (2011, 2012) identified several problems and limitations in trying to calculate the ROI of PR. First, ROI is quite specifically defined and understood in business and finance. Watson describes ROI as 'a ratio of monetary value created, divided by the costs incurred and multiplied by 100' (2013, para. 5) – although, strictly

TABLE 7.2 ROI formulae and calculations

Source	Description	Formula	ROI
Watson (2013, para. 5)	'a ratio of monetary value created, divided by the costs incurred and multiplied by 100'	*If monetary value is gross:* $150,000 ÷ $50,000 × 100 = 300 *If monetary value is net:* $100,000 ÷ $50,000 × 100 = 200	*Percentage* ROI = 300% ROI = 200%
Meng and Berger (2012, p. 333)	'ROI = net profits (or savings) ÷ by investment'	$100,000 ÷ $50,000 = 2	*Ratio* ROI = 2:1
Stacks and Bowen (2013, p. 27)	'Net financial return (gross financial return minus the financial investment) divided by the financial investment × 100'	$150,000 − $50,000 ÷ $50,000 × 100 = 200	*Percentage* ROI: 200%

speaking, this formula yields a percentage return rate, not a ratio (for example, $100,000 profit ÷ $50,000 costs × 100 = 200%). Also, it is not clear in this definition whether 'monetary value created' is gross or net financial return. Drawing on Flamholtz (1985), Juan Meng and Bruce Berger give a more specific ratio formula for calculating ROI as 'ROI = net profits (or savings) ÷ investment' (2012, p. 333). In the latest edition of the *Dictionary of Public Relations Measurement and Research*, Stacks and Bowen define ROI as 'net financial return (gross financial return minus the financial investment) divided by the financial investment × 100' and support Watson's view that ROI is usually expressed as a percentage (2013, p. 27). However, each of these definitions produces different formulae and can produce different ROI results, as shown in Table 7.2.

As well as encountering difficulties in calculating profit attributable to PR, practitioners calculate and use ROI in 'loose' and 'fuzzy' ways, according to the global study by Watson and Zerfass (2011, 2012). In addition to confusing gross and net returns (income vs profit), PR practitioners often miscalculate ROI by comparing returns with *operating expenditure* ('opex') only, when it should be calculated as profit compared with total costs composed of opex and *capital expenditure* ('capex').

Typical of business and finance industry views, *Investopedia* (2013) notes that ROI is calculated in different ways in different sectors of business, such as marketing and finance, but says that a financial analyst is most likely to evaluate a product 'by dividing the net income of an investment by the total value of all resources that have been employed to make and sell the product' (para. 5). This indicates that non-financial versions of ROI and shortcut derivatives are unlikely to have credibility with financially oriented management. This concern prompted Watson and Zerfass (2011, p. 11) to recommend that practitioners 'refrain from using the term in order to keep their vocabulary compatible with the . . . management world'. Philip Sheldrake, author of *The Business of Influence*, has gone further, stating:

> I dislike any attempt to hijack the term ROI. Accountants know what ROI means and they can only view any softening or redirection or substitution of its meaning by marketers trying to validate their investment plans as smoke and mirrors.
>
> *(Sheldrake, 2011, p. 117)*

Beyond the risk of presenting 'smoke and mirrors' in calculations of alleged PR ROI (Watson & Zerfass, 2012), a second problem with ROI is that many PR activities do not seek or have a financial return (for example, government and non-profit PR). Also, there is a valid argument that some of the outcomes of PR are long-term, such as building relationships, and do not have a short-term effect on the financial 'bottom line'. As Watson and Zerfass concluded, in many cases 'the complexity of communication processes and their role in business interactions means it is not possible to calculate return on investment in financial terms' (2011, p. 11).

Return on marketing investment (ROMI), return on expectations (ROE) and other ROI derivatives

To try to accommodate the varying outcomes of PR and recognize results other than financial returns, a range of what Watson and Zerfass (2012) call 'quasi-ROI' measures have been advocated. For example, the Institute of Practitioners in Advertising (IPA) champions *return on marketing investment* (ROMI), arguing that ROMI can be calculated based on (a) the value of incremental sales (that is, the additional sales that can be attributed to the campaign), *plus* (b) retailer margin, *less* (c) the total cost of a campaign, including all media and production costs and agency fees (IPA, 2016b). The IPA also argues that, with this data plus statistics on variable cost per unit and total variable costs of the campaign, the percentage contribution to profit can be calculated. The organization defines ROMI as follows:

$$\text{ROMI} = \left(\text{Incremental net profit}\right) \div \left(\text{Cost of campaign}\right) \times 100\%$$

(IPA, 2016b)

However, causality remains a challenge in such calculations, because advertising is rarely the only influence on sales and rarely occurs in a vacuum. With integrated marketing and communication increasingly used, sales can be influenced by in-store promotions and retailer tactics, such as discounts, media publicity, professional and peer reviews, social media discussion, word of mouth and other factors. Even if causality can be established, ROMI calculations are quite complex.

In PR literature, four further variations of ROI have been proposed for evaluating media publicity by Fraser Likely, David Rockland and Mark Weiner (2006), as follows:

- *return on impressions* (ROI), which assumes that a certain number of media impressions will lead to awareness, and then a proportion will change their attitudes and behaviour as a result – a 'domino' effect argument that the authors themselves admit is problematic;
- *return on media impact* (ROMI), which compares media coverage and sales data over a period to try to determine cause and effect;
- *return on target influence* (ROTI), which uses surveys before and after exposure to media coverage to evaluate changes in awareness or intention to buy; and
- *return on earned media* (ROEM), which is essentially AVEs by another name.

Even further, Stacks and Michaelson (2010) propose *return on expectations* (ROE) as a more broad-based derivative of ROI for PR to cover non-financial, as well as financial, returns and to differentiate PR measurement from the accounting formula of ROI. These proposals further 'muddy the waters' with a plethora of terms rather than provide clear methods for identifying and describing the value of PR. Return on expectations also raises the question of *whose* expectations (senior management, the communication practitioner or stakeholders?) and continues to leave unanswered the question of *how* these are quantified.

Yet more derivatives of ROI for PR measurement have been proposed by Meng and Berger (2012), drawing on the marketing communication concepts of *return on brand investment* (ROBI), also referred to as *return on brand communication* (Schultz, 2002) and *return on customer investment* (ROCI) (Schultz & Schultz, 2004). Meng and Berger acknowledge that practitioners and scholars in the marketing communication and integrated marketing fields 'believe that using a single metric to assess marketing communication performance is problematic', and instead call for 'the development of appropriate techniques for not only measuring short-term return on customer investment (ROCI) but also long-term value of customer relationships' (2012, p. 334). Nevertheless, they go on to discuss *return on communication investment*, another form of ROCI, as a metric for financial and non-financial returns from investment in PR (Meng & Berger, 2012, p. 334).

Social return on investment (SROI, or social ROI)

In *Social Media ROI: Managing and Measuring Social Media Efforts in Your Organization*, Olivier Blanchard (2011) has added yet another variation to the rubric of ROI. However, Blanchard simply applies traditional 'loose' PR interpretations of ROI to social media and relies on basic metrics, such as likes and follows, as evidence.

A related ROI concept, *social return on investment* (SROI, or social ROI), has been surprisingly little mentioned in PR literature and the measurement and evaluation standards debate, even though it has been widely discussed in government and the non-profit sector. Social ROI is not the same thing as social media ROI, as discussed by Blanchard (2011) and others, such as Guy Powell, Simon Groves and Jerry Dimos (2011) and Brian Solis (2010). The term 'social ROI' was first used in 2000 by the Roberts Enterprise Development Fund (REDF), a San Francisco-based philanthropic fund (Millar & Hall, 2012, p. 4). Social ROI uses cost–benefit analysis and social accounting to calculate the value of a range of activities conducted by organizations that do not have direct financial returns. A report prepared by social ROI consultants, in partnership with the Centre for Social Impact and PriceWaterhouseCoopers (PWC), provides this definition:

> SROI is a form of stakeholder-driven evaluation blended with cost-benefit analysis tailored to social purposes. It tells the story of how change is being created and places a monetary value on that change and compares it with the cost of inputs to achieve it.
>
> *(Social Ventures Australia Consulting, 2012, p. 3)*

The SROI Network, established in 2006, collaborated with the Impact Reporting and Investment Standards organization (IRIS) in 2009–2010 to create a common set of terms and definitions for describing the social and environmental performance of organizations – a move towards standards that mirrors the search for legitimacy and recognition in PR. Publications produced by the SROI Network (for example, SROI Network, 2012) and proponents of SROI, including Nicholls, Mackenzie and Somers (2007) and Peter Scholten, Jeremy Nicholls, Sara Olsen and Brett Galimidi (2006), explain that SROI goes beyond description of outcomes and applies 'proxy' financial values to impacts identified by stakeholders that do not typically have market values, using various formulae and algorithms applied in calculation guides and software programs. For example, along with Social E-valuator™, the Dutch tool that guides users through ten steps in developing an SROI analysis, Social Asset Measurements Inc., a Canadian software and consulting company, has developed the Social Return Intelligence Suite™, which comprises two interlinked software products: the Ira Impact Reporting and Management Suite (IIRM), and the Sabita Indicator and Financial Proxy Database Service (SDS). Sabita houses more than 500 indicators and financial proxies, which are graded according to the 'SAM Factor' – a proprietary algorithm that provides a 0–10 rating based on the quality of the sources used in creating the financial proxy. Ira allows practitioners to create monetized and non-monetized impact reports within the SROI framework.

This broader concept of measuring and evaluating public communication beyond the organization's objectives offers an innovative sociocultural approach. However, like some methods of media publicity evaluation, SROI has its critics because of its use of 'black box' algorithms and because the 'proxy' financial values used tend to be arbitrary and subjective. Also, it needs to be recognized that SROI is mainly appropriate to social enterprises – that is, organizations that operate primarily to 'serve the community's interest (social, societal, environmental objectives) rather than profit maximization' (European Commission, 2013, n.p.). The method is mainly applicable to non-profit organizations such as charities, community groups, foundations, trusts and cooperatives. Furthermore, SROI refers to the overall impact and outcomes of the operations of these enterprises, not only to communication – although public education, awareness-raising and behaviour change campaigns, such as health communication, can generate SROI. Thus while SROI may have some application to activities in the non-profit and non-governmental organization (NGO) sectors, it is a specific field of impact assessment and does not offer an outcome measurement strategy for public communication generally.

The proliferation and use of 'quasi-ROI' terms, such as PR ROI, *return on impressions* (also ROI), ROMI, ROTI, ROEM, ROE and social media ROI, use of marketing communication derivatives such as ROBI and ROCI, or appropriation of the concept of SROI are unlikely to facilitate either understanding or standards, given the variations in methods used and unanswered questions about their validity. A progress report on standards for measurement and evaluation presented at the fourth European Summit on Measurement in Dublin in 2012 recommended that 'ROI should be strictly limited to measurable financial impact' when this occurs (Marklein & Paine, 2012) – an approach supported by Watson and Zerfass (2012) and Likely and Watson (2013).

Econometrics

Econometrics is described as 'the quantitative analysis of actual economic phenomena based on the concurrent development of theory and observation, related by appropriate methods of inference' (Samuelson, Koopmans & Stone, 1954, p. 142). If that sounds complex, that is an accurate reflection of econometrics from the perspective of a communication scholar or practitioner. Usually, knowledge of advanced statistics and economic modelling is required to use the various methods applied in econometrics.

In simpler terms, econometrics is a branch of economics that uses mathematics, statistical methods and computer science to establish an empirical basis for economic relations and to make economic predictions. Econometric calculations are used to construct econometric models and hence this field incorporates, and is also referred to as, *econometric modelling*. But whereas economic models are a set of assumptions that describe the behaviour of an economy, econometric models use statistical techniques such as *regression analysis* to show and explain how various factors affect economic performance and to forecast future economic trends.

Big claims are made for econometrics and econometric modelling. For example, one leading firm specializing in this field, Brand Science, argues that clients can use econometrics to 'know exactly how much the following campaign will bring you, which medium will work the best, or even what format or [advertising] spot length to choose in order to achieve your desired result' (Brand Science, 2016, para. 1). The company's promotional materials go on to say:

> These questions and much more can be answered by econometric modelling . . . we can measure the impact of your communication on sales or profit. Thanks to the econometric model . . . we can predict what effect will your future campaigns have or what will be the return of your investments.
>
> *(Brand Science, 2016, para. 2)*

Despite its advanced statistical processes and lofty claims, econometrics relies on a number of assumptions and interpretations, and is not as precise or accurate as proponents claim. Its protagonists live in the 'village of Quant' (see Chapter 6), and believe that science can explain and control every aspect of the human world, including humans themselves. However, human behaviour continues to confound, and human emotions and agency refuse to be explained by science and statistics alone. Nevertheless, econometrics offers the benefit of rigorous scientific data to explain economic relationships and outcomes when these are sufficiently discoverable or predictable within the complex social, cultural and political context in which people live.

As well as specialist service providers offering econometric services, econometric software applications are available such as STATA[15] to help to navigate the calculations involved. Novices might find it useful to start with a basic text such as *Econometrics for Dummies* (Pedace, 2013). For those who are comfortable with statistics and economics, there are a number of scholarly journals devoted to econometrics and books (for example, Wooldridge, 2016 – all 793 pages of it). However, in most instances in the field of public communication, specialists will be employed if econometrics are to be applied.

Benefit–cost ratio (BCR)

Benefit–cost ratio (BCR) is a mathematical calculation that compares the total financial cost of a programme or activity with the actual or estimated financial returns (gross income) to calculate a ratio and a net return. For example, a BCR of 2:1 means that for every $1,000 spent, the financial benefit or return is $2,000. In the third edition of their *Dictionary of Public Relations Measurement and Research*, Stacks and Bowen describe BCR as an *outcome* level of evaluation (2013, p. 3). However, they note that BCR can measure 'expected benefits (or financial returns) over expected costs', as well as actual costs and benefits. When applied *ex post*, BCR is similar to ROI, but BCR calculations also can be used as part of formative evaluation to help to make decisions about a proposal or 'to choose between several alternative ones by comparing the total expected costs of each option against the total expected benefit' (Stacks & Bowen, 2013, p. 3). Thus BCR can be used either at input (planning) or outcomes stages of a programme.

Cost–benefit analysis (CBA)

Cost–benefit analysis (CBA) uses BCR calculations, but is normally conducted after activities are undertaken to calculate actual financial return. Evaluation based on CBA is widely favoured by management focused on quantitative data and economic factors in particular. However, it is criticized as a narrow approach to identifying returns and benefits by some researchers. This has led to some proponents of CBA seeking to position the method as broader than a measure of financial return. For example, in a presentation to the 2015 'Evaluation Conference' of the New South Wales (NSW) government, which requires CBA of major public communication programmes, Professor Peter Abelson (2015) stated that 'cost–benefit analysis should not be seen narrowly', asserting that 'it is a misnomer to call it economic analysis' and that 'benefits' included 'increases in human well-being' (n.p.) – and yet, in a subsequent slide in Professor Abelson's presentation, cost–benefit analysis was described as 'the leading method of economic evaluation'. In the vast majority of implementations, CBA applies *economic appraisal* and is focused predominantly, if not exclusively, on quantifiable economic benefits.

As an RMIT University 2005 evaluation of a 'Stronger Families and Communities' initiative noted, there are methodological problems in monetizing many benefits of information and communication for citizens and communities. As an example, the RMIT study stated: 'We cannot attach a monetary value to a mother's greater satisfaction with her relationship with her child', gained as a result of family support services (RMIT University, 2005, p. 9). The World Health Organization (WHO) has similarly pointed to the importance of non-economic benefits such as improved mental health (WHO, 2014), and a number of studies have identified the necessity for qualitative factors to be considered in evaluating quality of life and well-being (for example, Angner, 2011; Campbell, Converse & Rodgers, 1976).

Cost–benefit analysis is also controversial because, despite claims of statistical reliability based on quantitative research and economic modelling, it relies on a number of variables that require assumptions. For instance, even in major commercial projects such as the construction of a shopping centre, CBA uses assumptions about occupancy (the number of retailer leases that can be negotiated) and traffic (projected numbers of customers) to estimate likely net returns. A specialist in evaluation of intangibles states that 'almost every variable in a cost–benefit analysis is uncertain' (Hubbard, 2007 [1999], para. 3).

In an attempt to broaden the application and relevance of CBA, the inclusion of qualitative factors has been advocated and implemented by some researchers such as Allison Ziller and Peter Phibbs (2003). The RMIT University study cited previously used an adaptation of Ziller and Phibbs' *integrative cost–benefit matrix*, which it said 'gives social impacts equal standing with other impact variables and unquantified data equal standing with quantified data allowing the evaluation to consider the vast range of costs and benefits' (RMIT University, 2005, p. 11). However, CBA remains predominantly a measure of economic returns.

This is particularly problematic if applied to evaluating public communication for several reasons, including the following:

1. Many public communication activities and campaigns are not designed to achieve financial outcomes, even in commercial organizations. Sometimes, public communication is undertaken simply to create awareness (for example, of an issue, policy or law), to change attitudes or to build reputation.

2. Almost 50 per cent of public communication worldwide is undertaken by public-sector and non-profit organizations that do not have financial objectives, making CBA mostly irrelevant.

3. Many public communication activities are integrated with other interventions, such as regulatory measures (for example, increased fines for driving offences), enforcement activities and other strategies, making causality difficult to identify and prove.

4. The effects of communication campaigns are often long-term beyond the period in which CBA is required.

Notwithstanding, some organizations, including a number of government bodies, mandate CBA for evaluation. For example, the NSW government in Australia requires CBA for all advertising and communication campaigns costing more than AU$1 million in a year. Also, CBA is required *in advance* to gain approval for such campaigns. Interviews with senior communication staff in a number NSW government departments and agencies conducted as part of an independent review of the government's communication evaluation processes revealed that insistence on CBA was counterproductive in a number of respects (Macnamara, 2015d). Interviewees reported that the requirement for CBA prior to major public communication campaigns and programmes:

- added significantly to the costs of public communication, such as advertising campaigns, with several government agencies reporting that they had to hire financial consultants to conduct CBAs costing AU$50,000–100,000 a year; and
- delayed public communication in some cases, with heads of communication in government departments reporting that some campaigns can take 12–18 months to plan, gain approval and implement, with onerous evaluation processes such as CBAs contributing up to six months of this lead time (Macnamara, 2015d, pp. 28–30).

Comments from heads of communication in the NSW government who were interviewed also included:

> The submission and evaluation processes slow down campaigns and create considerable extra work.

> The costs are high in both time and money. This takes money away from other campaigns.

> The CBA processes create a nightmare for us.

> We are being asked to operate with one hand tied behind our back, caught up in bureaucracy.

> *(Anon., personal communications, October 20–November 15, 2015)*[16]

The independent review of evaluation of public communication conducted for the NSW government recommended that:

> A number of other evaluation methods and metrics should be applied to evaluate potential for, and achievement of, non-financial objectives such as creating awareness, changing attitudes, and improving quality of life and wellbeing (i.e., social benefits). Other evaluation methods recommended for use include behaviour tracking, surveys, stakeholder interviews, well-being and quality of life measures, and Social Return on Investment (SROI) . . . Agencies conducting campaigns . . . should be able to choose an evaluation method relevant to their objectives informed by social research literature for submission to the Standing Committee on Government Communication and Advertising.
>
> *(Macnamara, 2015d, p. 9)*

Cost-effectiveness analysis

Cost-effectiveness analysis (CEA) is often confused with CBA and also with evaluating effectiveness, but it is actually quite different from both of these methods. Cost-effectiveness analysis is a comparative analysis conducted to estimate whether one form of public communication is more or less cost-effective than other forms of intervention that could achieve the same objectives (Salmon & Murray-Johnson, 2013, p. 105). For example, if a media campaign is proposed to increase rates of cervical cancer screening among women aged 40–65 by 10 per cent over a two-year period (a SMART objective), the cost of this can be compared with other options such as a community-based programme involving doctors and community health workers using local leaflet distribution, information seminars, and so on.

Cost-effectiveness analysis is most productively conducted before activities and programmes are undertaken, and therefore can be a method for formative evaluation at the inputs or activities stage. Empirical data should be used as far as possible in evaluating the cost-effectiveness of various strategies and tactics, although *ex ante* CEA relies on projections and estimates based on precedents (similar activities conducted previously by the organization or others) and modelling. For example, published data on cancer screening programmes around the world can provide evidence of the results of various types of programme and sometimes their cost for comparison – an example of the importance of secondary data.

Cost-effectiveness analysis usually requires a researcher who is neutral in relation to the various communication options available. An advertising agency, for example, will be reluctant to recommend a community-based programme if it means giving up lucrative media commissions. Similarly, a PR firm is likely to favour approaches that earn it fees. This is a result of what is referred to as the *law of the instrument* – that is, a tendency to apply whatever instrument or tool we have at our disposal and with which we are familiar – also known as *Maslow's hammer* after Abraham Maslow who said, 'I suppose it is tempting, if the only tool you have is a hammer, to treat everything as if it were a nail' (1966, p. 15).

Social network analysis (SNA)

Social network analysis (SNA) is the method of investigating social structures and interconnections through the application of network theory (Freeman, 2004). It is usually reported in visualizations such as cluster diagrams and specialist *sociograms* – that is, graphic representations of social links showing connections as lines between individuals represented as dots, with the size of dots increasing as the number of connections to them increase. Visualizations of social networks are often referred to as *social network mapping*. While SNA can involve some qualitative assessment, it is largely quantitative, based on the number of connections and frequency of connections. Hence this method is included in this chapter.

Key concepts in SNA are:

- *nodes* – individuals or organizations in a network (represented as small dots);
- *hubs* – individuals or organizations that become central to a substantial number of interconnections (usually represented as larger dots scaled proportional to their number of connections);
- *clusters* – closely interconnected groups of nodes and hubs;
- *centrality* – the degree to which nodes and hubs are central to a cluster and therefore important;
- *structural holes* – an absence of links between two parts of a network;
- *bridges* – links between clusters (noting that, in some cases, a single or small number of links may connect one cluster to another, which means that these are important bridges); and
- *homophily* – the extent to which nodes form ties that are similar to them versus dissimilar others.

While some believe SNA to be a new method developed in the era of social media, the method evolved in sociology and has been extensively used in anthropology, biology, economics, history, organizational studies, political science, social psychology, development studies and information science, as well as communication studies. In communication and media studies, SNA has gained a resurgence in interest given its obvious application to analysis of online social networks.

Social network analysis can be used in formative, process and summative evaluation to identify key influencers (for example, hubs) and their centrality to relevant clusters, bridges to important clusters and, sometimes, 'outliers' with which an organization wishes to engage. Organizations also can use SNA to plot their own position in debates and conversations, as well as to track competitors. The sample of a social network map in Figure 7.2 illustrates that the anonymized person

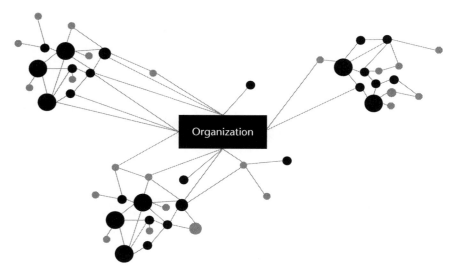

FIGURE 7.2 Sample social network map

or organization has several substantial clusters within their network. However, it shows a relatively small number of direct connections to the large cluster on the right. These connections are therefore very important for maintaining connectivity to the hubs and nodes in the right-hand cluster.

Customer journey mapping

Customer journey mapping (CJM), or what McKinsey consultants call the *customer decision journey*, identifies steps and stages of communication such as those discussed by W. J. McGuire (2001) in the context of commercial marketing, the desired outcome of which is sales and the desired impact revenue and profits. This concept can also be referred to as the *journey to the sale*.

There are several phases in CJM.

1. One maps the journey that a customer takes and their experiences along the way from the first point of contact with a brand or product to purchase, based on data such as web page views, downloads and social network connections, as well as inquiries, registrations, responses to surveys, and so on.
2. Then, CJM increasingly looks beyond sales to consider customer loyalty and retention. For example, McKinsey identifies the key steps along its customer decision journey as awareness, familiarity, consideration, purchase and loyalty (Court, Elzinga, Mulder & Vetvik, 2009).
3. A further type of CJM specifically examines a customer's journey through the organization with a view to streamlining processes and maximizing satisfaction with this experience.

Aware	Inquiry	Pricing	Purchase	Support	Complaint	Upgrade	Renew

• Advertising   • Call centre   • Retail   • Service   • Complaints   • Telesales
• PR   • Website   experience   centre   department
• Sales   • Online help
  promotion
• Web
• Social media

FIGURE 7.3   Sample internal customer journey map, showing key organization 'touch points'

Both internal and external 'touch points' are important in the journey of customers, whether they are *customers* in the traditional sense of buying consumer products or potential members of an organization, recruits for the military, students enrolling in university or the users of government services. The notion of multiple 'touch points' in the journey from being disinterested and unaware to supportive action mirrors the multiple steps and stages of communication discussed in Chapter 2, and it emphasizes the 'mini-steps' (Weiss, 1995) along what Atkin and Freimuth call the 'response chain' (2013, p. 58). It is important, in planning and evaluation for an organization, to know what these touch points are for its customers, how the organization performs in relation to internal touch points, what external touch points influence customers and potential customers, and how these might be optimized in terms of customers' experience (see Figure 7.3 for a sample customer journey map).

Attribution modelling

Attribution modelling involves the use of mathematical calculations to 'divide up credit for a conversion amongst touch points preceding it', so that marketers can identify which activities are working effectively and which are not, and adjust their strategy and investments accordingly (Yamaguchi, 2014, para. 9). Attribution is thus a method for identifying causality within a 'customer journey' in precise ways. The techniques employed range from simple rules-based modelling methods to advanced algorithmic modelling.

However, a number of assumptions are made, as they are in calculating BCRs and CBA. For example, data may indicate that a customer journey included viewing advertisements online, accessing an independent online review (editorial content) and following an advocate in social media – but which one of these had the most impact? In most cases, attribution modelling relies on quantitative data, such as which channel or content generates the most inquiries or leads. In some cases, to attempt to identify conversions, modelling focuses on the 'last touch' – that is, the information or experience that immediately preceded the conversion required (for example, a sale, a vote, joining a fitness programme, etc.). Others argue that 'first touch' is also important, because this information or experience is what attracted the citizen or consumer in the first place. While the marketing industry in particular searches for the 'Holy Grail' of evaluation metrics and methods using computer algorithms, proof of causality is challenging, as identified previously, and precise attribution of effects within multi-touch, multimedia communication programmes is extremely difficult.

Market mix modelling

Chapter 2 included a warning about assuming that *correlations* between public communication activities and desired outcomes mean that the communication caused the outcomes and impact (that is, that there is *causality*). There is an old adage in relation to causation that says: 'Success has many fathers and mothers; failure is an orphan.' In public communication practice – particularly in the case of integrated communication involving multiple channels and activities, and sometimes multiple agencies – successes are likely to be claimed to be the result of advertising, PR, direct marketing, digital communication, field staff and retailer activities, and so on. Public communication practitioners frequently fail to establish causality in claiming outcomes and impact, and need to know and employ methods for doing this. As noted in Chapter 2, causality can be complex at times, because outcomes and impact are often the result of multiple influences. Few people buy a car, for instance, because of any single influence or intervention. The 'journey to the sale' often involves multiple 'touch points', such as advertising, media publicity, word of mouth, website information and online reviews, social media comments, and so on. Furthermore, those impacted cannot always accurately recall what information and influences they encountered and what created the 'tipping point' for their decisions. However, some methods for identifying the influence and impact of specific public communication activities are available.

One of these used in marketing communication is *market mix modelling* (MMM). Market mix modelling involves adjusting the 'marketing mix' to add and delete various elements, while simultaneously tracking outcomes and impact. It is a type of experiment in which various forms of public communication are 'turned on or off' to identify differentials in results. For example, if advertising and media publicity generated by PR are both appearing in a particular market sector (for example, a geographic area), MMM could involve cessation of PR for a period and continuing to track inquiries, registrations or subscriptions, sales, or other metrics. If these metrics remain constant, there is no evidence that PR was having an impact; if these metrics decline, the differential can be attributed to PR. Conversely, PR can be turned back on and, provided that there are no other changes in public communication, any increase in key metrics can be attributed to PR. Similarly, websites, social media communication and other forms of public communication can be used in stages and differentials in results tracked.

Sometimes, 'found experiments' are available for MMM. For example, in some markets, advertising may be used only in some areas such as major cities. By using other methods of public communication in non-advertising areas, the outcomes and impact of these other methods can be isolated from advertising, and they can be measured and their cost-effectiveness evaluated. Mark Weiner (2006) has championed MMM for many years and Don Bartholomew (2016) argued that the method deserves much more attention in conducting evaluation (p. 36).

It should be noted that *ex post* surveys and interviews also can be used for identifying causality when they include questions that ask respondents about what sources of information and forms of communication they accessed, what sources of information and forms of communication they found most useful or credible, and so on. Such responses are not highly accurate, because respondents often cannot remember what they read, saw or heard, and sometimes they are uncertain about what caused them to make certain decisions. However, such research gives some useful indications of what is effective and what is not.

Behavioural insights

An emerging mainly quantitative method of research used for formative, as well as summative, evaluation is *behavioural insights*. The field of behavioural insights is closely related to *behavioural economics* in that both are based on a combination of behavioural science, particularly psychology, and economics. However, despite the terms often being used interchangeably, there are some distinct differences. Behavioural economics is a field of study within economics that explores how and why humans make economic decisions that are not rational – rationality being a basis of classical economics (Samson, 2016). Behavioural insights involve the practical application of behavioural sciences (the study of why humans behave as they do, in simple terms), with the aim of changing behaviour. Behavioural insights are applied to economic, as well as non-economic, decisions. In terms of evaluation of communication, which can have a wide range of objectives, behavioural science is the most relevant field from which to draw knowledge and hence the practice of behavioural insights is the focus here. The central underlying principles of behavioural insights are that:

1. people have two systems for processing information and decision-making – what behavioural insights and behavioural economics calls the *automatic* approach (also called 'System 1') and the *reflective* approach (referred to as System 2) (Kahneman, 2011), whereby 'automatic' refers to a system of decision-making that is typically intuitive and unconscious, requiring little cognitive effort or time, and the reflective approach is typically slower, conscious, rational, more effortful and more time-consuming – which idea is similar (if not the same thinking under a different name) to *elaboration likelihood theory* and *systematic* versus *heuristic* information processing, as referred to in Chapter 2;
2. human behaviour is largely automatic (that is, instinctive and habitual), rather than rational and deliberative; and
3. human behaviour is significantly influenced by the environment and context in which choices are made.

These three factors have led to behavioural insights being described as *choice architecture*, because its focus is understanding the influences – *triggers*, if you will – that shape people's choices in relation to certain behaviours and then manipulating those influences to create the desired behaviours (Thaler & Sunstein, 2008, p. 6). In particular, behavioural insights draw on social psychology to 'explain why people behave in ways that deviate from rationality as defined by classical economics' (Marteau, Ogilvie, Roland, Suhrcke & Kelly, 2011, p. 263).

Because behavioural insights are sought to stimulate desired behaviours in people, the field has become known colloquially as *nudge communication*, also referred to as *nudge marketing*, a term that was created by the pioneers of this field of practice, Richard Thaler and Cass Sunstein (2008) in their book *Nudge: Improving Decisions about Health, Wealth, and Happiness*. As Thaler and Sunstein describe it, 'a "nudge" entails any aspect of the choice architecture that alters people's behaviour in a predictable way without forbidding any options or significantly changing their economic incentives' (2008, p. 6).

Given that behavioural insights are sought to manipulate choice architectures and change people's behaviour, it needs to be said that nudge techniques should be applied ethically. Sunstein and Thaler (2003) argue that nudges belong to a political and economic 'third way' that they call *libertarian paternalism*. They say that nudges constitute paternalism, because they believe 'it is legitimate for private and public institutions to attempt to influence people's behaviour' and to 'steer people's choices in directions that will improve the choosers' own welfare' (Sunstein & Thaler, 2003, pp. 1162). They claim that this approach is 'libertarian' because they propose that nudges are applied in ways that preserve 'freedom of choice' for people to either comply or not comply (Sunstein & Thaler, 2003, pp. 1160, 1162). However, a number of researchers are not so sure, and argue that nudges can be coercive and open to abuse. At the very least, critics say, nudges rely on subjective decisions by authorities about what is good for people (Gigerenzer, 2015; Mitchell, 2005).

Critics also question the definition of behavioural insights, saying that the field is ill-defined and unscientific. For example, Marteau and colleagues say that:

> There is no precise, operational definition of nudging. This may reflect a reality – namely, that nudging is at best a fuzzy set intended to draw attention to the role of social and physical environments in shaping our behaviour and not to inform a scientific taxonomy of behaviour change interventions.
>
> *(Marteau et al., 2011, p. 263)*

However, the UK government has invested substantially in behavioural insights or nudge marketing, setting up a behavioural insights team, also known as the 'Nudge Unit', in the Cabinet Office in 2010. Number 10 Downing Street subsequently divested the unit in 2014 as a social purpose company jointly owned by the Cabinet Office, employees and Nesta. The Behavioural Insights Team (BIT),[17] as it is now called, is headed by British psychologist David Halpern.

Other countries are also turning to behavioural insights to inform policy-making and to influence citizens' behaviour. In the US, Harvard University's John F. Kennedy School of Government has established the Behavioural Insights Group

(BIG) and the White House set up a Nudge Unit in 2014 (Nesterak, 2014). In Australia, the NSW government has established a Behavioural Insights Community of Practice[18] to share knowledge across departments and agencies.

In the UK, the Department of Health and its arm's-length bodies (ALBs), such as NHS England and NHS Blood and Transplant, have applied behavioural insights in public communication campaigns. While behavioural insights are initially gained for strategic planning of communication, their application also involves detailed evaluation, as the following two examples show. In the first, researchers identified that 5.5 million hospital outpatient appointments were missed in 2012–2013 (NHS England, 2014) – a 'did not attend' (DNA) rate of 9.3 per cent of total health and medical appointments in the year. Missed appointments waste healthcare resources (for example, doctors and other health professionals being paid to attend facilities unnecessarily) and were estimated to cost British taxpayers £225 million a year (National Audit Office, 2014).

Two RCTs were conducted in 2013–2014 to test various forms of reminder and the content of reminder messages (Hallsworth, Berry, Sanders, Sallis, King, Vlaev et al., 2015). These found that short message service (SMS) text messages performed better than other reminder methods, such as telephone calls or email. Four different SMS text messages, as listed below, were then tested, with 10,000 patients in the 'nudge' trial to identify the most effective wording of reminders.

1. Appt at <clinic> on <date> at <time>. To cancel or rearrange call the number on your appointment letter.
2. Appt at <clinic> on <date> at <time>. To cancel or rearrange call <NUMBER>.
3. We are expecting you at <clinic> on <date> at <time>. Nine out of ten people attend. Please call <NUMBER> if you need to cancel or rearrange.
4. We are expecting you at <clinic> on <date> at <time>. Not attending costs NHS £160 on average, so call <NUMBER> if you need to cancel or rearrange.

(Berry, 2014, n.p.)

The trials found that adding a conformity message (that is, most others keep their appointments), as in the third SMS text, increased attendance. Furthermore, the research identified three characteristics for the most effective communication (SMS text 4):

1. using personalized language, including directly addressing recipients as 'you';
2. identifying the cost to the NHS of each missed appointment; and
3. listing the phone number to call for cancellations.

Use of this form of reminder reduced missed appointments from 11.7 per cent in the control group to 8.3 per cent, saving millions of pounds a year (Hallsworth, Berry & Sallis, 2014; Hallsworth et al., 2015).

In the second 'nudge' project, 1 million people were exposed to eight variants of message designed to prompt organ donation (more than 135,000 exposures of each) – one of the largest RCTs ever conducted in the UK. Adoption of the

TABLE 7.3 The Mindspace checklist of influences on our behaviour

Influence	Description
Messenger	We are heavily influenced by who communicates information.
Incentives	Our responses to incentives are shaped by predictable mental shortcuts, such as strongly avoiding losses.
Norms	We are strongly influenced by what others do.
Defaults	We 'go with the flow' of pre-set options.
Salience	Our attention is drawn to what is novel and seems relevant to us.
Priming	Our acts are often influenced by subconscious cues.
Affect	Our emotional associations can powerfully shape our actions.
Commitments	We seek to be consistent with our public promises and reciprocate acts.
Ego	We act in ways that make us feel better about ourselves.

Source: Dolan, Hallsworth, Halpern, King and Vlaev (2010)

best-performing message was estimated to generate 96,000 additional registrations of organ donors a year (Harper, 2013).

A summary of some of the influences identified in behavioural insights and used in nudge communication and nudge marketing is shown in Table 7.3. Another approach to applying behavioural insights is the *behaviour change wheel* (Michie, van Stralen & West, 2011). This identifies change strategies by increasing opportunity, or capability, or motivation, or a combination of the three using one or more of nine approaches – namely, persuasion, education, training, incentives, enablement or restrictions (for example, through regulation), environmental restructuring and coercion (such as through legislation).

'Big data' analysis

The business world is awash with excitement and even euphoria about *big data*, although there is considerable hype and confusion in relation to the concept. Business analysts such as McKinsey claim that the vast quantities of data now held by big companies, governments and other organizations can be used to identify patterns, predict trends and gain insights into target audiences, which in turn can create opportunities for increased sales through more precise targeting and customization, improved planning, better stakeholder and customer relationships, and lots more. In fact, if you believe the hype, big data is going to transform our world in myriad positive ways.

While there remains a lack of clear definitions, the term 'big data' is used to refer to data sets with sizes beyond the capability of commonly used computer software tools to capture, curate, manage and process data within a reasonable time (Snijders, Matzat & Reips, 2012, p. 1). What constitutes 'big' in data terms is a movable feast. In the early 2000s, it was a few gigabytes; in the second decade of the twenty-first century, databases routinely hold *terabytes*, *petabytes* and even *zettabyes* of data, with predictions that we will soon be dealing with *yottabytes* and *brontobytes* – the latter being 10 to the power of 27 bytes, or 1,000,000,000,000,000,000,000,000,000 bytes (Oxford Math Center, 2016).

Big data analysis incorporates a number of technologies and practices. A 2011 McKinsey Global Institute report describes the main components of big data as:

- techniques for advanced analysis of data, such as *machine learning* and *natural language processing* (NLP);
- big data technologies, such as databases, business intelligence applications[19] and *cloud computing*; and
- visualization techniques, such as charts, graphs and other displays of the data.

(Manyika et al., 2011)

Big data is discussed only briefly here, because it is a highly specialized subject and its implementation is likely to be beyond the skills of most public communication professionals. Analysis of so-called big data will, in most instances, be undertaken by specialists or 'data scientists'. However, public communication professionals should be aware of the growing potential to query large data sets to gain insights about many aspects of audience behaviour.

Summary

- This chapter has examined almost 20 quantitative research methods that can be used for evaluating public communication. Public communication practitioners need to be familiar with the major quantitative research methods to produce reliable empirical data as the basis of evaluation, as well as understand their benefits and weaknesses.
- Advanced quantitative research methods include experiments – particularly randomized controlled trials (RCTs), which are considered to be the 'gold standard' in scientific research – as well as observational trials and various forms of physiological testing of response to communication, such as eye movement tracking, brain pattern analysis, blood pressure testing and galvanic skin response measures.
- The most widely used quantitative research methods are surveys and polls. These can be implemented in various ways, including as cross-sectional, longitudinal or Delphi studies, and can use a range of question types and scales to quantify target audience awareness, opinions, perceptions, attitudes, beliefs and intentions.
- The reliability of quantitative research methods such as surveys and polls is highly dependent on the method of sampling used. While sample size is often seen as the key factor determining reliability, how samples are selected (the sampling method) is just as, or even more, important.
- Advanced methods and evaluation techniques such as social network analysis, customer journey mapping, attribution modelling, market mix modelling and

behavioural insights should be considered by those seeking to advance their career by demonstrating the effectiveness of public communication. Quantitative data is a key element of an evidence-based approach.

- Nevertheless, public communication practitioners need to be aware that qualitative research is also required to evaluate many of the outtakes, outcomes and impacts of public communication (see Chapter 8).

Notes

1 See www.abc.org.uk.
2 See www.circulationaudit.ca.
3 For example, see www.auditbureau.org.
4 See http://auditedmedia.com.
5 Panels are preselected groups of people who are representative of a target population or audience group. Panel members agree to periodically or regularly provide information, such as by completing surveys. Often, they are paid a small fee.
6 Audits of Great Britain (AGB) and Nielsen formed a joint venture (AGB–Nielsen Media Research) in 2004, and Nielsen fully acquired AGB in 2010, becoming Nielsen Audience Measurement.
7 See www.barb.co.uk.
8 See www.oztam.com.au.
9 Independent variables are usually referred to as *treatments* in medical experiments.
10 Independent variables are commonly referred to as *interventions* in health promotion and health communication
11 The *placebo effect* occurs when participants in an experiment or treatment anticipate that the treatment will positively affect them and react to a control treatment (e.g. a sugar pill that has no physical affect at all).
12 IMRB derives from the original name, Indian Market Research Bureau.
13 Originally established in 1934 as Gesellschaft für Konsumforschung (Society for Consumer Research), which now owns NOP.
14 Deepavali, known as the festival of lights, is the major Hindu celebration commemorating Lord Rama's return after vanquishing the forces of evil.
15 See www.stata.com.
16 Interviewees were de-identified under the terms of ethics approval for the research.
17 See www.behaviouralinsights.co.uk.
18 See http://bi.dpc.nsw.gov.au.
19 *Business intelligence* (BI) is a general umbrella terms for a variety of software applications that can analyse an organization's raw data.

8

QUALITATIVE AND MIXED METHODS TO EVALUATE PUBLIC COMMUNICATION

This chapter reviews a range of the most widely used qualitative methods of research that can be used for evaluation of public communication, as well as some mixed method approaches. As noted in Chapter 6, evaluation very often requires qualitative, as well as quantitative, data. For example, demonstrating a high volume of media publicity or gaining wide awareness of a product, service or policy is of little comfort to management if the content and perceptions are negative. Outcomes such as reputation and relationships are more about quality than quantity. Also, as noted in Chapter 4, some public communication is designed to facilitate quality of life and well-being among target audiences, such as promotion of the arts and mental health initiatives. Public communication professionals therefore need to be familiar with, and capable of implementing, qualitative research methods, and also must understand when such methods are appropriate, their strengths and their limitations. Thus this chapter provides a critical analysis, not simply a recitation of qualitative research methods.

In-depth interviews

The most common qualitative research method is interviewing. When undertaken qualitatively, interviews are usually referred to as *in-depth interviews*, or simply *depth interviews*. Unlike structured interviews conducted as part of quantitative research that administer a survey asking a predetermined set of questions seeking responses from a range of options (such as Likert scales or ratings), in–depth qualitative interviews are open–ended and exploratory. This is not to say that they have no structure: usually, an interview *question guide* is prepared for in–depth interviews to give some focus to the discussion and to achieve some consistency in the questions asked of each participant in the research. However, in-depth interviews allow participants to respond to questions in their own words – and even to speak at length to explain their views, perceptions or concerns. Also, qualitative interviewers ideally ask follow-up *probe questions* to clarify responses and to tease out information that participants might not reveal initially.

Interviews can be conducted in multiple modes, including face-to-face, via telephone, teleconference or video conference, or by *e-interview* – an increasingly popular approach that uses email exchanges to ask and respond to questions. Face-to-face, telephone, teleconference and video conference methods are usually recorded, so transcripts can be produced to ensure accurate reporting and understanding of responses, while an advantage of e-interviews is that responses are immediately available as text, saving considerable transcription costs.

Because the output of interviews is usually text in the form of transcripts or e-interview exchanges, data analysis requires *textual analysis* methods. Because similar analysis techniques are involved in content analysis (including media content analysis), and narrative and thematic analysis, these will be discussed specifically later in the chapter.

While in-depth interviews can gain deep insights into attitudes and perceptions, including concerns, interests, desires and needs, expert researchers issue the following warnings:

- People do not always tell the truth. While few tell bald-face lies in interviews, it is not uncommon for participants in research to exaggerate, report rumours or engage in conjecture.
- People do not always remember things accurately. This is particularly challenging in conducting research to identify the influences and information to which people have been exposed (for example, for establishing causality). For instance, people will often say that they heard about something in television ads, when there was no television advertising, or that they heard about it from a friend, when in fact they had read about it in the media.
- People sometimes tell you what they think you want to hear (a form of *response bias*).
- People use language in different ways, so interviewers need to make efforts to understand what participants mean, not only what they say. This is particularly important when interviewing speakers of other languages, people from cultures other than the interviewer's own, and people with low socio economic and education levels, who may not be able to clearly articulate their views.

(Berger, 2000, p. 124)

To gain the most accurate and complete responses in interviews, interviewers are encouraged to build empathy with participants and to make them feel comfortable. Interviewees who are intimidated or uncomfortable are unlikely to be open and honest. In addition, there are a number of practical tips and rules for interviewing with which researchers need to be familiar, such as not 'leading the witness' – that is, not putting words in their mouths with leading questions.

Because in-depth interviews require preparation by the interviewer, considerable administration to arrange individual appointments for interviews, an hour or more in the interview, and then transcription and textual analysis, in-depth interviews are a relatively time-consuming and expensive method of research. The upside is that they produce some of the deepest insights into audience attitudes, perceptions, concerns, interests, needs and preferences.

Focus groups

Focus groups are sometimes referred to as a form of interview involving small groups, usually of between eight and ten people, rather than one-on-one interaction with individual participants. This qualitative research technique was adapted by marketing researchers from group therapy (Krueger & Casey, 2009). In focus groups, individuals respond to questions posed by a *moderator*, who leads the groups, but the individuals can also engage with and respond to other members of the group in discussion. A focus group moderator builds rapport and comfort within the group, and also keeps the session on topic, while allowing a free-ranging, open-ended discussion (Atkin & Freimuth, 2013, p. 64). The aim of focus groups is to draw out the detail of views and opinions, such as why participants feel the way they do, from where they obtained their views and what they believe needs to be done.

Because qualitative research explores attitudes and perceptions within particular contexts, focus groups are usually made up of people with broadly similar social, cultural and economic backgrounds (for example, junior employees would not be mixed with management). Generally, the organizers of focus groups select participants from sectors based on *demographic, psychographic* or *socio economic* criteria. If a range of views across multiple sectors are to be explored, a number of focus groups composed of individuals from various sectors are conducted.

Focus groups should be held in neutral locations that are easily accessible for participants and not intimidating or alienating. For example, a focus group of employees held in an organization's boardroom is unlikely to make participants feel at ease. Often, hotel rooms or meeting rooms in public buildings are used. In addition, specialist facilities are available, with one-way mirrors to allow observation of focus groups and with facilities such as audio or video recording. Recording is recommended, because this keeps a complete and accurate record of discussion. However, if focus groups are to be observed or recorded, participants need to be advised of, and consent to, this as part of ethical research procedures.

Why would focus groups be observed and by whom? One example is when focus groups are conducted on behalf of an organization in which management is reluctant to believe feedback received. Researchers sometimes invite senior management to observe focus groups, so that they hear comments first-hand, rather than presenting them second-hand in reports that management may feel are exaggerated. Often, there is nothing as effective as management hearing comments directly out of the mouths of key audiences and stakeholders.

Both interviews and focus groups are popular research methods for pre-testing (for example, of strategies, creative concepts and messages), along with informal methods such as readability and usability testing.

Content analysis

Content analysis is widely used in public communication practices – particularly in public relations (PR) and corporate communication, where is it applied to media coverage to the extent that many refer to *media content analysis* as a specific research method (Macnamara, 2005b). Sociologists have been interested in media content since the early twentieth century, starting with Max Weber, who saw analysing media content as a means of monitoring the 'cultural temperature' of society (Hansen, Cottle, Negrine & Newbold, 1998, p. 92). Content analysis was introduced as a systematic method to study mass media by Harold Lasswell (1927), initially to study propaganda.

A widely used definition of content analysis that illustrates the early focus on *quantitative* analysis was provided by Berelson who described it as a 'research technique for the objective, systematic and quantitative description of the manifest content of communication' (1952, p. 18). Similarly, Kimberley Neuendorf, a prominent contemporary authority on content analysis, says that 'content analysis is a summarizing, quantitative analysis of messages that relies on the scientific method' (2002, p. 10). Neuendorf goes on to note that, being a quantitative method, content analysis should include 'attention to objectivity-intersubjectivity, *a priori* design, reliability, validity, generalizability, replicability, and hypothesis testing'[1] (p. 10).

However, content analysis has evolved over the decades to incorporate many techniques and procedures from closely related qualitative research methods, such as *textual analysis* (also called *text analysis*),[2] *narrative analysis*, *thematic analysis*, *semiotic analysis* and, in some cases, elements of *discourse analysis*. Pamela Shoemaker and Stephen Reese (1996) and Ellen Hijams (1996) are among prominent authors who reject the view that content analysis is a quantitative method, arguing that it can be conducted within both the behaviourist and humanist traditions. In either case, content analysis should be conducted systematically. Unfortunately, this is not always the case in the public communication field. 'Black box' analysis based on secret algorithms has already been noted in Chapter 4 as a questionable and mostly spurious practice. In other cases, content analysis is done manually without procedures in place to ensure that interpretations are reasonable.

As noted throughout this book, other specialist texts should be referred to for detailed descriptions of the various research methods discussed. Here, only some of the most salient points are noted about content analysis in terms of evaluation of public communication.

Quantitative content analysis

Quantitative content analysis relies primarily on counting and it focuses on *manifest* elements in content – that is, numbers, words and phrases that are physically present and countable. Quantitative content analysis can record and report volumes and frequencies, such as:

- the audited circulation or audience size of media in which articles appear;
- the number of unique visitors to websites;

- the number of viewers of videos;
- the number of articles published, broadcast or posted online (including social media posts, tweets, etc.);
- the number of likes, follows, shares, retweets and other social media metrics; and
- the number of mentions of key words and phrases, such as brand names, spokespersons and key messages (key words and phrases).

In addition, quantitative content analysis can categorize media or other content, such as by topic or issue, and count the number of mentions of these to produce charts, graphs and tables reporting analysis of the content.

Two main approaches are used in quantitative content analysis today. The first approach, which is the longest-standing and relatively common in the public communication field, is the use of *coding* to categorize words and phrases, based on coding lists or purpose-built dictionaries against which words or phrases in texts are matched manually by human analysts or, more recently, by computers using machine learning. The findings of quantitative content analysis are mostly counts of the frequency of key words and phrases (referred to as *mentions* in public communication). As well as reporting the volume or frequency of various characteristics in text, counts are also commonly converted to percentages.

The second, more recent, approach uses *natural language processing* (NLP) to produce *topic models* based on *latent Dirichlet allocation* (LDA). David Blei and colleagues, who developed LDA in the early twenty-first century,[3] describe the process as:

> A generative probabilistic [that is, statistical] model for collections of discrete data such as text corpora. LDA is a three-level hierarchical Bayesian model, in which each item of a collection is modelled as a finite mixture over an underlying set of topics.
>
> *(Blei, Ng & Jordan, 2003, p. 993)*

In simple terms, LDA allows the identification of major topics and their content in terms of the number of words related to each, and hence estimation of the prevalence of those topics within documents and across multiple documents. Findings are then able to be presented as graphical models. Professor Ken Benoit – head of the Department of Methodology at The London School of Economics and Political Science, and a world-leading authority on quantitative content and textual analysis – uses LDA in an *R*-based application he has coproduced called Quanteda (derived from *quantitative analysis of textual data*) (Benoit & Nulty, 2016). As its name makes clear, Quanteda uses quantitative statistical methods, but Benoit says that unstructured text (qualitative data) can be effectively and usefully turned into quantitative (that is, statistical) findings and reported accordingly.

Even human coding can be, and increasingly is, assisted by computer applications that can identify words and phrases and conduct categorization based on *key words in context* (KWIC), and generate tables, charts and graphs of metrics during specified periods. However, computer programs require projects to be 'set up' – for example, key words and phrases, such as the names of brands, products and spokespersons, and messages to be tracked have to be entered in dictionaries, libraries and coding lists used.

Qualitative content analysis

Qualitative content analysis is mostly based on human coding of text into categories such as by issue, source or message based on KWIC, and applies a series of judgements about the characteristics of the text based on predetermined parameters (for example, support for a particular viewpoint). Qualitative content analysis in uses such as analysing media reporting also frequently categorizes content as positive, negative or neutral, or by assigning a score for *sentiment, tone* or *favourability* based on a scale (for example, 0–5, 0–10 or 0–100), as discussed when examining metrics in Chapter 4. However, qualitative content analysis – referred to as *textual analysis* by some – involves much more than simple categorization and counting.

A key part of qualitative content analysis is examination of the *latent* elements and potential meanings in content. Neuendorf describes the latent meanings of content as 'consisting of unobserved concepts that cannot be measured directly' (2002, p. 23). In an 'Introduction to content analysis' in his book *Qualitative Research Methods for the Social Sciences*, Bruce Berg says that latent analysis involves 'an interpretive reading of the symbolism underlying the physical data' (2007, p. 242). For example, a photo of a politician or senior corporate executive looking angry or worried can be interpreted as symbolic of controversy, crisis or failure; a positive headline such as 'ACME says takeover will proceed', if followed by a question mark, will implicitly suggest that there is evidence, or at least suspicion, that the takeover will not proceed; a series of pauses and stammers by a spokesperson in a television interview can be interpreted as a sign of uncertainty or obfuscation. Latent analysis also can reveal conceptual frameworks and ideologies, such as sexism, racism, neoliberal capitalist values, and so on, which may be unsaid, but underpinning and implied in what is said.

Qualitative analysis therefore requires careful and time-consuming analysis, and draws on knowledge and interpretive techniques from semiotics, narrative analysis, thematic analysis and, sometimes, discourse analysis. Even though qualitative content analysis also is usually conducted using computer software programs, qualitative analysis relies heavily on human interpretation, including examination of latent elements in texts, consideration of context, and understanding of linguistic elements such as nuance, sarcasm, double-entendre, metaphors and figures of speech. These will be further examined in relation to textual, narrative and thematic analysis in the next section.

Analysis processes are made robust and trustworthy in both quantitative and qualitative content analysis by a number of procedures. The following are important procedures that are too seldom applied and which need to be considered to achieve high standards in evaluation.

- *Systematic coding* Coding of content into categories and identification of key messages that may appear in multiple variations (messages rarely appear verbatim) should be guided by a *coding book*, also known as a *coding sheet*. This is a list of categories, such as issues and messages for coding, with instructions on what should be included in each category and sometimes what should be excluded. As W. Lawrence Neuman notes in his social research methods text, a researcher undertaking content analysis 'carefully designs and documents procedures for coding to make replication possible' (1997, p. 274).[4] For example, if a key message to be tracked is 'innovator' or 'innovative', the coding list could include instructions such as shown in Table 8.1.
- Use of *multiple coders* To minimize bias in content analysis and to ensure that 'obtained ratings are not the idiosyncratic results of one rater's subjective judgement' (Tinsley & Weiss, 1975, p. 359), researchers recommend using multiple coders (but note the next point).
- *Intercoder reliability assessment* When multiple coders are used, intercoder reliability assessment can be conducted by having two or more coders 'double-blind' code a sample of items, ideally as a pilot study at the beginning of a content analysis project, for *analysis of variance* (ANOVA) and *analysis of co-variance* (ANCOVA). A number of formulae exist for intercoder reliability assessment, such as Scott's pi (π), Cohen's kappa (κ), Spearman's rho (ρ), Pearson's correlation coefficient (r), Krippendorf's alpha (α) and Lin's concordance correlation coefficient (rc) (Lombard, Synder-Duch & Bracken, 2003; Neuendorf, 2002). These produce a score in which 1.0 is complete correlation in coding. Recognizing that human interpretation will vary, most researchers agree that correlation coefficients of 0.7–0.8 indicate high reliability (Ellis, 1994; Frey, Botan & Kreps, 2000; Neuendorf, 2002). When correlation in coding is below the recommended level, coding should stop, and the coding guidelines should be clarified and made more explicit.

Many researchers suggest that a productive approach is to combine manifest and latent analysis, thus supporting a mixed method approach to content analysis involving both quantitative and qualitative approaches. For example, Berg (2007) discusses the merits of a 'blended' approach and Neuendorf says that 'it is more useful to think of a continuum from highly manifest to highly latent' (2002, p. 24).

TABLE 8.1 Sample coding guidelines for two key messages

No.	Key message	Coding guidelines
001	Innovator/innovative	Code if text mentions 'innovative', 'thought leader', 'leader in products/services/market', 'first to market', 'new/fresh approach' or similar terms
002	Quality products	Code if text reports independent comment about quality, quality awards or research findings reporting quality Do NOT code self-promotion statements about quality

Media content analysis can be very beneficial in evaluation of public communication for two key reasons. First, to the extent that media reporting *reflects* public opinion and public comments, media content analysis can provide insights into what stakeholders and audiences are saying and thinking. Social media content analysis, in particular, affords access to stakeholders' and publics' responses and comments in their own words. Second, to the extent that media content can *influence* audiences, media content analysis potentially provides insights into 'public opinion in the making'.

However, it is important to point out and emphasize, as does Neuendorf (2002), that no matter how rigorously content analysis is conducted, inferences cannot be made as to producers' intent or audiences' interpretation from content analysis alone. Neuendorf and other content analysis specialists argue that an integrated approach involving use of content analysis, along with other research such as audience studies (that is, triangulation), is required to reliably draw inferences and predictions about audience effects of media or other content.

Textual, narrative and thematic analysis

Qualitative textual analysis pays close attention to characteristics such as visuals (for example, photos, graphics, including cartoons, and factors such as facial expressions in images), as well as language elements – particularly adjectives and adverbs, and figures of speech such as *metaphors*, *metonyms* and *synecdoche*. Whereas nouns and verbs are relatively neutral words, meaning derived from texts is most likely to be influenced by use of *adjectives* and *adverbs* (that is, describing and qualifying words). For example, the sentence 'The CEO addressed the shareholders' is quite neutral and factual, but the addition of two adjectives, so that it reads 'The embattled CEO addressed the angry shareholders', quite substantially changes and shapes its likely meaning for readers. Suddenly, there are implications that the company is in some sort of trouble, the chief executive officer (CEO) is at risk of losing their job and shareholders are unhappy over performance or management decisions. All of these interpretations come from two adjectives.

Metonyms are names of places or things used to denote something else through a familiar association, such as using the term 'White House' to refer to the offices and home of the US president, or simply 'London' or 'Canberra' to denote the national government of the UK and Australia, respectively. *Synecdoche* is the use of a part of something to denote the whole, such as using the word 'wheels' to mean a car or 'hired hands' to refer to workers. Such uses of language might sound trivial, but using the term 'wheels' to refer to a car suggests a youth culture, while referring to labourers as 'hired hands' draws attention to the fact that they are hired and that they are involved only in manual work – therefore of a low level and potentially precarious.

Narrative analysis looks beyond specific words and phrases in content to identify the overarching story that is being told. This form of analysis includes a number of specialized approaches, such as *syntagmatic analysis*, which focuses on the series of words and phrases that sequentially describe something (the facts of the matter), while *paradigmatic analysis* explores the concepts behind the syntagm and subtexts that may exist. Syntagmatic analysis reveals the story on the face of it: who says what to whom. Paradigmatic analysis looks behind the surface story to identify what deeper or broader meanings could be gained from a text. For example, a story about a criminal being caught by the police may, beyond the specific details of one person's malfeasance, be a lesson that crime does not pay; the comeuppance of the flamboyant CEO of a high-tech company may be a story about hubris. Paradigmatic analysis explores what a text says conceptually – not only what it says literally. Also, paradigmatic analysis looks at opposites and binaries in texts – that is, what is present and what is absent. For example, a politician's speech announcing new funding for education in maths and the sciences is as significant for what it does *not* say about funding and government priorities for the arts and humanities as what it says explicitly.

These few examples are designed to illustrate that there is much more to content and textual analysis than buying a software application, such as Brandwatch, or hiring the lowest cost service provider. Advanced content, textual, narrative and thematic analyses involve systematic procedures and require relevant knowledge and skills.

Greater attention is needed to content and textual analysis, because most organizations today acquire large volumes of unstructured data in text form through correspondence (letters, emails and inquiries), complaints, interview and focus group transcripts, and public consultation submissions. Such data is a potentially rich source of in-depth insights into the opinions, perceptions, interests and concerns of stakeholders and publics. An example of the importance of textual analysis tools and capabilities was witnessed by the author during ethnography and participatory action research conducted to inform this analysis. The 'NHS Mandate' is one of the largest public consultations to have been conducted by the UK government, designed to canvass views from health professionals and citizens on their expectations of the National Health Service (NHS) and its future, in terms of policy, funding, structure and management. In 2015, the NHS Mandate public consultation attracted 127,400 submissions, many of them involving multiple pages. In total, around half a million pages of text were received via online forms and emails. (To add context, it should be noted that the UK Department of Health conducted 56 public consultations in 2015 and only slightly fewer in 2016.) However, staff in the department did not have the tools to conduct qualitative data analysis on large volumes of unstructured data, such as text, and were forced to conduct manual analysis based on 'skim reading'.

Some 12 months later, during research conducted to inform this book, detailed analysis of the 127,400 submissions was conducted to address this deficiency using Method52, a sophisticated textual analysis web application that incorporates active machine learning. Method52 was developed by the University of Sussex in collaboration with DEMOS. No endorsement of this particular application is intended; the tool was selected collaboratively by staff in the Digital Insights unit of the Department of Health and this researcher as part of the participatory action research conducted. Academics regularly use specialist applications such as NVivo, part of the NUD*IST (an acronym for *non-numerical unstructured data indexing, searching and theorizing*) range of data analysis tools produced by QSR[5]. Other well-known textual analysis applications include the IBM Text Analytics, SAP Text Analytics and SAS Text Analytics packages, MAXQDA,[6] Leximancer[7] and R,[8] an open-source software (OSS) text-mining and sentiment analysis package.

Reanalysis of the 2015 NHS Mandate public consultation submissions confirmed some of the findings derived manually by Department of Health staff, including concerns about privatization of the NHS. In addition, it identified several other very important findings, including concerns among stakeholders and the publics that:

1. an insufficient period of time is allowed for consultation;
2. consultation documents contain jargon that is difficult to understand; and
3. many respondents do not trust government consultation, believing that their views will not be considered and that the government already has its mind made up on the issues allegedly open for consultation.

The third finding above is particularly important, because it identifies a lack of trust in the process of public consultation. Such evaluation informs policy-making, as well as public communication strategy, in important ways. Furthermore, the reanalysis of the 2015 NHS Mandate public consultation submissions found that several thousand were from health professionals, including doctors and nurses with 20 or more years of experience. Given that these expert groups are highly unlikely to attend focus groups, their comments and feedback constitute hard-to-get, valuable information. Similarly, the submissions included NHS patients reporting their experiences – again, a valuable source of insights from a key stakeholder group. This example underlines the importance of public communication professionals having the capability to undertake qualitative analysis of unstructured data, including text.

On receiving the report of the reanalysis of the NHS Mandate public consultation, a senior Department of Health policy adviser said in an email to the analysis team:

> There are two key benefits that are very clear . . . You were able to carry out your analysis in a fraction of the time, and using a fraction of the resources that we required last year . . . your analysis identified a number of trends and patterns that we had no means to identify. Not only would M52 or a similar tool enable us to analyse engagement data more efficiently, it would also enable a much greater depth of analysis and much more value to be obtained from both existing and future data sets . . .
>
> *(Anon., personal communication, September 2, 2016)*

Qualitative data analysis tools can be used to analyse any unstructured data, such as text, collected through correspondence, complaints and transcripts of interviews and focus groups, as well as public consultation submissions.

Case studies

Many public communication professionals do not recognize that case studies can be used as a method of research and even some researchers ignore or question case study analysis (Yin, 2009, p. 17). This is understandable to some extent because case study analysis is somewhat ambiguous in that it is not a specific *method*. Rather, it is undertaken using other research methods such as interviews, content analysis and sometimes ethnography (observation). Neither are case studies really a *methodology* because they are studied using either quantitative methodology (Yin, 2009) or qualitative methodology (Neuman, 2006; Silverman, 2000; Stake, 2008; Yin, 2009). It is probably more accurate to describe cases (whether they are events, campaigns or projects) as *units of analysis* for study using quantitative or qualitative methodology and a range of appropriate research methods – although Yin (2009) says that a number of specific units of analysis need to be selected in examining case studies (p. 27).

As Schramm noted: 'The essence of a case study . . . is that it tries to illuminate a decision or set of decisions: why they were taken, how they were implemented, and with what result' (1971b, p. 21). Case studies worthy of analysis can include whole campaigns, specific activities such as the handling of a crisis, events or particular functions such as internal communication. For example, during planning of a health communication project to increase rates of breast screening among women in BAME/CALD[9] communities (see this case study in Chapter 10), cancer screening promotions among similar groups in several countries were analysed to identify strategies that had proved effective and those that had not. Another example of effective use of case studies is in planning crisis communication. There is rarely time for primary research during a crisis, so, rather than rely on intuition, a public communication professional planning for, or facing, a crisis can examine what other organizations have done in similar situations. Many case studies are documented and reported in books of case studies, journals and online. These examples show that case studies are particularly useful for formative research.

One or multiple cases can be studied. Some ask how one case study can provide reliable or useful insights. Here, again, is the difference between qualitative and quantitative research: to gain generalized insights, multiple cases need to be studied – for example, to identify common approaches to using social media for internal communication. As Stake (1994) says, case study analysis is extended to cover several cases to learn more about a phenomenon, population or general condition (pp. 236–247). However, sometimes, detailed in-depth understanding of a particular case is useful. For example, in the instance of a crisis, an organization facing a crisis similar to one that another organization has weathered previously can benefit from gaining a deep understanding of that organization's experience and learning. In that instance, a single case could be an appropriate focus.

Cases worthy of analysis can be:

- *critical* cases, such as crises or 'critical incidents' – that is, any occurrence that has a significant impact on an organization or its operations;
- *extreme* or unique cases;

- *representative* cases, which can identify common practice and norms; or
- *revelatory* cases, such as product recalls, mergers and acquisitions, or launches that were very successful – or alternatively those that were abject failures.

Methods used to examine cases include ethnography (observation), interviews, and content analysis of documents such as plans, reports, speeches, policy statements, media coverage, speeches, and so on, as well as archival research and examination of artefacts in some instances (Yin, 2009).

Case study analysis is not particularly difficult to do, and usually involves little cost and only some time. It is therefore an example of a useful and cost-effective research method that can be applied in evaluation.

Ethnography

As partially explained in Chapter 1 in outlining the methodology used in researching this book, *ethnography* is a deep qualitative research method conducted to learn and understand phenomena that reflect the knowledge and system of meanings guiding the life of a particular group of people (Geertz, 1973). The method was developed in anthropology by famous names such as Frank Hamilton Cushing, Bronislaw Malinowski and Margaret Mead, but is now widely used in social and marketing research.

A benefit of ethnographic findings is that they provide what Geertz (1973) described as 'thick description', meaning that such analysis is based on detailed observation and interpretation during an extended period of fieldwork.[10] Casual informal observation does not constitute ethnography. As Barbara Tedlock notes, ethnographers live in a society for a considerable period of time, which she identifies as 'two years ideally' (2008, p. 151). This immersion in a group is important. In contrast with 'thin description', 'thick description' includes context and details of those involved, the place, time period and background information that helps to explain what is observed. This intense – sometimes microscopic – level of research cannot be achieved by short-term cursory observations or surveys, or even through structured or semi-structured interviews.

Participant observation

As Geertz (1973) noted, a primary research method used in ethnography is *participant observation*. However, ethnography also uses other methods to inform and validate observations, including informal interviews, discussion groups, analysis of documents such as plans, reports and historical records, and sometimes participation by the researcher. This combination of information sources is important because it is one of the ways in which subjectivity is addressed in ethnography, as will be further discussed in the following.

A further key methodological feature of ethnography is that the observation occurs in the *natural setting* of who or what is observed. For example, if a study is to explore the eating habits of families at breakfast, ethnography has to occur in the kitchens and dining rooms of those studied. This method differs substantially from laboratory research and even from other qualitative research, such as interviews and focus groups, which are often done in venues such as special focus group discussion rooms. John Creswell (2009) defines ethnography as 'a strategy of inquiry in which the researcher studies an intact cultural group in a natural setting over a prolonged period of time by collecting, primarily, observational and interview data' (p. 13). Unlike the claimed 'objective' and detached standpoint of the 'scientific method' of research, ethnography involves intensive study using observation, and sometimes participation, inside the world of those studied, as well as interviews. Interviews are necessarily in-depth, or may take the form of open-ended conversations over a period of time, with data collected in notes, audio or video recordings, diaries and other records such as documents (for example, minutes of meetings, transcripts of speeches and statements, etc.).

While all ethnography involves observation, this method of research is undertaken from two different perspectives that determine the relationship between the researcher (the observer) and the group under study (the observed). An *etic* ethnographic approach involves observation from outside the group under study. In this approach, the researcher does not become involved in the studied group or participate in studied activities in any way. The observations are therefore the interpretations of the observer. Conversely, an *emic* approach observes from within the social group – up close to the action, as it were – and sometimes even participating in the activities of the group under study. This approach seeks to discover and report the worldview and interpretations of the observed as intimately and in as much detail as possible from a first-hand perspective.

Elaborating on Geertz's classic definition, W. Lawrence Neuman emphasizes an emic approach, saying that ethnography is 'very detailed description of a . . . culture from the viewpoint of an *insider* in the culture to facilitate understanding of it' (2006, p. 381, emphasis added). While some studies focus on one or other approach, Jensen states that cultural expressions, including communication, 'can and should be studied from both internal and external perspectives' (2012, p. 267).

Both etic and emic approaches throw up some challenges to be addressed by users of this method, however. An etic approach runs the risk of an outsider misunderstanding and not gaining sufficient immersion in the culture and practices of the group studied. Conversely, an emic approach runs the risk of what anthropologists call 'going native' – that is, become emotionally involved with the group under study and losing the critical perspective required of a researcher. Recognizing these risks, the validity and reliability of ethnographic observations are addressed in several ways.

First, reflexivity needs to be applied in both senses in which it is understood in the social sciences. *Reflexivity* involves (a) researchers being conscious of and acknowledging their presence in the research and what effects that might have, and (b) recognizing the situated nature of research – that is, all research occurs in a particular context (Finlay & Gough, 2003). In the first instance, the researcher needs to be mindful of how power relations and the researcher's own worldview and perspective might influence the research. This is addressed through applying self-critique as part of the analysis and reflecting 'with the benefit of time' that affords some distance.

Reflexivity also requires a researcher to consider how they might become social-ized into the group being studied. This is addressed through the second approach for ensuring validity: as far as possible, interpretations of observed practices are compared with other research and records to verify and contextualize observations. For example, observations can be compared with published records, historical and archival material, policies, speeches, events, and first-hand statements and interviews with members of the observed group to confirm or challenge observations.

Video ethnography

While early ethnography relied on researchers' notes of their observations and sometimes sound recordings, the availability of compact portable video cameras has facilitated the use of *video ethnography*. Video recording provides accurate records of discussions and behaviours, including body language, location, background, and so on. Uses range from marketers installing video cameras in the kitchens and dining rooms of homes to observe breakfast eating habits (with permission, of course), to video recording the facial expressions and gestures of people with dementia as they view artworks as part of evaluating an 'art and dementia' programme designed to enhance quality of life and well-being (for example, Kenning, 2016).

However, it must be remembered that a video camera can be intrusive in research, and can make those observed shy and reluctant to act normally or can cause them to 'play to the camera'. The availability of very small cameras such as GoPros has reduced this risk and if the camera is located discretely, those observed often forget about it after a short time.

Autoethnography

In some circumstances, the researcher's own experiences provide valid and useful insights. This is particularly the case when the researcher has been a witness to, or participant in, major events or developments. This has given rise to *autoethnography*, in which a researcher reflects on and analyses their own experiences and observa-tions. It has to be said that some researchers reject claims that autoethnography is a valid research method, arguing that it is selective (that is, one person's observations) and subjective (for example, Shields, 2000).

However, Barbara Tedlock (2008) rejects the binary separation of 'objective observation' associated with 'scientific' research and subjective autobiographical accounts. The ethnographic research method of autoethnography recognizes the value of personal first-hand accounts and experiences. What separates ethnographic and autoethnographic research from mere stories, according to Garance Maréchal (2010), is reflexivity and the connection of observations to wider cultural, political and social meanings and understandings. In other words, as in ethnography, the researcher should carefully and mindfully reflect on their position in the research and also look for other evidence that might confirm or disconfirm personal observations.

Netnography

With the proliferation of online interaction via the Internet, including conversations, public comment and production of artefacts ranging from text and videos to designs and even products, ethnography has gone online. Observation of behaviour on the Internet is a relatively new method of research referred to as *netnography*. This involves observing the online behaviour of individuals and groups. Data collected includes posts and comments such as tweets and microblogging, as well as recording digital interrelationships using methods such as *social network analysis* (as discussed in Chapter 7). Whereas anthropologists observe the cultural norms, behaviours and interrelationships of individuals, tribes and other forms of physical communities, netnography applies ethnography to study the digital trails and data deposits that people and groups leave as they move around and interact in cyberspace.

Ethnomethodology

Another research method that is variously described as a particular form of ethnography, or more broadly as a twentieth-century phenomenological challenge to US sociology, is *ethnomethodology*. The field was pioneered by Harold Garfinkel (1974), among others, and refers to the study of how people make sense of their world and form communities and societies through mundane, everyday interactions and activities. Ethnomethodology emerged as a challenge to empiricist approaches in sociology that built grand theories about society and human behaviour based on expert studies conducted using formal quantitative surveys and experiments. Ethnomethodologists argue that you cannot simply ask a person what norms they apply, or how and why they decide to act in certain ways in various circumstances, because most people are not able to articulate or describe these factors. Also, they are often unconscious of the social rules and 'social facts' that they ingest and apply in their daily lives.

Garfinkel and his followers claimed that people construct a common-sense knowledge of society and negotiate shared values, such as knowing how to dress and behave publicly, through everyday interactions as much as, or more than, through formal rules and regulations. Ethnomethodologists claim that studying these everyday interactions and activities can reveal the processes of meaning-making and social construction better than externally conducted scientific research.

One of the ways in which ethnomethodology identifies important everyday interactions is by disrupting a social norm and then closely observing how people react and respond to restore social equilibrium. For example, in the case of dress, an ethnomethodologist might introduce to a group some individuals who are dressed very differently from the norm of the group and then observe interactions. Usually, members of the group will not confront the newcomers who are considered to be dressed inappropriately. However, through a series of mundane interactions, either the newcomers will modify their dress or the group will come to understand and accept the newcomers' mode of attire. For instance, members in a group may avoid interacting with a woman wearing a very revealing outfit (the men may fear repriaals from their wives and partners if they do so, and women might interpret the newcomer's behaviour as predatory or anti-feminist). Thus the woman who dressed in a way that she thought would attract attention and social inclusion may be left standing alone in social gatherings, which is likely to cause her to reassess her attire. Similarly, a woman wearing a hijab might initially be avoided and provoke negative reactions in a Western group – but if she is afforded an opportunity to tell her story, and to explain her beliefs and views, the group may modify its social norms and come to accept that wearing a hijab is normal for many people. The ways in which groups negotiate such accommodations to maintain social equilibrium and a level of consensus about what is 'normal' and 'right' – or do not – is the focus of ethnomethodology. Ethnomethodology seeks to understand the mostly unnoticed influences and processes that shape attitudes and behaviour.

In a work environment, ethnomethodology could be used to examine the everyday interactions that shape corporate culture. Beyond the formal lines of communication and organization values and policies that are the explicit manifestations of corporate culture, a whole underworld of interactions and social norms and rules exists and shapes attitudes and behaviour. Many organizations know too little of these influences and could benefit from using ethnomethodology. Like ethnography, ethnomethodology is an approach to research – more a methodology than a method – because it employs a number of specific methods. One of the major criticisms of ethnomethodology is that it does not specify any particular research method: ethnomethodologists gather information and insights in any way they deem appropriate. However, close observation (ethnography and netnography), as well as many of the other methods discussed in this chapter, can be applied including in-depth interviews, focus groups, content analysis and social network analysis.

Conversation analysis

A related research method that is sometimes considered a form of ethnomethodology is *conversation analysis*, which records and analyses the conversations of people within specific groups and in specific situations. For instance, conversation analysis can centre on everyday conversations about issues to identify how people come to understand and make sense of them, or even conversations between patients and doctors (for example, to understand how patients interpret and explain their conditions). The latter, of course, requires written consent from both doctors and patients. Whereas conversation could be considered part of mundane, everyday sense-making and therefore a form of ethnomethodology, conversation analysis has evolved as a specialist research method because it focuses on the specific speech acts in conversations such as the language and terms used, mode of expression (such as voice volume and pitch), *phatic* expressions and non-verbal elements. Non-verbal elements examined can include *kinesics* (body language), *proxemics* (distance and spacing between those conversing), *haptics* (touch), *oculesics* (eye contact) and *paralanguage* (such as gestures). However, conversation analysis does not consider context, and this is a key difference between this method and ethnomethodology, which examines behaviour within a context and seeks to understand the social environment.

Action research

Action research is not widely understood or used in evaluation of public communication, but it offers significant potential. As the name suggests, it is the conduct of research during action – that is, during an activity in real time, not *ex post*. However, it is more than *process* evaluation, because action research is undertaken throughout a project from early planning through to evaluation of impact and acquiring learning to inform future communication. The purpose of action research is usually to solve a particular problem, such as to identify ways of reducing costs, to increase performance or efficiency, or to develop alternatives by studying the action or activity *in situ*.

Some regard all action research as participative – that is, as involving those responsible for the action or actions being studied. For example, an Open University guide provides a simple definition of action research as 'any research into practice undertaken by those involved in that practice with an aim to change and improve it' (Open University, 2005, p. 4). Similarly, Bob Dick (2000), who has written extensively about action research, describes its key characteristics as *participative, qualitative* and *reflective* (para. 3). However, others separately identify *participatory action research* (PAR) as action research undertaken collaboratively with those normally involved in the action(s) being studied. In this narrower view, action research simply refers to research that studies particular actions *in situ* in real time. Thus action research can be conducted by one or more researchers, with those involved in the action studied being 'subjects' or 'respondents' in the study. However, most action research today stresses a participatory approach.

Participatory action research (PAR)

Whereas the studied group goes about its activities in the normal way in traditional action research (that is, they do the actions) and the researcher is responsible for conducting the research, in PAR the group being studied are co-researchers. Members of the group are encouraged to observe and to critically reflect on their actions (see Figure 8.1). These characteristics make this research approach very different from other methodologies and methods.

Typical methods used in action research are ethnography (observation), supported by note-taking and record-keeping, as well as interviews and content analysis

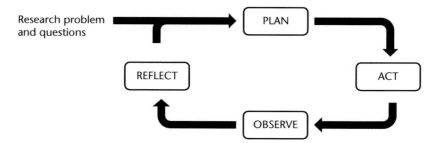

FIGURE 8.1 The process of participatory action research

(for example, of documents such as plans, communication materials and reports, in the case of public communication). Also, as Dick (2000) notes, PAR places emphasis on *critical reflection*. During and after participants carry out actions, they are encouraged to 'step back' and reflect on what was done. This includes asking questions such as what worked well, what did not work well, what could be improved and how the action(s) might be done differently with better results.

Dick and other advocates of PAR also point out that this approach is *responsive* and *emergent*. Participants in PAR projects need to respond to circumstances in a dynamic way. For example, if an action is not working as intended, the collaborators should be encouraged to reflect on the reasons why and adjust the approach – ideally, in a consensual way through discussion. Also, findings emerge throughout the project. Unlike surveys or experiments from which findings are revealed after analysis of all of the data, PAR can yield findings at any point during the action – and they are often discovered unexpectedly.

A key benefit of action research is that the research is undertaken inside the activity, rather than looking in from outside. This affords deep 'immersion in the data pool', to paraphrase Kimberley Neuendorf's recommendation in relation to content analysis, which can lead to deep insights (2002, p. 72). Also, it involves those most intimately familiar with the activity studied. As a result, PAR can provide practical solutions and have impact because its findings are already in action, unlike some research findings that languish in academic journal articles or reported laboratory experiments.

However, it must be pointed out in the interest of balance that there are disadvantages and potential pitfalls in action research. As with ethnography, one risk is what anthropologists call 'going native' – that is, the coordinating researcher becomes assimilated into the group and/or activity that is the subject of study and loses their critical and analytical perspective. The opposite problem is losing control of a project and it descending into chaos. Even PAR projects require a lead researcher who convenes meetings, ensures data is reliably collected and recorded, and keeps the project on track in terms of its objectives and research questions being investigated. The lead researcher needs to carefully balance control, on one hand, and open collaboration and emergence, on the other. This requires *reflexivity* on the part of the researcher – that is, being aware of, and regularly reviewing, their role and potential influence on the activities or people studied and biases that may occur. Another threat to action research projects is politics. Action research projects can become caught up in organizational politics, ranging from senior managers trying to inject their views, to defensiveness on the part of participants who may feel threatened by the open, critical nature of the research. Again, the leadership of the senior researcher is important in maintaining the integrity of the research and usually very experienced researchers lead PAR projects.

Sense-making methodology (SMM)

A recently developed advanced method of planning, implementing and evaluating public communication is *sense-making methodology* (SSM). While sometimes narrowly understood as a method of making sense of data (that is, analysis and interpretation), SSM is in fact a broad methodology for research, planning and implementation that is focused on genuine, open *dialogue* among individuals and between organizations and their publics that reaches beyond the tokenistic efforts that often characterize government and corporate engagement, consultation and research.

There are at least four key interrelated principles that inform SMM. First, at a philosophical level (an underpinning starting point of all research), SSM is based on the tenet that people make sense of the world and things in it by 'talking them over' and 'talking them through'. It is often in the course of talking things over with friends, peers or even strangers that people form and consolidate their own views and attitudes. These others sometimes function as 'sounding boards' offering feedback, but also meaning-making comes out of the talking itself – not only the advice or suggestions received or questions asked. Furthermore, this 'talking' involves both internal dialogue (talking to oneself), as well as external dialogue with others. Often, these dialogues involve the *hermeneutic circle* (Heidegger, 1962 [1927]), a cognitive process of moving back and forth from micro to macro perspectives and from one viewpoint to contrary viewpoints and back, in an iterative circular thought process or series of circles. Colloquially, this is often referred to as 'mulling something over' or 'chewing it over'.

Furthermore, this 'mulling over' involves reflection – that is, quiet space between spoken or unspoken statements in which to think. From the outset, this philosophical stance of sense-making through dialogue (internal and external), including reflection, makes it quite different from traditional quantitative and qualitative research methodologies in which participants are put on the spot to express their views and give answers in a survey, interview or even a focus group without time for discussion or thinking reflectively.

A second key principle of SMM is that it recognizes that people move through space and time, and that circumstances and context change as they do so. This is relevant at two levels. At a macro level, SMM contrasts traditional approaches to mass communication and public communication that assume or 'imagine' audiences as static groups identifiable by stable demographic and psychographic data (Anderson, 1991 [1983]). Conversely, SMM recognizes that people are in a constant state of growth and change. Therefore, SMM proponents argue that traditional audience segmentation works only for identifying habitual ways of thinking and behaviours, and they see traditional market research and quantitative statistics, such as demographics, as blunt instruments with which to measure audience attitudes, perceptions, interests and needs. Sense-making methodology tries to understand the *person in situation* – in other words, the person within the social, cultural, political and economic context in which they exist at a particular point in time using more open-ended qualitative methods. At a micro level, implementation of an SMM approach recognizes the importance of allowing people space and time to talk things over – either reflectively to themselves or with others.

Hence SMM typically uses focus groups and discussion forums. In these, one particular SMM technique is *sense-making journaling*, in which participants are asked to write down their reactions to subjects being discussed and their thoughts. The journal comments are kept private, but they allow participants time for internal dialogue and for reflection to prepare their thoughts before speaking to answer questions or to express their views. Brenda Dervin and Lois Foreman-Wernet, who have written about SMM extensively, say that 'reflective communicating with the self' is suppressed in traditional interviews and focus groups that focus on and strive for agreement and consensus, while in private journaling 'space is opened for what is usually left unsaid' (2013, p. 155). The methodology is cautious towards consensus, recognizing that consensus can be a majority view imposed on others or a creation of the loud and impetuous that renders others silent.

A third key principle of SMM is that, in implementing methods for creating dialogue, it adopts a verbing approach and avoids nouning. *Nouning* refers to the naming of people, not in terms of their first or family names, but with category signifiers. While some categorization is essential in daily life (for example, when asking for 'a doctor'), the naming of people carries with it a tendency to categorize individuals and groups of people as, for instance, 'workers', 'unemployed', 'low socio economic', 'conservative', 'radical', and so on. This naming is often done in advance of research – psychographics being an example. Once so-named, these people are assumed to belong to this group, and are addressed and considered as being what they have been labelled. In contrast, *verbing* refers to allowing people to talk about what they do, think or feel at that point in time. The unemployed person may be starting at university and dreaming of a career in science – and thus their attitudes are likely to reflect what they are doing rather than the views of an 'unemployed' person. This approach requires open-ended research in which the researcher avoids imposing categories or labels that *speak for* people and allows the *person-in-situation* to be presented, rather than represented. Avoidance of nouning should also extend to pronouns such as the undefined 'we' and 'they'. Who precisely are 'we' and 'they'? Most often, they are imagined groups.

Dervin and Foreman-Wernet say that SMM approaches require well-meaning experts in marketing, research and communication to 'humble' their own knowledge, and subjugate their views and categorizations, in favour of allowing audiences to speak on their own terms (2013, p. 160). This methodology recognizes that the everyday experiences of people are valid and valuable sources of information that are often dismissed in favour of 'expert' views and external scientific data. Ultimately, audiences know more about their lives than anyone else; hence we should listen to them – often and intently. In the words of Dervin and Foreman-Wernet, in the SMM approach participants in research are 'theorists of their own worlds' (2013, p. 158).

A fourth key principle that makes SSM fundamentally different from other top-down and expert-led approaches to research and planning is that the methodology is based on an understanding and acceptance that 'both organizations and constituencies have expertise to share, common struggles to ponder, and capacities to teach and learn from each other' (Dervin & Foreman-Wernet, 2013, p. 160). Dervin and Foreman-Wernet state frankly: '[I]n SMM public communication is defined as the means to not merely change constituencies but to change organizations' (2013, p. 160). They summarize the SSM approach as:

> You listen to me, and I will listen to you; you learn from me, and I will learn from you; you trust my narratives about my material circumstances, and I may listen to the narratives within which you wrap your expertise. But you will also have to listen to my expertise.
>
> *(Dervin & Foreman-Wernet, 2013, p. 159)*

Thus SMM deploys open listening involving *interactivity* (Pelias & VanOosting, 1987), *receptivity* (Kompridis, 2011), *reciprocity*, which is one of the essential elements of engagement (Oullier, 2014), and what Roger Silverstone (2007) calls *hospitality*, and is contingent and ethical, whereas some forms of 'strategic listening' and intelligence gathering are questionable. (The concept of listening and its roles in evaluation will be further examined in concluding this chapter.)

Based on these key principles, SMM predominantly uses qualitative research to gain deep insights into audiences through open dialogue. Also, SMM goes further than facilitating dialogue with major *stakeholders*. As the Organizational Listening Project found, dialogue and consultation are often restricted to the 'usual suspects' – that is, major organizations such as business groups, trade unions and mobilized lobby groups that represent economic and political elites (Macnamara, 2016a, p. 180). In contrast, SMM requires open listening and engagement of *all* parties potentially affected by an organization, which often requires *outreach* rather than passive engagement such as waiting for submissions to consultations or relying on occasional surveys.

The reason that SMM is referred to as a 'methodology' is that, in addition to recommending particular research methods, it offers a broad set of principles and methods for working in a field of practice. As Dervin and Foreman-Wernet point out, SMM 'mandates refocussing communication attention on dialogue rather than transmission' of information, and goes on to identify a number of specific methods and techniques (2013, p. 154). Similarly, D. Lawrence Kincaid, Richard Delate, Douglas Storey and Maria Elena Figueroa say that public communication should be 'conceptualized as dialogue with the audience', noting that dialogue requires speaking and listening (2013, p. 305).

In this context, evaluation is '*systematic listening* to the audience' (Kincaid et al., 2013, p. 306, original emphasis) and should be done on an ongoing basis – not in annual surveys or occasional 'listening posts' or public consultations. Also relevant to evaluation is that SMM 'gives the audience a chance to speak first – to provide valuable information about their own situations, beliefs and values, current and past behaviour, and hopes and dreams for a better life' (Kincaid et al., 2013, p. 306). This equates to formative research, but SMM advocates a more open, active listening than traditional market research, environmental scanning, pre-testing and other methods provide.

A final explanation and warning comes from Dervin and Foreman-Wernet who say: 'Communication is ultimately a quid pro quo. People are willing to listen to that which collides with or is new to their worlds when those communicating *at* them change to communicating *with* them' (2013, p. 153, emphasis added).

Approaches such as SMM are rarely used in PR, corporate, marketing, government or political communication, or even in research, but offer much to create a listening organization, a learning organization and an adaptive organization. Sense-making methodology is an approach that can reduce the organization-centricity that is identified and critiqued in many evaluation models. The organization that does not listen, learn and adapt inevitably faces fractious issues and crises, and potentially an uncertain future. Conversely, open listening informs strategy (formative research), provides a constant stream of feedback (evaluation), and can build productive relationships and trust.

To provide an overview of the methods discussed in this and the preceding chapter, Table 8.2 draws on 36 case studies examined in the Organizational Listening Project that identified research as one of the key methods of organizational listening, along with public consultation, customer and stakeholder relations, social media, correspondence and other channels (Macnamara, 2014a, 2015a, 2015b, 2016a, 2016b). This table rates the frequency of use of the research methods discussed among the organizations studied on a 10-point scale from 0 (not at all) to 10 (very regular use by all organizations studied), based on interviews, document analysis and observations. This shows that all, or the vast majority of, the organizations regularly use audited circulation statistics, content analysis (particularly of media publicity) and surveys. Structured interviews, reputation studies, return on investment (ROI), in-depth interviews, focus groups, and ROI derivatives such as return on marketing investment (ROMI) and return on expectations (ROE) are also widely used, along with people meters to track broadcast and cable viewing. Overall, this reveals a dominant focus on quantitative methods, with eight of the ten most widely used research methods being fully or predominantly quantitative.

TABLE 8.2 Metrics and quantitative and qualitative research methods used by organizations

Research and analysis methods	Frequency of use										
	0	1	2	3	4	5	6	7	8	9	10
Audited circulation statistics											✓
Content analysis											✓
Surveys										✓	
Structured interviews									✓		
Reputation studies									✓		
Return on investment								✓			
In-depth interviews								✓			
Focus groups							✓				
ROMI, ROE, etc.						✓	✓				
People meters					✓						
Case studies				✓							
Econometrics			✓								
Benefit–cost ratio			✓								
Cost–benefit analysis			✓								
Cost-effectiveness analysis		✓									
Physiological testing		✓									
Experiments, incl. RCTs		✓									
Social network analysis		✓									
Textual analysis		✓									
Big data analysis		✓									
Ethnography		✓									
Action research		✓									
Market mix modelling		✓									
Behavioural insights		✓									
Social ROI	✓										
Sense-making methodology	✓										

Note: 0 = not at all; 5 = occasionally by most organizations; 10 = very regularly by all organizations

Source: Based on Macnamara (2015a, 2016a)

(While content analysis and reputation studies can be done qualitatively, they are mostly implemented using quantitative methods.) A number of other quantitative methods, including econometrics, benefit–cost ratio and cost–benefit analysis, are also more popular than qualitative methods such as textual analysis, ethnography and action research. 'Big data' analysis is talked about extensively, but was not being undertaken in most organizations at the time of this study. Advanced methods such as behavioural insights, market mix modelling and sense-making methodology were used rarely or not all by most organizations studied.[11]

Evaluation as listening

Many aspects of evaluation involve and depend on listening. While, ultimately, evaluation requires the interpretation and application of findings, listening is crucial along the way. However, listening remains quite narrowly understood and deployed in many organizations, based on case studies examined in the Organizational Listening Project. Often, listening is associated with *intelligence* and, as discussed previously, many practitioners profess and practise strategic listening. In simple terms, *strategic listening* can be interpreted as an organization listening for what it wants to know and to gain insights that provide it with strategic advantage – not necessarily listening to what its audiences want to say. A detailed discussion of organizational listening based on an expansive literature analysis and critical review of 36 case studies is provided in *Organizational Listening: The Missing Essential in Public Communication* (Macnamara, 2016a) and in an online report (Macnamara, 2015a). This study argued that organizations need to create an 'architecture of listening' and identified eight key features. Based on extensive empirical evidence, the study proposed that organizations need:

1. An organizational *culture* that is open to listening (i.e., an organization must want to listen and be prepared to listen to those who wish to say something to it);
2. *Policies* that specify and require listening;
3. *Systems* that are open and interactive, such as websites and social media pages that allow visitors to post comments and questions, vote, etc.;
4. *Technologies* to aid listening, such as monitoring tools or services for tracking media and online comment; automated acknowledgement systems; textual analysis software for sense-making, and even specialist argumentation software to facilitate meaningful consultation and debate;
5. *Resources* including staff to operate listening systems and do the work of listening, such as establishing forums and consultations, inviting comment, and monitoring, analysing, and responding to comments and questions;
6. *Skills* for listening; and
7. *Articulation* of the voices of stakeholders and publics to policy-making and decision-making. While listening does not imply or necessarily require agreement, unless there is a link to policy-making and decision-making for consideration

of what is said to an organization, voice has no value, engagement with the organization is hollow, and disengagement is likely to follow.

(Macnamara, 2016a, pp. 247–272)

Along with public consultation, customer relations, processing correspondence, handling complaints, engaging in social media and special forums that solicit feedback, research requires listening. Good research should involve attentive open listening, which the Organizational Listening Project defined as made up of 'seven canons of listening':

1. *Recognition* of others (i.e., avoiding marginalization and discrimination);
2. *Acknowledgement* of those who speak;
3. Paying *attention* to those who speak;
4. *Interpretation* of what others say as fairly and empathetically as possible;
5. Gaining an *understanding* of others' perspectives, views, arguments, and proposals;
6. Giving *consideration* to what others say; and
7. *Responding* in some appropriate way, which may or may not be agreement and acceptance.

(Macnamara, 2016a, pp. 41–43)

Summary

*   There is a wide range of qualitative research methods that can be used to evaluate public communication. Ten or more methods have been examined in this chapter. Public communication professionals need to be familiar with at least a significant number of these. As noted throughout this analysis, those requiring more detailed explanation of these research methods should undertake wider reading of research methods texts, or consider a course in research methodology and methods.
*   The most widely used qualitative research methods are in-depth interviews, focus groups, and various forms of qualitative content analysis and textual analysis. All public communication practitioners need to have a sound understanding of these methods. Content and textual analysis can be applied to a wide range of content, including media articles, social media posts and comments, transcripts of interviews and focus groups, complaints, correspondence (that is, letters, emails and online inquiries) and submissions to public consultations. Such analysis can identify key themes, patterns and trends, and may even provide geolocation breakdowns.
*   In the digital age, evaluators should consider netnography, as well as social network analysis, in addition to basic social media monitoring and social media content analysis.
*   Approaches to qualitative, as well as quantitative, research have much to learn from sense-making methodology.

- Research methods overviewed in this chapter can be used to evaluate the outcomes and impact of public communication activities on stakeholders, publics and society generally, beyond those intended by organizations. Also, they can evaluate the outcomes and impact of public communication activities on organizations themselves – for example, whether they learned, adapted or changed as a result. A more open, bidirectional view of outcomes and impact should be considered by public communication professionals if two-way communication and relationships are to be more than normative theories.

Notes

1 Many contemporary scholars, particularly those in the arts and humanities, argue that humans cannot be objective. Poststructuralist thinkers use the term *intersubjectivity* to differentiate shared understandings and meanings developed through research, analysis and rational thought from personal subjectivity.

2 Most researchers refer to specific methods of analysing textual content as *textual analysis*. However, a number of applications and references also use the term *text analysis* interchangeably.

3 Jonathan Pritchard, Stephens and Donnelly (2000) are reported to have also developed latent Dirichlet allocation (LDA) around the same time.

4 Neuman is mainly discussing quantitative content analysis in referring to *replication*. However, qualitative content analysis should be designed so that a high level of consistency can be achieved.

5 See www.qsrinternational.com.

6 See www.maxqda.com.

7 See http://info.leximancer.com.

8 See www.r-project.org.

9 The description *black, Asian and minority ethnic* (BAME) is used in the UK and parts of Europe, while *culturally and linguistically diverse* (CALD) is used in some other countries to describe non-Anglo communities. Both terms are criticized, but there is no consensus on suitable alternatives.

10 The term *thick description* was first used by philosopher Gilbert Ryle (1949) and was applied to anthropology by Clifford Geertz (1973).

11 It should be noted that these estimates are based on qualitative research, including interviews, observations and content analysis of documents, not quantitative research, and are therefore estimates.

9
REPORTING AND USING EVALUATION

This chapter includes a brief, but important, review of the key steps and methods for reporting and using evaluation. This is a vital stage because, after all the hard work of collecting, analysing and interpreting data, the benefits of evaluation are realized only if findings are articulated into future decisions, policy-making and strategies. Too many research reports and studies sit on bookshelves or in filing cabinets or on hard disks with their findings largely ignored or only partially implemented at best. The reasons for this include management resistance, in some cases. But researchers and public communication practitioners themselves are also partly responsible for translating findings into practice, as is discussed in the following sections.

Research reports

The findings of research studies will usually be presented in a *research report*. A detailed research report is standard practice when external research and analysis companies are commissioned to undertake evaluation of some kind. In addition, research reports can be produced from internal research studies such as staff surveys.

Research reports vary widely in size and format. Academic research reports usually include a comprehensive literature review. As noted in Chapter 5, conducting a review of existing published research relevant to the study at hand is a worthwhile step because it identifies existing data and findings that may be informative, it can help to guide the approach and it avoids duplication of effort. Furthermore, academic research texts also recommend inclusion of a detailed outline of the methodology used for conducting the primary research. For example, Lawrence Frey, Carl Botan and Gary Kreps (2000) list the sections of a research report as: (a) *title*; (b) *abstract*; (c) *introduction*; (d) *review of literature*; (e) *research questions* or *hypotheses* explored; (f) the *methodology* used, including specific procedures such as sampling type and method, research methods and data analysis method; (f) *results* or *findings*;

(h) *discussion*; and (i) *references* (p. 67). Arthur Asa Berger (2000) presents what he calls the *IMRD model* of a research report, comprising: (a) an *introduction*, including background, literature review and research questions or hypotheses; (b) *method*; (c) *results*; and (d) *discussion*, including recommendations (pp. 255–256).

In professional practice, a lengthy literature review followed by a detailed description of the methodology of the study is likely to encounter reader resistance. Particularly in the case of presenting research findings to busy management, research reports need to get to the point quickly. A review of more than 60 research reports conducted while researching this book[1] – including many produced externally by research companies, as well as internally – found that over half were more than 40 pages in length, and a third did not present the key findings and recommendations until near the end. This makes digestion of the findings and data difficult, and such reports are likely to be 'skimmed' by management at best. However, it is important that information about how the research was conducted and supporting material, such as data tables, are included in the interests of transparency and trustworthiness.

A number of researchers recommend formats for research reports that can meet the potentially conflicting requirements of brevity and comprehensiveness. In his *Social Research Methods*, W. Lawrence Neuman (1997) recommends starting with (a) a short *abstract* and (b) an *executive summary*, which overviews the study and presents the key findings, followed by (c) defining the *problem*, (d) the *methods* used, (e) the *findings* in detail, (f) *discussion* and (f) *conclusions* (pp. 495–496). Public relations (PR) evaluation specialist Don Stacks (2002) proposes that research reports can be structured thus: (a) an *executive summary*; (b) *literature review*; (c) *method*; (d) *results*; (e) *discussion*; and (f) *appendices* (pp. 296–300).

An even more direct approach to reporting findings can be used without compromising transparency or rigour by providing only a brief summary of the methodology in the body of a research report, the detail of which (such as the sampling frame and method, response rates, research methods used, data analysis techniques, and so on) is contained in an appendix. This allows a research report to be structured as follows.

- *Title* page, with copyright details, date, author details, etc.;
- *Contents* page;
- Short *introduction*, including the problem explored and the methodology in overview;
- *Executive summary* of key findings, conclusions and recommendations;
- *Findings* in detail;
- *Conclusions* and *recommendations* in detail;
- *Appendices*, including a detailed description of the methodology and other relevant materials, such as supporting data tables;
- *References*.[2]

In this way, research reports can be easy to read, highlight key findings and contain the detail necessary for reporting rigorous research in a transparent way.

Regular research reports such as those presented on a monthly or quarterly basis by media analysis companies can be particularly tedious if they are repetitive or largely repetitive. A review of such reports found that many contain the same sections and paragraphs updated with slightly changed numbers such as 'media sentiment in the period averaged 7.6 on a 0–10 scale, compared with last month's 7.4'. Is this significant? If not, why not *say* that there was no significant change or a very minimal improvement? Research reports should not be formulaic, and should focus on inferences and predictions, not simply description, as discussed in relation to key concepts and procedures in research in Chapter 6.

Presenting findings including the power of visuals

In addition to written reports, findings of formative, process and summative evaluation usually need to be presented to various groups, such as management meetings, conferences, seminars and workshops. Presentations are important because they actively put research findings in front of relevant individuals and groups, such as senior managers and management teams, rather than passively rely on them to read research reports. Presentations can also combine the influence of interpersonal communication and rhetoric (the art of persuasion) through speaking and visual communication.

Visualization of research findings is particularly important, given the orientation of modern and contemporary societies towards visual communication (Smith, Moriarty, Barbatsis & Kenney, 2011). The presentation of charts and graphs summarizing quantitative findings is very common. However, qualitative data also can be summarized visually. For instance, key issues or themes found in unstructured data, such as interview and focus group transcripts or public consultation submissions, can be represented in word clouds, graphic timelines, or illustrations such as drawings and diagrams. Also, key comments by research participants can be recorded on video and played (with the participants' permission) in presentations with significantly more impact than words on paper.

Key performance indicators (KPIs)

Most organizations adopt a number of *key performance indicators* (KPIs) against which evaluation is reported. Some organizations adopt a limited number of overall KPIs for public communication, such as 'increase brand equity' and 'increase sales', while others develop specific KPIs for each functional unit or programme. The latter is most common. Whichever approach is taken, the key with KPIs is the first word. KPIs should not be so numerous that they try to evaluate everything. The central concept of KPIs is that they identify the *key* metrics or qualitative factors that are considered to be essential for success, and serve to focus attention and resources on evaluating these.

The question is often asked: 'How many KPIs should a functional unit have?' There is no single answer, but, generally speaking, most functional units have no fewer than three KPIs, while any more than six or seven can make evaluation onerous and potentially expensive. From analysis of company and government strategic communication plans and evaluation reports, between three and five KPIs seems to be a manageable number.

Key performance indicators are usually short statements containing numbers that represent targets. Examples of KPIs for public communication identified in reports examined included:

- 85 per cent of media coverage favourable;
- 65 per cent awareness of the new structure among staff;
- 75 per cent top-of-mind brand recall within target markets;
- 7/10 or above satisfaction rating among corporate website users; and
- 10 per cent or above increase in membership applications based on communication activities.

Indicators for public communication should ideally be derived from collaboration between senior management and public communication professionals. This ensures that management agrees with the targets that are set. However, public communication professionals also need to be involved to provide specialist knowledge of key steps and stages of communication that can be measured. This leads to the question of where KPIs come from – that is, how are they identified?

The frameworks and models of evaluation of public communication presented and discussed in Chapter 3 provide the basis for KPIs and most other forms of evaluation reporting. These frameworks identify the various steps and milestones that need to be achieved at inputs, outputs, outtakes, outcomes and impact stages. A number of the most relevant metrics and milestones from these frameworks can be selected as KPIs. Importantly, however, KPIs should not all be at output level. Ideally, one or more KPIs should be identified and evaluated at each key stage of communication, to include outputs, outtakes, outcomes and impact.

Balanced scorecards

Developed by Robert Kaplan and David Norton (1992), *balanced scorecards* have been applied to public communication practices such as PR by a number of researchers (for example, Fleisher & Mahaffy, 1997). The notion of 'balanced' comes from the development of *triple bottom-line* thinking espoused by John Elkington (1994, 1998). This concept proposed that, in addition to the financial bottom line (that is, sales and profits), which traditionally has been the primary, or even sole, basis for reporting performance, organizations, including corporations, need to pay attention to the social and environmental impacts of their operations. Hence the triple bottom line has come to be colloquially known as 'people, planet, profits'. An important element of Elkington's argument and that of management authors such as Charles Fombrun is that businesses should invest in people and the planet not only because it is ethical and socially responsible to do so, but also because it makes good business sense. Ultimately, they argue, businesses are more successful and survive longer if they address the 'triple bottom line' rather than narrowly pursue financial self-interest. Many organizations today publish sustainability reports and subscribe to voluntary reporting frameworks such as the Global Reporting Initiative (GRI)[3] and the AccountAbility 1000 (AA1000) Series of Standards.[4] These require reporting of up to five areas of material impact, such as economic, environmental, marketplace, workplace (that is, employees) and community. The *international integrated reporting framework* (IIRF) promoted by the International Integrated Reporting Council (IIRC, 2013), discussed in Chapter 3, is another example of an approach that extends beyond reporting financial results.

Balanced scorecards reflect this broader thinking and establish a set of targets across key areas of operations and performance. In the case of public communication, a balanced scorecard could identify metrics and milestones that can be achieved through communication to support overall environmental, workplace, community and other goals. For example, these could include creating awareness of an organization's environmental policies and activities, creating open two-way communication with employees to increase morale, satisfaction and retention, and building harmonious relationships with key community groups.

As in designing SMART objectives, developing KPIs and/or balanced scorecards for public communication requires that these are aligned to overall organization KPIs, scorecards and goals.

Benchmarking

The term *benchmark* comes from surveying, in which, before the era of theodolites, surveyors chiselled marks in stone blocks into which they inserted an iron rod that served as a level indicator. Subsequently, changes in factors such as water levels could be compared with the benchmark.

Benchmarking is not a particular method of research, but it is a useful technique in evaluation. Benchmarks can be identified for many public communication objectives and activities, such as awareness, understanding, support, satisfaction, trust, inquiry rates, volume of complaints, and so on, by measuring these at a point in time (the benchmark) and then comparing future measures of the same factors. Benchmarks can be metrics derived inside one's own organization for evaluating self-improvement over time, or industry standards obtained from external research to compare with industry leaders (that is, best practice) or averages.

Dashboards

While balanced scorecards seem to have declined in popularity after becoming a corporate *cause célèbre* in the late 1990s, *dashboards* are the 'new big thing' in evaluation reporting. Organizations such as the UK Government Communication Service (GCS) mandate dashboards as a method of reporting, both to save management time by simplifying multiple complex data sets and to create standards of reporting for comparative analysis. The UK Department of Transport gave permission for one of its dashboards reporting public communication to be published as an example (see Figure 9.1). This shows a summary of evaluation data in relation to: the volume and favourability of media coverage (an output); website interactions and searches, including referrals (outtakes); feedback from major stakeholders (outtakes); and public opinion and satisfaction in relation to public transport (an outcome). Thus this dashboard reports evaluation at three of the key stages of communication.

At the time of undertaking this research, the UK GCS was trialling a new dashboard tool from Datorama.[5] The product is described as a 'marketing integration engine' that allows users 'to create API-like connections with any data source'[6] to produce interactive dashboards and 'instant analytics' with a range of visualization capabilities (Datorama, 2016, n.p.).

Usually, dashboards are restricted to one page, the concept being based on the dashboard of a motor vehicle. While there are many hundreds of processes in the operation of a car or truck that could be evaluated, dashboards typically present drivers with between four and six indicators of performance, such as a speedometer, a rev counter (that is, a dial counting engine revolutions per minute, or rpm), an oil pressure gauge and a battery charge meter. Furthermore, most motor vehicle dashboards visualize this data in the form of dials, coloured lights and, increasingly, as digital graphics – even projected 'head up' displays – to make key information available in a highly understandable and easily digestible way.

Dashboards for reporting evaluation of public communication seek to emulate the performance reporting of modern motor vehicles in which drivers do not need to stop or even take their eyes off the road to see important information. Two potential pitfalls of dashboards, however, are oversimplification in reducing complex issues such as public attitudes and concerns to a single chart or table and, paradoxically, complexity when too much information is crammed into a dashboard. Public communication managers and practitioners need to be wary of becoming 'slaves to dashboards'. This occurs when focus shifts from producing effective public communication and doing rigorous evaluation to producing dashboards and 'pretty' charts and graphs as objectives in themselves. Dashboards should be only one form of evaluation reporting: a short, visual summary, with more detailed information available in reports and other documents such as PowerPoint presentations.

Integrated reporting

The IIRF developed by the IIRC, discussed in Chapter 3, provides a framework to show the value of public communication with key stakeholders, including employees, communities and others, as 'capital' of the organization alongside other forms of capital, such as financial, human, intellectual and manufactured capital (IIRC, 2013). Progressive, knowledgeable public communication professionals could introduce such broader methods of evaluation and reporting to their organizations.

DfT Group Communications Strategy - Evaluation and KPI trackers – JULY 2016

UK Public Opinion

Overall satisfaction fell to 80% (83%). But regional variations in key determinants driving satisfaction. Punctuality and handling of delays 5 points lower in L&SE.

Just 23% of peak time passengers in L&SE thought they got value for money.

As passenger numbers increase, satisfaction with room to sit or stand has dropped.

NPS June 2016

Overall satisfaction: National vs L&SE

National Autumn 15 National Spring 16   L&SE Spring 16

Satisfied   Neither   Dissatisfied

Punctuality experience: National vs L&SE

National Autumn 15 National Spring 16   L&SE Spring 16

Satisfied   Neither   Dissatisfied

Value for money: National vs L&SE

National Autumn 15 National Spring 16   L&SE Spring 16

Satisfied   Neither   Dissatisfied

MEDIA – Overall net sentiment of DfT print / broadcast

% age sentiment published stories by theme

Growth - May   Growth - June   Economy - May   Economy - June   Safety - May   Safety - June

Positive   Neutral   Negative

No. of print articles fell in June. But % age of positive coverage increased by 7%, and negative coverage fell by 11%.

Story sentiment by publication

City AM   Ind   Times   FT   Metro   D Tel   G'dian   Sun   Mirror   Mail

Positive   Neutral   Negative

Increase in articles about electric and driverless vehicles, largely positive. Negative perceptions largely around impacts of Brexit.

Performance of digital channels and content

DfT news stories - visitor sessions 2015 vs 2016

2015   2016

Visitors to DfT news stories - 2016 vs 2015 - down 20% YTD (all content down 12% YTD) Very little content published in June due to EU ref purdah

Social referrals down by 70% vs May Correlation fresh content / social – no new content = no shares.

Google trends UK for 'electric cars'

Google trends UK for 'driverless cars'

June media coverage

Google trends UK for 'drug drive'

Drug drive 'Am I fit to drive?' most popular press release on Gov UK. Peak in searches coincides with Glastonbury weekend.

STAKEHOLDER - Qualitative review of key transport stakeholders

CBI 'We're seeing the biggest investment programme in rail since Victorian times, and the biggest road-building programme since the ... A decision on a new runway must be...top domestic priority'

RHA '...this is also an opportunity to cut red tape and get a new deal on many issues for UK hauliers.'

SIEMENS 'We're here for the long-term ..... We're staying because the UK is a good place to do business.'

JAGUAR LAND ROVER / centreforcities '[This] doesn't change our overall strategy...Our commitment to our existing operations in the UK...'

'...serious risk that the Gov't's devolution agenda will come to a standstill...'

easyJet '...has been working on a number of options to allow it to continue flying in all of its markets... until terms of EU negotiations are made we have no plans to move from Luton.'

FIGURE 9.1 A dashboard reporting outputs, outtakes and outcomes of public communication

Source: Courtesy of the UK Department of Transport (2016)

Learning from evaluation to improve programmes

Beyond doing and reporting evaluation, the final – and perhaps most important – step is obtaining and applying *learning* from evaluation to future public communication planning and strategy development. An interesting observation was made at the 2016 AMEC International Summit on Measurement in London, which included reports of a number of case studies, as well as presentation of the AMEC Global Effectiveness Awards at a gala dinner during the summit. From all of the presentations at that and previous summits, no one could recall a case study or report of a public communication campaign or project that failed. Failures tend to be like shameful relatives: they are kept away from public attention and seldom talked about. Often, they are swept under the carpet by public communication practitioners out of fear that they will result in negative assessments and repercussions such as reduced budgets.

However, some of the most important learning about public communication comes from evaluation that shows what has *not* worked and, very importantly, *why*, if this can be determined. As discussed in Chapter 1, it is not only unlikely, but impossible, for all human communication to produce the intended effects. Even among families, parents struggle to get their children to do as they wish – and children struggle to make their parents understand them, particularly as they reach teenage years and begin to turn into autonomous adults. Even good friends sometimes fall out because of misunderstandings. If communication within our most intimate and closest relationships is challenging and sometimes fails, how much more difficult and contingent is communication with stakeholders, publics and audiences who are relative strangers?

Failures and breakdowns in public communication occur frequently because of a range of contextual factors such as competing messages, competitor activity, cultural issues or lack of necessary supporting interventions, such as regulation or industry, professional or personal support. Public communication also can fail to achieve desired outcomes and impact because of audience factors such as reactance, cognitive dissonance and phenomenological issues, such as interpretation based on past experiences or tradition. Public communication inevitably fails when a promoted product, service or policy does not meet audience expectations in terms of quality, integrity or performance. Sometimes, public communication fails because of poor planning, such as a lack of formative research or flawed execution. Whatever the reasons, those responsible for the often large expenditures committed to public communication should want to learn so that they can advise their organizations on better approaches or necessary changes, to design alternative strategies that circumvent barriers and obstacles to communication, and to apply continual improvement to their own activities.

Too many public communication professionals are defensive and use the oft-cited excuses identified in Chapter 1, such as lack of budget and lack of time, to avoid evaluation. Many proceed tentatively at best, fearful of even the slightest hint that communication is anything but a powerful mix of science and art in which they are unfailing experts. Most public communication practitioners particularly eschew discussing failures and suboptimal outcomes because of insecurity and lack of confidence.

Learning to inform continual improvement is one of the most important benefits of evaluation. A productive element of evaluation is to review completed public communication activities to ask questions such as 'what worked?', 'what didn't?' and 'what did we learn?'

Making evaluation practical

While this analysis has emphasized the importance of basing evaluation on sound theory, it is important that evaluation is practical in two respects. First, the findings of evaluation need to be applied in practice. Producing research reports that are easily readable, highlighting key findings in presentations to management and those responsible for activities, particularly with clear, high-impact visuals, and learning from failures help to ensure that the findings of evaluation are applied and productively used.

Second, evaluation needs to be practical in the more mundane sense of being doable within the reality of budgets and available time. The various management reporting systems discussed in this chapter provide mechanisms for identifying priorities. The format and content of KPIs, balanced scorecards and dashboards should be agreed with management, and therefore identify the key metrics, milestones and results that management expects. Ideally, these also should be those that are most indicative of the effectiveness of activities in achieving objectives. Measurement and evaluation should therefore focus on these.

This implicitly points towards what many will not come out and say explicitly: it is usually not practical, or even necessary, to evaluate *everything*. While rejecting lack of time and cost as reasons for not doing *any* evaluation, time and cost *are* parameters within which practitioners need to work. Trying to evaluate all activities can be prohibitively time-consuming and/or expensive. Also, arbitrary guidelines such as allocating 10 per cent of communication budgets to evaluation, which were noted in Chapter 1, are not based on any empirical evidence in relation to effectiveness. A prioritization approach focused on reporting KPIs and producing balanced scorecards or dashboards provides one avenue for identifying what should be evaluated. In addition, as noted in Chapter 1, practitioners should consider focusing evaluation on big-budget campaigns and projects, high-risk activities such as first-time undertakings and those for which there is little existing research, as well as those with difficult and challenging objectives. Such public communication activities may deserve 20 per cent or more of the available budget spent on research. Conversely, it can be reasonable to undertake little or no evaluation of repeat activities that have been successful previously and of low-budget, non-critical activities.

Summary

- Research reports should comprehensively present a summary of any literature review undertaken, the methodology of the primary research, key findings, conclusions and recommendations. However, for readability and impact, research reports can be arranged with an executive summary at the front reporting key findings, conclusions and recommendations, and detailed description of the methodology attached as an appendix.

- Research findings should be presented to management in clear and persuasive ways, using visualizations such as charts, tables, diagrams, word clouds and even videos showing comments first-hand, if they are to have the greatest chance of acceptance and adoption of recommendations.
- Key performance indicators (KPIs) identify a limited number of salient indicators that are evaluated regularly. Focusing on KPIs allows professionals to avoid trying to evaluate everything, making evaluation manageable and reporting simpler than lengthy reports.
- Balanced scorecards are another summarized form of reporting evaluation focused on key metrics, but they introduce additional elements such as environmental, workplace and community performance measurement.
- Most evaluation should incorporate benchmarking, either against previous internal levels or against external metrics such as industry or competitor averages. Benchmarks are a form of baseline date against which future performance can be compared.
- Some of our most important learning comes from failure. Evaluation should report the range of responses, outcomes and impacts. Furthermore, evaluation can include post-mortem discussions specifically focused on 'what did we learn?' and 'what could we do better?' This is the approach of *total quality management* (TQM) and *Six Sigma* programmes (Tennant, 2001), which can be productively adopted within public communication to improve professionalism and performance.

Notes

1 Research reports examined included more than 30 summaries entered in effectiveness awards conducted by the International Association for Measurement and Evaluation of Communication (AMEC) and the Institute of Practitioners in Advertising (IPA), along with more than 30 detailed research reports reviewed during primary research undertaken with the UK Government Communication Service (GCS) and its Evaluation Council, and with UK government departments.

2 Research reports often use endnotes for references, rather than academic methods of in-text citation, to make documents easier to read for professionals, as well as academic researchers.

3 See www.globalreporting.org/Information/about-gri/Pages/default.aspx.

4 See www.accountability.org/standards/.

5 See http://datorama.com.

6 An *application programming interface* (API) is a set of subroutine definitions, protocols and tools (that is, computer code) provided by the developers of databases and websites to allow others to build software applications that link to those databases and websites.

PART III
Case studies in evaluation

10

LEARNING FROM BEST (AND WORST) PRACTICE

International case studies

As noted in Chapter 8, case study analysis is a research method that can be undertaken quantitatively, when a representative sample of cases are analysed, or qualitatively, when one or a few cases are examined in depth. Case study analysis is a way of learning from what others have done. Thus it is grounded in practice. But such analysis also facilitates theory-building, because it can provide knowledge that can be generalized or transferred to other situations to allow us to replicate successful approaches and to avoid the mistakes that others have made. As practitioners would say, findings can inform future strategy and tactics. It seems fitting in this book – which reports research about research, including interviews and ethnography in relation to latest developments and practices, as well as literature review (desk research) – to conclude with case studies, particularly recent ones.

This chapter presents a dozen case studies of evaluation of public communication undertaken in 2015 and 2016. Some of the case studies reported are those in which this author has been engaged as an evaluator and on which this author can report from an insider's first-hand perspective – but there are also many others. To provide insights related to best practice, a number of cases have been sourced from among recent winners of the International Association for Measurement and Evaluation of Communication (AMEC) Global Effectiveness Awards and the Institute of Practitioners in Advertising (IPA) Effectiveness Awards. In addition, several cases have been purposively selected because they show what can be learned when public communication does not go the way it was planned.

The following case studies include evaluation of public communication by corporations, government departments and agencies, non-governmental organizations (NGOs) and non-profit organizations. They include examples of evaluation of advertising, public relations (PR), government communication, specialist campaigns such as health communication and health promotion, digital communication including social media, and integrated communication. Cases are drawn from Australasia, Europe, the Middle East, South Africa, the UK and the US to provide a range of international perspectives.

The case studies in this chapter are presented with an independent overview and some critical analysis, particularly in three personally observed and researched by this author. Those for which information has been provided by third-party organizations have been selected and edited by this author. However, to ensure accuracy and faithfulness to the original reports, minimal editing has been applied to those provided by third-party organizations. Some language and terminology that would usually be changed in scholarly writing, such as 'press releases', 'comms' (as a common abbreviation of communication) and 'measurement' (to mean measurement and evaluation) are retained to illustrate the focus and status of evaluation practice. Overt self-promotion has been removed as far as possible without eroding the detail and context of the cases. But readers are encouraged to critically review these cases as examples of the best and the worst, as well as the typical, in public communication evaluation.

Case study 10.1 Repositioning beauty: how commercial marketing promoted social good

Unilever's Dove

Unilever won silver awards for 'Best dedication to effectiveness' and 'Best commercial effectiveness for good' in the 2016 Institute of Practitioners in Advertising (IPA) Effectiveness Awards[1] for its ongoing campaign for Dove that has sought to reposition perceptions of female beauty. The authors of the award-winning Dove entry in the 2016 IPA Effectiveness Awards, Marie Maurer and Sam Pierce from Ogilvy & Mather, the Dove team at Unilever, and Jakob Kofoed from Data2Decisions said:

> Dove's *Campaign for Real Beauty* was a defining moment in brand communications. It kick-started a debate about the portrayal of women in the media that continues to this day. It drove $280 million global incremental revenue, spawned hundreds of copycat campaigns, and granted the brand fame.
>
> *(Maurer et al., 2016, n.p.)*

Background

Lever Brothers, in conjunction with Ogilvy, launched the 'Dove Beauty Bar' of soap in the US in 1957. The product established a stronghold in the US market and by the mid-1990s it was available in 55 countries. Dove subsequently underwent rapid expansion, becoming a global brand in 80 countries and five product categories.

However, by the turn of the century, the personal care and beauty products market was crowded. And times were changing, as Bob Dylan noted. Criticism was being directed at the manufacturers and advertisers of a number of women's products, including clothing and beauty products.

There have been three approaches in Dove communications over the past half-century:

1. product or category advertising;
2. master brand advertising; and
3. 'social mission' content developed as part of what the brand team calls its 'Self-Esteem Project' (Maurer et al., 2016, n.p.) – the latest approach adopted.

Strategy

The contemporary vision created for Dove is a world in which beauty is a source of confidence and not anxiety. From that, the mission developed for the Dove personal care brand is:

> To invite all women to realise their personal potential for beauty by engaging them with products that deliver superior care. Dove believes that beauty should be for everyone – because looking and feeling your best makes you feel happier.
>
> *(Maurer et al., 2016, n.p.)*

Unilever, in conjunction with Ogilvy & Mather and several PR agencies, launched the *Dove Campaign for Real Beauty* in 2007. Three different campaigns have been rolled out since then: 'Sketches', 'Patches' and 'Choose beautiful' – featuring videos distributed via television, social media, outdoor advertising and PR events. The 'Sketches' campaign alone has gained more than 170 million views, making it one of the most watched online ads of all time.

The campaigns

This first 'real beauty' campaign, 'Sketches' (2013), is well known. It features an FBI-trained sketch artist behind a curtain drawing images of women according to their own self-image. This is contrasted with the descriptions of strangers who describe the women much more positively than their self-image.

The campaign used television advertising, but extended well beyond traditional mass media. It started by launching the content with Dove's Facebook fans. Second, it activated influencers among US bloggers known to have high affinity with the female audience. This was followed and supported by a PR campaign that included taking sketch artists on a media tour to demonstrate the experimental basis of the campaign. Concurrently, a Twitter campaign was launched, along with content on YouTube. The campaign used programmatic digital video advertising tools, including Brightroll, TrueView and Unruly, to maximize reach.

'Patches' (2014) took the 'real beauty' approach a step further. This involved another experiment. This time, women were offered a 'beauty patch' to wear. Many women wearing the patch reported a new-found confidence. The conclusion of the video revealed that the patch was a placebo and that their new-found confidence was psychologically based. One participant described the experiment as a 'life-changing experience' (Maurer et al., 2016, p. 8).

'Patches' was again seeded online via social media and resulted in further worldwide conversation about female beauty using the #dovepatches hashtag.

The most recent Dove 'real beauty' campaign was informed by the largest study ever conducted for the brand, *The Real Truth about Beauty: Revisited* (Dove, 2010). This global research conducted in 20 countries, involving 6,400 telephone interviews with women aged 18–64, found that 'beauty-related pressure increases while body confidence decreases as girls and women grow older – stopping young girls from seeing their real beauty' (Dove, 2016, para. 2). Specific findings included:

- only 4 per cent of women consider themselves beautiful;
- only 11 per cent of girls are comfortable describing themselves as 'beautiful';
- 72 per cent of girls feel pressure to be beautiful;
- 80 per cent of women agree that every woman has something about her that is beautiful, but do not see their own beauty; and
- more than half of women globally (54 per cent) agree that, when it comes to how they look, they are their own worst critic.

(Dove, 2016, para. 2)

Researchers also concluded that it was no longer unrealistic beauty ideals in magazines that were to blame for this lack of self-esteem and self-confidence; rather, it was a negative inner voice that drew attention to a woman's flaws. One third of women commented that 'the pressure I put on myself to be beautiful' was their greatest source of anxiety (Maurer et al., 2016, p. 6).

Based on this, the brief was to prove that women were wrong about their own self-image. This enabled the brand to retain a strong point of view (POV), without facing criticism for being hypocritical or attacking its own industry. The result was a theme: 'You are more beautiful than you think'. However, psychological research indicated that the campaign would not be successful if it were simply to tell women what to think; the preferred approach was to let women discover this for themselves.

'Choose beautiful' (2015) was tasked with changing the way women feel and turned to behavioural science such as the work of Robert Cialdini who concluded that 'commitments are most effective in changing a person's self-image and future behaviour when they are active, public, and effortful' (2007, p. 92).

The campaign featured videos of women entering a building faced with a choice of two doors: one labelled 'average' and one labelled 'beautiful'. The campaign commenced with online conversation and PR in more than 70 countries simultaneously. Data and video content were shared through Dove digital channels with the aim of convincing women to #choosebeautiful. Every woman who chose 'beautiful' after watching the video drove up a global counter on Tumblr, which in turn encouraged other online viewers to make their own choice between 'beautiful' and 'average'. Outdoor advertising on highly visible public sites such as bus shelters kept the choice top of mind offline and Dove's sponsorship of *Women in the World* – a two–day event involving some of the world's most inspiring and impressive women from 17 countries coming together to tell their stories through journalistic narratives, videos and provocative debate – took the debate to a global stage.

Outtakes

All three of the 'real beauty' campaigns for Dove sent social media into a spin. Maurer et al. reported that 'Sketches' received 133,364 social media mentions, 'Patches' received 53,365 social media mentions and 'Choose beautiful' received 156,290 social media mentions (2016, p. 13). To put these numbers into perspective, when Kim Kardashian set out to 'break the Internet' with her 2014 naked photo on the cover of *Paper* magazine (Spedding, 2016), she gained 141,000 social media mentions.[2] In total, the Dove 'real beauty' campaigns ('Sketches', 'Patches' and 'Choose beautiful') have earned 13.9 billion global impressions.

The Dove team and Ogilvy & Mather employed a variety of evaluation techniques, including media metrics, pre- and post-campaign surveys, and econometric modelling, to isolate the effect of various communication strategies. Evaluation research identified that:

- the price of Dove products remained stable relative to the market during the period of the campaigns;
- media spend for Dove remained relatively flat during the period of the campaigns; and
- investment in other promotions, such as in-store, did not increase during the period.

These factors and others established causation – that is, that the communication campaigns caused the results obtained.

One aspect of evaluation of the Dove campaign that can be criticized is that it cited extensive worldwide earned media coverage, which was reported as 'adding up to a total media value of €82 million' (approximately US$87 million) – a use of advertising value equivalents (AVEs), which are rejected as a valid measure of media coverage by most researchers and communication industry bodies, as discussed in Chapter 4.

Nevertheless, the 'Choose beautiful' campaign prompted 3.7 million women around the world to declare on a Tumblr site that they were beautiful. A Google Brand Lift study commissioned to monitor the impact of the campaign revealed a 6 per cent overall uplift in women feeling beautiful among those who had been exposed to the videos. A BrandZ study that measures the degree to which consumers feel affinity towards a brand reported a 'meaningful' rating of 31 for Dove in 2015, making Dove the most meaningful brand in the category.

TABLE 10.1 Incremental sales generated by the Dove 'real beauty' marketing communication

Category	Sales revenue (US$)
Dove personal wash	23,635,000
Dove deodorants	3,893,000
Dove hair	5,174,000
TOTAL	**32,792,000**

Outcomes and impact

Furthermore, Dove enlisted Nielsen to build econometric models in the US between 2011 and 2014 to measure the sales impact and return on investment (ROI) of Dove's investment in category and master brand advertising. The multivariate analysis evaluated sales across Dove's product portfolio and isolated the sales contribution of communications, controlling for factors such as price, distribution, seasonality, consumer promotions, trade activity and new product launches.

Nielsen marketing mix modelling in the US showed that incremental sales generated by the marketing communication in 2013–2014 totalled almost US$33 million, as shown in Table 10.1.

As a whole, the Dove 'real beauty' campaigns have generated an ROI of US$4.42 for every $1 spent on marketing communication. This is more than three times the average fast-moving consumer goods (FMCG) marketing ROI of $1.27 (Data2Decisions, as cited in Maurer et al., 2016, p. 16). The campaigns also have made Dove a household name and, through its *Self Esteem Project47*, Dove reportedly has reached 19.4 million girls in 112 countries, helping to ensure that the next generation grows up with a positive view and confidence in how they look (Maurer et al., 2016, p. 20).

Case study 10.2 Strategic stakeholder engagement through influencer network analysis

International Diabetes Federation

The International Diabetes Federation (IDF) is the global federation of 231 national diabetes associations in 170 countries. The IDF has been leading the global diabetes community since 1950. Its objectives are to provide a global voice for people living with diabetes and those at risk, to campaign for a world without diabetes, and to promote diabetes care and prevention. It is the recognized global authority on diabetes, and advocates with policy-makers on multinational political platforms such as the G7, G20 and the UN General Assembly.

The project

In 2014, the IDF engaged Commetric to identify advocates and influencers to enhance its stakeholder outreach. Employing its *influencer network analysis* methodology (a form of social network analysis), Commetric analysed a relevant sample of international media coverage, identified the most prominent influencers and stakeholders in media conversations, and illustrated how these influencers are linked.[3]

This information helped the IDF to become more targeted and efficient in its stakeholder outreach, and was used to develop its overall communication strategy. Actionable insight from the research, such as an intelligence-informed influencer outreach list, contributed to tangible results. Examples of outcomes include diabetes being the second most mentioned topic on Twitter in connection with the G7,[4] despite the topic not being on the summit agenda.

Goals

The three key goals of the project were to:

1. inform future campaign planning;
2. identify active influencers for potential advocacy and communications partnerships; and
3. provide external validation that this strategy would lead to positive outcomes for the organization.

Challenges

In 2012, the World Health Organization (WHO) announced an aspirational set of targets to drive progress on diabetes and non-communicable diseases, including the first ever global target to halt the rise of diabetes. This specific target indicated a need for the diabetes community to forge partnerships and advocates outside the 'diabetes world'.

Eric Drosin, IDF's director of communications and advocacy, said:

> The IDF understood that achieving the WHO target is a global and cross-sectoral challenge and requires us to broaden our conversations and partnerships with a wider range of stakeholders. This is why we were looking for allies in all spaces. Media research helped us to identify these allies.
>
> *(E. Drosin, personal communication, February 26, 2016)*

Informed by media listening and mindful that the debates surrounding diabetes, sugar and obesity were converging, the IDF knew that it needed to engage outside the 'diabetes world', which is made up of national member organizations, healthcare professionals, academics and corporate stakeholders. Building strategic alliances and partnerships across all sectors – the UN, governments, civil society and the private sector – was necessary to strengthen the IDF's impact.

The IDF also needed to stake its position in the media debate surrounding diabetes, sugar and obesity, based on informed insights and intelligence. A landscape and stakeholder analysis from Commetric was commissioned to inform the team's actions.

Approach

Business titles and online sources with a global spread were identified to reflect the IDF's broad target audience, which consists of multiple stakeholders. Commetric's influencer network analysis methodology mapped stakeholders central to the discussion in English, French and Spanish articles published between October and March 2015.

The research explored media and stakeholder discussion in relation to nutrition, sugar and obesity, all factors impacting diabetes prevalence. Content analysis identified topics receiving attention and highlighted potential partners for advocacy collaboration. The research also identified dominant and emerging themes, which assisted the IDF in its message formulation.

The communications and advocacy team was keen to tap into the 'middle tier' of influencers, which sit between global policy-making platforms (G7) and front-line diabetes prevention and care advocates, including the IDF's members (national diabetes associations). The team needed a better understanding of the content being shared and discussed by these influencers. The findings would also give structure and focus to future communications and stakeholder engagement planning.

Commetric worked with the IDF to develop a media search strategy to source a relevant coverage sample. Key words relating to nutrition, consumption, diabetes, prevention and sugar were agreed (and translated), returning 1,401 articles for analysis by Commetric's media analysts. This sample was large enough to provide meaningful data, yet focused enough to fit the budget.

Names of individuals and organizations within the discussion were automatically identified using entity extraction software. Articles were read for relevancy and duplicates, and irrelevant items were removed. Each influencer's role was identified and coded under categories such as healthcare professionals, celebrities, academics, regulators, NGO representatives and journalists. Similarly, Commetric identified subtopics in the discussion and coded each influencer's sentiment towards the discussion (positive, negative or neutral towards the sugar and nutrition debate). This provided input for network maps and tables illustrating those central to the discussion, what topic or topics they were discussing (providing intelligence for targeted message outreach), and which sources and journalists were promoting or supporting this messaging (aiding future campaign planning).

The study also ranked how central each individual and organization was to discussion of the topic. This social network analysis identified individuals who are primary influencers of change, regardless of where they existed in a formal hierarchy. For example, a person or organization connected with many others in a conversation network was ranked higher than someone more isolated. If these connections, in turn, were linked with many others in the network, the person or organization ranked even higher. This insight helped to prioritize outreach efforts to target the most relevant and influential stakeholders.

The sentiment analysis, combined with ranking of how central a person or an organization is in the discussion, provided insight into the 'advocates', 'swing voters'

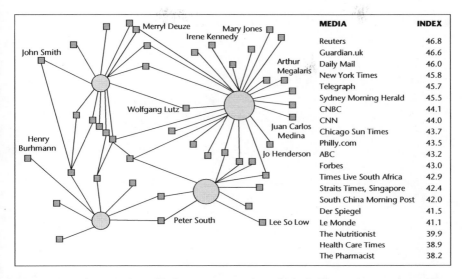

MEDIA	INDEX
Reuters	46.8
Guardian.uk	46.6
Daily Mail	46.0
New York Times	45.8
Telegraph	45.7
Sydney Morning Herald	45.5
CNBC	44.1
CNN	44.0
Chicago Sun Times	43.7
Philly.com	43.5
ABC	43.2
Forbes	43.0
Times Live South Africa	42.9
Straits Times, Singapore	42.4
South China Morning Post	42.0
Der Spiegel	41.5
Le Monde	41.1
The Nutritionist	39.9
Health Care Times	38.9
The Pharmacist	38.2

FIGURE 10.1 A recreation of influencer network analysis similar to that conducted by Commetric for the International Diabetes Federation

and 'critics' within the relevant conversations. This provided the IDF with actionable intelligence for 'comms' planning and stakeholder engagement.

Results, return on investment and future plans

Objective 1: Inform future campaign planning

Research revealed that key messages originating from the IDF were being amplified and spread by stakeholders. Local member organizations helped to spread the message, as did others in the IDF's network, including Jamie Oliver's Food Revolution and Consumers International, as well as corporate supporters from AstraZeneca, Novartis and Lilly.

Analysis revealed differences in the strength of interconnectedness of influencers in English-language media versus French and Spanish media, suggesting that different outreach approaches for advocacy and communications may be appropriate for different markets.

Objective 2: Identify active influencers

The report gave the IDF a list of external stakeholders to target. This intelligence was used successfully in its G7 'Call to Action' campaign. Social media outreach efforts targeting influencers contributed to diabetes being the second most mentioned topic in connection with the G7 on Twitter, despite the topic not being on the summit agenda. The report findings guided the IDF to reach out to organizations and individuals for direct interaction. From this outreach, meetings were held with Food Revolution, World Obesity Federation and Action on Sugar, from which new ideas have sprung and seeds for potential partnerships have been sown.

Objective 3: Provide external validation

Using external data with a broader outlook to inform policy and positioning provided the team with context and insight, resulting in better alignment of IDF's work with its target audiences.

Intelligence helped to strengthen the IDF's working relationships with members. Diabetes UK and the American Diabetes Association were identified as among the most central organizational influencers in the debate, initiating discussions internally aimed at strengthening the cut-through of diabetes prevention and care messages.

The IDF has acknowledged the high level of 'intelligence and mileage derived from Commetric's report'. Eric Drosin, director of communications and advocacy, said that the report opened the eyes of those within the IDF to the need to take an outward-looking view at the influencer and advocacy landscape to effect change. He added: 'If we were not ready to fight the war we could already begin the skirmishes. The key was to find allies' (E. Drosin, personal communication, February 26, 2016).

The research has encouraged the IDF to involve Commetric earlier in future as it formulates policy. It also informed action across the organization up to board level. The positive reception to the research internally has 'helped the team break the cycle of those above asking "what are you doing and why?" and has helped the team become more proactive in its outreach', Drosin said. He added: 'To be an authority you not only need to provide expertise, you need to be forward looking and provide thought leadership. Commetric's research helped us to do that' (personal communication, February 26, 2016).

The findings contributed towards communication and advocacy planning for World Diabetes Day in November 2015 and the World Diabetes Congress in Vancouver on November 30, 2015.

The IDF reports that it intends to have all major projects informed by landscape and stakeholder mapping in future.

Case study 10.3 Increasing life-giving blood donations
UK NHS Blood and Transplant

NHS Blood and Transplant (NHSBT) is a special health authority that forms part of the National Health Service (NHS) of the UK. Clearly, as the name suggests, the NHSBT is responsible for the promotion and management of blood and organ donations.

Background: the brief

The NHSBT provides a wide range of services to the NHS that save and improve lives. The authority encourages people to donate organs, blood, stem cells and tissues. It also ensures that a safe and adequate supply of blood and blood components is delivered to hospitals across England and north Wales. Each year, donors give around 3,500 organs and 2 million blood donations. These contributions save and transform countless lives. For instance, research shows that:

- on average, three people a day die in need of an organ donor;
- one organ donor can help as many as nine people; and
- every blood donation can help up to three people.

The communications team of the NHSBT plan and implement a series of campaigns each year to raise public awareness of blood and organ donation. In June 2015, as part of National Blood Week, the NHSBT launched the 'Missing Type' campaign to increase donations of specific types of blood that were in short supply[5] in response to the following facts.

- There has been a 40 per cent reduction in new blood donors over the past decade.
- Some 204,000 new volunteers were needed in 2015 to meet patient needs.
- Half of the NHSBT's current donors are over the age of 45.
- Black, Asian and minority ethnic (BAME) people make up 14 per cent of the eligible donor population of England and north Wales, but only 5 per cent of the BAME population had given blood in the previous 12 months.

Objectives

The two key objectives of the NHSBT's 'Missing Type' blood donation campaign of June 2015 were to:

1. gain 40,000 new volunteers to register as blood donors during June 2015 (National Blood Week); and
2. gain more blood donors from two key target audiences – young adults and ethnic minorities.

Strategy

To achieve these targets, the NHSBT created a PR strategy to raise public awareness of its research findings and to reveal the decline in new donor numbers. Central to this strategy was a social media campaign that won the PR agency responsible (Engine) a Masters of Marketing award. The central creative idea was to remove the letters 'A', 'O' and 'B' (names of blood types) from well-known names of places and brands, and to encourage individuals and organizations to create social media content and discussion on the theme of 'missing type'.

The campaign involved a number of partner brands, including Odeon Leicester Square, Waterstones in Trafalgar Square and the government authority responsible for the famous sign on Downing Street, Whitehall (see Figure 10.2). These

FIGURE 10.2 Illustration of the street sign of Downing Street, Westminster after the letters 'A', 'O' and 'B' were deleted from street signs in support of the NHSBT campaign

organizations helped to launch the campaign by removing letters from their signs in the run-up to National Blood Week.

In addition, the NHSBT issued a series of press releases[6] to promote key facts about blood donation and promoted patient stories through case studies.

Evaluation was undertaken pre- and post-campaign to track implementation of the strategy (for example, raising awareness) and achievement of the ultimate objectives as follows.

Pre-campaign (formative) evaluation

Step 1: Raising awareness about the decline in new blood donors

Research undertaken before the campaign helped to determine the messages that would be most effective. This included the hard-hitting fact that if not enough new donors come forward and some blood types become unavailable in years to come, there will not be enough blood available when patients need it. Case studies were also promoted, with a focus on patient survival stories. These patients came forward to help to raise awareness about the decline in the number of new blood donors and to urge people to register.

Media content analysis during this stage helped to identify whether the PR tactics were working and whether the messages were being picked up by key journalists and reported in the right way.

Step 2: Prompting people to donate and getting people to encourage others to donate

An important step for the NHSBT was to make sure that, once people were aware of the need for new donors, they knew where to go to register as donors. The NHSBT set up a series of calls to action, including its website, telephone number, and YouTube and Facebook pages, to motivate people to register as a blood donor. It also encouraged the public to take the discussion online and encourage others to register.

Media content analysis during this stage identified the percentage of articles featuring a call to action and which calls to action achieved the highest success rate.

Post-campaign (summative) evaluation

Step 3: The effect on target audiences: gaining 40,000 new donors, including young adults and ethnic minorities

During National Blood Week, the NHSBT monitored the number of people who registered to donate blood and released statistics on the results of the campaign. These results were used to formulate a second set of messages (after National Blood Week). Gorkana also received internal blood registration figures for all UK adults, young adults and ethnic minorities throughout June, and compared these results with the volume of mainstream and social media coverage over times. Social media were also monitored throughout the campaign to identify what conversations were happening outside of the campaign and who the key influencers were.

Evaluation addressed both media outputs and audience outcomes that were aligned to the organization's and the campaign's objectives. All mainstream media coverage was coded by experienced analysts to ensure that metrics such as message delivery and favourability were tracked accurately and effectively. Social media coverage was monitored by Gorkana's social media tools, capturing mentions across multiple channels. The analysis focused on three overall outcomes, as well as specific PR tactics, which enabled the NHSBT to evaluate which parts of the campaign worked well and which could be improved on.

Before the campaign launched, the NHSBT formed relationships with journalists from different regions to gain a wide range of local coverage. Media analysis showed the NHSBT the volume of coverage achieved in each region and which key journalists were driving coverage for that region. This allowed the organization to work out which areas of England and north Wales were underperforming and which media contacts should be targeted in future.

Another section of the report focused on understanding the relationship between the media coverage aimed at key audiences and the resulting blood registration figures for those audiences. To understand whether audiences had been targeted effectively, NHSBT integrated market research conducted in partnership with YouGov (a survey of 10,000 people, representative of the UK population), which enabled the communication team to identify specific audiences, such as ethnic groups and young adults, as well as the media that they consumed. This enabled the team to calculate the reach of the coverage within these audiences. This, in turn, enabled correlation of media messaging with the resulting number of registrations for each audience day by day as the campaign developed.

To work out the effect that social media played in influencing people to register and donate, evaluation also included analysis of key conversations in social media and identified key influencers in social content.

Effectiveness

The NHSBT generated some very successful results within mainstream and social media. Volumes for mainstream coverage saw a threefold increase on the previous year's results owing to the 'buzz' created by the social media campaign (19,749 mentions across social media spaces during June 2015).

Message delivery, which was a key metric for the NHSBT, increased by 16 per cent to 97 per cent. It became clear that the statistics that the NHSBT released were crucial in providing an effective 'news hook' for the campaign. This was reflected in the Gorkana evaluation report. The message that 40 per cent fewer new volunteers had come forward to give blood in the previous year compared with a decade ago featured in 78 per cent of all content, while the message that 204,000 new volunteers needed to come forward featured in 63 per cent of all coverage. These figures informed the NHSBT's subsequent strategy and the organization continues to use them to garner support for its campaigns.

As noted previously, it was also crucially important that people knew where to go to register as a blood donor. Website analytics showed that, between June 5 and 14, 10,933 people visited the main campaign page and 1,805 people (16.5 per cent) clicked through to book an appointment to give blood. This resulted in only 90 appointments (a 5 per cent conversion rate). This led the NHSBT to investigate whether there were enough appointment times available for the public and whether people were being notified that their local clinics operated a walk-in system to give blood. These learnings are being used to inform future campaign activity to improve conversion rates. Overall, the NHSBT concluded that investing more time and resource in web analytics would be useful in future, given the insights and learnings it provided during the 'Missing Type' campaign.

Evaluation showed which media tactics worked well and this learning was used to inform planning. For example, one of the key insights for the NHSBT was the effectiveness of press releases to regional or local media to highlight the number of people who had signed up in the area compared with the same period in the previous year. This was an experimental PR tactic that resulted in a positive response (83 articles), leading the NHSBT to employ this approach again in subsequent campaigns.

Another key learning was gained through the second campaign press release to national and regional media. The release focused on the results of a survey about people's knowledge of their own blood group and facts that they were not likely to know. The media failed to respond to this, because they were still covering the national and regional story from the initial launch. This led the NHSBT to plan the timing for each activity more strategically.

The social media element of the campaign was very successful. Data showed that Facebook accounted for over 46 per cent of total referring traffic and 29 per cent of total referring traffic was from Facebook mobile. This statistic will be used to justify why additional budget should be allocated to optimize web pages for mobile audiences when launching future campaigns. The NHSBT also concluded that more time should be allowed for planning social media campaigns to ensure that they are as creative as possible and also to allocate more resources for Twitter outreach, because this was an effective way in which supporters could convey the correct message and hashtag.

The integration of data on donor registrations with data on media coverage provided a range of important insights. It showed that there was a direct correlation between mainstream or social coverage and new donor registration across June

2015, with registrations peaking on June 5 – the day on which the main story of the campaign appeared in media.

Evaluation also drew on data from a survey of 10,000 people across the UK to compare mainstream media coverage and the percentage of coverage reaching the BAME and young adults audience groups with awareness and attitudes in relation to blood donation. Findings revealed a strong correlation on June 8, when the NHSBT gained coverage in publications including Metro.co.uk and Yahoo (when 46 per cent of these target audiences were reached). The most effective part of the campaign to reach the BAME audience group was on June 5, when the NHSBT successfully targeted 70 per cent of the BAME audience.

Ultimately, the main aim of the campaign was to persuade people to donate blood. Donation records revealed that:

- from June 1 to June 21, 2015, 46,756 registrations were received compared with 22,489 in the same period in 2014 – a 108 per cent increase – and total blood donor registrations for the full month of June 2015 reached 56,877;
- from June 5 to 14, 2015, BAME registrations were 2,113 compared with 1,390 in the same period in 2014 – a 52 per cent increase – and the highest responses came from the Indian and Black Caribbean communities; and
- in 2015, 7,856 young adults registered as blood donors compared with 3,442 young adult registrations in 2014 – a 128 per cent increase.

Andrea Ttofa, head of media and PR at the NHSBT, reported that the Gorkana media content analysis was indispensable to the organization's success, saying:

> We see Gorkana as a vital ingredient of our campaigns. Their evaluation reports give us a real understanding of both the media, social media and, more importantly, the business impact of campaigns such as #MissingType and valuable insights for future activity. Knowing what works well and taking learning forward is vital as the media and social media landscape is constantly changing and we absolutely must constantly evolve to ensure we publicly promote donation as effectively as possible to continue saving lives.
>
> *(A. Ttofa, personal communication, February 26, 2015)*

Case study 10.4 Increasing breast screening in BAME/CALD communities 120 per cent above target

New South Wales Multicultural Health Communication Service

Australian Bureau of Statistics (2013a, 2013b) data shows that people from India and Sri Lanka are one of the largest and fastest growing culturally and linguistically diverse (CALD) communities in Australia, and particularly in the state of New South Wales (NSW). Immigration patterns indicate that, over the coming years, there will be a substantial increase in women aged 50–74 within these cultural groups. This is the age group in which women are most susceptible to breast cancer.

However, Cancer Institute NSW data shows that women from India and Sri Lanka living in Australia have among the lowest rates of breast screening (mammograms) – the primary recommended strategy for early detection and treatment of breast cancer.

In 2014, Cancer Institute NSW awarded AU$100,000 to the NSW Multicultural Health Communication Services (MHCS) to conduct a 12-month project from July 1, 2014 to June 30, 2015 to increase awareness and rates of breast screening among Indian and Sri Lankan women aged 50–74 in NSW. As a result of the success of the project reported here, it was subsequently extended to June 30, 2016.[7]

Objectives

The objectives of the project were to:

- increase breast cancer screening rates among Indian and Sri Lankan women aged 50–74 in NSW by at least 5 per cent from the baseline rate;
- increase knowledge of enablers and barriers to address current low rates of screening among Indian and Sri Lankan women in NSW;
- increase awareness of and influence positive community attitudes towards breast screening; and
- increase the capacity of screening services to engage effectively with the target communities.

To facilitate achievement and demonstration of its objectives, MHCS engaged a team of academic researchers at the University of Technology Sydney (UTS), led by Professor Jim Macnamara,[8] to assist in conducting formative and evaluative research to guide and report on the project.

MHCS also established a Project Steering Group comprising key stakeholders. This is in line with recommendations of the European Commission in its *Toolkit for the Evaluation of Communication Activities* (European Commission, 2015c). Members included representatives of the NSW Refugee Health Service and BreastScreen Liverpool, a breast screening clinic in an area of Indian and Sri Lankan migrant concentration, as well as MHCS senior executives and UTS academics. The Project Steering Committee also consulted with local area health services (for example, South-West Sydney Local Health District).

The strategy adopted took account of the fact that a number of previous campaigns have been conducted and that these used *mass media* and top-down information approaches. Also, a key observation was that information materials for Indian and Sri Lankan communities were direct translations of English-language materials.

Formative research

As the first step, extensive formative research was conducted to inform the project, which included:

1. a *survey* of 250 women in the target audience to identify their knowledge, awareness and attitudes towards cancer, particularly breast cancer, and to gain

insights into their motivations and/or de-motivations in relation to breast cancer screening and their primary sources of information in relation to health, which survey was administered online and in intercept interviews during gatherings of Indian and Sri Lankan women (for example, Deepavali celebrations);

2. *focus groups* among Indian and Sri Lankan women in the target age range; and
3. a *global literature review* of academic and professional research in relation to cancer detection programmes targeting CALD communities, including screening for breast and cervical cancer, which review produced a 24-page report detailing international research findings in relation to promotion of cancer detection services.

(Macnamara, Dunston & Monden, 2014)

Formative research revealed that:

• while Indian and Sri Lankan women in the target age group use mass media, including ethnic newspapers, as a source of local news, they do not use or attach credibility to mass media as a major source of information about health issues; and
• they rely mostly on their peers, families and local communities for health information, including local Indian and Sri Lankan doctors and community leaders.

Formative research also revealed a number of barriers and challenges that needed to be overcome to increase breast screening rates among Indian and Sri Lankan women, including:

• a lack of knowledge about breast cancer;
• lack of understanding of English and poor translations of information materials from English;
• deep-seated fears and superstitions (for example, that attending screening for breast cancer could indicate ill health in a family and reduce the chances of marriage for daughters);
• concern for family honour if cancer is detected;
• modesty, including concerns about exposure in front of men working in breast screening clinics; and
• a resulting 'culture of silence' (that is, cancer is not something to talk about).

Based on the above research findings, MHCS developed a strategy that involved the following:

1. Establishment of *community partnerships* with a wide range of organizations representing and interacting with Indian and Sri Lankan women   As well as members of the Project Steering Group, such as the NSW Refugee Health Service and BreastScreen NSW clinics in relevant areas, these included the Sri Lankan Health Professionals' Association, the Indian Doctors' Association, the Sri Lankan and Indian Welfare Association, Migrant Resource Centres, and women's health services in local health districts.
2. Identification of *community champions*   Through the partnerships established, a number of 'community champions' and leaders were identified and engaged

in spearheading the project. These included Indian and Sri Lankan doctors, community and religious leaders, and some women who had survived breast cancer and were willing to support the project.

Based on these partnerships and their outreach into Indian and Sri Lankan communities, a *community-based collaborative planning and design approach* was taken in developing the project. This included collaborative design of all materials, from naming of the project and logo design, to planning all activities undertaken as part of the project (see 'The "Pink Sari" Project').

3. Provision of all *information materials 'in language'* by native speakers of each of the key languages — not as translations of English-language content. This included information materials written in Tamil, Hindi and Sinhalese — the three main language groups.

4. *Collaborative planning and design* to produce a range of education and communication materials and resources tailored to the interests, needs and cultural preferences of the target audience (see 'The "Pink Sari" Project').

5. A study of the *cultural competency* of a breast screening clinic in an area with a high Indian and Sri Lankan population. This study examined factors such as the level of cultural understanding among staff (for example, of issues identified in research such as fears, superstitions and modesty concerns), of the availability of interpreters, and of the knowledge and skills to meet the preferences and expectations of the target audience.

Evaluation methodology

The project was evaluated at output, outcome and impact levels, using analysis of reports from participating community groups, including reports of attendance at events and minutes of meetings, and website statistics and social media content analysis, plus, most importantly:

*   content analysis of traditional and social media coverage;
*   statistical data on breast screening by women in NSW collected and provided by Australian Medical Aid Foundation, BreastScreen NSW and Cancer Institute NSW; and
*   post–project interviews conducted in August 2016 with senior spokespersons of five key stakeholder groups, including a breast screening clinic in the key target area of Western Sydney, the Australian Medical Aid Foundation, the Resourceful Australian Indian Network (RAIN) and the newly formed Pink Sari Inc., as well as a multicultural health liaison officer.[9]

The 'Pink Sari' Project

Based on the in-depth research and the community-based collaborative approach adopted, the following activities were undertaken in the 12-month period July 2014–June 2015:

1. creation of the 'Pink Sari' name, logo and artwork – based largely on ideas and suggestions from the community (see Figure 10.3);
2. development of a Pink Sari Project website (http://pinksariproject.org);
3. creation of a Pink Sari Facebook page (www.facebook.com/thepinksariproject);
4. a number of Pink Sari community leaders' forums, at which 'community champions' were briefed and engaged in the project;
5. community information sessions for Indian and Sri Lankan women;
6. a Pink Sari pledge, which encouraged women to write a pledge to have a breast screen and/or to encourage other women to have one (see Figure 10.4);
7. a march of 100 Indian and Sri Lankan women in pink saris in the *Parramasala* parade through the streets of Parramatta, Sydney, in October 2014 (*Parramasala* being a major festival involving street parades, food stalls, music, dance, poetry, film, art and street performances);
8. a Pink Sari fashion show, held in June 2015, planned and organized by volunteers;
9. a Pink Sari photo exhibition of 14 breast cancer survivors, held in the Black-town Arts Centre on August 27, 2015 (planned during the project period), for which Indian and Sri Lankan women came up with the idea and volunteered, and 14 leading photographers donated their time to create the exhibition, which was publicly displayed for several months;
10. another innovative initiative in the Pink Sari Project was to enlist daughters, who are mostly more educated and Westernized than older generations, to encourage their mothers to have a breast screen through online videos, pledges and personal communication;
11. favourable media publicity was gained as a result of the various activities undertaken;
12. a study of the cultural competency of a BreastScreen NSW clinic was under-taken and recommendations were made to increase cultural competency as a key enabler of increased breast screening for CALD groups.

Additional activities undertaken in 2016 when the project was extended included:

13. production of five in-language video interviews with breast cancer survivors from Indian and Sri Lankan backgrounds to use in ongoing awareness raising and education;
14. additional information sessions with religious, women's, and senior and youth groups from Indian and Sri Lankan backgrounds;
15. rural outreach to Indian and Sri Lankan women living in rural and remote areas;
16. a Pink Sari Project Songwriting Competition that attracted 18 entries from which a winner was selected in November 2016;
17. the capacity of key volunteers was developed to the extent that a group of community supporters set up an incorporated association to continue the work of the Pink Sari Project beyond the period of Cancer Institute NSW funding; Pink Sari was officially handed over to Pink Sari Inc. at a morning tea on October 26, 2016.

PINK S&RI

FIGURE 10.3 The 'Pink Sari' name and logo created by the Indian and Sri Lankan community (produced in bright pink)

Activities and outputs

- In total, 55 Pink Sari events were attended by 10,462 women from Indian, Sri Lankan or other Asian backgrounds during the 12 months.
- 100 Tamil doctors voluntarily engaged in outreach to Indian and Sri Lankan women in their communities to encourage breast screening.
- 100 women turned out in pink saris to participate in the *Parramasala* parade through the streets of Parramatta in October 2014 and again in 2015.
- The Pink Sari fashion show was a sell-out and generated a large amount of effective publicity.
- 14 Indian and Sri Lankan women who survived breast cancer and 14 leading photographers volunteered to produce the Pink Sari photo exhibition.
- The value of volunteer time and resources contributed to the project is estimated at $300,000 (for example, donation of pink saris, donation of photo exhibition space and video production, volunteer workers, free media space to promote Pink Sari events, etc.) – a 3:1 ROI.[10]
- The Pink Sari Facebook site gained 951 likes (fans) overall – a significant number given that the target audience of Indian and Sri Lankan women aged 50–74 living in NSW totals fewer than 2,500. In addition, the Pink Sari Project Facebook site attracted:
  - ○ 1,796 likes of 140 posts (including text, photos and videos);
  - ○ 73 comments, of which all except one were positive;
  - ○ 565 shares; and
  - ○ 7,589 video views.
- Almost 1,000 video views were gained on YouTube (951).
- While media publicity was not a primary communication channel in the project, supporting media publicity in city, local and ethnic press included:

  - ○ 47 media articles in city and suburban media;
  - ○ 252 placements of key messages (see Figure 10.5); and
  - ○ 99.5 per cent of media coverage was positive.

Independent data collected and provided by the Cancer Institute NSW (2016) shows that, in the financial years July 1, 2014–June 30, 2015 and July 1, 2015–June 30, 2016 (the period of the Pink Sari Project), there was:

FIGURE 10.4 An example of a pledge used in the daughters' campaign to encourage their mothers to have a breast screen

- an increase of 25 per cent in the total number of Indian and Sri Lankan women aged 50–69[11] living in NSW having a breast screen in 2015–2016 compared with 2013–2014 (the year before the Pink Sari Project started), which was made up of an 8 per cent increase in 2014–2015 over the previous year (3 per cent more than the target objective, or 62.5 per cent ahead of the target), followed by a 17 per cent increase in 2015–2016 over 2014–2015 (see Figure 10.6);
- an extraordinary 39 per cent increase in the number of Indian and Sri Lankan women aged 50–69 living in NSW having a breast screen for the first time in 2015–2016 compared with 2013–2014 (the year before the Pink Sari Project started), which was made up of a 7 per cent increase in the number of first-time screeners in the first year of the Pink Sari Project (2014–2015) and a 32 per cent increase in the number of first-time screeners in 2015–2016 compared with the previous year, as the project gained momentum (see Figure 10.7);
- a 12 per cent increase in the number of Tamil women aged 50–69 living in NSW having a breast screen in 2015–2016 compared with 2013–2014 (the year before the Pink Sari Project) – 7 per cent more than the Pink Sari Project target objective, or 120 per cent ahead of the target;

- a 17 per cent increase in the number of Hindi women aged 50–69 living in NSW having a breast screen in 2015–2016 compared with 2013–2014 (the year before the Pink Sari Project) – 12 per cent more than the target objective;
- a 15 per cent increase in the number of Sinhalese women aged 50–69 living in NSW having a breast screen in 2015–2016 compared with 2013–2014 (the year before the Pink Sari Project) – 10 per cent more than the target objective;
- a 51 per cent increase in the number of Hindi women aged 50–69 living in NSW having a breast screen for the first time in 2015–2016 compared with 2014–2015; and
- while first-time screening by Tamil women in 2015–2016 had declined slightly over 2014–2015 (by 2 per cent), this followed a 48 per cent increase in the number of Tamil women aged 50–69 living in NSW having a breast screen for the first time in 2014–2015 compared with 2013–2014 and a shift in focus to increase first-time screening among Hindi women.

The impact of such increases in breast screening is predicted by health officials to lead to more effective treatment of breast cancer and, ultimately, to saving lives. It is also important to note that the cultural competency study of a BreastScreen clinic found significant failings in meeting the needs of CALD communities, including a failure of staff to offer translators in many cases, unavailability of translators and lack of understanding of important cultural issues, and made recommendations for cultural competency training and improved cultural knowledge in screening clinics that will further improve future breast screening rates.

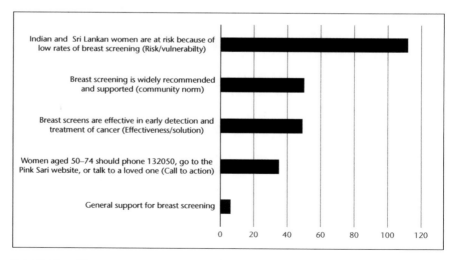

FIGURE 10.5 Key messages communicated through media publicity based on media content analysis

Source: Macnamara (2015e, p. 19)

Stakeholder satisfaction and feedback

In August 2016, the independent evaluators interviewed senior representatives of five of the stakeholder groups most involved in the Pink Sari Project. Interviewees were encouraged to comment as widely as they wished on their experience and perceptions of the project. While a small sample, the interviewees were senior professionals and community workers engaged with Indian and Sri Lankan communities in NSW, including doctors and presidents and chief executive officers (CEOs) of key organizations. Under ethics guidelines, several elected to be de-identified. Key findings were as follows.

- Overall, all stakeholder group representatives rated the Pink Sari Project a success, with two rating it 9 out of 10. One pointed to areas for improvement, but rated the project a success overall.
- Stakeholder groups were unanimous in saying that the Pink Sari Project should be continued.
- One of the organizers of workshops for Indian and Sri Lankan women reported that some were 'attended by 100 health professionals' and brought a 'breast screen van' to an area as part of a health expo, with the result that 'we were able to screen 47 women this weekend, mainly first timers' (Anon., personal communication, August 6, 2016).
- The same professional commented that participation of health professionals is very important, but that it was low in some cases, and indicated that this is an area for improvement.
- The same health professional also saw the Pink Sari Project as capable of being applied to bowel and cervical screening, rates of which are also low.

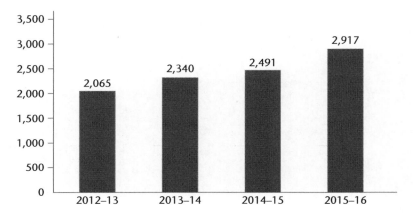

FIGURE 10.6 Overall increase in Indian and Sri Lankan women aged 50–69 having a breast screen

Source: Cancer Institute NSW (2016)

- The president of RAIN, Sudha Natharajan, who agreed to be quoted, said:'Sub-continent women who are generally shy are reluctant to have mammograms. The Pink Sari concept made a great impact on them and out of 150 who turned out for the Pink Sari Day, more than 90 wore pink saris.' She added that the Pink Project was 'well planned and well carried out' (S. Natharajan, personal communication, August 5, 2016).
- Associate Professor Nirmala Pathmanathan, service director of the Westmead Breast Cancer Institute in Sydney, who also agreed to be quoted, confirmed that 'word of mouth' and 'community events that are fun to attend' are the key to engagement. In addition, she said that engaging 'community champions' who 'latched on to the project' and led a 'succession of events' contributed to the success and scalability (N. Pathmanathan, personal communication, August 6, 2016).
- A multicultural health liaison officer said that the 'Portraits in Pink' photo exhibitions, information events and survivor stories told on video had reduced the stigma associated with breast cancer and changed community attitudes. He also said that the collaborative approach taken in engaging stakeholders and community groups had built trust and shown the benefits of 'working truly collaboratively' (Anon., personal communication, August 6, 2016).
- Several senior representatives of stakeholder groups said that a project such as Pink Sari needed to be funded and conducted over several years to have real impact, suggesting between two and three years of commitment.

International recognition

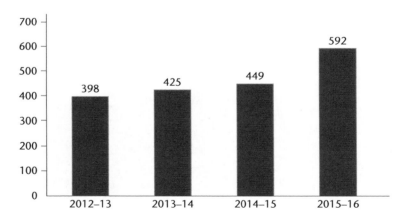

FIGURE 10.7 Increase in Indian and Sri Lankan women aged 50–69 having a breast screen for the first time in 2014–2015 and 2015–2016 compared with previous years

Source: Cancer Institute NSW (2016)

In 2016, the Pink Sari Project took two of the top awards in the AMEC Global Communication Effectiveness Awards presented in London (AMEC, 2016c, and see n. 7).

Conclusions

The Pink Sari Project is an exemplar in health promotion and public communication in that it:

- gained extensive community involvement and engagement;
- generated information resources and activities far in excess of the available budget through community support and volunteering;
- achieved outcomes far in excess of the 5 per cent target increase in breast screening rates among Indian and Sri Lankan women living in NSW; and
- created sustainability and scalability through high levels of community engagement during the project and generating sufficient community support for the project to be established as a non-profit incorporated association, enabling it to access alternative sources of funding and continue.

Case study 10.5 Make peace, not war: building military–community relations

US Army

In recent years, there has been a growing disconnect between the American population and the US Army. Indeed, many Americans receive information about the Army by knowing someone who serves or has served. Yet less than 1 per cent of Americans serve in the US military today, so most people are not exposed to Army service, what the Army's missions are, what service entails and what soldiers do. Recent budget cuts have led to a reduction in the force. As the Army shrinks to its smallest size in decades, fewer Americans in the future will serve or know someone who serves. Over the past 15 years, media have been key communication channels informing Americans about the Army due to attention focused on missions in Iraq and Afghanistan.

However, as the Army withdraws from these conflicts and attention shifts elsewhere, the media are informing fewer people about the Army. This combination of factors indicated to Army leadership that more had to be done to keep Americans informed about the force to maintain its connection with the American public. Keeping Americans connected to the Army is an important objective that contributes to the Army's organizational goal to maintain the American public's trust and confidence. This, in turn, develops a deeper relationship with the American public, furthering their support of the Army's missions by encouraging their sons and daughters to join the all-volunteer force and by funding the Army with their tax dollars.

'Meet your Army'

In an effort to inform and maintain its connection, the Army decided to renew its emphasis on telling the Army story to the American public through interpersonal outreach and media engagements. To spearhead these efforts, the US Army public affairs office launched a new programme in the summer of 2015 initially called 'Community Connect', with the theme 'Meet your Army'.[12] The programme was designed to bring the Army and soldiers to communities around the country – primarily those without a significant Army presence – and engage with the local public through outreach events. Events were conducted at a variety of venues, including schools, universities, veteran service organizations, and meetings with business and civic leaders, with additional outreach through the press[13] and social media. Events were designed to create interpersonal engagement between soldiers and community members, and also to present the Army story through press and social media.

The context/background

Fewer Americans today have contact with those who serve in the Army and fewer are aware of the Army's mission, because:

- less than 1 per cent of Americans serve in the military – thus most Americans do not have exposure to the Army;
- the wind-down or withdrawal from high-profile missions in Iraq and Afghanistan has meant less news on what the Army is doing; and
- budget cuts have reduced the size of the Army, resulting in fewer Americans serving or knowing someone who serves.

Organizational goal

The overarching organizational goal was to maintain the American public's trust and confidence in the Army so that they continue to encourage their sons and daughters to join the all-volunteer force and continue to fund the Army with tax dollars.

Communication objectives

The communication objectives were:

- through the 'Meet your Army' programme, to tell the Army story through outreach and media engagements to keep Americans informed of, and connected to, the Army;
- to increase Army connections with communities where Army presence is low or infrequent; and
- to increase Army messaging through communication channels in communities visited.

Strategy

Barbaricum integrated several measurement instruments, including cutting-edge tools that were new to Army Public Affairs, to inform planning and assess the results of event execution. A robust measurement strategy was crucial to help the Army to increase connections with communities where Army presence is low, as well as increase Army messaging through communication channels. Measurement was vital to the planning process, and ensured that the Army engaged the right communities and stakeholders with the right strategies and tactics to maximize outreach impact. Measurement of results was essential to confirm objectives were met and, if not, to recommend adjustments to planning and execution.

Budget constraints were another key reason it was vital for Barbaricum to use an integrated and innovative measurement strategy. The Army had limited resources at the onset of the 'Meet your Army' programme, which narrowed the number and scale of the events. Also, measurement had to be conducted remotely, as it was unable to fund travel to assess programme results. Thus Barbaricum chose the following integrated and innovative measurement tools to help the Army to boost results despite budget constraints.

Traditional and social media analysis

Barbaricum leveraged its database of three years of media coverage of the US Army, monitored and coded by Vocus to identify locations where Army news coverage and messaging was infrequent. Coverage coded after 'Meet your Army' outreach events was then used to measure increased coverage and messaging.

Crimson Hexagon was used to analyse social media discussion about the Army before, during and after outreach events.

Geocoded mapping

Tableau, a mapping tool not previously used by Army Public Affairs, was used to overlay data sets from the US census, Army records and media data provided by Vocus on a map of the United States to consider multiple research factors when selecting locations for 'Meet your Army' events.

Social network analysis

Dunami, another tool not previously used by Army Public Affairs, was used to conduct social network analysis to analyse stakeholder relationships on Twitter. Engaging stakeholders who are most connected to the community on Twitter maximized and targeted the Army's messaging reach.

Open source research

Barbaricum also collected and used a range of open source data to track and evaluate the effectiveness of the 'Meet your Army' outreach programme, including:

- *US census data* on population by zip code, to select areas with the largest populations to maximize potential engagement and message reach;
- *US Army records* of the location and size of Army bases around the country, to identify areas for outreach where the Army's physical presence is absent or minimal;
- *Lexis Nexis* data, to identify potential stakeholders to engage, such as local government authorities, community leaders, academic institutions and media outlets; and
- *Internet research*, to gain additional background information in relation to potential stakeholders and organizations to help to inform Army leadership prior to outreach.

Execution/implementation

The first two 'Meet your Army' outreach events were considered pilots. These took place in East Lansing, Michigan, and Indianapolis, Indiana, in the summer of 2015. These two events were executed by the Army's chief of public affairs and were test cases to establish best practices for developing a strategy for the following year. During these events, the chief of public affairs engaged local government, business and civic leaders, media outlets, academic institutions and veterans' organizations.

Barbaricum employed social network analysis, geocoded mapping, traditional and social media analysis, and open source research to evaluate the pilot 'Meet your Army' events and help to shape the programme's long-term strategy. All research was aimed at maximizing the Army's potential to achieve its objectives to increase Army connections with communities where Army presence is infrequent and increase messaging in communities visited. Evaluation was focused on assessing these objectives based on event results.

The key stages of the 'Meet your Army' pilot programme were as follows.

- **Select locations.** Barbaricum combined data from multiple measurement tools to provide the Army with the best insight possible to inform location selection. The agency used US census databases to obtain statistics on US population by zip code, Army databases to identify locations and population size of Army bases in the US, and Vocus to export coded data of media coverage about the Army. Barbaricum then used the mapping tool Tableau to geocode this data into a map of the US, providing robust insight to inform Army planning. This triangulation of data pinpointed areas in the US with substantial population, but where the Army's physical presence and media messaging are low or infrequent.
- **Identify stakeholders.** Barbaricum then used multiple tools, including Vocus, Lexis Nexis, Crimson Hexagon and open source Internet research, to identify

community leaders for Army leadership to engage. Research identified their background information, interests and visibility in the media. This information was compiled into reports that provided Army Public Affairs with insight on individuals to engage that would help to further Army connections and message reach.

- **Maximize outreach impact.** While the intent of the 'Meet your Army' programme was to tell the Army story to Americans through outreach and media engagements, limited funding for travel and events created challenges in reaching these objectives. With only one trip scheduled every few months, Barbaricum had to be creative in helping the Army to find ways to reach as many people as possible during each event. Social media allowed for two-way dialogue, and was an excellent way to facilitate connections and relationship-building without an increase in budget. While the social media monitoring tools that Barbaricum typically used provided data on users and content, richer insight on the relationships and connections between users was needed. For 'Meet your Army', Barbaricum used Dunami and social network analysis to create visual displays of the Twitter networks in communities that identified the most connected stakeholders in geographic locations, as well as within subgroups such as business, government, sports and academics. Because tweets from influential Twitter users had the potential to reach the most people, Barbaricum provided reports with recommendations on which stakeholders the Army should engage on Twitter to increase connections and messaging reach within the community.

- **Measure results.** Following the first two pilot 'Meet your Army' events, Barbaricum used its integrated suite of measurement tools to compare data gathered before and after events to determine if they achieved the Army's objectives. Barbaricum used Dunami, Vocus, Crimson Hexagon and Lexis Nexis to measure both increased connections and messaging. Using Dunami and Crimson Hexagon, Barbaricum quantified increased social media connections and potential message reach on Twitter based on the number of community stakeholders connected to the Army on Twitter and the number of tweets and retweets of Army content by these stakeholders. Barbaricum quantified the use of hashtags, photos and referrals to identify indicators driving interest and engagement. Using Vocus and Lexis Nexis, Barbaricum quantified Army messages by examining local news articles during and after the 'Meet your Army' outreach events. Media analysis included volume, tone, key stakeholder quotes, message penetration and media outlet reach.

Effectiveness

Data collected during the first two pilot events demonstrated effectiveness in achieving the Army's communication objectives to increase connections with, and messaging to, local communities. Results included:

- 20 local news reports (8 online print, 9 radio broadcasts and 3 television broadcasts) about the Army communicating key messages compared with none in months prior to the events;
- 470 tweets about 'Meet your Army' directed to the local community for a total of 4.5 million impressions, compared with none in the local community prior to the events;
- a near-quadrupling of tweet volume from the first to the second 'Meet your Army' pilot event, most tweets being the result of engagement with the Army (for example, retweets of Army tweets);
- 47 per cent of 'Meet your Army' tweets containing the #meetyourarmy hashtag, which was established following the first pilot event; and
- an increase in the Twitter followership of the Army chief of public affairs by 43 per cent during the second pilot trip.

Recommendations from learning and insights

Based on the insights gained from the two 'Meet your Army' pilot events, Barbaricum made a range of recommendations to the US Army, many of which resulted in actions by Army senior leadership. These included the following:

- **Dedicated hashtag.** After the first pilot outreach event in Lansing, Michigan, Barbaricum's social media measurement showed that there was no consistent use of a hashtag for its community engagement activities and recommended designating #meetyourarmy as the official hashtag for use in all outreach events. Army Public Affairs liked the suggested hashtag so much that it rebranded the entire campaign as 'Meet your Army'.
- **US Army goes on Twitter.** Barbaricum's social network analysis of community stakeholder relationships on Twitter showed the Army how using this platform to engage influential stakeholders could be a cost-effective way to increase connections and message reach. Barbaricum recommended that the Army chief of public affairs join Twitter and engage influential users. Subsequently, the chief did so, and now regularly tweets and follows community stakeholders. Barbaricum's social media measurement showed that most tweets about 'Meet your Army' occurred during specific days and hours of the day, and recommended timely use of Twitter before, during and after events to increase tweets over a longer period of time —a recommendation that the Army chief of public affairs has adopted.
- **Geolocation targeting.** As a result of Barbaricum's use of geocoded data in Tableau to pinpoint US locations with significant populations, but where Army presence and messaging were low, Army Public Affairs requested that Barbaricum update the map every quarter to inform selecting of location for future outreach events.

Case study 10.6 How CEOs sleeping on the street broke charity fund-raising records

CEO SleepOut™, South Africa

The CEO SleepOut™ is a global movement that sees business leaders sleep under the stars on one of the longest and coldest nights of the year to raise awareness and funds for the homeless. The movement was founded in 2006 by Australian business leader Bernard Fehon, who coordinated the first CEO SleepOuts in Sydney.

Ali Gregg, founder of The Philanthropic Collection, engaged Bernhard Fehon in 2012 to extend the concept to South Africa and imported The CEO SleepOut™ concept and brand from Australia. In 2015, the movement was officially launched in South Africa,[14] with The CEO SleepOut™ aspiring to ignite a new wave of philanthropy in South Africa to create social change to assist with one of the country's most pressing problems: vulnerable children and youth living on the streets. Girls and Boys Town, the largest private childcare organization in South Africa, was identified as the ideal beneficiary partner for the inaugural event.

Introduction

Thursday June 18, 2015 saw Gwen Lane in Johannesburg playing host to CEOs and business leaders, giving them the opportunity to experience life on the streets, and to meet with Girls and Boys Town alumni, but, most importantly, to raise awareness and funds to create social change.

The CEO SleepOut™ approached Ornico to provide social media monitoring services for the event. In addition to the initial engagement, Ornico volunteered its full suite of monitoring and analytical services, identifying the opportunity to promote the Barcelona Principles by creating a best measurement practice showcase report to be distributed to all participating CEOs and business leaders post-event.

A month later, the stakeholder auditing partner firm BDO SA announced that a record-breaking R26,054,869[15] had been collected. It was the largest sum ever raised by a single South African charity event and, worldwide, it is the largest amount of funds raised by any inaugural CEO SleepOut™ event.

Objectives

The objectives of the CEO SleepOut™ in South Africa were to:

1. recruit 250 CEOs or senior business leaders to participate and donate R100,000 each;
2. raise R25 million in total donations for Girls and Boys Town;
3. increase awareness of the plight of homeless and vulnerable children through media coverage; and
4. create multiple campaign benchmarks for future events.

(van Dyk, 2016, n.p.)

Strategy

Being a charitable organization, The CEO SleepOut™ had limited resources available, and had to secure the services of several partners, sponsors and friends in fields such as hospitality, communications, media and measurement. Sun International and Radio 702 were secured as joint title partners for the 2015 event.

In addition to gaining partnerships, the strategy involved:

- direct invitation to 800 key business leaders to participate;
- using partners and influencers to reach out to the target audience and provide endorsements;
- creating exposure and awareness of the event through nominations and challenges among peers;
- creating advance knowledge of the CEO SleepOut™ through media coverage in the lead-up to the event;
- creating a CEO SleepOut™ app;[16]
- providing easy access to information regarding the event, including how to register, donate or challenge peers;
- creating visibility for participants and partners through their association with the event; and
- through all of the above, creating a sustainable event that is viewed positively by the targeted audience and public.

(van Dyk, 2016, n.p.)

Evaluation plan

Planned evaluation included:

- content analysis of media coverage in print, broadcast, online, social and owned media to identify the volume and tone of coverage and key messages;
- a participant survey post-event; and
- use of the All Media Products Survey (AMPS) to collect public feedback post-event.

Implementation

The CEO SleepOut™ made extensive use of its key media partner Radio 702 to generate coverage of the event. On-air nominations, as well as personal invitations to potential participants, were a key part of the strategy. The event was rolled out as follows:

- April 1, 2015 – Monitoring and evaluation commenced;
- April 14, 2015 – Media launch of The CEO SleepOut™;
- April 14–30, 2015 – Hand delivery of direct invitations to 800 CEOs;
- June 18, 2015 – The CEO SleepOut™ event;
- July 18, 2015 – Campaign analysis report due date.

Evaluation of effectiveness

The AMEC Valid Metrics Framework[17] informed the selection of measurement and evaluation metrics for each key step of the communication phases and processes. Ornico's monitoring capabilities enabled the data to be collected and collated, with analysts providing qualitative interpretation and insight.

* **Traditional media analysis.** A total of 634 media articles were generated. These were analysed according to the following quantitative and qualitative variables:
  o media source;
  o title partner and sponsor mention;
  o beneficiary partner mention;
  o stakeholder, influencer and friends mentions;
  o companies mentioned;
  o companies challenged or nominated;
  o sympathy SleepOuts (other events arranged in support);
  o key message alignment;
  o commitment and endorsement;
  o knowledge transfer based on eight criteria;
  o advocacy of event based on six criteria;
  o tonality; and
  o prominence.

* **Website visits.** Ornico analysts were given direct access to the CEO SleepOut™ website and identified more than 50,000 unique visitors to the web pages promoting the SleepOut™. Web analysis identified bounce rate, as well as region and sources of traffic.
* **Social media analysis.** The event gained 29,000 mentions on Twitter.
* **App user analysis.** The CEO SleepOut™ app usage data was also collected and analysed, showing 603 downloads of the event app.
* **Participants' survey.** All of the participants on the evening also completed a detailed survey for further analysis.

The CEO SleepOut™ held in Johannesburg on June 18, 2015 holds the record for the biggest ever single South African event. Ornico's monitoring and evaluation services were utilized on a daily basis to keep track of developments and to adjust strategy accordingly – so even ambush marketing attempts could be successfully thwarted.

In addition to reporting outputs and outtakes, Ornico was able to demonstrate the following outcomes and impact of the first South African CEO SleepOut™ included in its evaluation report:

* 104 per cent of the fund-raising target was achieved (R26,054,869);
* 98 per cent of the participant target was reached (247 CEOs and business leaders);

- 70 per cent media coverage contained the key message concerning the homeless and vulnerable;
- There was an average monthly increase of 45 per cent in media coverage focusing on the plight of the homeless after the event (measured across all 12 months);
- 60 per cent of CEOs nominated on radio participated in the event;
- 14 unofficial 'Sympathy SleepOuts' were held, as identified in analysed media;
- High media advocacy for the event in analysed media items (rated 7.2 on a 0–10 scale);
- 74 per cent overall positive sentiment in media coverage;
- Only 4 per cent of post-event media coverage was negative, with some commentators stating that CEOs used the event as 'a PR exercise';
- There was a social media engagement rate of 3.4 per cent on Twitter and an average of 9.4 likes and 1.9 shares per post on Facebook;
- Multiple measurement benchmarks were set for future events.

(van Dyk, 2016, n.p.)

The Ornico campaign analysis report was made available in an e-book format, as well as a printed 48-page full-colour report, which was hand delivered to all participants after the event, reinforcing and providing independent evidence of the success of the event, as well as encouraging future participation. Additional research on media channels, prominent influencers and partner performance was also conducted in support of the main campaign analysis, guiding the communications and partner strategy for 2016.

Major changes planned include the omission of a main media partner, focusing instead on smaller media partnerships plus a bigger focus on social media. The spontaneous 'Sympathy SleepOuts' identified gained great public support, which will now be leveraged by launching up to three additional official SleepOut™ brands in 2016.

Case study 10.7 Ex-smokers turn negative messaging to positive results in Europe

Directorate-General for Health and Food Safety, European Commission

The 'Ex-smokers are unstoppable' awareness-raising campaign ran for two-and-a-half years from June 2011 to the end of 2013 across 27 European countries.[18] It targeted the 28 million smokers in Europe aged 25–34 (European Commission, 2016). The European Commission's Directorate-General for Health and Food Safety (DG Health and Consumers, at the time) was responsible for the campaign, and hired a consortium led by Saatchi and Saatchi Brussels[19] to design and implement it, with active involvement from national ministries, health associations and NGOs across the European Union (EU). Evaluation was subsequently contracted to Coffey, a Tetra Tech Company, at the conclusion of the campaign.[20]

Background: situation analysis

Cigarette smoking is one of the major causes of human death and illness globally. In 2012, it was estimated that around 28 per cent of Europeans were smokers, with much higher rates in some EU countries, such as Greece, which has an estimated smoking rate of 40 per cent. It is estimated that 700,000 deaths occur annually across the EU as a result of tobacco-related diseases (European Commission, 2012). The EU has a mandate to take action in public health as long as it complements efforts by the member states and, in this capacity, the European Commission had supported communication campaigns on this issue since 2002.

Communicating the dangers of smoking was a well-worn approach at both EU and national levels. It was also noted that scare tactics had been used in other campaigns and that their impact was likely to wane with repeated use. Furthermore, it was considered important to avoid the Commission telling people how to live their lives. As the third EU anti-smoking campaign, a fresh approach was considered necessary.

The budget allocated to the campaign was €33 million over two and a half years – €13.2 million a year. Therefore, it was important that evaluation was conducted to ensure effectiveness.

Organizational objectives

The Commission had three interlinked, overarching goals in relation to smoking as follows:

1. to raise awareness of the dangers of smoking;
2. to encourage citizens to stop smoking and help them to quit; and
3. by doing so, to contribute to the Commission's long-term objective of a smoke-free Europe.

Communication objectives

There were four communication objectives, as follows:

1. To achieve high *reach* of smokers in the EU through traditional and social media (*exposure*);
2. To generate emotional *engagement* and *response* to the campaign;
3. To create *intention* to stop smoking;
4. To gain *registration* in the 'quit smoking' programmes offered as part of the campaign (*conversion*).

Targets/KPIs

The campaign involved a range of key performance indicators (KPIs) for years one, two and three, including:

- reach more than 20 million smokers across the 27 member states through paid media advertising;

- generate 2,000 editorial media articles in print and online across the 27 member states involved;
- place at least three of the campaign messages in 50 per cent of the news articles generated; and
- generate high volumes of likes, shares and comments in social media supporting the campaign and smokers in quitting.

There were also targets for the percentage of smokers who found the campaign helpful in quitting smoking (identified by an independent post-campaign survey conducted by GfK) and registrations in the iCoach application. However, there were no specific targets set for quitting rates.

These KPIs show a predominant focus on output measures, with only some outtake evaluation (consideration of quitting and intention to quit) and early outcome targets (registrations in iCoach). This, along with other factors discussed later, limited evaluation of this campaign.

Communication strategy

Instead of focusing on the negative consequences of smoking, this campaign focused on the positive message that life is better when smokers stop smoking. It also recognized that many, if not most, smokers want to give up smoking in their lifetime – for example, the *Eurobarometer 385* study reported that 31 per cent of smokers in the EU had tried to give up smoking in the previous 12 months and 28 per cent had tried to give up between one and five times (European Commission, 2012).

The strategy adopted was to present 'real life' ex-smokers talking about the benefits of not smoking in public communication, backed up by support materials, including a free tool to help smokers to quit: a downloadable 'app', iCoach, available in 23 languages. The theme adopted in the communication was 'Ex-smokers are unstoppable'. This was supported by research including an online pre-test survey conducted in France, Poland, Sweden and UK using a quota sample based on age, gender and smoking status.

iCoach involved the completion of a smoking self-assessment, after which intending quitters received daily tips according to their profile. Users were also encouraged to log in regularly to reassess progress, during which tips were updated. The 'app' encouraged and supported smokers to move through five identified steps to becoming an ex-smoker.

Using real ex-smokers including celebrity ex-smokers from each of the then 27 EU member states provided authentic inspirational stories from people with whom smokers could identify.

The campaign prioritized EU countries with a high smoking prevalence, in which it could best complement existing national cessation structures and campaigns, and where there were opportunities for partnerships. A PR partner in each participating country identified local opportunities to maximize campaign impact and a number of 'Ex-smoker' sub-campaigns were conducted locally in member states, including some that sought to make the most of moments of reflection such as the end of summer holidays, Christmas and New Year.

To maximize the link between healthy living and non-smoking, the 'Ex-smokers are unstoppable' campaign also involved sponsorship of several high-profile sporting events, including the Berlin, Poznan, Athens, Dublin and Venice marathons, and the Brussels 20 kilometre run, as well as, most notably, FC Barcelona (FCB). The football club conducted a special sub-campaign under the theme 'Quit smoking with Barça',[21] timed to coincide with the UEFA Champions League. Well-known staff and players gave out daily personal tips, information and exercises on motivation, health, food, movement, stress and quitting strategy via an adapted FCB version of iCoach.

The campaign concluded with a final push to move the target audience from awareness to registration in iCoach with 'Day of the Ex-smoker' (DOES).

Key messages

The key messages of the campaign were:

- 'Ex-smokers are unstoppable' (the campaign theme);
- the European Commission is conducting this campaign to help smokers to quit (branding);
- iCoach is a free downloadable tool to help smokers to quit smoking; and
- information and the tool are available on the Unstoppable website.

Evaluation: outputs

Key output metrics reported following the 'Ex-smokers are unstoppable' campaign included the following:

- Paid advertising reached 19.3 million smokers aged 25–34 across the 27 countries in year one and more than 20 million of the target audience in subsequent years, achieving the output KPI set.
- Some 5,535 media articles were generated in print and online media across the 27 countries, of which 50 per cent incorporated at least three of the campaign messages. Media content analysis reported that, on average, the 'Ex-smokers are unstoppable' message was included in 91 per cent of media coverage, the European Commission brand appeared in 92 per cent of media coverage and the iCoach application was mentioned in 83 per cent of media coverage. Media coverage achieved was well in excess of the target.

Evaluation: outtakes

Registration and conversion data showed that there were 408,334 registrations in iCoach in total. In year one, 9 per cent of visitors to the iCoach website registered with the tool.

The FCB interface was particularly successful, generating 55.7 per cent of iCoach registrations during year two of the campaign.

Evaluation: outcomes

A post-campaign survey found that:

- 30 per cent of smokers said they talked about stopping smoking with other people as a result of the campaign;
- 28 per cent of smokers said that they considered stopping smoking as a result of the campaign;
- 22 per cent of smokers said that they recommended the campaign materials to someone; and
- 18 per cent of smokers visited the campaign website (see Figure 10.8).

Most importantly, it was estimated that 65,200 smokers quit with support from iCoach, which represented around 36 per cent of registered users and a cost per converted smoker of €511. At a conservative estimate, this resulted in seven quality-adjusted life years (QALYs) gained per converted smoker, with a cost per QALY of €73.[22]

Insights and learning

A team led by Andrea Kobilsky and Melanie Kitchener from Coffey was tasked with a retrospective evaluation of the 'Ex-smokers are unstoppable' campaign. The brief focused on three dimensions:

- evidence of behavioural change – that is, smoking cessation attempts;
- communication awareness – that is, impact, relevance, effectiveness of awareness activities; and
- complementarity and synergies with national smoking cessation structures.

A number of lessons emerged from *ex post* evaluation, including the following.

- The simple, positive campaign messages were well received. They contrasted with the negative images and slogans about smoking that some had seen previously – but many people were not willing to share their personal stories (for example, via social media).
- While the positive contribution of iCoach was clear, most who registered had already decided to quit and might have quit anyway without the quit tool.
- Having a tangible product such as iCoach to offer in addition to communication made it easier to engage the target audience and partners, including FCB.
- Partnerships were key to campaign success. Several other football clubs also expressed an interest, but this interest was not taken up, which was a significant missed opportunity. It was also noted that while local PR partners were important in each country, there was a need for better integration of the pan-European campaign with national and local health initiatives.
- The focus on sports, in particular football, meant greater engagement with men than women. There were also significant differences in engagement across

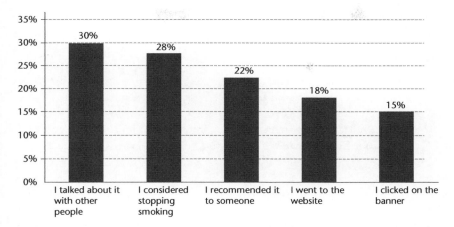

FIGURE 10.8 Average impact of the call to take an action over three years based on an independent post–campaign survey

Source: Coffey (2015)

different countries, with lower engagement in Nordic countries and higher engagement in Eastern Europe.

- Pre- and post-tests provided vital insights into paid advertising effectiveness – but there was no baseline data to help understanding of impacts.
- Also, the evaluators concluded that there was a need for better mechanisms to capture data from iCoach and events. For example, evaluation of the effectiveness of events relied on people's memories collected in interviews conducted up to several years afterwards.

Overall, a key lesson from this campaign is that rigorous evaluation was not designed into the campaign from the outset, with the result that there was a lack of SMART objectives, particularly in relation to outcomes. Even though a large amount of data was collected, the evaluators employed *post hoc* were not able to influence the design of measurement mechanisms or to ensure SMART objectives were set for outputs, outtakes and outcomes.

Particularly when large budgets are involved, SMART objectives and design of evaluation at the planning stage are essential and can lead to even greater effectiveness in important public health, as well as other types of campaign.

Case study 10.8 Raising eyebrows and sales of a sagging media brand with 25:1 ROMI

The Economist, UK

The credibility of *The Economist* as a media brand is inarguable. Its content is perceived as of high quality and it is trusted. However, since the early 2000s, its subscriptions have plateaued and, by 2014, they were beginning to fall (see Figure 10.9). Even digital conversions slowed as the publication's traditional prospect base was exhausted.

The Economist's iconic poster advertising over two decades cemented its reputation as the publication for the 'man that wants to get ahead' – particularly in finance and business. This positioning worked so well that most people saw themselves as outside the target audience: *The Economist* was not seen as relevant to their lives. Research found that many potential readers dismissed the journal as a 'handbook for the corporate elite' (Burnett, Baker, Brown, Noakes & Peace, 2016).

The authors of the campaign for *The Economist* that won a Gold award in the 2016 IPA Effectiveness Awards,[23] Darren Burnett, Nick Baker and Sarah Brown from Proximity London Ltd, Iain Noakes from *The Economist* and Neil Peace from UM London, said that the iconic media brand needed to reach out to a new, much younger, 'progressive' audience and also address the historical gender imbalance by bringing more women to *The Economist*. They reported:

> We needed to open up a brand-new audience by spurring a sudden re-evaluation of everything they thought they knew about us. We needed to persuade them to raise their hand and allow us to show them how *The Economist* was relevant to them so that we could turn these rejecters into readers – and ultimately, into subscribers.
>
> *(Burnett et al., 2016, p. 4)*

The campaign developed had ambitious communication objectives, as well as overarching marketing and commercial objectives, as follows:

- *Communication objectives*
  - Prompt 650,000 previously unseen targets to click, read content and join the prospect pool to re-target with future marketing activity (*primary objective*).
  - Shift perceptions of *The Economist* among a younger audience, particularly in terms of consideration, willingness to recommend and specific brand attributes (*relevance, shareable content*).

- *Marketing objectives*
  - Create a global pool of previously unseen prospects that can be re-targetted for future conversion.
  - Shift the subscriber profile away from an older, very male profile to create a platform for future growth.

- *Commercial objectives*
  - Deliver profitable subscription growth globally (with a target of 9,000 subscriptions).
  - Help *The Economist* to return to circulation growth.

Formative research

Formative research informing the campaign asked non-readers to draw and describe a typical reader of *The Economist*. Participants drew male figures dressed in conservative suits and ties, usually with glasses and carrying a briefcase. Descriptions included 'wears a business suit, kind of hates his life, studied economics, ended up working for Barclays. Kind of disillusioned, grey kind of guy, has a bleeper that warns him when stocks are down' (AMV prospect research, as cited in Burnett et al., 2016, p. 5).

The Economist was described by non-readers as 'unreadably dense; pompous academic tone; predictably conservative; just finance, business, politics; a right wing newspaper pushing free markets', while readers described the publication as 'ultimate simplicity, concise, clear, accessible; sharp, fresh, witty editorial style; surprising counter-intuitive views – often liberal; very broad coverage of arts, culture, people, tech; balanced analysis that recognizes its own bias' (Burnett et al., 2016, p. 6).

Research also told the agency and the organization that there was a large potential audience of people 'who have a thirst to understand the important issues around the world', who have a 'detached macro-economic view of current affairs' and who seek insights 'almost entirely removed from political bias'. The campaign team referred to this potential audience as 'progressives', describing them as 'true global citizens seeking to objectively understand international issues' in relation to a broad range of topics, including the arts, culture, technology and people, as well as business and finance (Burnett et al., 2016, p. 6).

The campaign

This research led to a campaign aiming to provoke non-readers and pique their curiosity to read an article in *The Economist*. The creative approach involved using

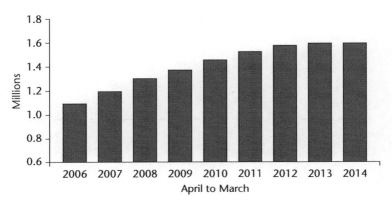

FIGURE 10.9 Global print and digital subscriptions to *The Economist*

Source: The Economist Group (2015, p. 3)

The Economist's own editorial content for advertising. As the campaign team explained:

> We used *The Economist's* own content to stop people in their tracks and make them want to find out more. We scoured recent editions for the most provocative insights, the most fresh and arresting views, which may run counter to common wisdom.
>
> We spoke to issues of the moment . . . We addressed topics far outside business and finance and, of course, we showcased *The Economist's* characteristic dry wit, tailored to this new audience.
>
> We built a live newsroom with a direct line to editorial meetings. As soon as articles were approved for publication, we created ads on the spot to put *The Economist* at the centre of current debate.
>
> *(Burnett et al., 2016, p. 8)*

The articles selected from *The Economist* to feature in online media and mobile device advertising were not traditional finance news. For example, under the headline 'Is pregnancy about to become a disability?', the campaign challenged non-readers' perceptions of the publication by linking to an article critically examining an upcoming court decision that could allow employers to put workers engaged in physically onerous jobs who become pregnant on unpaid leave. Another online ad for *The Economist* featured the headline 'Bad back? Do it doggy style', which linked to an article exploring how people with back pain can copulate in comfort.

The campaign also introduced innovative speed-reading style *blipverts* containing 10-second summaries of major news items, which demonstrated *The Economist's* ability to 'condense complex issues into concise take-outs' (Burnett et al., 2016, p. 10).

To put the provocative creative content in front of the right audience, the campaign used tailored programmatic media buying to find more than 5 million potential readers who had not previously been targeted by *The Economist*. The campaign team explained:

> Facebook and Twitter covered social, whilst ShareThrough and Outbrain delivered *Economist* content into a long tail of quality publications such as *Wall Street Journal* and CNN.
>
> We mixed dynamic ads (display ads composed of *Economist* content and built in real-time) with dynamically targeted prebuilt ads and matched them to page context and viewer profile. We used a feed from *The Economist* containing thousands of articles, infographics and special reports to build dynamic creative. And we crafted over 100 executions that could be deployed in the right context.
>
> *(Burnett et al., 2016, p. 10)*

The campaign conducted in 2014 and 2015, with a total annual budget of US$2 million, surprised many non-readers and broke down negative stereotypical views.

Outcomes

The campaign provoked 5.2 million non-readers to explore content in *The Economist*, according to campaign tracking.

Survey-based post-campaign research (summative evaluation) by Universal McCann (UM) showed that audiences exposed to the advertising have been made more likely to consider *The Economist*, to want to recommend it to others and to recognize it as relevant to them. For example, in the UK, 32 per cent of those surveyed said they were 'very likely' or 'likely' to consider subscribing to *The Economist* and 24 per cent said that they were willing to recommend it to others. In the US, where *The Economist* faced lack of awareness, as well as negative perceptions, awareness among target audiences increased by 64 per cent, consideration rose by 22 per cent and willingness to recommend rose by 10 per cent (Burnett et al., 2016, p. 14).

Impact

During a period when ad spending was down, newsstand sales were down, and pricing and promotions were static, the campaign increased paid subscriptions to *The Economist* by 64,405 as at early 2016. With more than 5 million re-targetable potential readers reached, there is also the likelihood of further subscriptions arising from the campaign.

In evaluating the impact of the campaign, the agency stressed that only digital subscriptions prompted through paid search or clickthroughs from placed links were counted as being causally related to the campaign. All offline acquisitions and other digital acquisition channels not explicitly linked to one of the ads that could have influenced results, such as social media, were excluded from reported results.

Using the projected lifetime value of subscribers, *The Economist* estimates that, as at early 2016, the campaign was already responsible for delivering £51.7 million in lifetime revenue – a return on marketing investment (ROMI) of over 25:1 on the year one spend of £2.03 million.

Case study 10.9 Evaluating a year of learning across 190 countries

UNICEF

UNICEF's communication staff and advisers have been leading a transformative initiative that aims to introduce an evidence-based approach to communications. In this sense, UNICEF's *Global Communication and Public Advocacy Strategy (2014–2017)* not only helped to unify the outlook on communications across UNICEF's offices in more than 190 countries, but also led to the development of a dedicated multi-market monitoring and evaluation (M&E) framework and is a natural next step towards providing an overarching methodology of measurement. At the same time, it aims to capture the diversity across a geographically decentralized organization present in more than 190 countries and to allow learning from the wealth of information and experiences globally in more systematic ways. The development and implementation of this framework in 2015 was referred to as the 'year of learning'.[24]

The M&E framework, which was developed in full alignment with the Barcelona Principles and with the involvement of Ketchum Research and Gorkana, outlines a measurement rationale rooted in the *theory of change*. It endeavours to measure the impact of the communication function, its alignment with UNICEF's strategic policy and programmatic priorities, and its contribution to the organization's objectives, grounded in protecting and advocating for the rights of every child.

Objectives and KPIs

To this end, the framework proposes a set of KPIs. The KPIs were developed taking into account the strategy's three main objectives, which were:

1. to be the leading voice for and with children;
2. to reach 1 billion people; and
3. to engage 50 million people by 2017.

Even though most KPIs are very specific, the framework allows different country offices to expand their measurement criteria to capture the local contexts and to best inform the work of local communications teams, giving them the flexibility to track the metrics that reflect their work.

The KPIs tracked at global level – aggregated by context – can be applied to inform decisions and budgets, to contribute to collective learning, and ultimately to shape and strengthen communication and public advocacy efforts across UNICEF.

Strategy: the rollout of the M&E framework globally

Translating the global framework into the local context represented one of the key challenges. Therefore, the M&E framework was developed with an iterative mindset. After a consultative process with the pilot and early adopter countries, the collected recommendations have been incorporated and reflected in the list of suggested KPIs. As part of the implementation plan, UNICEF's central Division of Communication (DOC) has been closely supporting, training and guiding more than 30 country offices and 24 national committees through a rigorous three-part process, as follows:

1. Local communications teams are introduced to the M&E framework through DOC-supported webinars, bilateral virtual meetings and/or normative guidance documents, such as toolkits and handbooks.

2. Communications teams develop their country scorecards using the most relevant KPIs under each category of voice, reach and engagement.
3. They hire a local or regional media monitoring company to help them to monitor and analyse, on a continuous basis, various campaigns and initiatives.
4. Finally, they report on quarterly bases, which are then aggregated into the global scorecards (which are separately tracked at the global level capturing all 27 KPIs).

Implementation

The first year of implementation witnessed extensive collaborations between the DOC and offices globally, on the one hand, and with internal partners across other divisions of UNICEF, on the other. While constantly learning from the established process, baselines have been defined at headquarters and in implementing countries, with the objective of capturing data to realistically define targets and to establish benchmarks for future analysis and assessments. The key metrics that the DOC has been tracking to the time of this publication are considered an initial step towards developing data analysis and research, with the overall aims not only of tracking progress against the main goals of the strategy, but also of helping to inform communication plans and strategies to ensure that collective advocacy and communication efforts drive change for children. In this sense, the first year of the implementation was a year of collective learning.

Effectiveness

The following are some of the key lessons that the global M&E team responsible for the programme learned in the first year of implementation after extensive consultation.

1. **Keep it simple.** Simplicity and flexibility have been essential to implementing such a complex global programme, to allow the M&E framework to be adapted to various country contexts, in terms of both size and situation. Initially, the M&E team developed an exhaustive list of KPIs, but soon discovered that KPIs needed to have the flexibility to be tailored for each country due to differences in budget, office size and local context. Countries are encouraged to track as many KPIs as possible, particularly those that matter the most to them, but the M&E programme is flexible enough to allow countries to move forward at their own pace. The *Handbook for the Implementation of KPIs* developed by the DOC has proved to be a valuable tool that is being used widely to explain key concepts and rationale, and to detail techniques to calculate each of the KPIs.
2. **Be serious about evidence-based communication: M&E should not be an afterthought.** This was the first time that UNICEF had undertaken such a strategic approach to measurement and evaluation in its communication efforts. All strategies, including the global strategy and national strategies based upon the global strategy and adapted to the local context, are informed

by data collected both in advance of the implementation phase and during it. This provides the opportunity to take the time to reflect on what has contributed to the success or failure of the campaigns and initiatives that UNICEF implements. The DOC and many country offices have organized evaluation sessions to identify areas for improvement and to better interpret achievements to replicate or bring to scale models of success.

3. **Data and impact analysis help to change the way UNICEF does business and the way it communicates.** This new approach to measurement is contributing to change the way UNICEF works and the way it communicates. Staff are now able to get a better idea of the reach and impact of communication initiatives and to identify gaps, as well as progress. The use of frequent monitoring of data has informed timely course corrections in plans and strategies of communication and public advocacy efforts. This has also led efforts to be more responsive to the reality on the ground and has helped to accelerate sustainable results for all children.

4. **Hire the right people, develop human capital and invest in capacity-building.** Investing in human capital has been found to be fundamental. Creating new positions, bringing in new skills and developing the capacity of the existing communication teams are a priority to ensure proper implementation of such an ambitious M&E plan. Candidates with relevant and up-to-date skills allow the organization to keep up with the ongoing changes in the digital and media world. The DOC, in collaboration with the seven regional communication offices, is regularly providing training and capacity-building to field staff through webinars, bilateral calls and guidance tools.

5. **Work with the right partners – you cannot do it alone!** It is simply not possible to implement a truly global and multifaceted framework like that designed by UNICEF without collaborating with external vendors and partners. The DOC is working with several industry leaders that provide technical support, including Ketchum Global Research and Analytics. The service provided by Gorkana, the vendor contracted for the global monitoring and analysis, is complemented by Brandwatch (social media), Factiva (paid content), TV Eyes (TV and radio clips) and other tools. The DOC encourages offices to utilize external media monitoring companies to assist in tracking KPIs. Even in the best-funded and staffed offices, having an external service provider partner provides both quantitative and qualitative analysis to better inform communication activities. A local media monitoring company can also fill the gaps that a global provider may not be able to address (for example, local languages/dialects, print media as opposed to online editions, etc.).

6. **Seek advice and do not reinvent the wheel.** It is important to remember that others may have already found a solution to the problems an organization encounters. At the headquarters level, Ketchum Global Research and Analytics (KGRA) provides strategic advice and helps to coordinate the work of an advisory board, which includes representatives from private-sector companies along with large global operations, global NGOs and academic institutions. The advisory board meets biannually, and provides UNICEF with guidance and feedback on the approach and direction of its evaluation. The forum is

also a place to share expertise and to discuss potential solutions and additional innovations to common challenges. UNICEF is greatly benefiting from the expertise and know-how of these senior communication professionals.

7. **Fail fast, fail cheaply, try again, improve and scale up.** Experience from the 'year of learning' has shown that when support and guidance are shared at all levels, country offices are able to produce results greater than initially envisioned. Each month, the DOC produces a monthly compendium of examples of how the 'voice, reach and engagement' pillars of the strategy are being put into action at country level, as well as facilitating case studies on the M&E framework implementation that can be useful learning tools for other offices tracking KPIs.

8. **Share data and insights in a timely manner.** Sharing data and insights is important, but if it is to have impact, it must be clear and shared in a timely manner. Data can be useful in decision-making, but it can also create confusion if not explained well. It is therefore important to be clear when communicating to audiences that may not understand the technicalities or the assumptions behind the metrics.

   To this end, the DOC launched two new internal communication products in 2015: (a) a set of daily email alerts that keep colleagues informed about the main articles appearing in top-tier media that mention UNICEF and issues related to children; and (b) a monthly newsletter that includes the best examples of external communication and public advocacy campaigns from UNICEF teams around the globe. The DOC also continues to produce biweekly 'communication highlights', which are widely distributed internally. Information is also packaged for senior managers in a straightforward and transparent way, allowing them to better understand UNICEF's presence in the global media landscape.

9. **Measurement and evaluation is an art: do not try to apply the same model in all countries.** The organization's aim is to have all country and national committee offices implementing the M&E framework. This requires the creation of tailored solutions to respond to the local needs and realities in each of the countries. The M&E team realized that it would be a mistake to try to use the same model in all regions around the globe. Each country has its own needs and local contexts, which include the various human and financial capacities of each office.

Next steps

Starting in 2016, taking into account the lessons learned, the DOC expanded the scope of its research to answer the following questions.

- **Who is the audience?** To assist UNICEF's digital production team in creating more relevant and engaging content for UNICEF's global audience, the team has started to conduct literature reviews and to evaluate the demographic profile of various social media platforms.
- **What do the numbers mean?** To have meaningful benchmarks to evaluate social media posts, UNICEF has been developing detailed weekly, as well as

monthly, global scorecards. After initially focusing on Facebook and Twitter, the new scorecards are expanding to track emerging social media networks and platforms including LinkedIn, Instagram and Pinterest.

*   **What learning can be shared?** The DOC is promoting knowledge-sharing, such as through newsletters, showcasing the best initiatives as a way of providing concrete examples of success so that other country offices can adopt and further tailor their own efforts without reinventing the wheel. This is in line with the organizational vision of efficiency and effectiveness.

Case study 10.10 Media analysis to track brands across multiple markets

Samsung Electronics, Middle East and North Africa

Since 2010, Samsung Electronics, Middle East and North Africa (MENA) offices have used CARMA to analyse media coverage of Samsung and competitor brands across multiple countries in the MENA region. Over the years, the media analysis report has evolved from a simple Excel sheet with a few quantitative charts to become an in-depth analysis report that measures not only quantity, but also the quality of media coverage. The data for the analysis report is provided by the agencies working for Samsung in each country.

In 2015, Samsung MENA collaborated with CARMA to devise a more regimented, qualitative, multi-market measurement programme suitable for all countries across the region.[25]

Objectives

The objectives of the revised media analysis programme were to:

*   measure the success of the communications efforts of the in-country agencies;
*   focus on the analysis of locally generated stories;
*   focus on key media within each country;
*   assess the quality of the articles in a way that allows reliable comparisons between divisions, countries and over time;
*   encourage agencies to use more innovative communication techniques with less reliance on press releases;
*   achieve consistent and impartial analysis across all 16 countries – namely, the Gulf Cooperation Council (GCC) countries (United Arab Emirates, Bahrain, Oman and Qatar), Turkey, Iran, the Levant countries (Jordan, Lebanon, Syria and Palestine), Pakistan, Algeria, Egypt, Morocco, Saudi Arabia and Tunisia; and
*   have a reporting format that is easy to use and segmented for onward distribution.

Strategy

CARMA worked in partnership with Samsung MENA to agree on a new analysis framework and reporting structure to evaluate the qualitative effectiveness of media coverage. The following elements were considered key to a successful outcome:

- *categorization* of local and global coverage (that is, whether the story was about local issues or Samsung's international activities) using a media tier schema (Tier 1, Tier 2, etc.);
- devising an *in-depth coding frame* for local coverage, including all elements that contribute to a high-profile 'quality' article, as well as breakdown of coverage by business units, products, key messages and spokespersons;
- creating a *bespoke database* to capture agency code sheets uniformly;
- creating a *coverage evaluation matrix* (CEM) as an article scoring system; and
- *segmentation* of reporting overall, by business unit and by country, with countries grouped by media/publication size (small, medium, large) to afford fair comparison.

A simple, yet effective, set of KPIs was developed, and media coverage was benchmarked month-on-month for each country and overall by media type (based on Tier 1 and 2 for local coverage) on the basis of:

- total volume of coverage;
- positive/negative ratio;
- percentage of local coverage;
- percentage of quality stories; and
- average CEM score.

Implementation

CARMA's Insights team worked closely with the internal information technology (IT) development team to create a bespoke database and reporting system exclusively for Samsung MENA. The programme was coordinated by a dedicated account manager, who agreed a workflow with Samsung MENA whereby contracted PR agencies sent coded Excel sheets to the account manager, who conducted a thorough quality check to ensure clean data and accurate coding before importing into the custom database. The account manager also provided feedback on their coding to ensure quality control.

The database was designed to assign the correct score and weighting to elements coded on the Excel sheet, and to calculate a rounded score for each of the articles. The same database was used to produce data for the charts and tables in the newly redesigned monthly report. The report comprised a dashboard format, with sections for the MENA regional overview, country overview (grouped into small, medium and large countries), results by country (16 countries) and a business unit breakdown.

Each country dashboard included the following metrics (based on Tier 1 and 2 local coverage, except where stated), for easy comparison:

- KPIs table;
- share of voice (SOV) of top competitors (all coverage);
- global/local breakdown;
- tonality breakdown (all coverage);
- volume by CEM ranking (from excellent to poor);
- media focus breakdown (for example, business, lifestyle, news outlet, technology, trade, etc.); and
- average CEM score over time.

Succinct narrative reported key highlights each month and allowed easy comparison of:

- volume increases in percentages by country month-on-month;
- top stories in coverage of business units, including identification of percentage share for each business unit;
- percentage of local news that is agency-generated and percentage of local news that comprises verbatim press release material; and
- proportion of 'high-quality' articles with explanations of positive/negative coverage (for example, causes, issues involved, etc.).

An annual round-up analysis report was added to the programme in 2015 to allow Samsung MENA to review trends over the previous year and to plan for the coming one.

Effectiveness

The solution provided by CARMA met Samsung MENA's objectives in several ways, as follows:

- The coding frame segregated global and local coverage so that local stories can be analysed in greater depth. The bespoke database was designed to be flexible enough to handle different coding criteria for each type of coverage.
- The scoring methodology allows Samsung MENA to assess the quality of locally focused articles in a systematic way, allowing valid comparison between countries and business units, and over time.
- Article ranking allows Samsung MENA to instantly identify which countries are performing best by virtue of the percentage of quality articles each month.
- The percentage of agency-generated stories and press releases documented in the narrative each month gives Samsung MENA a snapshot of which countries are having the greatest PR success and what proportion of local news stories make it into the media due to the agency's communication efforts, as well as the use of press releases verbatim.

- Because this information is set out in the same place on the dashboard for each country month after month, management can easily see which countries are improving over time.
- Implementation of a robust bespoke database to store the data, instead of Excel sheets, has meant that the data is uniform, stable and capable of being repurposed for ad hoc reports at short notice.
- The appointment of a dedicated account manager, who manages the coding sheet and workflow with the PR agencies, has saved a great deal of administration time for Samsung MENA. The account manager also has raised the quality of analysis through rigorous data quality control and feedback.
- The new format provides an easy-to-read, consistent, visually appealing and informative report that, because of the uniformity and slide-by-slide segmentation, can be used by all of Samsung MENA's stakeholders – country managers, PR agencies, business unit managers, senior management and global management.

Jane Yun, public relations manager of Samsung MENA, said:

> The Middle East and North Africa region is such a dynamic market with diverse media landscapes and characteristics. When it comes to measuring or understanding the value of media coverage, it is often underestimated or inaccurately measured. Hence, given the nature of the region, Samsung Electronics, MENA created an internal KPI structure and algorithm to measure media coverage beyond quantity.
>
> The objective of the [CEM] is to evaluate the quality of coverage being produced in Tier 1 and 2 media and the effectiveness of PR activities being executed across the markets. CARMA's role was crucial to translate these data points to an analytical report by countries. Working with CARMA is a pleasure and to date the team continues to provide their consultancy to better our in-depth analysis segregated by countries, reinforcing our understanding on each country's strength and weakness, resulting in long and short term fixes to further excel in our communication activities across the MENA region.
>
> *(J. Yun, personal communication, February 26, 2016)*

Case study 10.11 Learning from crisis mismanagement by a mining company

Hazelwood coal mine fire, Victoria, Australia

While evaluation in the previous case studies has demonstrated effectiveness and success, evaluation can also reveal failures to communicate and provide insights to inform future strategy, as this case study shows.

In February 2014, in the heat of the Australian summer, savage bushfires swept through the Latrobe Valley in the southern Australian state of Victoria, causing substantial damage to houses, livestock, wildlife and the environment. In addition to constituting a crisis in themselves, the bushfires sparked a much longer-lasting and potentially disastrous crisis when they ignited the Hazelwood open-cut coal mine. Brown coal in the mine caught alight and burned for 45 days before being extinguished. In the process, the coal mine fire spread thick smoke and ash containing potentially dangerous chemicals and particles over the adjoining town of Morwell.

Burning brown coal emits carbon monoxide, methane, sulphur and nitrogen oxides, volatile organic compounds (VOCs), particulate matter, and potentially toxic trace elements such as arsenic and mercury, making it potentially very hazardous to human health and the environment when emissions reach high levels or occur over an extended period of time, as was the case at Hazelwood.

Not surprisingly, the 14,000 residents of Morwell – many living within a few kilometres of the mine – became concerned and soon were reporting respiratory problems and sickness caused by alleged carbon monoxide poisoning, as well as substantial damage to their homes and rainwater tanks caused by the smoke and falling ash.

As the fire burned out of control, the Department of Health in Victoria ordered the evacuation of the elderly and those with respiratory ailments. The local school was closed and students were moved to a nearby town. By the second week, even the local courthouse closed and hearings were adjourned to another location. After several weeks, with the fire still burning, residents became angry and rallied in protest at community meetings organized by emergency agencies, as well as the locally established 'Voices of the Valley' community action group.

Subsequently, in March 2014, the State Government of Victoria appointed a board of inquiry into management of the crisis, with terms of reference including independent review of the effectiveness of public communication by the mining company, GDF Suez Australian Energy,[26] and health and emergency services. The Hazelwood Coal Mine Fire Inquiry took place in Morwell, Victoria, in May and June 2014, after the mine fire, which began on February 9, was finally extinguished on March 25.

Jim Macnamara, professor of public communication at the UTS, was appointed on May 14 to conduct an independent evaluation of communication by the mining company and health and emergency services during the crisis and to serve as an expert witness. He subsequently submitted a 60-page report to the inquiry on May 26 (Macnamara, 2014d) and appeared before the inquiry on June 5. The inquiry concluded its hearings on June 13 and handed down its report on August 29, 2014 (Hazelwood Mine Fire Inquiry, 2014).

The board of inquiry estimated that the cost of the fire to the Victorian government, the mining company and the local community exceeded AU$100 million (US$85–90 million), and made 18 recommendations for improving response to such emergencies in future, including in relation to public communication. These were informed by the independent evaluation, which is summarized in the following sections. The full evaluation report is available online (Macnamara, 2014d).

Methodology

Crisis communication was examined through content analysis of more than 4,000 pages of public statements, media releases, government authority notices and warnings, transcripts and videos from public meetings and media conferences, and statements by witnesses to the board of inquiry, including those issued by:

* the Country Fire Authority (CFA) of Victoria and its incident controller of the site;
* the Victorian Environment Protection Authority (EPA);
* the Department of Health in Victoria;
* the state's chief health officer (CHO);
* the Department of Human Services (DHS);
* the Latrobe City Council; and
* the mine company, GDF Suez Australian Energy.

Also, statements and media releases issued by the Premier of Victoria, the Minister for Health and Ageing, and other government leaders were analysed. In addition, media coverage of the fire was reviewed through access to media clippings, video recordings and transcripts provided to the Hazelwood Coal Mine Fire Inquiry by a media monitoring company, and the content of the Twitter and Facebook accounts of all of the above government departments and authorities and the mine operator during the period of the crisis was analysed.

Content analysis of relevant statements and documents was conducted qualitatively in accordance with academic standards (Neuendorf, 2002; Shoemaker & Reese, 1996). An initial stage of open *in vivo* coding was undertaken to identify categories and major themes in statements and reporting. This inductive coding stage identified discussion related to: (a) the *cause* of the fire (for example, accidental ignition by a bushfire, mine fault or arson/sabotage); (b) *preparedness* by the mine company and government bodies; (c) *operational response* (that is, firefighting); (d) *public information*, including timeliness, comprehensibility and tone; (e) *community engagement*; (f) *public health and safety*; (g) *environment*; (h) *industry/energy supply*; and (i) *local business* (including economic effects). Texts were then analysed in further detail using qualitative content analysis to examine what the community was told, when and in what form. Specifically, this sought to identify the key messages, information and advice that were provided to the community on key issues such as safety, public health, and so on. Coding was done manually by two analysts independently and then compared to ensure maximum trustworthiness of the data.

The actions, statements and information provided to citizens identified from extensive content analysis of documents were compared with best practice crisis communication outlined in textbooks, research literature, and manuals and handbooks.

Research questions

The research questions explored in this evaluative research were as follows:

1. What information and messages were distributed to those affected by the crisis?
2. How timely was information provided to those affected by the crisis?
3. How appropriate was information and communication for those affected by the crisis (for example, in terms of medium, format, language and tone)?
4. How effective was public communication during the crisis?

While the researcher did not have access to interview authorities or community leaders involved, his appointment as an independent researcher and expert witness to review public communication and advise the board of inquiry, which had legal powers to access all relevant records and information, afforded him unrestricted access to public information and communication, as well as submissions and witness statements to the board of inquiry given under oath. Therefore, this analysis was conducted from a position of in-depth knowledge supported by direct access to relevant public communication materials and extensive witness statements.

Context

An important context for understanding and evaluating this crisis communication case study is that the population of Morwell is largely of low socio economic status (SES), made up of mine workers and their families, along with people involved in support services and agriculture in the surrounding area. As well as having relatively low education levels and low incomes, Morwell's population has an above-average proportion of elderly people, and Internet connectivity and use is much lower than Australia's high online national average at the time of 87 per cent (Internet World Statistics, 2015). These factors were known to government authorities responsible for community health, support and welfare, and are important in evaluating the public communication that followed the outbreak of the Hazelwood coal mine fire.

Three other important points to note are that:

- the rural area around Morwell in the Latrobe Valley is prone to bushfires;
- brown coal combusts at relatively low temperatures and a number of coal mines around the world have caught fire – most notably, the Centralia coal mine in the US, which has been burning unchecked since 1962, and Burning Mountain in Australia,[27] as well as a number in China (O'Carroll, 2010); and
- the Hazelwood mine had already caught fire previously in 2005, 2006, 2008 and 2012.

(The Australian, May 26, 2014, para. 2)

Findings and conclusions

While there was much to admire in the stalwart, and sometimes heroic, efforts of the firefighters, volunteer organizations and many individuals who rallied to provide support to concerned citizens, management of public communication during the Hazelwood coal mine fire failed to follow crisis communication and emergency communication theory and best practice principles. Six key findings were reported, as follows:

1. **Silence and evasion by the mining company.** The first serious and troubling finding of evaluation was that the mining company failed to follow basic crisis communication best practice by remaining silent and evasive. Somewhat inexplicably, GDF Suez Australian Energy did not make any statement in the early days and weeks of the crisis nor did it attend any of the public meetings held to brief the local community and answer questions. The company issued its first public statement on March 11 – 28 days after the fire started and two weeks after the board of inquiry was announced. No further statement or media release was issued until May.

   This approach is in direct contradiction of best practice crisis communication advice to 'be quick, be consistent, and be open' (Coombs, 2006, p. 172). As Coombs explicates: '[T]he organization should tell stakeholders everything they know about the crisis as soon as the organization receives the information' (2006, p. 173). When the mining company did become involved in public communication, it was a case of 'too little, too late'.

2. **Lack of preparation.** Analysis revealed that the mining company and a number of government departments also failed in relation to another basic principle of crisis management and crisis communication: preparation. Craig Lapsley, fire services commissioner of Victoria, told the inquiry that a *draft* communications and stakeholder engagement strategy had been provided to him, the incident control centre and the regional control centre on February 16 – a week after the coal mine fire started. It was not 'incorporated into the State Strategy Support Team briefs' or implemented until after February 20 – a full 11 days after the crisis began (Lapsley, 2014, p. 28). In short, the key emergency services did not have a communication strategy in place for such an emergency.

   In defending their approach and actions, the mining company and authorities such as the EPA argued that the coal mine fire was 'unprecedented' (for example, EPA Victoria, 2014; GDF Suez Australian Energy, 2014). However, given the frequency of bushfires in the area, the low combustive nature of brown coal and previous fires at the mine, there clearly were precedents and clear evidence that such a crisis was not only possible, but likely.

3. **Misreading of the situation.** Evaluation also revealed that key emergency services misread the situation and made gross errors of judgement. For instance, in giving evidence about events during the week following the outbreak of the fire, Merita Tebain, director of media and corporate communications of the Victoria Police and chair of the Emergency Management Joint Public Information Committee (EMJPIC), told the inquiry that 'as the week progressed, the significance of the Hazelwood Coal Mine fire became more apparent as

the risk to energy supply diminished and the community effects came to light' (Hazelwood Mine Fire Inquiry, 2014, p. 3). This statement illustrates that the Victoria Police and those responsible for public communication perceived the fire as simply a threat to electricity supplies and failed to recognize the risks to public health until a week after the fire started.

4. **Delays in providing necessary information and communication.** Misreading of the extent and nature of the crisis resulted in a fourth failing in crisis communication: delays. While the EPA issued 76 smoke alerts during the period of the fire, starting February 11 (two days after the mine fire broke out), and its CEO John Merritt participated in media conferences in Morwell on February 9, 27 and 28 and March 17, the first *News and Update* in relation to testing air quality at Morwell was not issued until February 17 – eight days after the coal mine fire started. The first media release from the EPA was issued on February 20 – 11 days after the fire broke out.

The chief health officer for Victoria issued a number of *advisories* for residents in relation to health risks and evacuation during the crisis, but the first of these did not appear until February 17, the same day as the first EPA *News and Update* – eight days after the crisis began. Also, significantly, neither the chief health officer nor any representative of the Department of Health attended the first public meeting in Morwell to discuss the fire and its impact on the community.

The Victorian Department of Human Services (DHS) provides considerable information on its website in relation to 'Preparing for emergencies'. This includes information on disruption to essential services and 'Managing stress during emergencies', with links to the Victorian Bushfire Information Line (VBIL), St John's Ambulance, Lifeline and other support groups. However, the DHS was accused of doing little for the community, and the Community and Public Sector Union (CPSU) claimed that the department even neglected the health and welfare of its own employees at the Morwell Centrelink office, a government unemployment agency (Nelson, 2014, p. 7).

Even the CFA, which was the most active of government agencies in terms of public communication, did not publish the first issue of its *Mine Fire Newsletter* until five days after the fire started and its first 'Mine Fire Update' was posted online on February 17 – eight days after the outbreak. And, as noted previously, the mining company did not make any statement until almost a month after the fire started.

5. **Inappropriate media and messages.** When information was provided to residents of Morwell and the surrounding area, most of it was provided online. As noted in the background provided under 'Context', Morwell has low Internet use due to the low SES and age of most residents. This meant that most residents in the area did not access the information provided.

Furthermore, much of the information provided by authorities was highly technical and scientific in nature, such as tables of chemicals and their emission levels – for example, *dichlorodifluormethane*, *ethylbenzene* and *butadlene* (see Figure 10.10). These were mostly unintelligible to local residents.

6. **Confusing information with communication.** An overarching failing in crisis communication by the mining company and all government agencies involved, with the exception of the CFA, was that information dissemination and transmission was erroneously considered to be communication. The *Emergency Management Manual Victoria*, which was used and referred to by several government bodies during the crisis, defines 'communications' as 'the practice of sending, gathering, managing and evaluating information. This can occur before, during and after (both long and short term) emergencies' (Emergency Management Victoria, 2014, p. 57). This definition in the state's key reference for emergency and crisis communication reveals a focus on *information* rather than communication and a *transmissional* view of communication rather than a transactional, interactive approach. The Victorian government's emergency management manual and the communication attempts of authorities during the crisis demonstrated a lack of attention to reception and interpretation of information – that is, what the Morwell community interpreted and understood – as well as a lack of community interaction and engagement.

The fire services commissioner of Victoria acknowledged in his statement to the Hazelwood Mine Fire Inquiry that there were 'things that could have been done better', including 'messaging that better integrates fire, health and environmental information', 'messaging must be distributed to match the profile and technology use of a community' and 'community connection' (Lapsley, 2014, p. 29).

What has the VOC testing found so far?

Of the 64 chemicals tested for, 50 were not found. The 14 chemicals that were found are listed in the table.

Chemical	Unit	Morwell East		Morwell Bowling Club		Maryvale Crescent Early Learning Centre		Air Quality Guideline Value
		26 Feb	27 Feb	26 Feb	27 Feb	26 Feb	27 Feb	24 hr ppb
Propene (Propylene)	ppb	4.7	5.7	42	28	24	16	232.4
Dichlorodifluoromethane(Freon12)	ppb	0.89	0.89	0.81	0.84	0.83	0.86	101000
Chloromethane (methyl chloride)	ppb		1.5	1.9	2.0	2.5	1.9	155
1,3-Butadiene	ppb			2.5	1.6	1.6	0.70	145
Acetone	ppb	1.9	2.2	8.0	7.0	5.8	6.2	497
Ethanol	ppb	2.9	94.9	7.2	8.4	5.3	5.4	10084
Carbon disulfide	ppb						0.81	106
2-Butanone (MEK)	ppb			1.1	0.93	0.75	0.82	339
Hexane	ppb			1.2	0.89	0.77		284
Benzene	ppb	1.7	2.1	14	9.7	9.2	6.0	9
Heptane	ppb			0.91	0.70	0.61		2684
Toluene	ppb	0.70	0.92	4.7	3.4	3.0	2.1	531
Ethylbenzene	ppb				0.57			230
Naphthalene	ppb			0.97	1.6			4.29

FIGURE 10.10 Sample information provided in Victorian Department of Health factsheets

Source: Victorian Department of Health (2014)

John Merritt, CEO of the EPA, also acknowledged, in his witness statement to the Hazelwood Mine Fire Inquiry, that:

> As the incident unfolded, it became clear that more information was required by the community. The challenge was that . . . the information, such as individual test results started to introduce more complex scientific ideas, principles and concepts and as such required substantially more explanation and translation into easily understood terms.
>
> *(Merritt, 2014, p. 8)*

The report of the Hazelwood Mine Fire Inquiry (2014), released in August 2014, accepted and endorsed the key findings of this author's independent evaluation of communication by the mining company and relevant government agencies, stating that:

- the mine company was 'inadequately prepared to manage the fire' (p. 16);
- 'the State Control Centre's initial request for the EPA's support and advice in responding to the Hazelwood mine fire came too late and the EPA was ill-equipped to respond rapidly' (p. 23);
- '[t]here were significant shortcomings by government authorities, as well as GDF Suez, in communicating throughout the emergency' (p. 28); and
- '[c]ommunication did not reach many people in a timely way and in some cases, not at all' (p. 28).

The report further noted:

> Members of affected communities felt they were not listened to and were not given appropriate and timely information and advice that reflected the crisis at hand and addressed their needs . . . communication was largely one-way with information being transmitted, but not received or understood by the intended recipients . . . government departments and agencies did not engage to any significant extent in listening to, or partnering with local residents and community groups.
>
> *(Hazelwood Mine Fire Inquiry, 2014, p. 28)*

Insights to inform future strategy

Beyond the coal-mining industry, there are important lessons in this case study for all companies and government departments and agencies. Most particularly, the findings of this evaluation underline the key principles of crisis communication, including:

- preparation based on scenario development and 'worst case' forecasting;
- having a strategic communication plan in place;

- understanding stakeholders and communities affected, so that they can be addressed through appropriate methods and media in appropriate language;
- consulting with, and listening to, those affected, to supplement desk research with direct communication and engagement; and
- demonstrating empathy and considering the human dimensions of a crisis – not only the operational, technical, scientific and legal aspects.

In addition, this analysis indicates a need for educating and training management in the fundamentals of communication, as distinct from information distribution. This analysis also supports Kent's (2010) call for crisis communication research, particularly within the field of PR, to take a broader approach that looks beyond the organization's reputation, image and recovery, and includes more focus on stakeholder and community welfare, recovery and renewal (Macnamara, 2015f).

Case study 10.12 'Big Change Starts Small' obesity campaign gets big results

Y&R New Zealand

Obesity is a growing health issue in many countries, but this chapter ends with a positive case study of how award–winning evaluation[28] helped to identify effective strategies in an integrated communication campaign.

Background

The *Annual Update of Key Results 2014/15: New Zealand Health Survey* (New Zealand Ministry of Health, 2015a) found that both adult and child obesity rates in New Zealand are increasing, as they are in many other developed countries. It reported that 31 per cent of New Zealand adults and 11 per cent of New Zealand children aged 2–14 are now obese. In announcing a plan to combat obesity, New Zealand's Health Minister and Sport and Recreation Minister Jonathan Coleman said, in a press release, that 'being overweight or obese is expected to overtake tobacco as the leading preventable risk to health in New Zealand within the next 12 months' (New Zealand Ministry for Culture and Heritage, 2015, n.p.).

New Zealand's Childhood Obesity Plan

The Childhood Obesity Plan (New Zealand Ministry of Health, 2015b) launched by the New Zealand government in October 2015 aims to prevent and manage obesity in children and young people up to 18 years of age. The plan includes 22 initiatives involving multiple government and private-sector agencies, communities, schools and families, and is focused on three areas:

1. targeted interventions for those who are obese;
2. increased support for those at risk of becoming obese; and
3. broad approaches to make healthier choices easier for all New Zealanders.

'Big Change Starts Small' campaign

One of the first initiatives taken was a multimedia advertising campaign developed by Y&R New Zealand on behalf of the Health Promotions Agency (HPA) to raise awareness and generate conversations about childhood obesity under the theme 'Big Change Starts Small'. Launched on November 12, 2015 and running until December 31, 2015, the campaign included television, radio, digital and outdoor advertising, an information website, and supportive messages and endorsements from five high-profile athletes. The advertisements were focused on the role of food in families (encouraging parents and families to think about the quantity and quality of food they are providing to their children) and inactivity (suggesting that children are spending too much time on sedentary activities such as playing video games), while the website provided information on affordable meals and ideas for family activities.

Objectives

The overarching objective of the Childhood Obesity Plan is to create social change – that is, to reduce obesity. However, because behaviour change takes time, the objective of the 'Big Change Starts Small' campaign was to increase discussion, and therefore recognition, of obesity and its related problems. Key channels to achieve these outcomes were identified as traditional and social media.

Traditional and social media analysis

Y&R New Zealand contracted Isentia, a leading Asia Pacific supplier of media intelligence software and services, to evaluate the impact of the 'Big Change Starts Small' campaign using quantitative and qualitative media content analysis. In accordance with the objectives, media content analysis was designed to:

1. evaluate the effectiveness of the campaign in increasing discussion about obesity;
2. analyse how obesity, particularly childhood obesity, was discussed in traditional and social media (that is, what attitudes, concerns and intentions were expressed); and
3. identify the key commentators and influencers in discussions about obesity.

Isentia analysed the content of both traditional and social media coverage, including Facebook, Twitter, blogs and online forums, to assess reception of the Minister's announcement of the Childhood Obesity Plan and comments about the campaign, and to evaluate the campaign's impact in terms of creating discussion of childhood obesity and ways of reducing obesity.

Editorial media coverage and social media comment were sourced from two proprietary databases using key word searches, as well as selection of a purposive sample from a pool of general media content based on defined criteria. The sample for analysis included content containing mentions of:

- the campaign by name;
- campaign elements, including the ambassadors (by name) and the website (www.eatmovelive.co.nz);
- the Childhood Obesity Plan;
- obesity and/or related health issues, particularly those affecting children;
- exercise and/or lifestyle-related activities, particularly involving children or in a family context; and
- food and food consumption, particularly involving children or in a family context.

This ensured that the content analysed was not limited to specific mentions and discussion of the 'Big Change Starts Small' campaign, but also included analysis of discussion about the Childhood Obesity Plan and childhood obesity in general. Coverage was analysed from October 1 to December 31, 2015 using computer-aided research and media analysis (CARMA) methodology, based on a customized coding framework designed to examine discussion of each of the above issues and topics (and see the description of content analysis methodology in Chapter 8).

Particular attention was paid to how social media commentators and journalists positioned responsibility for childhood obesity – for example, with the government, communities, parents, extended families or others.

Isentia also obtained the schedule of campaign activities from Y&R, which enabled media content analysis to link coverage and discussion to the various communication activities undertaken.

Effectiveness

Isentia's analysis showed a marked increase in conversation and discussion about obesity in the reporting period compared with the previous three months. While a large proportion of traditional media coverage and social media conversations in October 2015 focused on the Minister's announcement of the Childhood Obesity Plan, this discussion declined substantially after a few weeks, as is common in a news cycle. However, the ongoing campaign was shown to be successful in regenerating and extending discussion of obesity, as evidenced by a significant increase in the volume of media reporting and social media comment about the campaign and its key messages in relation to food, exercise and health.

The analysis showed that the significance of obesity as an issue was widely recognized, with 'Obesity is a critical issue' found to be the leading message in the period of analysis. The government's efforts to tackle childhood obesity were regularly acknowledged, and other leading messages included both praise and criticism of the government's approach to the issue. This indicates that, for many media outlets and social media users, childhood obesity is an issue that is closely tied to government policy and political debate.

It was therefore significant that the message 'The government's approach to childhood obesity is effective' was prevalent in November and December 2015, following the launch of the 'Big Change Starts Small' campaign. Just as importantly, this was accompanied by a sharp decline in mentions of unfavourable messages, such as 'The government is not doing enough to improve childhood obesity rates' and 'The government's approach to tackle childhood obesity is ineffective/misguided'. This indicated that the campaign was recognized as an effective measure (see Figure 10.11).

The leading issues in relation to obesity reported in traditional media were largely consistent with those discussed in social media, demonstrating a high level of interaction between the two. However, social media posts were markedly less favourable compared with traditional media reports. Social media users were often more critical of the government's approach to childhood obesity, although online criticisms were rarely aimed directly at the campaign.

Traditional media reports and social media posts that mentioned the campaign and ambassadors achieved very high favourability ratings. Overall, the campaign was almost universally received positively, its advertisements and ambassadors were frequently praised, and, most importantly, it was directly credited with encouraging and increasing constructive discussion about obesity.

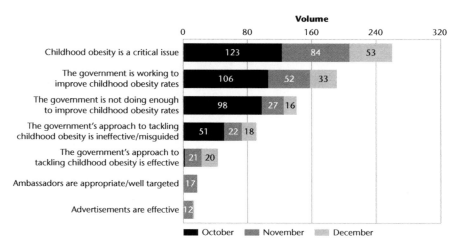

FIGURE 10.11 Key messages communicated in the 'Big Change Starts Small' campaign

Source: Isentia

As part of the analysis, secondary data from a similar government announcement on changes to the tax system that used a paid advertising campaign were used to demonstrate the typical media cycle for this kind of announcement and serve as a benchmark. This comparative analysis demonstrated that the 'Big Change Starts Small' campaign by Y&R was more effective in generating ongoing discussion than other similar announcements.

Impact

- The Isentia media analysis report provided important empirical evidence for Y&R's post-campaign review and analysis, and was presented directly to the HPA.
- The HPA used the report to demonstrate the success of the campaign to its stakeholders.
- This success of the campaign will help the HPA to gain further funding to continue the campaign.
- The report also will play an important role in planning the next stages of the campaign. The report has provided a benchmark for future campaigns, which will be evaluated using the same or similar methodology to allow ongoing comparative tracking. Also, now that the nature of conversations about obesity has been identified, the next stage will include evaluation of how conversations change and evolve, and whether they point towards behaviour change.
- The evaluation directly contributed to a number of award entries submitted by Y&R and won an international AMEC award (see n. 28).

Client satisfaction

While regularly using traditional advertising metrics, Y&R had not previously used this type of evaluation. This project demonstrated the value of qualitative content analysis of traditional and social media as an extension of quantitative media metrics, especially when tracking the outcomes of communication campaigns in relation to complex social issues.

Grant Maxwell, general manager of Y&R New Zealand, said of the evaluation:

> Isentia's analysis of the 'Big Change Starts Small' campaign is an instrumental piece of research which will not only help inform the running of subsequent initiatives under the Childhood Obesity Plan, but also help us direct other social change campaigns in the future. This is the first time that we have done any evaluation of this nature, and the findings of this report gave us a great insight into the interaction between a campaign, traditional media news, and social media conversations. One of the major challenges of running a publicly funded social change campaign is to show that money has been well spent,

and this report enabled us to demonstrate that we have achieved the desired outcome from an awareness point of view.

(G. Maxwell, personal communication, December 15, 2016)

Notes

1 The Institute of Practitioners in Advertising (IPA) Effectiveness Awards are claimed to be 'recognized by agencies and clients as the world's most rigorous award scheme' in the advertising and marketing industry (IPA, 2016c, n.p.). Dame Dianne Thompson OBE, chair of the judges in 2016, described them as 'the most valuable and important of all' industry awards that provide 'proof that marketing and advertising create real returns to stakeholders' (Thompson, 2016, n.p.).

2 This figure refers to comments, not views. Kim Kardashian's *Paper* magazine photos reportedly received 50 million views in one day (Spedding, 2016).

3 The influencer network analysis conducted by Commetric for the International Diabetes Federation won the Gold Award for 'Most impactful client recommendations arising from a measurement study' in the 2016 International Association for Measurement and Evaluation (AMEC) Global Effectiveness Awards.

4 The Group of Seven (G7) is an informal group of industrialized democracies (the US, Canada, France, Germany, Italy, Japan and the UK) that meets annually to discuss issues such as global economic governance, international security and energy policy.

5 The 'Missing Type' blood donation campaign by NHS Blood and Transplant, including research by Gorkana, won Gold Awards for 'Best measurement of a public sector campaign' and 'Best use of integrated communication measurement/research' in the 2016 AMEC Global Effectiveness Awards.

6 Many PR practitioners continue to use terms such as *press releases*, even though broadcast media have been part of mainstream media for most of the past century and social media are now increasingly important.

7 Evaluation of the Pink Sari Project by the University of Technology Sydney on behalf of the New South Wales Multicultural Health Communication Service won the Gold Award for 'Best campaign in the public and not-for-profit sectors' and the Grand Prix Platinum Award for 'Most effective PR consultancy or in-house communications team campaign' in the 2016 AMEC Global Effectiveness Awards.

8 While this author was chair of the judges for the AMEC awards in 2016, as noted in Chapter 1, he was not a judge and had no role in judging awards in the categories in which this project was successful.

9 A number of the participants in interviews asked to be de-identified because of their organization's policies.

10 The value of editorial media publicity, sometimes calculated using advertising value equivalents (AVEs), is not included in this calculation, in compliance with the Barcelona Principles of Communication Measurement and Best Practice.

11 Until 2014, Cancer Institute NSW collected breast screening data only for those aged 50–69, not for those aged 70–74. Hence this age range was used to allow comparison with previous years.

12 Evaluation of the US Army community relations programme implemented by Barbaricum won the Gold Award for 'Innovation in new measurement methodologies' in the 2016 AMEC Global Effectiveness Awards.

13 The strategic plan and evaluation reports of this activity used the term *press* to refer to media including newspapers, radio and television. This remains a dated but common practice in PR.

14 Evaluation of The CEO SleepOut™ in South Africa conducted by Ornico won the Gold Award for 'Best use of measurement for a single event' and the Gold Award for 'Best

measurement of a not-for-profit campaign' in the 2016 AMEC Global Effectiveness Awards.

15 South African rand, equivalent to around US$1.9 million.

16 A mobile software application.

17 The AMEC Valid Metrics Framework was a predecessor to the AMEC Integrated Evaluation Framework (IEF) launched in 2016, as discussed in Chapter 3.

18 Croatia became the 28th member state of the European Union after the campaign was launched.

19 The consortium, led by Saatchi and Saatchi Brussels, involved European Service Network (ESN), Huntsworth Health, Zenithoptimedia, GFK, Tonic Solutions and BrandNewHealth.

20 This case study was produced with the help of Melanie Kitchener, senior consultant in evaluation and research, and other staff of Coffey, a Tetra Tech Company, in London. The evaluation report on which it is based was commissioned and published by the European Commission.

21 *Barça* is a popular colloquial term referring to Futbol Club Barcelona, the professional football club based in Barcelona, Catalonia, Spain, also known as 'FC Barcelona'.

22 All data in this section is taken from the *Ex-post Evaluation Ex-smokers Campaign: Final Report* prepared for the European Commission by Coffey (2015).

23 The 'Raising eyebrows' campaign for *The Economist* won the Gold Award for 'Best new learning' (The Channon Prize) in the 2016 IPA Effectiveness Awards presented in London.

24 Evaluation of the UNICEF 'Year of Learning' won a Gold Award for 'Best multi-market reporting' in the 2016 AMEC Global Effectiveness Awards.

25 Evaluation of Samsung's media coverage and promotion in the Middle East by CARMA won a Gold Award for 'Best multi-market reporting' in the 2016 AMEC Global Effectiveness Awards.

26 GDF Suez Australian Energy changed its name to ENGIE in April 2015 (Engie, 2015).

27 Burning Mountain near the town of Wingen around 220 kilometres (140 miles) north of Sydney is the oldest known underground coal mine fire, estimated to have been burning for 6,000 years.

28 Evaluation by Isentia of Y&R's integrated multimedia campaign 'Big Change Starts Small' won the Gold Award for 'Plain English simplicity in campaign effectiveness measurement and reporting' in the 2016 AMEC Global Effectiveness Awards.

REFERENCES

Aakar, D., & Myers, J. (1975). *Advertising management*. Englewood Cliffs, NJ: Prentice-Hall.

Abelson, P. (2015). Using cost benefit analysis: Don't be afraid. Presentation to NSW Government Evaluation Conference, University of Technology Sydney, June.

Ajzen, I. (1985). From intentions to actions: A theory of planned behavior. In J. Kuhl & J. Beckmann (Eds.), *Action control: From cognition to behavior* (pp. 11–39). Berlin and Heidelberg, Germany: Springer-Verlag.

Ajzen, I. (1988). *Attitudes, personality, and behaviour*. Chicago, IL: Dorsey Press.

Ajzen, I., & Fishbein, M. (1980). *Understanding attitudes and predicting social behaviour*. Englewood Cliffs, NJ: Prentice-Hall.

Albanese, I. (2007). *The 4Cs of truth in communications: How to identify, discuss, evaluate and present stand-out effective communication*. Ithaca, NY: Paramount Market Publishing.

AMEC (Association for Measurement and Evaluation of Communication). (2010). Barcelona Declaration of Measurement Principles. London, UK: Author. Retrieved from http://amecorg.com/2012/06/barcelona-declaration-of-measurement-principles

AMEC (Association for Measurement and Evaluation of Communication). (2012). AMEC standards plan. London, UK: Author. Retrieved from http://amecorg.com/2012/01/amec-standards-plan

AMEC (Association for Measurement and Evaluation of Communication). (2015). Barcelona principles 2.0. London, UK: Author. Retrieved from http://amecorg.com/barcelona-principles-2-0

AMEC (Association for Measurement and Evaluation of Communication). (2016a). NFP research shows comms measurement barriers. London, UK: Author. Retrieved from http://amecorg.com/2016/06/nfp-research-shows-comms-measurement-barriers

AMEC (Association for Measurement and Evaluation of Communication). (2016b). Integrated evaluation framework. London, UK: Author. Retrieved from http://amecorg.com/amecframework

AMEC (Association for Measurement and Evaluation of Communication). (2016c). Global communication effectiveness awards 2016 [Website]. London, UK: Author. Retrieved from http://amecorg.com/amec-awards-winners-2016

American University. (2016). What is public communication? [Website]. Retrieved from www.american.edu/soc/communication/what-is-public-communication.cfm

Anderson, A. (2005). *The community builder's approach to theory of change: A practical guide to theory and development.* New York, NY: The Aspen Institute Roundtable on Community Change.

Anderson, B. (1991). *Imagined communities: Reflections on the origin and spread of nationalism* (rev. ed.). New York, NY and London, UK: Verso. (Original work published 1983.)

Anderson, C. (2006). *The long tail.* New York, NY: Hyperion.

Anderson, C., Bell, E., & Shirky, C. (2012). Post-industrial journalism: Adapting to the present. Tow Center for Digital Journalism, Columbia Journalism School, Columbia University, New York, NY. Retrieved from http://towcenter.org/research/post-industrial-journalism

Angner, E. (2011). The evolution of eupathics: The historical roots of subjective measures of wellbeing. *International Journal of Wellbeing, 1*(1), 4–41.

Argyris, C., & Schön, D. (1978). *Organizational learning: A theory of action perspective.* Reading, MA: Addison-Wesley.

Ashe, G. (1972). *The art of writing made simple.* London, UK: W. H. Allen.

Atkin, C., & Freimuth, V. (2013). Guidelines for formative evaluation research in campaign design. In R. Rice & C. Atkin (Eds.), *Public communication campaigns* (4th ed., pp. 53–68). Thousand Oaks, CA: Sage.

Atkin, C., & Rice, R. (2013). Theory and principles of public communication campaigns. In R. Rice & C. Atkin (Eds.), *Public communication campaigns* (4th ed., pp. 3–19). Thousand Oaks, CA: Sage.

Australian Bureau of Statistics. (2013a). Australia's population by country of birth. Report 3412.0 – Migration, Australia, 2011–12 and 2012–13. Canberra, ACT: Author. Retrieved from www.abs.gov.au/ausstats/abs@.nsf/Lookup/3412.0Chapter12011-12%20and%20 2012-13

Australian Bureau of Statistics. (2013b). Estimated resident population, country of birth, state/territory, age and sex – 30 June 2011. Report 3412.0 – Migration, Australia, 2011–12 and 2012–13. Canberra, ACT: Author. Retrieved from www.abs.gov.au/AUSSTATS/abs@.nsf/DetailsPage/3412.02011-12%20and%202012-13?OpenDocument

Bailey, K. (1994). *Typologies and taxonomies: An introduction to classification techniques.* Thousand Oaks, CA: Sage.

Bakhtin, M. (1981). *The dialogic imagination: Four essays.* Austin, TX: University of Texas Press.

Bakhtin, M. (1984). *Problems of Dostoevsky's poetics* (C. Emerson, Ed. & Trans.). Minneapolis, MN: University of Minnesota Press. (Original work published 1963.)

Bandura, A. (1977). *Social learning theory.* Englewood Cliffs, NJ: Prentice-Hall.

Bandura, A. (1986). *Social foundations of thought and action: A social cognitive theory.* Englewood Cliffs, NJ: Prentice Hall.

Bandura, A. (1997). *Self-efficacy: The exercise of control.* New York, NY: W. H. Freeman.

Barcaccia, B., Esposito, G., Matarese, M., Bertolaso, M., Elvira, M., & De Marinis, M. (2013). Defining quality of life: A wild-goose chase. *Europe's Journal of Psychology, 9*(1), 185–203.

Barley, N. (1983). *The innocent anthropologist.* Long Grove, IL: Waveland Press.

Barnhurst, K. (2011). The new 'media affect' and the crisis of representation for political communication. *International Journal of Press/Politics, 16*(4), 573–593.

Barry, T., & Howard, D. (1990). A review and critique of the hierarchy of effects in advertising. *International Journal of Advertising, 9*(2), 121–135.

Barthes, R. (1977). Death of the author: Structural analysis of narratives. In *Image, music, text* (S. Heath, Trans.). London, UK: Fontana.

Bartholomew, D. (2007). Let's put outputs, outtakes, and outcomes in the outhouse [Web log post], *MetricsMan,* November 1. Republished in D. Bartholomew (Z. Chen, Ed.) (2016), *Metrics man: It doesn't count unless you can count* (pp. 63–64). New York, NY: Business Expert Press.

Bartholomew, D. (2008). A new model for social and traditional media measurement [Web log post], *MetricsMan,* August 29. Republished in D. Bartholomew (Z. Chen, Ed.) (2016), *Metrics man: It doesn't count unless you can count* (pp. 68–69). New York, NY: Business Expert Press.

Bartholomew, D. (2010). Social media measurement 2011: Five things to forget and five things to learn [Web log post], *MetricsMan,* December 30. Republished in D. Bartholomew (Z. Chen, Ed.) (2016), *Metrics man: It doesn't count unless you can count* (pp. 96–104). New York, NY: Business Expert Press.

Bartholomew, D. (2016). *Metrics man: It doesn't count unless you can count* (Z. Chen, Ed.). New York, NY: Business Expert Press.

Baskin, O., Hahn, J., Seaman, S., & Reines, D. (2010). Perceived effectiveness and implementation of public relations measurement and evaluation tools among European providers and consumers of PR services. *Public Relations Review, 36*(2), 105–111.

Bateson, G. (1955). A theory of play and fantasy. *Psychiatric Research Reports, 2,* 39–51.

Bauman, A., & Nutbeam, D. (2014). *Evaluation in a nutshell: A practical guide to the evaluation of health promotion programs* (2nd ed.). North Ryde, NSW: McGraw-Hill.

Baxter, L. (2011). *Voicing relationships: A dialogic perspective.* Thousand Oaks, CA: Sage.

Bell, P. (2010). *Confronting theory: The psychology of cultural studies.* Chicago, IL: Intellect.

Ben-Ari, A., & Enosh, G. (2011). Processes of reflectivity: Knowledge construction in qualitative research. *Qualitative Social Work, 10*(2), 152–171.

Bennett, W., & Iyengar, S. (2008). A new era of minimal effects? The changing foundations of political communication. *Journal of Communication, 58*(4), 707–731.

Benoit, J., & Nulty, P. (2016). Quanteda: Quantitative analysis of textual data [Website]. Retrieved from https://cran.r-project.org/web/packages/quanteda/README.html

Berelson, B. (1952). *Content analysis in communication research.* New York, NY: Hafner.

Berg, B. (2007). *Qualitative research methods for the social sciences* (6th ed.). Boston, MA: Allyn & Bacon.

Berger, A. (2000). *Media and communication research methods: An introduction to qualitative and quantitative approaches.* Thousand Oaks, CA: Sage.

Berger, P., & Luckmann, T. (1966). *The social construction of reality: A treatise in the sociology of knowledge.* New York, NY: Doubleday.

Berlo, D. (1960). *The process of communication: An introduction to theory and practice.* New York, NY: Harcourt/Holt, Rinehart & Winston.

Berry, D. (2014). Study to test the content of the most effective SMS reminder message to reduce missed appointments in hospital outpatient clinics. *BioMed Central,* ISRCTN. Retrieved from www.isrctn.com/ISRCTN49432571

Bessette, G. (2004). *Involving the community: A guide to participatory development communication.* Penang, Malaysia: International Development Resource Centre.

Better Evaluation. (2016). Realist evaluation [Website]. Melbourne, Vic: Author. Retrieved from http://betterevaluation.org/approach/realist_evaluation

Bhattacherjee, A. (2012). *Social science research: Principles, methods, and practices.* Textbooks Collection. Book 3 (2nd ed.). Retrieved from http://scholarcommons.usf.edu/oa_textbooks/3

Bickman, L. (1987). The functions of program theory. *New Directions for Evaluation, 33,* 5–18.

Bickman, L. (1990). Using program theory to describe and measure program quality. *New Directions for Evaluation, 47,* 61–72.

Blanchard, O. (2011). *Social media ROI: Managing and measuring social media efforts in your organization.* Indianapolis, IN: Que and Boston, MA: Pearson.

Blei, D., Ng, A., & Jordan, M. (2003). Latent dirichlet allocation. *Journal of Machine Learning Research, 3*(4–5), 993–1022.

Bloom, B., Hastings, J., & Madaus, G. (Eds.). (1971). *Handbook on the formative and summative evaluation of student learning*. New York, NY: McGraw-Hill.

Blumler, H. (1932). *Movies and conduct*. New York, NY: Macmillan.

Blumler, J. (2015). Core theories of political communication: Foundational and freshly minted. *Communication Theory, 25*(4), 426–438.

Bourdieu, P. (1990). *In other words: Essays towards a reflexive sociology*. Cambridge, UK: Polity.

Box, G. (1976). Science and statistics. *Journal of the American Statistical Association, 71*(356), 791–799. Retrieved from www.jstor.org/stable/2286841?seq=1#page_scan_tab_contents

Brand Science. (2016). Econometric modelling [Website]. Retrieved from http://brandscience.cz/?lang=en#ekonometrickemodelovani

Britain Elects. (2015). Britainelects.com [Website]. Retrieved from https://twitter.com/britainelects

Bronfenbrenner, U. (1999). Environments in developmental perspective: theoretical and operational models. In S. Friedman & T. Wachs (Eds.), *Measuring environment across the life span: Emerging methods and concepts* (pp. 3–28). Washington, DC: American Psychological Association Press.

Brooks, G. (2016). Reputation formation. In C. Carroll (Ed.), *The SAGE encyclopedia of corporate reputation* (pp. 639–641). Thousand Oaks, CA: Sage.

Broom, G. (2009). *Cutlip & Center's effective public relations* (10th ed.). Upper Saddle River, NJ: Pearson.

Broom, G., & Dozier, D. (1983). An overview: Evaluation research in public relations. *Public Relations Quarterly, 28*(3), 5–9.

Broom, G., & Dozier, D. (1990). *Using research in public relations: Applications to program management*. Englewood Cliffs, NJ: Prentice-Hall.

Broom, G., Casey, S., & Ritchey, J. (1997). Toward a concept and theory of organization-public relationships. *Journal of Public Relations Research, 9*(2), 83–98.

Brown, S. (2015). *The Government Communication Service Modern Communications Operating Model*. London, UK: Government Communication Service. Retrieved from https://gcs.civilservice.gov.uk/wp-content/uploads/2015/11/6.1288_CO_CP_Modern-Comms-Team-Document_for-print-FINAL-2-2.pdf

Bryman, A. (1988). *Quantity and quality in social research*. London, UK: Unwin Hyman.

Buber, M. (1958). *I and thou* (R. Smith, Trans.). New York, NY: Scribners. (Original work published 1923, 2nd ed. 1987.)

Buber, M. (2002). *Between man and man* (R. Smith, Trans.). London, UK: Kegan Paul. (Original work published 1947.)

Burnett, D., Baker, N., Brown, S., Noakes, I., & Peace, N. (2016). *The Economist*: Raising eyebrows and subscriptions. London, UK: Institute of Practitioners in Advertising.

Cacciatore, M., Meng, J., & Berger, B. (2016). Measuring the value of PR? An international investigation of how practitioners view the challenge and solutions. In *Proceedings of the 19th International Public Relations Research Conference*. Miami, FL, March.

Cameron, G. (1994). Does publicity outperform advertising? An experimental test of the third-party endorsement. *Journal of Public Relations Research, 6*(3), 185–207.

Cameron, W. (1963). *Informal sociology: A casual introduction to sociological thinking*. New York, NY: Random House.

Campbell, A., Converse, P., & Rodgers, W. (1976). *The quality of American life: Perceptions, evaluations, and satisfactions*. New York, NY: Russell Sage Foundation.

Cancer Institute NSW. (2014). Evidence to practice grants: Expression of interest brief. Sydney, NSW: Author.

Cancer Institute NSW. (2016). Breast screening rates monitored by BreastScreen NSW and analyzed by CINSW. Sydney, NSW: Author.

Canel, M., & Sanders, K. (2012). Government communication: An emerging field in political communication research. In H. Semetko & M. Scammell (Eds.), *The SAGE handbook of political communication* (pp. 85–96). London, UK: Sage.

Cappella, J., Fishbein, M., Hornik, R., Ahern, R., & Sayeed, S. (2001). Using theory to select messages in antidrug media campaigns: Reasoned action and media priming. In R. Rice & C. Atkin (Eds.), *Public communication campaigns* (3rd ed., pp. 214–230). Thousand Oaks, CA: Sage.

Carey, J. (2009). *Communication as culture: Essays on media and culture* (rev. ed.). New York, NY: Routledge.

Carroll, C. (2016). *The SAGE encyclopedia of corporate reputation*. Thousand Oaks, CA: Sage.

Carroll, T., & Stacks, D. (2004). Bibliography of public relations measurement. Gainesville, FL: Institute for Public Relations. Retrieved from www.instituteforpr.org/wp-content/uploads/PRM_Bibliography.pdf

CCR (Center for Corporate Reporting). (2016). How valuable is integrated reporting? Insights from best practice companies [Website]. Retrieved from www.corporate-reporting.com/artikel/how-valuable-is-integrated-reporting-insights-from-best-practice-companies

CDC (Center for Development Communication). (2016). Who are we? [Website]. Washington, DC: Author. Retrieved from www.cendevcom.org

Center, A., Jackson, P., Smith, S., & Stansberry, F. (2008). *Public relations practices, managerial case studies and problems* (7th ed.). Upper Saddle River, NJ: Pearson.

Center for Theory of Change. (2016a). What is theory of change? [Website]. Retrieved from www.theoryofchange.org/what-is-theory-of-change

Center for Theory of Change. (2016b). Backwards mapping and connecting outcomes [Website]. Retrieved from www.theoryofchange.org/what-is-theory-of-change/how-does-theory-of-change-work/example/backwards-mapping

Cha, M., Haddadi, H., Benevenuto, F., & Gummadi, K. (2010). Measuring user influence in Twitter: The million follower fallacy. Refereed proceedings of the Fourth International Conference on Weblogs and Social Media (ICWSM), pp. 10–17. Retrieved from http://snap.stanford.edu/class/cs224w-readings/cha10influence.pdf

Chaiken, S., Liberman, A., & Eagly, A. (1989). Heuristic and systematic information processing within and beyond the persuasion context. In J. Uleman & J. Bargh (Eds.), *Unintended thought* (pp. 212–252). New York, NY: Guilford Press.

Chartier, R. (Ed.). (1989). *A history of private life: Passions of the renaissance* (A. Goldhammer, Trans.). Cambridge, MA: Harvard.

Chavez, A. de, Backett-Milburn, K., Parry, O., & Platt, S. (2005). Understanding and researching well-being: Its usage in different disciplines and potential for health research and health promotion. *Health Education Journal, 64*(1), 70–87.

Chen, H. (1990) *Theory-driven evaluation*. Thousand Oaks, CA: Sage.

Chen, H., & Rossi, P. (1983). Evaluating with sense: The theory-driven approach. *Evaluation Review, 7*(3), 283–302.

Childers, L., & Grunig, J. (1999). Guidelines for measuring relationship in public relations. Gainesville, FL: Institute for Public Relations. Retrieved from www.instituteforpr.org/measuring-relationships

Cialdini, R. (2007). *Influence: The psychology of persuasion* (15th ed.). New York, NY: Collins. (Original work published 1984.)

CIPR (Chartered Institute for Public Relations). (2011). Research, planning and measurement toolkit. Retrieved from www.cipr.co.uk/sites/default/files/Non-member%20excerpt%202_0.pdf

Clandinin, D., & Connelly, F. (2000). *Narrative enquiry: Experience and story in qualitative research*. San Francisco, CA: Jossey-Bass.

Clark, H. (2004). *Deciding the scope of a theory of change*. New York, NY: ActKnowledge.

Clark, H., & Taplin, D. (2012). *Theory of change basics: A primer on theory of change*. New York, NY: ActKnowledge.

Coffey. (2015). *Ex-post evaluation ex-smokers campaign: Final report*. London, UK: Coffey.

Coffman, J. (2002). *Public communication campaign evaluation: An environmental scan of challenges, criticisms, practice, and opportunities*. Boston, MA: Harvard Family Research Project.

Colley, R. (1961). *Defining advertising goals for measured advertising results*. New York, NY: Association of National Advertisers.

Commission on Public Relations Education (2012). Educating for complexity: Standards for a Master's degree in public relations [Website]. Retrieved from www.commpred.org

Conclave on Social Media Measurement Standards. (2013 [2011]). The standards [Website]. Retrieved from http://smmstandards.wixsite.com/smmstandards/reach-and-impressions

Coombs, T. (2006). Crisis management: A communicative approach. In C. Botan & V. Hazelton (Eds.), *Public relations theory II* (pp. 171–198). Mahwah, NJ: Lawrence Erlbaum.

Court, D., Elzinga, D., Mulder, S., & Vetvik, O. (2009). The consumer decision journey. *McKinsey Quarterly*, June. Retrieved from www.mckinsey.com/business-functions/marketing-and-sales/our-insights/the-consumer-decision-journey

Craig, R. (1999). Communication theory as a field. *Communication Theory, 9*(2), 119–161.

Craig, R. (2015). The constitutive model: A 10-year review. *Communication Theory, 25*(4), 356–374.

Craig, R., & Muller, H. (Eds.). (2007). *Theorizing communication: Readings across traditions*. Thousand Oaks, CA: Sage.

Crawford, E., & Okigbo, C. (2014). Strategic communication campaigns. In C. Okigbo (Ed.), *Strategic urban health communication* (pp. 11–24). New York, NY: Springer.

Creswell, J. (2009). *Research design: Qualitative, quantitative, and mixed methods approaches* (3rd ed.). Thousand Oaks, CA: Sage.

Creswell, J., & Plano Clark, V. (2007). *Designing and conducting mixed methods research*. Thousand Oaks, CA: Sage.

Crifasi, S. (2000). Everything's coming up rosie. *Public Relations Tactics, 7*(9), 14–15. New York, NY: Public Relations Society of America.

Cronbach. L. (1982). *Designing evaluations of educational and social problems*. San Francisco, CA: Jossey-Bass.

Crossman, J., Bordia, S., & Mills, C. (2011). *Business communication for the global age*. North Ryde, NSW: McGraw-Hill Australia.

Curran, J. (2002). *Media and power*. London, UK: Routledge.

Cutler, A. (2004). Methodical failure: The use of case study method by public relations researchers. *Public Relations Review, 30*(3), 365–375.

Cutlip, S., & Center, A. (1952). *Effective public relations*. Englewood Cliffs, NJ: Prentice-Hall.

Cutlip, S., Center, A., & Broom, G. (1985). *Effective public relations* (6th ed.). Englewood Cliffs, NJ: Prentice-Hall.

Cutlip, S., Center, A., & Broom, G. (1994). *Effective public relations* (7th ed). Upper Saddle River, NJ: Prentice Hall.

Daniels, K. (2000). Measures of five aspects of affective well-being at work. *Human Relations, 52*(2), 277.

Daniels, M. (2012). Valid metrics frameworks. Presentation to the 4th European Summit on Measurement, Dublin, Ireland, June. Retrieved from http://amecorg.com/downloads/dublin2012/Valid-Metrics-Framework-Mike-Daniels.pdf

Datorama. (2016). Product [Website]. Retrieved from http://datorama.com/product

Deloitte. (2014). *2014 global survey on reputation risk*. Retrieved from www2.deloitte. com/global/en/pages/governance-risk-and-compliance/articles/reputation-at -risk.html

DeMers, J. (2014). 2014 is the year of digital marketing analytics: What it means for your company. *Forbes*, February 10. Retrieved from www.forbes.com/sites/jayson-demers/2014/02/10/2014-is-the-year-of-digital-marketing-analytics-what-it-means-for-your-company/#7fd6ff7d6619

Deming, W. (1986). *Out of crisis*. Boston, MA: MIT Press.

Denzin, N., & Lincoln, Y. (Eds.). (2008). *Strategies of qualitative inquiry*. Thousand Oaks, CA: Sage.

Denzin, N., & Lincoln, Y. (Eds.). (2013). *Strategies of qualitative inquiry* (4th ed.). Thousand Oaks, CA: Sage.

Department of Health. (2014). Air quality testing in Morwell: Volatile organic compounds. Hazelwood coal mine fire fact sheet, no. 1, March 13. Melbourne, Vic: Author.

Dervin, B., & Foreman-Wernet, L. (2013). Sense-making methodology as an approach to understanding and designing for campaign audiences. In R. Rice & C. Atkin (Eds.), *Public communication campaigns* (4th ed., pp. 147–162). Thousand Oaks, CA: Sage.

Dewey, J. (1916). *Democracy and education*, New York, NY: Macmillan.

Dick, B. (2000). *A beginner's guide to action research* [Online guide]. Retrieved from www.aral. com.au/resources/guide.html

Diener, E. (1984). Subjective well-being. *Psychological Bulletin, 95*(3), 542–575.

Diener, E. (2006). Guidelines for national indicators of subjective well-being and ill-being. *Applied Research in Quality of Life, 1*(2), 151–157.

Digital Analytics Association (2013) Social media standards definitions: Reach and impressions. Wakefield, MA. Available at www.smmstandards.com/wp-content/uploads/2013/03/SMM-Standard-Definitions_DAA_v4.pdf

Dillard, J., & Shen, L. (2005). On the nature of reactance and its role in persuasive health communication. *Communication Monographs, 72*(2), 144–168.

Dillard, J., Weber, K., & Renata, G. (2007). The relationship between the perceived and actual effectiveness of persuasive messages: A meta-analysis with implications for formative campaign research. *Journal of Communication, 57*(4), 613–631.

Dobson, A. (2014). *Listening for democracy: Recognition, representation, reconciliation*. Oxford, UK: Oxford University Press.

Dolan, P., Hallsworth, M., Halpern, D., King, D., & Vlaev, I. (2010). *MINDSPACE: Influencing behaviour through public policy*. London, UK: Institute for Government. Report for the Cabinet Office, UK. Retrieved from www.instituteforgovernment.org.uk/our-work/better-policy-making/mindspace-behavioural-economics

Dove. (2010). *The real truth about beauty: Revisited*. London, UK: Author.

Dove. (2016). Our research [Website]. London, UK: Author. Research report. Retrieved from www.dove.com/uk/stories/about-dove/our-research.html

Dozier, D. (1984). Program evaluation and the roles of practitioners. *Public Relations Review, 10*(2), 13–21.

Dozier, D. (1985). Planning and evaluation in public relations practice. *Public Relations Review, 11*(2), 17–25.

Dozier, D. (1990). The innovation of research in public relations practice: Review of program studies. *Public Relations Research Annual, 2*(1–4) 3–28.

DPC (Department of Premier and Cabinet). (2016). *New South Wales government evaluation framework for advertising and communication*. Sydney, NSW: Author.

DPRG/GPRA (Deutsche Public Relations Gesellschaft and Gesellschaft Public Relations Agenturen). (2000). *PR-evaluation: Messen, analysieren, bewerten – empfehlungen für die praxis*. Booklet des evaluationsausschusses von DPRG und GPRA, 2, Bonn, Germany.

DPRG/ICV (Deutsche Public Relations Gesellschaft and International Controller Verein). (2009). DPRG/ICV framework for communication controlling. Retrieved from www. communicationcontrolling.de/en/positions/framework.html

Draper, N. (2014). The new reputation custodians. In L. Lievrouw (Ed.), *Challenging communication research* (pp. 157–171). New York, NY: Peter Lang.

Dresner, H. (2008). *The performance management revolution: Business results through insight and action*. Hoboken, NJ: John Wiley & Sons.

Drypen. (2008). DAGMAR – Defining advertising goals for measured advertising results [Website]. Retrieved from www.drypen.in/advertising/dagmar-defining-advertising-goals-for-measured-advertising-results.html

Durkheim, E. (1982). *The rules of sociological method and selected texts on sociology and its method* (S. Lukes, Ed., W. Halls, Trans.). New York, NY: Free Press.

Dutta, M., & de Souza, R. (2008). The past, present, and future of health development campaigns: Reflexivity and the critical-cultural approach. *Health Communication, 23*(4), 326–339.

Dutta, M., Anaele, A., & Jones, C. (2013). Voices of hunger: Addressing health disparities through the culture-centered approach. *Journal of Communication, 63*(1), 159–180.

Dykes, B. (2010). Metrics manifesto: Raising the standard for metrics [Web log post]. *Digital Marketing Blog*, July 13. Retrieved from https://blogs.adobe.com/digitalmarketing/analytics/metrics-manifesto-raising-the-standard-for-metrics

Easton, V., & McColl, J. (1997). *Statistics glossary*, Version 1.1 [Website]. Retrieved from www.stats.gla.ac.uk/steps/glossary/sampling.html

EC (European Commission). (2012). *Eurobarometer 385: Attitudes of Europeans towards tobacco*. Brussels, Belgium: Author. Retrieved from http://ec.europa.eu/health/tobacco/eurobarometers/index_en.htm

EC (European Commission). (2013) Social entrepreneurship: The social business initiative. Brussels, Belgium: Author. Retrieved from http://ec.europa.eu/internal_market/social_business/index_en.htm

EC (European Commission). (2015a). Better regulation guidelines. Brussels, Belgium: Author. Retrieved from http://ec.europa.eu/smart-regulation/guidelines/toc_guide_en.htm

EC (European Commission). (2015b). External communication network code of conduct on measurement and evaluation of communication activities. Brussels, Belgium: Author. Retrieved from http://ec.europa.eu/dgs/communication/about/evaluation/documents/code-of-conduct-measurement-evaluation-communication-activities_en.pdf

EC (European Commission). (2015c). Toolkit for the evaluation of communication activities. Brussels, Belgium: Author. Retrieved from http://ec.europa.eu/dgs/communication/about/evaluation/documents/communication-evaluation-toolkit_en.pdf

EC (European Commission). (2016). Ex-smokers are unstoppable: 2014–16. [Website]. Retrieved from http://ec.europa.eu/health/tobacco/ex_smokers_are_unstoppable_en

Edelman. (2015). Edelman Trust Barometer. New York, NY: Author. Retrieved from www.edelman.com/insights/intellectual-property/2015-edelman-trust-barometer/trust-around-world

Edelman. (2016). Edelman Trust Barometer. New York, NY: Author. Retrieved from www.edelman.com/insights/intellectual-property/2016-edelman-trust-barometer

Egbert, N., & Reed, P. (2016). Self-efficacy. In D. Kim & J. Dearning (Eds.), *Health communication research measures* (pp. 203–211). New York, NY: Peter Lang.

Ehling, W. (1992). Estimating the value of public relations and communication to an organization. In J. Grunig (Ed.), *Excellence in public relations and communication management* (pp. 617–638). Hillsdale, NJ: Lawrence Erlbaum.

Eisenmann M., Geddes, D., Paine, K., Pestana, R., Walton, F., & Weiner, M. (2012). Proposed interim standards for metrics in traditional media analysis.

Gainesville, FL: Institute for Public Relations. Retrieved from www.instituteforpr.org/proposed-interim-standards-for-metrics-in-traditional-media-analysis

Eliasoph, N. (2004). Can we theorize the press without theorizing the public? *Political Communication, 21*(3), 297–303.

Elkington, J. (1994). Towards the sustainable corporation: Win-win-win business strategies for sustainable development. *California Management Review, 36*(2), 90–100.

Elkington, J. (1998). *Cannibals with forks: The triple bottom line of 21st century business.* Stony Creek, CT: New Society Publishers.

Elliot, J. (2014). How to apply the AIDA model to digital marketing [Web log post], May 6. Retrieved from www.hallaminternet.com/apply-aida-model-digital-marketing

Ellis, L. (1994). *Research methods in the social sciences.* Madison, WI: WCB Brown & Benchmark.

E-marketer. (2016). Worldwide ad spending growth revised downward [Website]. Retrieved from www.emarketer.com/Article/Worldwide-Ad-Spending-Growth-Revised-Downward/1013858

Emergency Management Victoria. (2014). *Emergency management manual Victoria,* Part 4. Retrieved from www.emv.vic.gov.au/policies/emmv

Engie. (2015). GDF Suez becomes Engie. Media release. Retrieved from www.engie.com/en/journalists/press-releases/gdf-suez-becomes-engie

Entman, R. (1993). Framing: Toward a clarification of a fractured paradigm. *Journal of Communication, 43*(4), 51–58.

EPA Victoria (Environment Protection Authority of Victoria). (2014). Q&A on the Latrobe valley mine fire. Retrieved from www.epa.vic.gov.au/latrobe-valley-mine-fire/latrobe-valley-mine-fire-q-and-a

Eurostat. (2015). Quality of life indicators – Measuring quality of life. Retrieved from http://ec.europa.eu/eurostat/statistics-explained/index.php/Quality_of_life_indicators_-_measuring_quality_of_life

Fairchild, M. (1997). *How to get real value from public relations.* London, UK: ICO.

Fairchild, M. (2001). *The IPR toolkit: Planning, research and evaluation for public relations success* (2nd ed.). London, UK: Chartered Institute of Public Relations.

Fairchild, M., & O'Connor, N. (1999). *The public relations research and evaluation toolkit: How to measure the effectiveness of PR.* London, UK: Institute of Public Relations (now CIPR).

Farquhar J. (1991). The Stanford cardiovascular disease prevention programs. *Annals of New York Academy of Sciences, 623,* 327–331.

Feld, K. (2003). Push polls: What are they? In R. Faucheux (Ed.), *Winning elections* (pp. 184–189). New York, NY: M. Evans & Co.

Felstehausen, H. (1973). Conceptual limits of development communications theory. *Sociologia Ruralis 13*(1), 39–54.

Festinger, L. (1957). *A theory of cognitive dissonance.* Palo Alto, CA: Stanford University Press.

Figueroa, M., Kincaid, D., Rani, M., & Lewis, G. (2002). Communication for social change: An integrated model for measuring the process and its outcomes. In B. Byrd (Ed.), *The communication for social change working paper series, 1.* New York, NY: The Rockefeller Foundation.

Finlay, L., & Gough, B. (2003). *Reflexivity: A practical guide for researchers in health and social sciences.* Oxford, UK: Blackwell.

Fishbein, M. (1963). An investigation of relationships between beliefs about an object and the attitude toward that object. *Human Relations, 16*(3), 233–240.

Fishbein, M., & Ajzen, I. (1975). *Belief, attitude, intention, and behaviour: An introduction to theory and research.* Reading, MA: Addison-Wesley.

Fiske, J. (1989). *Understanding popular culture.* Boston, MA: Unwin Hyman.

Fiske, S., & Kinder, D. (1981). Involvement, expertise, and schema use: Evidence from political cognition. In N. Cantor & J. Kihlstrom (Eds.), *Personality, cognitions, and social interaction* (pp. 171–190). Hillsdale, NJ: Lawrence Erlbaum.

Flamholtz, E. (1985). *Human resource accounting: Advances in concepts, methods and applications.* San Francisco, CA: Jossey-Bass.

Fleisher, C., & Mahaffy, D. (1997). A balanced scorecard approach to public relations management assessment. *Public Relations Review, 23*(2), 117–123.

Flew, T., Spurgeon, C., Daniel, A., & Swift, A. (2012). The promise of computational journalism. *Journalism Practice, 6*(2), 157–171.

Flora, J., Maccoby, N., & Farquhar, J. (1989). Communication campaigns to prevent cardiovascular disease: The Stanford Community Studies. In R. Rice & C. Atkin (Eds.), *Public communication campaigns* (2nd ed., pp. 233–252). Newbury Park, CA: Sage.

Fombrun, C., Ponzi, L., & Newburry, W. (2015). Stakeholder tracking and analysis: The RepTrak system for measuring corporate reputation. *Corporate Reputation Review, 18*(1), 3–24.

Fox, E. (2012). Rethinking health communication in aid and development. In R. Obregon & S. Waisbord (Eds.), *The handbook of global health communication* (pp. 52–69). Hoboken, NJ: John Wiley & Sons.

Francis, R. (2013). Report of the Mid-Staffordshire NHS Foundation Trust public inquiry. Retrieved from http://webarchive.nationalarchives.gov.uk/20150407084231/http://www.midstaffspublicinquiry.com/report

Fransden, F., & Johansen, W. (2017). Strategic communication. In C. Scott & L. Lewis (Eds.), *The international encyclopedia of organizational communication* (pp. 1–9). Hokoken, NJ: John Wiley & Sons.

Freeman, L. (2004). *The development of social network analysis: A study in the sociology of science.* Vancouver, BC: Empirical Press.

Freeman, R. (1984). *Strategic management: A stakeholder approach.* London, UK: Pitman.

Freud, S. (1973). *Introductory lectures on psychoanalysis* (J. Strachey, Trans.). Harmondsworth, UK: Pelican.

Frey, B., & Stutzer, A. (2000). Maximising happiness? *German Economic Review, 1*(2), 145–167.

Frey, L., Botan, C., & Kreps, G. (2000). *Investigating communication: An introduction to research methods* (2nd ed.). Needham Heights, MA: Allyn & Bacon/Pearson.

FTC (Federal Trade Commission). (2013). Blurred lines: Advertising or content? – An FTC workshop on native advertising. Washington, DC: Author. Retrieved from www.ftc.gov/news-events/events-calendar/2013/12/blurred-lines-advertising-or-content-ftc-workshop-native

FTC (Federal Trade Commission). (2015). Identity theft tops FTC's consumer complaint categories again in 2014 [Press Release], February 27. Retrieved from www.ftc.gov/news-events/press-releases/2015/02/identity-theft-tops-ftcs-consumer-complaint-categories-again-2014

Fukuda-Parr, S. (2003). The human development paradigm: Operationalizing Sen's ideas on capabilities. *Feminist Economics, 9*(2–3), 301–317.

Funnell, S. (1997). Program logic: An adaptable tool for designing and evaluating programs. *Evaluation News and Comment, 6*(1), 5–7.

Funnell, S., & Rogers, P. (2011). *Purposeful program theory: Effective use of theory of change and logic models.* San Francisco, CA: Jossey-Bass.

GAO (US General Accounting Office). (2011). Performance measurement and evaluation: Definitions and relationships. Retrieved from www.gao.gov/assets/80/77277.pdf

Garfinkel, H. (1974). *Studies in ethnomethodology.* Englewood Cliffs, NJ: Prentice-Hall.

Gauntlett, D. (2005). *Moving experiences: Media effects and beyond*. Eastleigh, UK: John Libbey Publishing.

GCS (Government Communication Service). (2014). *GCS evaluation capability standards*. London, UK: Cabinet Office. Retrieved from https://gcn.civilservice.gov.uk/wp-content/uploads/2014/03/GCS-Evaluation-Capability-Standards.pdf

GCS (Government Communication Service).(2015). *Government communications plan 2015/16*. London, UK: Cabinet Office. Retrieved from https://communication.cabinetoffice.gov.uk/government-comms-plan.

GCS (Government Communication Service). (2016a). GCS evaluation framework. London, UK: Cabinet Office. Retrieved from https://gcs.civilservice.gov.uk/wp-content/uploads/2015/11/GCS_GCS-Evaluation-framework_A4-_191115.pdf

GCS (Government Communication Service). (2016b). Modern communications operating model (MCOM) skills survey 2016/7: Key findings and proposed actions. Report to the GCS Evaluation Council, London, UK.

GDF Suez Australian Energy. (2014). Written submission of GDF Suez Australian Energy. Submission to the Hazelwood Mine Fire Inquiry, Morwell, Victoria, June 18. Retrieved from http://hazelwoodinquiry.vic.gov.au/wp-content/uploads/2014/06/GDF-Suez.pdf

Geertz, C. (1973). Thick description: Toward an interpretive theory of culture. In *The interpretation of cultures: Selected essays* (pp. 3–30). New York, NY: Basic Books.

Gerbner, G. (1956). Toward a general model of communication. *Audio Visual Communication Review, 4*(3), 171–199.

Getuiza, C. (2014). Californians grade the state with new report card app. *CA FWD*, January 29. Retrieved from www.cafwd.org/reporting/entry/californias-citizens-grade-the-state-with-new-report-card-app

Gibbons, F., & Gerrard, M. (1997). Health images and their effects on health behaviour. In B. Buunk & F. Gibbons (Eds.), *Health, coping and well-being: Perspectives from social comparison theory* (pp. 63–94). Mahwah, NJ: Erlbaum.

Gibbons, F., Gerrard, M., & Lane, D. (2003). A social-reaction model of adolescent health risk. In J. Suls & K. Wallston (Eds.), *Social psychological foundations of health and illness* (pp. 107–136). Oxford, UK: Blackwell.

Gibson, R., Williamson, A., & Ward, S. (2010). *The Internet and the 2010 election: Putting the small 'p' back in politics*. London, UK: Hansard Society.

Giddens, A. (1984). *The constitution of society: Outline of the theory of structuration*. Berkeley, CA: University of California Press.

Giddens, A. (1991). *Modernity and self-identity: Self and society in the late modern age*. Cambridge, UK: Polity.

Gigerenzer, G. (2015). On the supposed evidence for libertarian paternalism. *Review of Philosophy and Psychology, 6*(3), 361–383.

Glanz, K., Rimer, B., & Viswanath, K. (Eds.). (2008). *Health behaviour and health education: Theory, research, and practice* (4th ed.). San Francisco, CA: Jossey-Bass.

Gobe, M. (2010). *Emotional branding: The new paradigm for connecting brands to people*. New York, NY: Allworth Press.

Goffman, E. (1974). *Frame analysis*. Cambridge, MA: Harvard University Press.

Gohr, T. (2013). Interview series: Thought leaders in PR measurement. Communication Controlling [Website]. Retrieved from www.00525.i24-cs02.clickstorm.de.k2811.ims-firmen.de/index.php?id=114&type=98&tx_ttnews[tt_news]=766&L=3

Gorini, R. (2003). Al-Haytham the man of experience: First steps in the science of vision. *Journal of the International Society for the History of Islamic Medicine, 2*(4), 53–55.

Graber, D. (1988). *Processing the news: How people tame the information tide* (2nd ed.). New York, NY: Longman.

Greenwood, D., & Levin, M. (2006). *Introduction to action research: Social research for social change.* Thousand Oaks, CA: Sage.

Gregory, A. (1996). *Planning and managing a public relations campaign.* London, UK: Kogan Page.

Gregory, A., & Watson, T. (2008). Defining the gap between research and practice in public relations programme evaluation: Towards a new research agenda. *Journal of Marketing Communications, 24*(5), 337–350.

Gregory, A., & White, T. (2008). Introducing the Chartered Institute of Public Relations initiative. In B. van Ruler, A. Verčič, A., & D. Verčič (Eds.), *Public relations metrics: Research and evaluation* (pp. 307–317). New York, NY: Routledge.

Griffin, E. (2000). *A first look at communication theory* (4th ed.). Boston, MA: McGraw-Hill.

Griffin, E. (2009). *A first look at communication theory* (7th ed.). New York, NY: McGraw-Hill.

Griffin, E., Ledbetter, A., & Sparks, G. (2015). *A first look at communication theory* (9th ed.). New York, NY: McGraw-Hill.

Grunig, J. (1979). The status of public relations research. *Public Relations Quarterly, 20*(1), 5–8.

Grunig, J. (1983). Basic research provides knowledge that makes evaluation possible. *Public Relations Quarterly, 28*(3), 28–32.

Grunig, J. (2008). Conceptualizing quantitative research in public relations. In B. van Ruler, A. Verčič, & D. Verčič (Eds.), *Public relations metrics: Research and evaluation* (pp. 88–119). New York, NY: Routledge.

Grunig, J. (2014). Thought leaders in PR measurement. Communicationcontrolling.de [Website]. Retrieved from www.communicationcontrolling.de/index.php?id=302&L=3

Grunig, J., & Hunt, T. (1984). *Managing public relations.* Orlando, FL: Holt, Rinehart & Winston.

Grunig, L., Grunig, J., & Dozier, D. (2002). *Excellent organizations and effective organizations: A study of communication management in three countries.* Mahwah, NJ: Lawrence Erlbaum.

Guba, E., & Lincoln, Y. (1981). *Effective evaluation: Improving the usefulness of evaluation results through responsive and naturalistic approaches.* San Francisco, CA: Jossey-Bass.

Guba, E., & Lincoln, Y. (2005) Paradigmatic controversies, contradictions, and emerging confluences. In N. Denzin & Y. Lincoln (Eds.), *Handbook of qualitative research* (3rd ed., pp. 191–215). Thousand Oaks, CA: Sage.

Guth, D., & Marsh, C. (2007). *Public relations: A values-driven approach* (3rd ed.). Boston, MA: Pearson Education.

Guttman, L. (1944). A basis for scaling quantitative data. *American Sociological Review, 9*(2), 139–150.

Guttman, L., & Levy, S. (1982). On the definition and varieties of attitude and well-being. *Social Indicators Research, 10*(2), 159–174.

Habermas, J. (1989). *The structural transformation of the public sphere.* Cambridge, UK: Polity. (Original work published 1962.)

Habermas, J. (2006). Political communication in media society: Does democracy still enjoy an epistemic dimension? The impact of normative theory on empirical research. *Communication Theory, 16*(4), 411–426.

Hall, S. (1993 [1973]). Encoding/decoding. Reprinted in S. Hall, D. Hobson, A. Lowe, & P. Willis (Eds.), *Culture, media, language* (pp. 26–27). London, UK: Hutchinson.

Hall, S. (1993). Encoding/decoding. In S. During (Ed.), *The cultural studies reader* (pp. 90–103). New York, NY: Routledge. (Original work published 1973.)

Hallahan, K. (1993). The paradigm struggle and public relations practice. *Public Relations Review, 19*(2), 197–205.

Hallahan, K. (1999). No, Virginia, it's not true what they say about publicity's 'implied third-party endorsement' effect. *Public Relations Review, 25*(3), 331–350.

Hallahan, K., Holtzhausen, D., Van Ruler, B., Verčič, D., & Sriramesh, K. (2007). Defining strategic communication. *International Journal of Strategic Communication*, 1(1), 3–35.

Hallsworth, M., Berry, D., & Sallis, A. (2014). Reducing missed hospital outpatient appointments through an SMS intervention: A randomized controlled trial in a London hospital. Division of Health Psychology Annual Conference, New York, NY. Retrieved from http://abstracts.bps.org.uk/index.Cfm?&Resultstype=abstracts&resultset_id=12039&formdisplaymode=view&frmshowselected=true&localaction=details

Hallsworth, M., Berry, D., Sanders, M., Sallis, A., King, D., Vlaev, I., & Darzi, A. (2015). Stating appointment costs in SMS reminders reduces missed hospital appointments: Findings of two randomized controlled trials. *PLOS One*. Retrieved from http://journals.plos.org/plosone/article?id=10.1371/journal.pone.0137306

Hansen, A., Cottle, S., Negrine, R., & Newbold, C. (1998). *Mass communication research methods*. London, UK: Macmillan.

Hansen, H. (2005). Choosing evaluation models: Discussion on evaluation design. *Evaluation*, 11(4), 447–462.

Hansson, M. (2007). *The private sphere: An emotional territory and its agent*. New York, NY: Springer.

Harper, H. (2013). Applying behavioural insights to organ donation: Preliminary results from a randomized controlled trial. Retrieved from www.behaviouralinsights.co.uk/sites/default/files/Applying_Behavioural_Insights_to_Organ_Donation_report.pdf

Harris Poll. (2016). Six dimensions of reputation [Website]. Retrieved from www.theharris-poll.com/reputation-quotient

Harvard University. (2015). *Trust in institutions and the political process*. Boston, MA: Institute of Politics. Retrieved from www.iop.harvard.edu/trust-institutions-and-political-process

Hatry, H., Houten, T., Plantz, M., & Greenway, M. (1996). *Measuring program outcomes: A practical approach*. Alexandria, VA: United Way of America.

Hazelwood Mine Fire Inquiry. (2014). Hazelwood mine fire inquiry report. Melbourne, Vic: Government of Victoria. Retrieved from http://report.hazelwoodinquiry.vic.gov.au/print-friendly-version-pdf

Healey, J. (1974). A model of communication impact and consumer response. *Advances in Consumer Research*, 1, 384–392.

Heath, R. (2002). Issues management: Its past, present and future. *Journal of Public Affairs*, 2(2), 209–214.

Heath, R. (2013). The journey to understand and champion OPR takes many roads, some not yet well travelled. *Public Relations Review*, 39(5), 426–431.

Heath, R., & Johansen, W. (Eds.). (forthcoming). *The international encyclopedia of strategic communication*. Hoboken, NJ: Wiley-Blackwell.

Heidegger, M. (1962). *Being and time* (J. Macquarrie & E. Robinson, Trans.). New York, NY: Harper and Row. (Original work published 1927.)

Heider, F. (1946). Attitudes and cognitive organisation. *Journal of Psychology*, 21(1), 107–112.

Hendrix, J., & Hayes, D. (2010). *Public relations cases* (8th ed.). Boston, MA: Wadsworth Cengage.

Henert, E., & Taylor-Power, E. (2008). *Developing a logic model: Teaching and training guide*. Madison, WI: University of Wisconsin-Extension Program. Retrieved from www.alnap.org/pool/files/logic-model-guide.pdf

Henert, E., Jones, L., & Taylor-Power, E. (2003). *Enhancing program performance with logic models*. Madison, WI: University of Wisconsin-Extension Program. Retrieved from http://fyi.uwex.edu/programdevelopment/logic-models

Henningsen, A., Traverse Healy, K., Gregory, A. Johannsen, A., Allison, R., Bozeat, N., & Domaradzki, L. (2014). *Measuring the European Commission's communication: Technical and methodological report*. London, UK: ICF GHK. Retrieved from http://ec.europa.eu/dgs/communication/about/evaluation/index_en.htm

Hijams, E. (1996). The logic of qualitative media content analysis: A typology. *Communications, 21*(1), 93–109.

Hoggart, R. (2004). *Mass media in a mass society: Myth and reality*. London, UK and New York, NY: Continuum.

Holmes, B. (2011). *Citizens' engagement in policymaking and the design of public services*. Research Paper No. 1, Parliamentary Library Information, Analysis, Advice. Canberra, ACT: Department of Parliamentary Services. Retrieved from www.aph.gov.au/About_Parliament/Parliamentary_Departments/Parliamentary_Library/pubs/rp/rp1112/12rp01

Hoofnagle, C., & Meleshinsky, E. (2015). Native advertising and endorsement: Schema, source-based misleadingness, and omission of material facts. *Technology Science*. Retrieved from http://techscience.org/a/2015121503

Hornik, R. (Ed.). (2002). *Public health communication: Evidence for behaviour change*. Mahwah, NJ: Lawrence Erlbaum.

Hovland, C. (1954). Effects of the mass media of communication. In G. Lindzey (Ed.), *Handbook of social psychology*, Vol. 2 (pp. 1062–1103). Cambridge, MA: Addison-Wesley.

Hovland, C., & Weiss, W. (1951). The influence of source credibility on communication effectiveness. *Public Opinion Quarterly, 15*(4), 633–650.

Hovland, C., Janis, L., & Kelley, H. (1953). *Communication and persuasion*. New Haven, CN: Yale University Press.

Hovland, C., Lumsdaine, A., & Sheffield, F. (1949). *Experiments on mass communication*. New York, NY: Wiley.

Hubbard, D. (2007). The IT measurement inversion. *CIO Magazine*, June 13. Retrieved from www.cio.com/article/2438748/it-organization/the-it-measurement-inversion.html (Original work published 1999.)

Hubbard, D. (2010). *How to measure anything: Finding the value of intangibles in business* (2nd ed.). Hoboken, NJ: John Wiley & Sons.

Huhn, J., Sass, J., & Storck, C. (2011). *Communication controlling: How to maximize and demonstrate the value creation through communication*. Berlin, Germany: German Public Relations Association (DPRG). Retrieved from www.communicationcontrolling.de/fileadmin/communicationcontrolling/sonst_files/Position_paper_DPRG_ICV_2011_english.pdf

ICCO (International Communications Consultancy Organization). (2013). ICCO world report [Website]. Retrieved from www.akospr.ru/wp-content/uploads/2014/01/World-Report_en.pdf

IIRC (International Integrated Reporting Council). (2013). International integrated reporting framework. London, UK. Author. Retrieved from www.theiirc.org/international-ir-framework

Interactive Advertising Bureau. (2012). Ad recall [Website]. Retrieved from https://wiki.iab.com/index.php/Ad_recall

Interactive Advertising Bureau. (2014). *Digital video in-stream ad metric definitions*. New York, NY: Author. Retrieved from www.iab.com/guidelines/digital-video-in-stream-ad-metric-definitions

Internet World Statistics. (2015). World Internet users and population statistics. Retrieved from www.internetworldstats.com/stats6.htm

Investopedia. (2013). Definition of return on investment – ROI [Website]. Retrieved from www.investopedia.com/terms/r/returnoninvestment.asp

IPA (Institute of Practitioners in Advertising). (2016a). The IPA is widely recognised as the world's most influential professional body for practitioners in advertising and marketing communications [Web site]. London, UK: Author. Retrieved from www.ipa.co. uk/about

IPA (Institute of Practitioners in Advertising). (2016b). ROMI calculator [Website]. London, UK: Author. Retrieved from http://romi.ipa.co.uk/index.php/calculator

IPA (Institute of Practitioners in Advertising). (2016c). *IPA Effectiveness Awards 2016*. Back cover. London, UK: Author.

IPRA (International Public Relations Association). (1994). *Public relations evaluation: Professional accountability*. Gold Paper No. 11. Geneva, Switzerland; Author.

Ipsos MORI. (2009). *Social grade: A classification tool*. London, UK: Author. Retrieved from www.ipsos-mori.com/DownloadPublication/1285_MediaCT_thoughtpiece_Social _Grade_July09_V3_WEB.pdf

ITVE. (2010). TV ratings and TV audience measurement across the world [Website]. Retrieved from www.international-television.org/tv_audience_measurement_research _boards_and_institutes.html

Iyengar, S., & Kinder, D. (1987). *News that matters*. Chicago, IL: University of Chicago Press.

Iyengar, S., Peters, M., & Kinder, D. (1982). Experimental demonstrations of the 'not-so-minimal' consequences of television news programs. *American Political Science Review, 76*(4), 848–858.

Jalonen, H., & Jussila, J. (2016). Developing a conceptual model for the relationship between social media behaviour, negative consumer emotions and brand disloyalty. In Y. Dwividi, M. Mäntymäki, M. Ravishankar, M. Janssen, M. Clement, E. Slade et al. (Eds.), *Social media: The good, the bad, and the ugly*. Refereed proceedings of the 15th IFIP Conference on e-business, e-services and e-society, Swansea, UK, September 13–15 (pp. 134–145). Switzerland: Springer.

Jauss, H. (1982). Toward an aesthetic of reception (T. Bahti, Trans.). Minneapolis, MN: University of Minnesota Press.

Jeffries-Fox, B. (2003). *Advertising value equivalency (AVE)*. Gainesville, FL: Institute for Public Relations. Retrieved from www.instituteforpr.org/wp-content/uploads/2003_AVE1.pdf

Jenkins, H. (2006). *Convergence culture: Where old and new media collide*. New York, NY: New York University Press.

Jensen, K. (2012). *A handbook of media and communication research* (2nd ed.). Abingdon, UK: Routledge.

Jo, S. (2004). Effect of content type on impact: Editorial vs. advertising. *Public Relations Review, 30*(4), 503–512.

Joint Committee on Standards for Educational Evaluation. (1994). *The program evaluation standards: How to assess evaluations of educational programs*. Thousand Oaks, CA: Sage.

Julian, D. (1997). The utilization of the logic model as a system level planning and evaluation device. *Evaluation and Program Planning, 20*(3), 251–257.

Kahneman, D. (2011). *Thinking, fast and slow*. New York, NY: Farrer, Straus & Giroux.

Kaplan, R., & Norton, D. (1992). The balanced scorecard: Measures that drive performance. *Harvard Business Review, 70*(1), 71–79.

Karpf, D., Kreiss, D., & Nielsen, R. (2014). A new era of field research in political communication. In L. Lievrouw (Ed.), *Challenging communication research* (pp. 43–57). New York, NY: Peter Lang.

Katz, E. & Lazarsfeld, P. (1955). *Personal influence*. New York, NY: Free Press.

Kellogg Foundation. (2004). *Logic model development guide*. Battle Creek, MI: Author. Retrieved from www.smartgivers.org/uploads/logicmodelguidepdf.pdf (Original work published 1998.)

Kellogg Foundation. (2010). *W. K. Kellogg Foundation evaluation handbook.* Battle Creek, MI: Author. Retrieved from www.wkkf.org/resource-directory/resource/2010/w-k-kellogg-foundation-evaluation-handbook

Kendall, R. (1997). *Public relations campaign strategies: Planning for implementation* (2nd ed.). New York, NY: Addison-Wesley.

Kenning, G. (2016). *Arts engagement for people with dementia: Independent evaluation of the Art Access Program, Art Gallery of New South Wales.* Sydney, NSW: University of Technology Sydney and Art Gallery of New South Wales.

Kent, M. (2010). What is a public relations crisis? Refocusing crisis research. In T. Coombs & S. Holladay (Eds.), *The handbook of crisis communication* (pp. (705–712). Oxford, UK: Wiley-Blackwell.

Kerlinger, F., & Lee, H. (2000). *Foundations of behavioural research* (4th ed.). New York, NY: Harcourt.

Kim, D., & Dearning, J. (Eds.). (2016). *Health communication research measures.* New York, NY: Peter Lang.

Kim, M., & Ebesu Hubbard, A. (2007). Intercultural communication in a global village: How to understand 'the other'. *Journal of Intercultural Communication Research, 36*(3), 223–235.

Kim, S., & Hancock, J. (2016). How advertorials deactivate advertising schema: MTurk-based experiments to examine persuasion tactics and outcomes in health advertisements. *Communication Research* (Pre-print online). Retrieved from http://crx.sagepub.com/content/early/2016/04/21/0093650216644017.short

Kincaid, D., Delate, R., Storey, D., & Figueroa, M. (2013). Closing the gaps in practice and in theory. In R. Rice & C. Atkin (Eds.), *Public communication campaigns* (4th ed., pp. 305–319). Thousand Oaks, CA: Sage.

Kindon, S., Pain, R., & Kesby, M. (Eds.). (2007). *Participatory action research approaches and methods: Connecting people, participation and places.* Abingdon, UK: Routledge.

Kirkpatrick, D. (2001). *Evaluating training programs: The four levels* (2nd ed.). San Francisco, CA: Berrett-Koehler.

Klapper, J. (1960). *The effects of mass communication.* New York, NY: Free Press.

Knowles, E., & Linn, J. (Eds.). (2004). *Resistance and persuasion.* Mahwah, NJ: Lawrence Erlbaum.

Knowlton, L., & Phillips, C. (2013). *The logic models guidebook: Better strategies for great results* (2nd ed.). Thousand Oaks, CA: Sage.

Kompridis, N. (2011). Receptivity, possibility, and democratic politics. *Ethics and Global Politics, 4*(4), 255–272.

Korpela, J. (2010). Human communication. *IT and Communication* [Website]. Retrieved from www.cs.tut.fi/~jkorpela/wiio.html

Kotler, P. (1991). *Marketing management* (7th ed.). Englewood Cliffs, NJ: Prentice Hall.

Kotler, P., Rackman, N., & Krishnaswamy, S. (2006). Ending the war between sales and marketing. *Harvard Business Review,* July/August. Retrieved from https://hbr.org/2006/07/ending-the-war-between-sales-and-marketing

Koyré, A., & Cohen, B. (Eds.). (1972). Isaac Newton's *Philosophiae Naturalis Principia Mathematica: The third edition (1726) with variant readings.* Cambridge, MA: Harvard University Press. (Original work *Philosophiæ Naturalis Principia Mathematica Book 3: On the system of the world: Book 3* published 1726.)

Krippendorff, K., & Bock, M. (2009). *The content analysis reader.* Thousand Oaks, CA: Sage.

Kroeber-Riel, W. & Esch, F. (2000). *Strategie und technik der Werebung.* Stuttgart, Germany: Kohlhammer.

Krueger, R., & Casey, M. (2009). *Focus groups: A practical guide for applied research.* Thousand Oaks, CA: Sage.

Krug, S. (2016). Reactions now available globally. Retrieved from http://newsroom.fb.com/news/2016/02/reactions-now-available-globally

Lacey, K. (2013). *Listening publics: The politics and experience of listening in the media age*. Malden, MA and Cambridge, UK: Wiley Blackwell/Polity.

Lamme, M., & Russell, K. (2010). Removing the spin: Towards a new theory of public relations history. *Journalism & Mass Communication Monographs, 11*(4), 281–362.

Lang, G., & Lang, K. (1981). Watergate: An exploration of the agenda-building process. In *Mass Communication Review Yearbook*, Vol. 2 (pp. 447–469). Beverly Hills, CA: Sage.

Lang, G., & Lang, K. (1983). *The battle for public opinion: The president, the press and the polls during Watergate*. New York, NY: Columbia University Press.

Lang, K., & Lang, G. (1968). *Voting and nonvoting: Implications of broadcasting returns before polls are closed*. Waltham, MA: Blaisdell.

Lapsley, C. (2014). Statement of Craig William Lapsley to the Hazelwood Coal Mine Fire Inquiry, Morwell, Victoria, May 20. Retrieved from http://hazelwoodinquiry.vic.gov.au/public-hearings

Lasswell, H. (1927). *Propaganda techniques in the world war*. New York, NY: Knopf.

Lasswell, H. (1948). The structure and function of communication in society. In L. Bryson (Ed.), *The communication of ideas* (pp. 37–51). New York, NY: Harper.

Laughey, D. (2007). *Key themes in media theory*. Maidenhead, UK: Open University Press.

Lavidge, R., & Steiner, G. (1961). A model for predictive measurements of advertising effectiveness. *Journal of Marketing, 25*(6), 59–62.

Lazarsfeld, P., Berelson, F., & Gaudet, H. (1944). *The people's choice: How the voter makes up his mind in a presidential campaign*. New York: Duell, Sloan & Pearce.

Leite, E. (2015). Why trust matters in business. Address to the World Economic Forum, Davos-Klosters, Switzerland, January 19. Retrieved from https://agenda.weforum.org/2015/01/why-trust-matters-in-business

Lennie, J., & Taachi, J. (2013a). *Evaluating communication for development: A framework for social change*. New York, NY: Routledge.

Lennie, J., & Taachi, J. (2013b). Moving beyond the paradoxes and contradictions in evaluating development initiatives: Towards a new paradigm for sustainable social change. Paper presented to the Australasian Evaluation Society International Conference, Brisbane, Australia, September 6.

Lerner, D. (1958). *The passing of traditional society: Modernizing the Middle East*. New York, NY: The Free Press.

L'Etang, J. (2008). *Public relations: Concepts, practice and critique*. London, UK: Sage.

Lewin, K. (1946). Action research and minority problems. *Journal of Social Issues, 2*(4), 34–46.

Lewin, K. (1951). *Field theory in social science: Selected theoretical papers* (D. Cartwright, Ed.). New York, NY: Harper & Row.

Lievrouw, L. (Ed.). (2014). *Challenging communication research*. New York, NY: Peter Lang.

Likely, F. (2000). Communication and PR: Made to measure. *Strategic Communication Management, 4*(1), 22–27.

Likely, F. (2016). CCOs and evaluation: Will the competition heat up? *Research Letter* [Web log post], September 6. Gainesville, FL: Institute for Public Relations. Retrieved from www.instituteforpr.org/ccos-evaluation-will-competition-heat

Likely, F., & Watson, T. (2013). Measuring the edifice: Public relations measurement and evaluation practice over the course of 40 years. In K. Sriramesh, A. Zerfass, & J. Kim, (Eds.), *Public relations and communication management: Current trends and emerging topics* (pp. 143–162). New York, NY: Routledge.

Likert, R. (1932). A technique for the measurement of attitudes. *Archives of Psychology, 22*(140), 5–55.

Lincoln, Y., & Guba, E. (1985). *Naturalistic inquiry*. Beverly Hills, CA: Sage.

Lindenmann, W. (1979). The missing link in public relations research. *Public Relations Review*, 5(1), 26–36.

Lindenmann, W. (1980). Hunches no longer suffice. *Public Relations Journal*, 36(6), 9–13.

Lindenmann, W. (1990). Research, evaluation and measurement: A national perspective. *Public Relations Review*, 16(2), 3–16.

Lindenmann, W. (1993). An 'effectiveness yardstick' to measure public relations success. *Public Relations Quarterly*, 38(1), 7–9.

Lindenmann, W. (1997a). Using research to measure the effectiveness of PR programs. *Quirk's Marketing Research*. Retrieved from www.quirks.com/articles/a1997/19970204.aspx

Lindenmann, W. (1997b). *Guidelines for measuring and evaluating PR effectiveness*. Gainesville, FL: Institute for Public Relations.

Lindenmann, W. (2003). *Guidelines for measuring the effectiveness of PR programs and activities*. Gainesville, FL: Institute for Public Relations. Retrieved from www.instituteforpr.org/wp-content/uploads/2002_MeasuringPrograms.pdf. (Revised version of original work 1997b.)

Lindenmann, W. (1998). Only PR outcomes count: That is the real bottom line. *Journal of Communication Management*, 3(1), 66–73.

Lindenmann, W. (2001). *Research doesn't have to put you in the poorhouse*. Gainesville, FL: Institute for Public Relations. Retrieved from www.instituteforpr.org/topics/research-savings

Lindenmann, W. (2005). *Putting PR measurement and evaluation in historical perspective*. Gainesville, FL: Institute for Public Relations. Retrieved from www.instituteforpr.org/wp-content/uploads/PR_History2005.pdf

Littlejohn, S., & Foss, K. (2008). *Theories of human communication* (9th ed.). Belmont, CA: Thomson-Wadsworth.

Livingstone, S. (2015). Active audiences? The debate progresses but is far from resolved. *Communication Theory*, 25(4), 439–446.

Lofland, J., & Lofland, L. (1984). *Analyzing social settings* (2nd ed.). Belmont, CA: Wadsworth.

Logsdon, R., Gibbons, L., McCurry, S., & Teri, L. (2005). Assessing changes in quality of life in Alzheimer's disease. In B. Vellas, M. Grundman, H. Feldman, L. Fitten, B. Winblad, & E. Giacobini (Eds.), *Research and practice in Alzheimer's disease and cognitive decline* (pp. 221–255). New York, NY: Springer.

Lombard, M., Synder-Duch, J., & Bracken, C. (2003). Content analysis in mass communication: Assessment and reporting of intercoder reliability. *Human Communication Research*, 29(3), 469–472.

Lull, J. (2000). *Media, communication, culture*. Cambridge, UK: Polity Press.

McCarney, R., Warner, J., Iliffe, S., van Haselen, R., Griffin, M., & Fisher, P. (2007). The Hawthorne Effect: A randomized, controlled trial. *BMC Medical Research Methodology*, 7(30), n.p. Retrieved from http://bmcmedresmethodol.biomedcentral.com/articles/10.1186/1471-2288-7-30

McCombs, M. (2004). *Setting the agenda: The mass media and public opinion*. Cambridge, UK: Polity.

McCombs, M., & Reynolds, D. (2002). News influence on our pictures of the world. In J. Bryant & D. Zillman (Eds.), *Media effects: Advances in theory and research* (2nd ed., pp. 1–18). Mahwah, NJ: Lawrence Erlbaum.

McCombs, M., & Shaw, D. (1972). The agenda-setting function of mass media. *Public Opinion Quarterly*, 36(2), 176–187.

McDavid, J., Huse, I., & Hawthorn, L. (Eds.). (2013). *Program evaluation and measurement: An introduction to practice* (2nd ed.). Thousand Oaks, CA: Sage.

Macey, W., & Schneider, B. (2008). The meaning of employee engagement. *Industrial and Organizational Psychology*, 1(1), 3–30.

McGuire, W. (1968). Personality and attitude change: An information processing theory. In A. Greenwald, T. Brock, & T. Ostrom (Eds.), *Pyschological foundations of attitudes* (pp. 171–196). San Diego, CA: Academic Press.

McGuire, W. (1969). The nature of attitudes and attitude change. In G. Lindzey & E. Aronson (Eds.), *Handbook of social psychology*, Vol. 3 (2nd ed., pp. 136–314). Reading, MA: Addison-Wesley.

McGuire, W. (1976). Some internal psychological factors influencing consumer choice. *Journal of Consumer Research*, 2(4), 302–319.

McGuire, W. (1985). Attitudes and attitude change. In G. Lindzey & E. Aronson (Eds.), *Handbook of social psychology*, Vol. 2 (3rd ed., pp. 233–346). New York, NY: Random House.

McGuire, W. (1989). Theoretical foundations of campaigns. In R. Rice & C. Atkin (Eds.), *Public communication campaigns* (2nd ed., pp. 43–65). Newbury Park, CA: Sage.

McGuire. W. (1999). *Constructing social psychology: Creative and critical processes.* Cambridge, UK: Cambridge University Press.

McGuire, W. (2001). Input and output variables currently promising for constructing persuasive communications. In R. E. Rice & C. K. Atkin (Eds.), *Public communication campaigns* (3rd ed., pp. 22–48). Thousand Oaks, CA: Sage.

McGuire W. (2013). McGuire's classic input-output framework for constructing persuasive messages. In R. Rice & C. Atkin (Eds.), *Public communication campaigns* (4th ed., pp. 133–145). Thousand Oaks, CA: Sage. (Original work published 1989.)

McLaughlin, J., & Jordan, J. (1999). Logic models: A tool for telling your program's performance story. *Evaluation and Program Planning*, 22(1), 65–72.

Macnamara, J. (1992). Evaluation of public relations: The Achilles heel of the public relations profession. *International Public Relations Review*, 15(2), 19–25.

Macnamara, J. (1999). Research in public relations: A review of the use of evaluation and formative research. *Asia Pacific Public Relations Journal*, 1(2), 107–133.

Macnamara, J. (2000a). The ad value of PR. *Asia Pacific Public Relations Journal*, 2(1), 90–103.

Macnamara, J. (2000b). *Jim Macnamara's public relations handbook*. Melbourne, Vic: Information Australia.

Macnamara, J. (2002a). Research and evaluation. In C. Tymson & P. Lazar, *The new Australian and New Zealand public relations manual* (21st century ed., pp. 100–134). Sydney, NSW: Tymson Communications.

Macnamara, J. (2002b). An international perspective on priority issues in public relations. Paper presented to the International Public Relations Association (IPRA) World Congress, Cairo, Egypt, November 14.

Macnamara, J. (2005a). *Jim Macnamara's public relations handbook* (5th ed.). Sydney, NSW: Archipelago Press.

Macnamara, J. (2005b). Media content analysis: Its uses, benefits and best practice methodology. *Asia Pacific Public Relations Review*, 6(1), 1–34.

Macnamara, J. (2009). Address to Journalism Forum, Pymble Ladies College (PLC), Croydon, Sydney, June.

Macnamara, J. (2012a). *Public relations theories, practices, critiques.* Sydney, NSW: Pearson.

Macnamara, J. (2012b). Democracy 2.0: Can social media engage youth and disengaged citizens in the public sphere. *Australian Journal of Communication*, 39(3), 65–86.

Macnamara, J. (2014a). Organizational listening: A vital missing element in public communication and the public sphere. *Asia Pacific Public Relations Journal*, 15(1), 90–108.

Macnamara, J. (2014b). Breaking the PR measurement and evaluation deadlock: A new approach and model. Paper presented to the International Summit on Measurement hosted by the Association for Measurement and Evaluation of Communication, Amsterdam, The Netherlands, June.

Macnamara, J. (2014c). *The 21st century media (r)evolution: Emergent communication practices.* New York, NY: Peter Lang.

Macnamara, J. (2014d). A review of public communication by the mine owner (GDF SUEZ Australian Energy) and government departments and agencies during the 2014 Hazelwood coal mine fire. Report to the Hazelwood Coal Mine Fire Board of Inquiry, June. Retrieved from http://hazelwoodinquiry.vic.gov.au/wp-content/uploads/2014/08/Report-of-Prof-MacNamara.pdf

Macnamara, J. (2015a). *Creating an 'architecture of listening' in organizations: The basis of engagement, trust, healthy democracy, social equity, and business sustainability.* Sydney, NSW: University of Technology Sydney. Retrieved from www.uts.edu.au/node/134066

Macnamara, J. (2015b). The work and 'architecture of listening': Requisites for ethical organization–public communication. *Ethical Space, 12*(2), 29–37.

Macnamara, J. (2015c). Overcoming the measurement and evaluation deadlock: A new approach and model. *Journal of Communication Management, 19*(4), 371–387.

Macnamara, J. (2015d). *Compliance and evaluation of NSW government advertising and communication.* Sydney, NSW: Department of Premier and Cabinet, NSW Government.

Macnamara, J. (2015e). *Evaluation of the Pink Sari project.* Sydney, NSW: Multicultural Health Communication Service, NSW Health.

Macnamara, J. (2015f). The Hazelwood coal mine fire: Lessons from crisis miscommunication and misunderstanding. *Case Studies in Strategic Communication, 4,* 54–87. Retrieved from http://cssc.uscannenberg.org/cases/v4

Macnamara, J. (2016a). *Organizational listening: The missing essential in public communication.* New York, NY: Peter Lang.

Macnamara J. (2016b). The work and 'architecture of listening': Addressing gaps in organization–public communication. *International Journal of Strategic Communication, 10*(2), 133–148.

Macnamara, J. (2016c). *A taxonomy of evaluation: Towards standards.* London, UK: Association for Measurement and Evaluation of Communication [Website]. Retrieved from http://amecorg.com/amecframework/home/supporting-material/taxonomy

Macnamara, J. (2017). *Creating a democracy for everyone: Strategies for increasing listening and engagement by government.* Report. Sydney, NSW: University of Technology Sydney. Retrieved from www.uts.edu.au/node/230356

Macnamara, J., & Camit, M. (2016). Effective CALD community health communication through research and collaboration: An exemplar case study. *Communication Research & Practice.* doi: 10.1080/22041451.2016.1209277

Macnamara, J., & Kumar, R. (2014). Metrics to insights: A model for researchers to convert data to insights. New York, NY: Ketchum.

Macnamara, J., & Likely, F. (2017). Revisiting the disciplinary home of evaluation: New perspectives to inform PR evaluation standards. *Research Journal of the Institute for Public Relations, 2*(2), 1–21.

Macnamara, J., & Watson, T. (2014). The rise and fall of IPRA in Australia: 1959 to 2000. *Asia Pacific Public Relations Journal, 15*(1), 23–36. Retrieved from https://ojs.deakin.edu.au/index.php/apprj/index

Macnamara, J., & Zerfass, A. (2012). Social media communication in organisations: The challenges of balancing openness, strategy and management. *International Journal of Strategic Communication, 6*(4), 287–308.

Macnamara, J., Dunston, R., & Monden, M. (2014). *Improving breast screening rates for Indian and Sri Lankan women in NSW: What research tells us.* Sydney, NSW: Multicultural Health Communication Service, NSW Ministry of Health.

Macnamara, J., Lwin, M., Adi, A., & Zerfass, A. (2016). PESO media strategy shifts to SOEP: Opportunities and ethical dilemmas. *Public Relations Review, 42*(3), 377–385.

McQuail, D. (1997). *Audience analysis.* Thousand Oaks, CA: Sage.

Manyika, J., Chui, M., Bughin, J., Brown, B., Dobbs, R., Roxburgh, C., & Byers, A. (2011). *Big data: The next frontier for innovation, competition, and productivity.* New York, NY: McKinsey Global Institute. Retrieved from www.mckinsey.com/business-functions/business-technology/our-insights/big-data-the-next-frontier-for-innovation

Maréchal, G. (2010). Autoethnography. In A. Mills, G. Durepos, & E. Wiebe (Eds.), *Encyclopedia of case study research,* Vol. 2 (pp. 43–45). Thousand Oaks, CA: Sage.

Marklein, T., & Paine, K. (2012). The march to standards. Presentation to the 4th European Summit on Measurement, Dublin, Ireland. Retrieved from http://amecorg.com/downloads/dublin2012/The-March-to-Social-Standards-Tim-Marklein-and-Katie-Paine.pdf

Marston, J. (1981). *Modern public relations.* New York, NY: McGraw-Hill.

Marteau, T., Ogilvie, D., Roland, M., Suhrcke, M., & Kelly, M. (2011). Judging nudging: Can nudging improve population health? *British Medical Journal, 342*(d228), 263–265.

Maslow, A. (1966). *The psychology of science: A reconnaissance.* Chapel Hill, NC: Maurice Bassett.

Maurer, M., Kofoed, J., & Pierce, S. in conjunction with Dove team at Unilever. (2016). *Beautifully effective: How Dove turned cultural resonance into ROI.* London, UK: Institute of Practitioners in Advertising.

Mead. G. (2014). *Telling the story: The heart and soul of successful leadership.* San Francisco, CA: Jossey-Bass.

Melcote, S., & Steeves, L. (2001). *Communication for development in the third world: Theory and practice for empowerment* (2nd ed.). London, UK: Sage

Meng J., & Berger, B. (2012). Measuring return on investment (ROI) organizations' internal communication effort. *Journal of Communication Management, 16*(4), 332–354.

Merriam–Webster. (2016). Evaluation. Retrieved from www.merriam-webster.com/dictionary/evaluate

Merritt, J. (2014). Statement of John Damian Merritt to the Hazelwood Coal Mine Fire Inquiry, Morwell, Victoria, May 14. Retrieved from http://hazelwoodinquiry.vic.gov.au/statement-of-john-merritt

Meyer, J., & Smith, C. (2000). HRM practices and organisational commitment: A test of a mediation model. *Canadian Journal of Administrative Services, 17*(4), 319–331.

Meyer, P. (2002). *Precision journalism: A reporter/s introduction to social science methods* (4th ed.). Lanham, MD: Rowman & Littlefield.

Michaelson, D., & Stacks, D. (2006). *Exploring the comparative communications effectiveness of advertising and media placement.* Gainesville, FL: Institute for Public Relations. Retrieved from www.instituteforpr.org/advertising-media-placement-effectiveness

Michaelson, D., & Stacks, D. (2007). *Exploring the comparative communications effectiveness of advertising and public relations: An experimental study of initial branding advantage.* Gainesville, FL: Institute for Public Relations. Retrieved from www.instituteforpr.org/wp-content/uploads/Michaelson_Stacks.pdf

Michaelson, D., & Stacks, D. (2011). Standardization in public relations measurement and evaluation. *Public Relations Journal, 5*(2), 1–22.

Michie, S., van Stralen, M., & West, R. (2011). The behaviour change wheel: A new method for characterising and designing behaviour change interventions. *Implementation Science, 6*(1), Article 42. Retrieved from https://implementationscience.biomedcentral.com/articles/10.1186/1748-5908-6-42

Miles, M., & Huberman, A. (1994). *Qualitative data analysis: A sourcebook of methods.* Thousand Oaks, CA: Sage.

Millar, R., & Hall, K. (2013). Social return on investment (SROI) and performance measurement. *Public Management Review, 15*(6), 923–941.

Mitchell, G. (2005). Libertarian paternalism is an oxymoron. *Northwestern University Law Review, 99*(3), 1245–1277.

Morley, D. (1992). *Television, audiences and cultural studies.* London, UK: Routledge.

Morrison, M., Haley, E., Sheehan, K., & Taylor, R. (2002). *Using qualitative research in advertising: Strategies, techniques, and applications.* Thousand Oaks, CA: Sage.

Moy, P., Bimber, B., Rojecki, A., Xenos, M., & Iyenger, S. (2012). Transnational connections: Shifting contours in political communication research. *International Journal of Communication, 6,* 247–254.

NatCen (National Centre for Social Research). (2016a). British Social Attitudes study, No 33. Retrieved from www.bsa.natcen.ac.uk/latest-report/british-social-attitudes-33/euroscepticism.aspx

NatCen (National Centre for Social Research). (2016b). EU referendum poll of polls [Website]. Retrieved from http://whatukthinks.org/eu/opinion-polls/poll-of-polls

National Audit Office. (2014). *NHS waiting times for elective care in England.* London, UK: Author. Retrieved from www.nao.org.uk/wp-content/uploads/2014/01/NHS-waiting-times-for-elective-care-in-England.pdf

National Council of Public Polls. (2015). Pollingreport.com [Website]. Retrieved from www.pollingreport.com/ncpp.htm

National Readership Survey. (2016). What's the difference between readership and circulation? [Website]. Retrieved from www.nrs.co.uk/nrs-print/readership-and-circulation-trends/readership-vs-circulation

Needham, J. (Ed.) (1986). Paper and printing. In *Science and civilization in China, Volume 5, Part 1: Chemistry and chemical technology.* Cambridge, MA: Cambridge University Press.

Nelson, L. (2014). Overwhelmed by smoke. *Latrobe Valley Express,* March 3. Retrieved from www.latrobevalleyexpress.com.au/story/2123570/overwhelmed-by-smoke

Nesterak, E. (2014). Head of White House 'nudge unit' Maya Shankar speaks about newly formed social and behavioural sciences team. *ThePsychReport,* July 13. Retrieved from http://thepsychreport.com/current-events/head-of-white-house-nudge-unit-maya-shankar-speaks-about-newly-formed-us-social-and-behavioral-sciences-team

Neuendorf, K. (2002). *The content analysis guidebook.* Thousand Oaks, CA: Sage.

Neugarten, B., Havighurst, R., & Tobin, S. (1961). The measurement of life satisfaction. *Journal of Gerontology, 16*(2), 134–143.

Neuman, W. (1997). *Social research methods: Qualitative and quantitative approaches.* Needham Heights, MA: Allyn & Bacon.

Neuman, W. (2006). *Social research methods: Qualitative and quantitative approaches* (6th ed.). New York, NY: Pearson.

Newbold, C., Boyd-Barrett, O., & Van Den Bulck, H. (2002). *The media book.* London, UK: Arnold Hodder Headline.

Newcomb, T. (1953). An approach to the study of communicative acts. *Psychological Review, 60*(6), 393–404.

New Zealand Ministry for Culture and Heritage. (2015). Plan to reduce childhood obesity. Retrieved from www.mch.govt.nz/plan-reduce-childhood-obesity

New Zealand Ministry of Health. (2015a). Annual update of key results 2014/15: New Zealand Health Survey. Retrieved from www.health.govt.nz/publication/annual-update-key-results-2014-15-new-zealand-health-survey

New Zealand Ministry of Health. (2015b). Childhood obesity plan. Retrieved from www.health.govt.nz/our-work/diseases-and-conditions/obesity/childhood-obesity-plan

NHS England. (2014). Quarterly hospital activity data [Website]. Retrieved from www.england.nhs.uk/statistics/statistical-work-areas/hospital-activity/quarterly-hospital-activity/qar-data

Nicholls, J., Mackenzie, S., & Somers, A. (2007). *Measuring real value: A DIY guide to social return on investment*. London, UK: New Economics Foundation.

Nielsen. (2015). Global trust in advertising: Winning strategies for an evolving landscape. New York, NY: Author. Retrieved from www.nielsen.com/content/dam/nielsenglobal/apac/docs/reports/2015/nielsen-global-trust-in-advertising-report-september-2015.pdf

Nielsen. (2016a). Television measurement [Website]. Retrieved from www.nielsen.com/eu/en/solutions/measurement/television.html

Nielsen. (2016b). About us [Website]. Retrieved from www.agbnielsen.com/aboutus/aboutus.asp

Nielsen, K., Stokes, J., & Laden-Andersen, K. (2015). *Managing reputation in the public sector. Q4 2014/2015*. Report to UK Cabinet Office, London, UK.

Noble, P., & Watson, T. (1999). Applying a unified public relations evaluation model in a European context. Paper presented to the Transnational Communication in Europe: Practice and Research Congress, Berlin, Germany.

Noblet, A., & LaMontagne, A. (2009). The challenges of developing, implementing, and evaluating interventions. In S. Cartwright & C. Cooper (Eds.), *The Oxford handbook of organizational well-being* (pp.466–496). Oxford, UK: Oxford University Press.

Nock, S. (1993). *The costs of privacy: Surveillance and reputation in America*. New York, NY: De Gruyter.

Norman, R. (2014). *Digital media for governments: Reaching audiences in an age of fragmentation and austerity*. London, UK: WPP-GroupM. Retrieved from www.wpp.com/govtpractice/~/media/wppgov/files/wppgovt-robnorman-digital.pdf

Norris, P. (2001). Political communication. In N. Smelser & P. Baltes (Eds.), *International encyclopaedia of the social and behavioural sciences* (pp. 11631–11640). Amsterdam, The Netherlands: Elsevier.

Nutbeam, D. (1998). Evaluating health promotion: Progress, problems and solutions. *Health Promotion International, 13*(1), 27–44.

Nutbeam, D., Harris, E., & Wise, M. (2010). *Theory in a nutshell: A practical guide to health promotion theories* (3rd ed.). Sydney, NSW: McGraw-Hill.

O'Carroll, E. (2010). Centralia, PA: How an underground coal fire erased a town. *Christian Science Monitor*, Bright Green blog [Web log post], February 5. Retrieved from www.csmonitor.com/Environment/Bright-Green/2010/0205/Centralia-Pa.-How-an-underground-coal-fire-erased-a-town

Ocean Tomo. (2015). *Annual study of intangible asset market value*. Chicago, IL: Author. Retrieved from www.oceantomo.com/blog/2015/03-05-ocean-tomo-2015-intangible-asset-market-value

O'Keefe, D. (1990). *Persuasion: Theory and research*. Newbury Park, CA: Sage.

O'Neil, J., & Eisenmann, M. (2016). How changing media formats impact credibility and drive consumer action. In B. Yook, Y. Ji, & Z. Chen (Eds.), *Refereed Proceedings of the 19th International Public Relations Research Conference, Miami, FL*. Retrieved from www.instituteforpr.org/wp-content/uploads/IPR19-proceedings.pdf. Gainesville, FL: Institute for Public Relations.

Open University. (2005). *Action research: A guide for associate lecturers*. Milton Keynes, UK: Centre for Outcomes-Based Education. Retrieved from www.open.ac.uk/cobe/docs/AR-Guide-final.pdf

Osgood, C. (Ed.). (1954). Psycholinguistics: A survey of theory and research problems. *Journal of Abnormal and Social Psychology, 49*. Morton Prince Memorial Supplement.

Osgood, C., Suci, G., & Tannenbaum, P. (1957). *The measurement of meaning*. Urbana, IL: University of Illinois Press.

Oullier, O. (2014). The science of engagement. Paper presented to the International Summit on Measurement, Association for Measurement and Evaluation, Amsterdam, The Netherlands, June. Retrieved from http://amecorg.com/2014/09/amec-2014-summit-presentations

Owston, R. (2007). Models and methods for evaluation. In J. Spector, D. Merrill, J. van Merriënboer, & M. Driscoll (Eds.), *Handbook of research on educational communications and technology* (3rd ed., pp. 605–617). New York, NY: Routledge.

Oxford Dictionary. (2016). Evaluation. Retrieved from www.oxforddictionaries.com/definition/english/evaluation

Oxford Math Center. (2016). From bits to brontobytes [Website]. Retrieved from www.oxfordmathcenter.com/drupal7/node/410

Paine, K. (2016a). Measurement 101 course for professors in a box [Website]. Retrieved from http://painepublishing.com/products/measurement-101-for-professors

Paine, K. (2016b). Making sense of measurement: How to navigate your way through standards, dashboards, modeling platforms, and correlations in order to tie communications to business results. Presentation to the Measurement and Evaluation Summit, Norwegian Business School, Oslo, Norway, November 10.

Panter-Brick, C., Clarke, S., Lomas, H., Pinder, M., & Lindsay, S. (2006). Culturally compelling strategies for behaviour changes: A social ecology model and case study in malaria prevention. *Social Science & Medicine, 62*(11), 2810–2825.

Park, H. (2016). Health belief model. In D. Kim & J. Dearing (Eds.), *Health communication research measures* (pp. 25–32). New York, NY: Peter Lang.

Patel, S. (2015). Why you should ignore vanity metrics and focus on engagement. *Forbes,* May 13. Retrieved from www.forbes.com/sites/sujanpatel/2015/05/13/why-you-should-ignore-vanity-metrics-focus-on-engagement-metrics-instead/#59ea320a574e

Patton, M. (1978). *Utilization-focused evaluation.* Beverly Hills, CA: Sage.

Patton, M. (2002). *Qualitative research and evaluation methods* (3rd ed.). Thousand Oaks, CA: Sage.

Pavlik, J. (1987). *Public relations: What research tells us.* Newbury Park, CA: Sage.

Pawson, R. (2013). *The science of evaluation: A realist manifesto.* London, UK, Sage.

Pawson, R., & Tilley, N. (1997). *Realistic evaluation.* London, UK: Sage.

Pawson, R., & Tilley, N. (2001). Realistic evaluation bloodlines. *American Journal of Evaluation, 22*(3), 317–324.

Pawson, R., & Tilley, N. (2004). Realist evaluation. Paper funded by the UK Cabinet Office. Retrieved from www.communitymatters.com.au/RE_chapter.pdf

Pedace, R. (2013). *Econometrics for dummies.* Hoboken, NJ: John Wiley & Sons.

Pelias, R., & VanOosting, J. (1987). A paradigm for performance studies. *Quarterly Journal of Speech, 73*(2), 219–231.

Peters, J. (1999). *Speaking into the air: A history of the idea of communication.* Chicago, IL: University of Chicago Press.

Petty, R., & Cacioppo, J. (1986). *Communication and persuasion: Central and peripheral routes to attitude change.* New York, NY: Springer-Verlag.

Pew Research Center. (2012). Winning the media campaign [Website]. Retrieved from www.journalism.org/2012/11/02/winning-media-campaign-2012

Piotrow, P., Kincaid, D., Rimon, J., & Rinehart, W. (1997). *Health communication: Lessons for public health.* New York, NY: Praeger.

Ponzi, L. (2016). Measurement challenges in the third era of reputation management. Presentation to the Measurement and Evaluation Summit, Norwegian Business School, Oslo, Norway, November 10.

Poole, M., Seibold, D., & McPhee, D. (1985). Group decision making as a structurational process. *Quarterly Journal of Speech*, *71*(1), 74–102.

Potter, W. (James). (2009). *Arguing for a general framework for mass media scholarship*. Thousand Oaks, CA: Sage.

Powell, G., Groves, S., & Dimos, J. (2011). *ROI of social media: How to improve the return on your social marketing investment*. Singapore: John Wiley & Sons.

Practical Concepts, Inc. (1971). *The logical framework*. Approach and training materials developed for US Agency for International Development, Washington, DC [Unpublished manuscript].

Practical Concepts, Inc. (1979). *The logical framework: A manager's guide to a scientific approach to design & evaluation*. Washington, DC. Retrieved from http://pdf.usaid.gov/pdf_docs/pnabn963.pdf

Pritchard, J., Stephens, M., & Donnelly, P. (2000). Inference of population structure using multilocus genotype data. *Genetics*, *155*(2), 945–959.

PRSA (Public Relations Society of America). (2014). Measurement resources [Website]. Retrieved from www.prsa.org/intelligence/businesscase/measurementresources

Public Health England. (2016). Change4Life behaviour change model. In *Change4Life: Making it easier for families to eat well and move more*. London, UK: Author.

Punch, K. (1998). *Introduction to social research: Quantitative and qualitative approaches*. London, UK: Sage.

PWC (PriceWaterhouseCoopers). (2015). *Global entertainment and media outlook 2015–2019*. Retrieved from www.pwc.com/gx/en/industries/entertainment-media/outlook/segment-insights/internet-advertising.html

Quebral, N. (1972–1973). What do we mean by 'development communication'? *International Development Review*, *15*(2), 25–28.

Quick, B. (2016). Psychological reactance. In D. Kim & J. Dearing (Eds.), *Health communication research measures* (pp. 173–181). New York, NY: Peter Lang.

Ragan/NASDAQ OMX Corporate Solutions. (2013). *PR Measurement*. Chicago, IL: Author. Retrieved from http://bit.ly/PRMeasureWPPR

Ready, R., & Ott, B. (2003). Quality of life measures in dementia. *Health and Quality of Life Outcomes*, *1*(11), open access online. Retrieved from http://hqlo.biomedcentral.com/articles/10.1186/1477-7525-1-11

Reichheld, F. (2008). *The ultimate question: Driving good profits and true growth*. Boston, MA: Harvard Business School Publishing.

Reputation Institute. (2016). Reptrak research methodology [Website]. Retrieved from www.reputationinstitute.com/reputation-measurement-services/reptrak-framework#methodology

Rhoades, L., Eisenberger, R., & Armeli, S. (2001). Affective commitment to the organization: The contribution of perceived organizational support. *Journal of Applied Psychology*, *86*(5), 825–836.

Rice, R., & Atkin, C. (2002). Communication campaigns: Theory, design, implementation, and evaluation. In J. Bryant & D. Zillman (Eds.), *Media effects: Advances in theory and research* (2nd ed., pp. 427–451). Mahwah, NJ: Lawrence Erlbaum.

Rice, R., & Atkin, C. (Eds.). (2013). *Public communication campaigns* (4th ed.). Thousand Oaks, CA: Sage.

Ritson, M. (2016). If you think the sales funnel is dead, you've mistaken tactics for strategy. *Marketing Week*, April 6. Retrieved from www.marketingweek.com/2016/04/06/mark-ritson-if-you-think-the-sales-funnel-is-dead-youve-mistaken-tactics-for-strategy

RMIT University. (2005). *Evaluation of the stronger families and communities strategy 2000–2004: Qualitative cost benefit analysis*. Melbourne, Vic: Author. Retrieved from http://mams.rmit.edu.au/phhpu3ty2nm5.pdf

Rogers, E. (1962). *Diffusion of innovations*. New York, NY: The Free Press

Rogers, E. (1995). *Diffusion of innovations* (4th ed.). New York, NY: The Free Press. (Original work published 1962.)

Rogers, E., & Shoemaker, F. (1971). *Communication of innovations: A cross-cultural approach* (2nd ed.). New York, NY: The Free Press.

Rogers, E., & Storey, J. (1987). Communication campaigns. In C. Berger & S. Chafee (Eds.), *Handbook of communication science* (pp. 817–846). Newbury Park, CA: Sage.

Rogers, P. (2008). Using programme theory to evaluate complicated and complex aspects of interventions. *Evaluation, 14*(1), 29–48.

Rogers, P., Petrosino, A., Huebner, T., & Hacsi, T. (2000). Program theory evaluation: Practice, promise, and problems. *New Directions for Evaluation, 87,* 5–13.

Rosen, J. (2006). The people formerly known as the audience. *Press Think* [Web log post], June 27. Retrieved from http://archive.pressthink.org/2006/06/27/ppl_frmr.html

Rossi, P., Lipsey, M., & Freeman, H. (2004). *Evaluation: A systematic approach* (7th ed.). Thousand Oaks, CA: Sage.

Russill, C. (2008). Through a public darkly: Reconstructing pragmatist perspectives in communication theory. *Communication Theory, 18*(4), 478–504.

Ryle, G. (1949). *The concept of mind*. London, UK: Hutchinson.

Salmon, C., & Murray-Johnson, L. (2013). Communication campaign effectiveness and effects. In R. Rice & C. Atkin (Eds.), *Public communication campaigns* (4th ed., pp. 99–112). Thousand Oaks, CA: Sage.

Salter, K., & Kothari, A. (2014). Using realist evaluation to open the black box of knowledge translation: A state-of-the-art review. *Implementation Science, 9*(115), 1–14.

Samson, A. (2016). *The behavioural economics guide 2016.* Behavioraleconomics.com [Website]. Retrieved from www.behavioraleconomics.com/the-behavioral-economics-guide-2016

Samuelson, P., Koopmans, T., & Stone, J. (1954). Report of the evaluative committee for Econometrica. *Econometrica, 22*(2), 141–146.

Satell, G. (2013). 4 failed marketing buzzwords that you really shouldn't use. *Forbes,* November 17. Retrieved from www.forbes.com/sites/gregsatell/2013/11/17/4-marketing-buzz-words-that-you-really-shouldnt-use/#658deb5e622e

Schirato, T., Buettner, A., Jutel, T., & Stahl, G. (2010). *Understanding media studies*. South Melbourne, Vic: Oxford University Press.

Schlag, P. (2010). Nudge, choice architecture and libertarian paternalism. *Michigan Law Review, 108*(6), 913–924.

Scholten, M. (1996). Lost and found: The information-processing model of advertising effectiveness. *Journal of Business Research, 37*(2), 97–104.

Scholten, P., Nicholls, J., Olsen S., & Galimidi, B. (2006). *Social return on investment: A guide to SROI analysis.* Amstelveen, The Netherlands: Lenthe.

Schramm, W. (1954). How communication works. In W. Schramm (Ed.), *The process and effects of communication* (pp. 3–26). Urbana, IL: University of Illinois Press.

Schramm, W. (1971a). The nature of communication between humans. In W. Schramm & D. Roberts (Eds.), *The process and effects of mass communication* (rev. ed., pp. 3–53). Urbana, IL: University of Illinois Press.

Schramm, W. (1971b). *Notes on case studies for instructional media projects.* Working paper for Academy of Educational Development, Washington, DC.

Schultz, D. (2002). Measuring return on brand communication. *International Journal of Medical Marketing, 2*(4): 349–358.

Schultz, D., & Schultz, H. (2004). *IMC: The next generation.* New York, NY: McGraw-Hill.

Scriven, M. (1967). *The methodology of evaluation.* Washington, DC: American Educational Research Association.

Scriven, M. (1972). Pros and cons about goal free evaluation. *Journal of Educational Evaluation,* *3*(4), 1–7.

Scriven, M. (1991). Beyond formative and summative evaluation. In M. McLaughlin & E. Phillips (Eds.), *Evaluation and education: A quarter century* (pp. 19–64). Chicago, IL: University of Chicago Press.

Severin, W., & Tankard, J. (2001). *Communication theories: Origins, methods and uses in the mass media* (5th ed.). New York, NY: Addison Wesley Longman.

Shannon, C., & Weaver, W. (1949). *The mathematical theory of communication.* Urbana, IL: University of Illinois Press.

Sheldon, A. (1911). *The art of selling.* Chicago, IL: The Sheldon School.

Sheldrake, P. (2011). *The business of influence: Reframing marketing and PR for the digital age.* London, UK: Wiley.

Shenton, A. (2004). Strategies for ensuring trustworthiness in qualitative research projects. *Education for Information, 22*(2), 63–75.

Shiavo, R. (2007). *Health communication: Theory to practice.* San Francisco, CA: Jossey-Bass.

Shields, D. (2000). Symbolic convergence and special communication theories: Sensing and examining dis/enchantment with the theoretical robustness of critical autoethnography. *Communication Monographs, 67*(4), 392–421.

Shoemaker, P., & Reese, S. (1996). *Mediating the message: Theories of influences on mass media content.* White Plains, NY: Longman.

Shute, V., & Becker, B. (Eds.). (2010). *Innovative assessment for the 21 century.* New York, NY: Springer.

Silverman, D. (2000). *Doing qualitative research: A practical handbook.* London, UK: Sage.

Silverstone, R. (2007). *Media and morality: On the rise of the mediapolis.* Cambridge, UK: Polity.

Sixsmith, J., Fox K., Doyle P., & Barry, M. (2014). *A literature review on health communication campaign evaluation with regard to the prevention and control of communicable diseases in Europe.* Stockholm, Sweden: European Centre for Disease Prevention and Control.

Smith, K., Moriarty, S., Barbatsis, G, & Kenney, K. (2011). *Handbook of visual communication: Theory, methods, and media.* New York, NY: Routledge.

Snijders, C., Matzat, U., & Reips, U. (2012). 'Big data': Big gaps of knowledge in the field of Internet. *International Journal of Internet Science, 7*(1), 1–5.

Snyder, L., & LaCroix, J. (2013). How effective are mediated health campaigns? In R. Rice & C. Atkin (Eds.), *Public communication campaigns* (4th ed., pp. 113–129). Thousand Oaks, CA: Sage.

Social Ventures Australia Consulting. (2012). *Social return on investment: Lessons learning in Australia.* Sydney, NSW: Author. Retrieved from http://socialventures.com.au/assets/SROI-Lessons-learned-in-Australia.pdf

Solis, B. (2010). ROI: How to measure return on investment in social media. *@Brian Solis* [Web log], February 22. Retrieved from www.briansolis.com/2010/02/roi-how-to-measure-return-on-investment-in-social-media

Sparks, G. (2006). *Media effects research: A basic overview* (2nd ed.). Belmont, CA: Thomsom Wadsworth.

Spedding, E. (2016). The man behind Kim Kardashian's *Paper* magazine cover on how to break the Internet. *Daily Telegraph,* April 18, Lifestyle-Fashion. Retrieved from www.telegraph.co.uk/fashion/people/the-man-behind-kim-kardashians-paper-magazine-cover-on-how-to-br

Spicer, C. (2007). Collaborative advocacy and the creation of trust: Toward an understanding of stakeholder claims and risks. In E. Toth (Ed.), *The future of excellence in public relations and communication management: Challenges for the next generation* (pp. 27–40). Mahwah, NJ: Lawrence Erlbaum.

SROI Network. (2012). *A guide to social return on investment 2012*. Haddington, East Lothian, Scotland. Retrieved from www.socialvalueuk.org/resources/sroi-guide

Stacks, D. (2002). *Primer of public relations research*. New York, NY: Guilford Press.

Stacks, D. (2011). *Primer of public relations research* (2nd ed.). New York, NY: Guilford Press.

Stacks, D., & Bowen, S. (2013). *Dictionary of public relations measurement and research* (3rd ed.). Gainesville, FL: Institute for Public Relations Measurement Commission. Retrieved from www.instituteforpr.org/dictionary-public-relations-measurement-research-third-edition

Stacks, D., & Michaelson, D. (2009). Exploring the comparative communications effectiveness of advertising and public relations: A replication and extension of prior experiments. *Public Relations Journal, 3*(3), 1–22.

Stacks, D., & Michaelson, D. (2010). *A practitioner's guide to public relations research, measurement, and evaluation*. New York, NY: Business Experts Press.

Stake, R. (1994). Case studies. In N. Denzin & Y. Lincoln (Eds.), *Handbook of qualitative research* (pp. 236–246). Thousand Oaks, CA: Sage.

Stake, R. (2008). Qualitative case studies. In N. Denzin & Y. Lincoln (Eds.), *The SAGE handbook of qualitative research* (3rd ed., pp. 119–149). Thousand Oaks, CA: Sage.

Stern, M., Farquhar, J., Maccoby, N., & Russell, S. (1976). Results of a two-year health education campaign on dietary behaviour: The Stanford Three Community Study. *Circulation, 54*(5), 826–833.

Stewart, D., Pavlou, P., & Ward, S. (2002). Media influences on marketing communications. In J. Bryant & D. Zillman (Eds.), *Media effects: Advances in theory and research* (2nd ed., pp. 353–396). Mahwah, NJ: Lawrence Erlbaum.

Story, D., & Figueroa, M. (2012). Toward a global theory of health behaviour and social change. In R. Obregon & S. Waisbord (Eds.), *The handbook of global health communication* (pp. 70–94). Malden, MA: Wiley-Blackwell.

Strong, E. (1925). Theories of selling. *Journal of Applied Psychology, 9*(1), 75–86.

Stufflebeam, D. (1973). An introduction to the PDK book: Educational evaluation and decision-making. In B. Worthern & J. Sanders (Eds.), *Educational evaluation: Theory and practice* (pp. 128–142). Belmont, CA: Wadsworth.

Stufflebeam, D. (2001). Evaluation models. *New Directions for Evaluation, 89*, 7–98.

Suchman, E. (1967). *Evaluative research: Principles and practice in public service and social action programs*. New York, NY: Russell Sage Foundation.

Sullivan, G. (2011). Getting off the 'gold standard': Randomized controlled trials and education research. *Journal of Graduate Medical Education, 3*(3), 285–289.

Sunstein, C., & Thaler, R. (2003). Libertarian paternalism is not an oxymoron. *University of Chicago Law Review, 70*(4), 1159–1202.

Svoronos. T., & Mate K. (2011). Evaluating large-scale health programmes at a district level in resource-limited countries. *Bulletin of the World Health Organization, 89*(11), 831–837.

Tanaka, A., Gaye, L., & Richardson, R. (2010). Co-production and co-creation: Creative practice in social inclusion. In R. Nakatsu, N. Tosa, F. Naghdy, K. Wong, & P. Codognet (Eds.), *Cultural computing* (pp. 169–178). Berlin and Heidelberg, Germany: Springer.

Taylor, M., & Kent, M. (2014). Dialogic engagement: Clarifying foundational concepts. *Journal of Public Relations Research, 26*(5), 384–398.

Taylor-Power, E., & Henert, E. (2008). *Developing a logic model: Teaching and training guide*. Madison, WI: University of Wisconsin. Retrieved from https://fyi.uwex.edu/program development/files/2016/03/lmguidecomplete.pdf

Teddlie, C., & Yu, F. (2007). Mixed method sampling: A typology with examples. *Journal of Mixed Methods Research, 1*(1), 77–100.

Tedlock, B. (2008). The observation of participation and the emergence of public ethnography. In N. Denzin & Y. Lincoln (Eds.), *Strategies of qualitative inquiry* (3rd ed., pp. 151–171). Thousand Oaks, CA: Sage.

Tennant, G. (2001). *Six Sigma: SPC and TQM in manufacturing and services* Aldershot, UK: Gower.

Tester, K. (1994). *Media, culture, and morality.* London, UK: Routledge.

Thaler, R., & Sunstein, C. (2008). *Nudge: Improving decisions about health, wealth, and happiness.* New Haven, CT: Yale University Press.

The Australian. (2014). Coal mine fires commonplace, hears inquiry into Hazelwood blaze. *The Australian,* May 26. Retrieved from www.theaustralian.com.au/news/nation/coal-mine-fires-commonplace-hears-inquiry-into-hazelwood-blaze/story-e6frg6nf-1226931 612282

The Economist Group. (2015). *Annual report 2015.* London, UK: Author. Retrieved from www.economistgroup.com/pdfs/Annual_Report_2015_FINAL.pdf

Thomas, J. (2008). Advertising effectiveness. Decision Analyst [Website]. Retrieved from www.decisionanalyst.com/publ_art/adeffectiveness.dai

Thomas, P., & van de Fliert, E. (2014). *Interrogating the theory and practice of communication for social change: The basis for a renewal.* Basingstoke, UK: Palgrave Macmillan.

Thompson, D. (2016). The very best in creativity, insight and strategy. *IPA Effectiveness Awards 2016,* Foreword. London, UK: Institute of Practitioners in Advertising.

Tilley, C. (2005). *Trust and rule.* New York, NY: Cambridge University Press.

Tinsley, H., & Weiss, D. J. (1975). Interrater reliability and agreement of subject judgements. *Journal of Counseling Psychology, 22*(4), 358–376.

Trochim, W. (2006). Evaluation research. In *Research methods knowledge base.* Retrieved from www.socialresearchmethods.net/kb/evaluation.php

Tyler, R. (1942). General statement on evaluation. *Journal of Educational Research, 35*(7), 492–501.

UK Department of Transport. (2016). *Evaluation dashboard.* London, UK: Author.

UNICEF and 3D Change. (2009). Communication for development (C4D) capability development framework, Module 1. Adapted from the Centers for Disease Control and Prevention (CDC), *The Social Ecological Model: A Framework for Prevention.* Atlanta, GA: Author. Retrieved from www.unicef.org/cbsc/files/UNICEF-C4D-Capability-Framework.doc

USC (University of Southern California) Annenberg Center for Public Relations & The Holmes Report. (2016). *Global communications report 2016.* Retrieved from www.holmesreport.com/docs/default-source/default-document-library/2016-global-communications-report.pdf?sfvrsn=2

Valente, T. (2001). Evaluating communication campaigns. In R. Rice & C. Atkin (Eds.), *Public communication campaigns* (3rd ed., pp. 105–124). Thousand Oaks, CA: Sage.

Valente, T. (2002). *Evaluating health promotion programs.* New York, NY: Oxford University Press.

Valente, T., & Kwan, P. (2013). Evaluating communication campaigns. In R. Rice & C. Atkin, *Public communication campaigns* (4th ed., pp. 83–97). Thousand Oaks, CA: Sage.

van Dyk, F. (2016). The CEO SleepOut South Africa: Engineering social change. Entry in the AMEC Global Effectiveness Awards. Sandton, South Africa.

VanSlyke Turk, J. (Ed.) (2006). The professional bond: Public relations education for the 21st century. Commission on Public Relations Education [Website]. Retrieved from www.commpred.org

Vergeer, M. (2013). Politics, elections and online campaigning: Past, present … and a peek into the future. *New Media and Society, 15*(1), 9–17.

Walker, G. (1992). Communicating public relations research. Unpublished paper presented to a research conference at the University of Technology Sydney, Australia.

Walker, G. (1994). Communicating public relations research, *Journal of Public Relations Research*, 6(3), 141–161.

Walker, G. (1997). Public relations practitioners' use of research, measurement and evaluation. *Australian Journal of Communication*, 24(2), 97–113.

Wasserman, T. (2013). Ad recall: Why that ad wasn't as awesome as you thought. *The Digital Marketer's Roadmap* [Web log post], November 27. Retrieved from http://mashable.com/2013/11/26/ad-recall-metrics/#dzb3XQqo1GqP

Watson, T. (1996). New models for evaluating public relations practice. In B. Baerns & J. Klewes (Eds.), *Jahrbuch public relations* (pp. 50–62). Dusseldorf: Econ Verlag.

Watson, T. (2012). The evolution of public relations measurement and evaluation. *Public Relations Review*, 38(3), 390–398.

Watson, T. (2013). ROE may be more accurate than ROI. *FiftyOneZeroOne* [Web log post], March 22. Retrieved from http://fiftyonezeroone.blogspot.com.au/2013/03/roe-may-be-more-accurate-than-roi.html

Watson, T., & Noble, P. (2007). *Evaluating public relations: A best practice guide to public relations planning, research and evaluation* (2nd ed.). London, UK: Kogan Page.

Watson, T., & Noble, P. (2014). *Evaluating public relations: A best practice guide to public relations planning, research and evaluation* (3rd ed.). London, UK: Kogan Page.

Watson, T., & Simmons, P. (2004). *Public relations evaluation – survey of Australian practitioners.* Making a Difference: Refereed Proceedings of the Annual Meeting of the Australia New Zealand Communication Association, University of Sydney. Retrieved from www.anzca.net/conferences/past-conferences/2004-conf/2004-conf-p2.html

Watson, T., & Zerfass, A. (2011). Return on investment in public relations: A critique of concepts used by practitioners from communication and management sciences perspectives. *PRism*, 8(1), 1–14. Retrieved from www.prismjournal.org/vol8_1.html

Watson, T., & Zerfass, A. (2012). ROI and PR evaluation: Avoiding 'smoke and mirrors'. International Public Relations Research Conference, Miami, FL. Retrieved from www.instituteforpr.org/iprwp/wp-content/uploads/Watson-Zerfass-ROI-IPRRC-Miami-20121.pdf

Weiner, M. (2006). *Unleashing the power of PR: A contrarian's guide to marketing and communication.* San Francisco, CA: John Wiley & Sons.

Weiner, M. (2012). Showcase to the social media world. *Kommunikations Manager*, 3, 6–10.

Weiner, M., & Bartholomew, D. (2006). *Dispelling the myth of PR multipliers and other inflationary audience measures.* Gainesville, FL: Institute for Public Relations. Retrieved from www.instituteforpr.org/wp-content/uploads/Dispelling_Myth_of_PR_Multiplier.pdf

Weiss, C. (1972). *Evaluation research: Methods of assessing program effectiveness.* Englewood Cliffs, NJ: Prentice Hall.

Weiss, C. (1995). Nothing as practical as good theory: Exploring theory-based evaluation for comprehensive community-based initiatives for children and families. In J. Connell, A. Kubisch, L. Schorr, & C. Weiss (Eds.), *New approaches to evaluating community initiatives, Vol. 1, Concepts, methods and contexts* (pp. 15–44). Washington, DC: Aspen Institute.

Weiss, C. (1998). *Evaluation: Methods for studying programs and policies.* Upper Saddle River, NJ: Prentice Hall.

White, J., & Blamphin, J. (1994). *Priorities for research into public relations practice in the United Kingdom.* London, UK: City University Business School and Rapier Marketing.

Wholey, J. (1979). *Evaluation: Promise and performance.* Washington, DC: Urban Institute Press.

Wholey, J. (1983). *Evaluation and effective public management.* Boston, MA: Little Brown & Co.

Wholey, J. (1987). Evaluability assessment: Developing program theory. In L. Bickman (Ed.), *Using program theory in evaluation*, New Directions for Evaluation, Vol. 33 (pp. 77–92). San Francisco, CA: Jossey-Bass.

Wholey, J., Hatry, H., & Newcomer, K. (Eds.). (2010). *Handbook of practical program evaluation* (3rd ed.). San Francisco, CA: Jossey-Bass.

Wiener, N. (1948). *Cybernetics: Or the control and communication in the animal and the machine.* Cambridge, MA: MIT Press.

Wiener, N. (1950). *The human use of human beings.* Cambridge, MA: Da Capo Press.

Wijaya, B. (2012). The development of hierarchy of effects model in advertising. *International Research Journal of Business Studies, 5*(1), 73–85.

Williams, R. (1976). *Communications.* Harmondsworth, UK: Penguin. (Original work published 1962.)

Wilsdon, J., Allen, L., Belfiore, E., Campbell, P., Curry, C., Hill, S., et al. (2015). *The metric tide: Report of the independent review of the role of metrics in research assessment and management.* London, UK: Higher Education Funding Council of England (HEFCE).

Wooldridge, J. (2016). *Introductory econometrics: A modern approach* (6th ed.). Boston, MA: Cengage.

World Health Organization. (2014). *Mental health: A state of well-being.* Geneva, Switzerland: Author. Retrieved from www.who.int/features/factfiles/mental_health/en

WPP. (2015). What we do: Behaviour change. London, UK: WPP – The Government and Public Sector Practice [Website]. Retrieved from www.wpp.com/govtpractice/what-we-do/#Behaviour-Change. Also published in WPP. (2015). *Integrated communication campaigns to support citizen behaviour change: A practical guide.* London, UK: Author.

Wrench, J., McCroskey, J., & Richmond, V. (2008). *Human communication in everyday life.* Upper Saddle River, NJ: Pearson Education.

Wright, D., & Hinson, M. (2012). Examining how social and emerging media have been used in public relations between 2006 and 2012: A longitudinal analysis. *Public Relations Journal, 6*(4), 1–40.

Wright, D., Gaunt, R., Leggetter, B., Daniels, M., & Zerfass, A. (2009). *Global survey of communications measurement 2009 – final report.* London, UK: Association for Measurement and Evaluation of Communication. Retrieved from http://amecorg.com/wp-content/uploads/2011/08/Global-Survey-Communications_Measurement-20091.pdf

Yamaguchi, K. (2014). 3 Challenges of attribution modelling: The bad, the bad and the ugly. *MarketingLand* [Website]. Retrieved from http://marketingland.com/3-challenges-attribution-modeling-bad-bad-ugly-101257

Yin, R. (2009). *Case study research: Design and methods* (4th ed.). Thousand Oaks, CA: Sage.

YouGov. (2015). Facebook: To dislike or emoji? [Website]. Retrieved from https://today.yougov.com/news/2015/10/19/facebook-dislike-or-emoji/?nh=find-solutions,omnibus

Zelizer, B. (2015). Making communication theory matter. *Communication Theory, 25*(4), 410–415.

Zerfass, A. (2007). Unternehmenskommunikation und kommunikationsmanagement: Grundlagen, wertschöpfung, Integration [Corporate communication and communication management: Basics, value creation, integration]. In M. Piwinger, & A. Zerfass (Eds.), *Handbuch Unternehmenskommunikation* [*Handbook of corporate communication*] (pp. 21–71). Wiesbaden, Germany: Gabler.

Zerfass, A. (2010). Assuring rationality and transparency in corporate communications: Theoretical foundations and empirical findings on communication controlling and communication performance management. In M. Dodd & K. Yamamura (Eds.), *Ethical issues for public relations practice in a multicultural world, 13th International Public Relations Research Conference* (pp. 947–966). Gainesville, FL: Institute for Public Relations. Retrieved from http://iprrc.org/paperinfo_proceedings

Zerfass, A., & Volk, S. (forthcoming). Aligning and linking communication with organizational goals. In V. Luoma-aho & M. Canel (Eds.), *Handbook of public sector communication*. London, UK: Wiley-Blackwell.

Zerfass, A., Verčič, D., Verhoeven, P., Moreno, A., & Tench, R. (2012). *European communication monitor 2012: Challenges and competencies for strategic communication*. Brussels, Belgium: European Association of Communication Directors (EACD), European Public Relations Education and Research Association (EUPRERA), and Helios Media.

Zerfass, A., Verčič, D., Verhoeven, P., Moreno, A., & Tench, R. (2015). *European communication monitor 2015*. Brussels, Belgium: European Association for Communication Directors (EACD) and European Public Relations Education and Research Association (EUPRERA) in association with Helios Media, Berlin. Retrieved from www.zerfass.de/ECM-WEBSITE/media/ECM2015-Results-ChartVersion.pdf

Zhel, M. (2016). The beginner's guide to the sales funnel [Website]. Retrieved from www.mailmunch.co/blog/sales-funnel

Ziller, A., & Phibbs, P. (2003). Integrating social impacts into cost benefit analysis: A participative method: Case study: The NSW Area Assistance Scheme. *Impact Assessment and Project Appraisal, 21*(2), 141–157.

INDEX

Figures are denoted in italics, tables are denoted in bold

Printed in Great Britain
by Amazon